The Complete How to Handbook for Jewish Living

Three Volumes in One

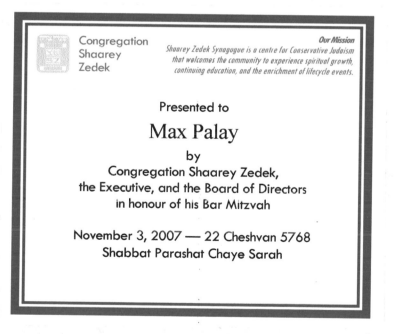

Congregation
Shaarey
Zedek

Our Mission
Shaarey Zedek Synagogue is a centre for Conservative Judaism
that welcomes the community to experience spiritual growth,
continuing education, and the enrichment of lifecycle events.

Presented to

Max Palay

by
Congregation Shaarey Zedek,
the Executive, and the Board of Directors
in honour of his Bar Mitzvah

November 3, 2007 — 22 Cheshvan 5768
Shabbat Parashat Chaye Sarah

The Complete How to Handbook for Jewish Living

Three Volumes in One

Rabbi Kerry M. Olitzky
and
Rabbi Ronald H. Isaacs

Illustrations by
Dorcas Gelabert

KTAV PUBLISHING HOUSE, INC.
JERSEY CITY, NEW JERSEY
2004

Library of Congress Cataloging-in-Publication Data

Olitzky, Kerry M.
  The complete how-to handbook for Jewish living / Kerry M. Olitzky and Ronald H.
Isaacs ; illustrations by Dorcas Gelabert.
      p. cm.
  Compilation of three previous volumes: The how-to handbook for Jewish living / Kerry
M. Olitzky and Ronald H. Isaacs, The second how-to handbook for Jewish living / Kerry
M. Olitzky and Ronald H. Isaacs, and The third "how to" handbook for Jewish living / by
Ron Isaacs and Kerry Olitzky.
  ISBN 0-88125-784-2
  1. Judaism--Customs and practices. 2. Jewish way of life. I. Isaacs, Ronald H. II.
Olitzky, Kerry M. How-to handbook for Jewish living. III. Olitzky, Kerry M. Second
how-to handbook for Jewish living. IV. Isaacs, Ronald H. Third "how to" handbook for
Jewish living. V. Title.
BM700.O425 2004
296.7--dc22

                            2004046581

Published by
KTAV Publishing House, Inc.
930 Newark Avenue
Jersey City, NJ 07306
Email: info@ktav.com
www.ktav.com
(201) 963-9524
Fax (201) 963-0102

Table of Contents

Table of Contents

Table of Contents

Preface

We learn best by example, observing the way things are done by our families, friends, and neighbors. When that is not possible, we turn to books in order to guide us and even reinforce our learning. But where do you go to find out all of the basic things you need to know to live the life of a Jew? There is really no one place—until now! In the pages of this book, you will find a step-by-step guide to doing things that make us unique as Jewish people. Just about all you need to know is included. And if you are so inclined, we have included basic sources and books to read if you want to know more. When the sources for a particular practice come to us through various paths in Jewish history and culture, we have listed only those that we feel are most relevant to you (and your teacher or parent). We have also included a section called "Instant Information" for those hard-to-find pieces of information that you just have to know but have no idea where to turn for the answer.

If you are just returning to Judaism and find all of these practices overwhelming, start with one today and two tomorrow. Judaism is a rich experience. We just want to get you started. This book is here to help.

Rabbi Ronald H. Isaacs
Rabbi Kerry M. Olitzky

Basic Berachot (Blessings)
בְּרָכוֹת

The source:

Berachot (Blessings) are attributed to the Men of the Great Assembly, who lived approximately 400–300 B.C.E.

What you need to know:

According to the great medieval Jewish philosopher Moses Maimonides (known as the RaMBaM), there are three types of blessings:

1. Blessings recited prior to eating, drinking, or smelling nice things, called *Birchot Hanehenin*.   בִּרְכוֹת הַנֶּהֱנִין

2. Blessings recited prior to the performance of a mitzvah, known as *Birchot Hamitzvot*.   בִּרְכוֹת הַמִּצְווֹת

3. Blessings that express praise of God and thanks to God, as well as those that ask God for things, called *Birchot Hodaah*.   בִּרְכוֹת הוֹדָאָה

בְּרָכוֹת
הַנֶּהֱנִין
*Birchot
Hanehenin*

Blessings for Taste

On eating bread:

בָּרוּךְ אַתָּה יְיָ אֱלֹהֵינוּ מֶלֶךְ הָעוֹלָם, הַמוֹציא לֶחֶם מִן הָאָרֶץ.

Baruch atah Adonai elohaynu melech ha'olam hamotzi lechem min ha'aretz.

Praised are You, Adonai our God, Sovereign of the Universe, who brings forth bread from the earth.

1

On eating foods other than bread prepared from wheat, barley, rye, oats, or spelt (such as cakes and cookies):

בָּרוּךְ אַתָּה יְיָ אֱלֹהֵינוּ מֶלֶךְ הָעוֹלָם, בּוֹרֵא מִינֵי מְזוֹנוֹת.

Baruch atah Adonai elohaynu melech ha'olam boray meenay mezonote.

Praised are You, Adonai our God, Sovereign of the Universe, who creates different kinds of nourishment.

On drinking wine:

בָּרוּךְ אַתָּה יְיָ אֱלֹהֵינוּ מֶלֶךְ הָעוֹלָם, בּוֹרֵא פְּרִי הַגָּפֶן.

Baruch atah Adonai elohaynu melech ha'olam boray pri ha'gafen.

Praised are You, Adonai our God, Sovereign of the Universe, who creates the fruit of the vine.

On eating fruit:

בָּרוּךְ אַתָּה יְיָ אֱלֹהֵינוּ מֶלֶךְ הָעוֹלָם, בּוֹרֵא פְּרִי הָעֵץ.

Baruch atah Adonai elohaynu melech ha'olam boray pri ha'eytz.

Praised are You, Adonai our God, Sovereign of the Universe, who creates the fruit of the tree.

On eating foods which grow in the ground, like potatoes:

בָּרוּךְ אַתָּה יְיָ אֱלֹהֵינוּ מֶלֶךְ הָעוֹלָם, בּוֹרֵא פְּרִי הָאֲדָמָה.

Baruch atah Adonai elohaynu melech ha'olam boray pri ha'adamah.

Praised are You, Adonai our God, Sovereign of the Universe, who creates the fruit of the ground.

A general blessing for other food and drink:

בָּרוּךְ אַתָּה יְיָ אֱלֹהֵינוּ מֶלֶךְ הָעוֹלָם, שֶׁהַכֹּל נִהְיָה בִּדְבָרוֹ.

Baruch atah Adonai elohaynu melech ha'olam she'hakol nihiyeh bidvaro.

Praised are you, Adonai our God, Sovereign of the Universe, at whose word all things come into existence.

Blessings for Smell

On smelling fragrant spices:

בָּרוּךְ אַתָּה יְיָ אֱלֹהֵינוּ מֶלֶךְ הָעוֹלָם, בּוֹרֵא מִינֵי בְשָׂמִים.

Baruch atah Adonai elohaynu melech ha'olam boray minay vesamim.

Praised are You, Adonai our God, Sovereign of the Universe, who creates different kinds of spices.

On smelling the fragrance of shrubs and trees:

בָּרוּךְ אַתָּה יְיָ אֱלֹהֵינוּ מֶלֶךְ הָעוֹלָם, בּוֹרֵא עֲצֵי בְשָׂמִים.

Baruch atah Adonai elohaynu melech ha'olam boray atzay vesamim.

Praised are You, Adonai our God, Sovereign of the Universe, who creates fragrant trees.

On smelling the fragrances of plants and herbs:

בָּרוּךְ אַתָּה יְיָ אֱלֹהֵינוּ מֶלֶךְ הָעוֹלָם, בּוֹרֵא עִשְׂבֵי בְשָׂמִים.

Baruch atah Adonai elohaynu melech ha'olam boray isvay vesamim.

Praised are You, Adonai our God, Sovereign of the Universe, who creates fragrant plants.

On smelling fragrant fruit:

בָּרוּךְ אַתָּה יְיָ אֱלֹהֵינוּ מֶלֶךְ הָעוֹלָם, הַנּוֹתֵן רֵיחַ טוֹב בַּפֵּרוֹת.

Baruch atah Adonai elohaynu melech ha'olam hanotayn rayach tov bapayrot.

3

Praised are You, Adonai our God, Sovereign of the Universe, who gives a pleasant fragrance to fruits.

On smelling fragrant oils:

בָּרוּךְ אַתָּה יְיָ אֱלֹהֵינוּ מֶלֶךְ הָעוֹלָם, בּוֹרֵא שֶׁמֶן עָרֵב.

Baruch atah Adonai elohaynu melech ha'olam boray shemen arayv.

Praised are You, Adonai our God, Sovereign of the Universe, who creates fragrant oil.

Blessings for Seeing Special Things

On seeing a rainbow:

בָּרוּךְ אַתָּה יְיָ אֱלֹהֵינוּ מֶלֶךְ הָעוֹלָם, זוֹכֵר הַבְּרִית וְנֶאֱמָן בִּבְרִיתוֹ וְקַיָּם בְּמַאֲמָרוֹ.

Baruch atah Adonai elohaynu melech ha'olam zocher ha'berit ve'ne'eman bivrito vekayam be'ma'amaro.

Praised are You, Adonai our God, Sovereign of the Universe, who remembers the covenant and is faithful in keeping promises.

On seeing trees blossoming for the first time in the year:

בָּרוּךְ אַתָּה יְיָ אֱלֹהֵינוּ מֶלֶךְ הָעוֹלָם, שֶׁלֹּא חִסַּר בְּעוֹלָמוֹ דָּבָר, וּבָרָא בוֹ בְּרִיּוֹת טוֹבוֹת וְאִלָנוֹת טוֹבִים לְהַנּוֹת בָּהֶם בְּנֵי אָדָם.

Baruch atah Adonai elohaynu melech ha'olam shelo chisar b'olamo davar uvara vo briyot tovot v'ilanot tovim l'hanot bahem b'nai adam.

Praised are You, Adonai our God, Sovereign of the Universe, who has withheld nothing from the world, and has created lovely creatures and beautiful trees for people to enjoy.

On seeing the ocean:

בָּרוּךְ אַתָּה יְיָ אֱלֹהֵינוּ מֶלֶךְ הָעוֹלָם, שֶׁעָשָׂה אֶת־הַיָּם הַגָּדוֹל.

Baruch atah Adonai elohaynu melech ha'olam she-asah et hayam hagadol.

Praised are You, Adonai our God, Sovereign of the Universe, who has made the great sea.

On seeing trees or creatures of unusual beauty:

בָּרוּךְ אַתָּה יְיָ אֱלֹהֵינוּ מֶלֶךְ הָעוֹלָם, שֶׁכָּכָה לּוֹ בְּעוֹלָמוֹ.

Baruch atah Adonai elohaynu melech ha'olam shekacha lo b'olamo.

Praised are You, Adonai our God, Sovereign of the Universe, who has such beauty in the world.

On seeing someone of abnormal appearance:

בָּרוּךְ אַתָּה יְיָ אֱלֹהֵינוּ מֶלֶךְ הָעוֹלָם, מְשַׁנֶּה הַבְּרִיּוֹת.

Baruch atah Adonai elohaynu melech ha'olam mishaneh ha'briyot.

Praised are You, Adonai our God, Sovereign of the Universe, who makes people different.

On seeing lightning, shooting stars, mountains, or sunrises:

בָּרוּךְ אַתָּה יְיָ אֱלֹהֵינוּ מֶלֶךְ הָעוֹלָם, עֹשֶׂה מַעֲשֵׂה בְרֵאשִׁית.

Baruch atah Adonai elahaynu melech ha'olam oseh ma'asey v'reshit.

Praised are You, Adonai our God, Sovereign of the Universe, Source of creation.

On seeing restored synagogues:

בָּרוּךְ אַתָּה יְיָ אֱלֹהֵינוּ מֶלֶךְ הָעוֹלָם, מַצִּיב גְּבוּל אַלְמָנָה.

Baruch atah Adonai elohaynu melech ha'olam matziv gevul almanah.

Praised are You, Adonai our God, Sovereign of the Universe, who restores the borders of the widow [Zion].

On seeing a person who is really knowledgeable about Torah:

בָּרוּךְ אַתָּה יְיָ אֱלֹהֵינוּ מֶלֶךְ הָעוֹלָם, שֶׁחָלַק מֵחָכְמָתוֹ לִירֵאָיו.

Baruch atah Adonai elohaynu melech ha'olam shechalak me'chochmato lirey'av.

Praised are You, Adonai our God, Sovereign of the Universe, who has given wisdom to those who revere God.

On seeing a person who knows lots of things about lots of things:

בָּרוּךְ אַתָּה יְיָ אֱלֹהֵינוּ מֶלֶךְ הָעוֹלָם, שֶׁנָּתַן מֵחָכְמָתוֹ לְבָשָׂר וָדָם.

Baruch atah Adonai elohaynu melech ha'olam she'natan me-chochmato l'vasar va'dam.

Praised are You, Adonai our God, Sovereign of the Universe, who has given wisdom to human beings.

On seeing a head of state (like a president):

בָּרוּךְ אַתָּה יְיָ אֱלֹהֵינוּ מֶלֶךְ הָעוֹלָם, שֶׁנָּתַן מִכְּבוֹדוֹ לְבָשָׂר וָדָם.

Baruch atah Adonai elohaynu melech ha'olam she'natan mi'kvodo l'vasar va'dam.

Praised are You, Adonai our God, Sovereign of the Universe, who has given special status to human beings.

Blessings on Hearing Something Special

On hearing thunder:

בָּרוּךְ אַתָּה יְיָ אֱלֹהֵינוּ מֶלֶךְ הָעוֹלָם, שֶׁכֹּחוֹ וּגְבוּרָתוֹ מָלֵא עוֹלָם.

Baruch atah Adonai elohaynu melech ha'olam she'kocho u'gevurato malay olam.

Praised are You, Adonai our God, Sovereign of the Universe, whose mighty power fills the entire world.

On hearing good news:

בָּרוּךְ אַתָּה יְיָ אֱלֹהֵינוּ מֶלֶךְ הָעוֹלָם, הַטּוֹב וְהַמֵּטִיב.

Baruch atah Adonai elohaynu melech ha'olam hatov v'hametiv.

Praised are You, Adonai our God, Sovereign of the Universe, who is good and causes good things to happen.

On hearing tragic news:

בָּרוּךְ אַתָּה יְיָ אֱלֹהֵינוּ מֶלֶךְ הָעוֹלָם, דַּיַּן הָאֱמֶת.

Baruch atah Adonai elohaynu melech ha'olam dayan ha-emet.

Praised are You, Adonai our God, Sovereign of the Universe, who is the true Judge.

בִּרְכוֹת הַמִּצְווֹת
Birchot Hamitzvot

On lighting Shabbat candles:

בָּרוּךְ אַתָּה יְיָ אֱלֹהֵינוּ מֶלֶךְ הָעוֹלָם, אֲשֶׁר קִדְּשָׁנוּ בְּמִצְוֹתָיו, וְצִוָּנוּ לְהַדְלִיק נֵר שֶׁל שַׁבָּת.

Baruch atah Adonai elohaynu melech ha'olam asher kidshanu be'mitzvotav vetzivanu l'hadlik ner shel Shabbat.

Praised are You, Adonai our God, Sovereign of the Universe, who has made us holy with mitzvot and instructed us to light Sabbath candles.

On lighting holiday candles:

בָּרוּךְ אַתָּה יְיָ אֱלֹהֵינוּ מֶלֶךְ הָעוֹלָם, אֲשֶׁר קִדְּשָׁנוּ בְּמִצְוֹתָיו,
וְצִוָּנוּ לְהַדְלִיק נֵר שֶׁל יוֹם טוֹב.

Baruch atah Adonai elohaynu melech ha'olam asher kidshanu be'mitzvotav vetzivanu l'hadlik ner shel yom tov.

Praised are You, Adonai our God, Sovereign of the Universe, who has made us holy with mitzvot and instructed us to light festival candles.

On washing hands:

בָּרוּךְ אַתָּה יְיָ אֱלֹהֵינוּ מֶלֶךְ הָעוֹלָם, אֲשֶׁר קִדְּשָׁנוּ בְּמִצְוֹתָיו,
וְצִוָּנוּ עַל נְטִילַת יָדָיִם.

Baruch atah Adonai elohaynu melech ha'olam asher kidshanu bemitzvotav vetzivanu al netilat yadayim.

Praised are You, Adonai our God, Sovereign of the Universe, who has made us holy with mitzvot and instructed us to wash our hands.

בִּרְכוֹת
הוֹדָאָה
*Birchot
Hodaah*

1. בָּרוּךְ אַתָּה יְיָ אֱלֹהֵינוּ מֶלֶךְ הָעוֹלָם, אֲשֶׁר נָתַן לַשֶּׂכְוִי בִינָה
לְהַבְחִין בֵּין יוֹם וּבֵין לָיְלָה.
2. בָּרוּךְ אַתָּה יְיָ אֱלֹהֵינוּ מֶלֶךְ הָעוֹלָם, שֶׁעָשַׂנִי בְּצַלְמוֹ.
3. בָּרוּךְ אַתָּה יְיָ אֱלֹהֵינוּ מֶלֶךְ הָעוֹלָם, שֶׁעָשַׂנִי יִשְׂרָאֵל.
4. בָּרוּךְ אַתָּה יְיָ אֱלֹהֵינוּ מֶלֶךְ הָעוֹלָם, שֶׁעָשַׂנִי בֶּן־ (בַּת־)חוֹרִין.
5. בָּרוּךְ אַתָּה יְיָ אֱלֹהֵינוּ מֶלֶךְ הָעוֹלָם, פּוֹקֵחַ עִוְרִים.
6. בָּרוּךְ אַתָּה יְיָ אֱלֹהֵינוּ מֶלֶךְ הָעוֹלָם, מַלְבִּישׁ עֲרֻמִּים.
7. בָּרוּךְ אַתָּה יְיָ אֱלֹהֵינוּ מֶלֶךְ הָעוֹלָם, מַתִּיר אֲסוּרִים.
8. בָּרוּךְ אַתָּה יְיָ אֱלֹהֵינוּ מֶלֶךְ הָעוֹלָם, זוֹקֵף כְּפוּפִים.

9. בָּרוּךְ אַתָּה יְיָ אֱלֹהֵינוּ מֶלֶךְ הָעוֹלָם, רוֹקַע הָאָרֶץ עַל הַמָּיִם.

10. בָּרוּךְ אַתָּה יְיָ אֱלֹהֵינוּ מֶלֶךְ הָעוֹלָם, שֶׁעָשָׂה לִי כָּל־צָרְכִּי.

11. בָּרוּךְ אַתָּה יְיָ אֱלֹהֵינוּ מֶלֶךְ הָעוֹלָם, הַמֵּכִין מִצְעֲדֵי־גָבֶר.

12. בָּרוּךְ אַתָּה יְיָ אֱלֹהֵינוּ מֶלֶךְ הָעוֹלָם, אוֹזֵר יִשְׂרָאֵל בִּגְבוּרָה.

13. בָּרוּךְ אַתָּה יְיָ אֱלֹהֵינוּ מֶלֶךְ הָעוֹלָם, עוֹטֵר יִשְׂרָאֵל בְּתִפְאָרָה.

14. בָּרוּךְ אַתָּה יְיָ אֱלֹהֵינוּ מֶלֶךְ הָעוֹלָם, הַנּוֹתֵן לַיָּעֵף כֹּחַ.

Praised are You, Adonai our God, Sovereign of the Universe:

1. . . . who helps Your creatures distinguish day and night.

2. . . . who made me in God's image.

3. . . . who made me a Jew.

4. . . . who made me a free person.

5. . . . who gives sight to blind people.

6. . . . who clothes the naked.

7. . . . who releases the imprisoned.

8. . . . who raises the downtrodden.

9. . . . who creates heaven and earth.

10. . . . who provides me with everything.

11. . . . who guides us on our path.

12. . . . who strengthens Israel with courage.

13. . . . who gives Israel glory.

14. . . . who restores strength to those who are tired.

Things to remember:

1. Blessings can be said in any language as long as they express thoughts similar to the Hebrew text and include the basic formula "Praised are You, Adonai our God, who. . . " בָּרוּךְ אַתָּה יְיָ אֱלֹהֵינוּ מֶלֶךְ הָעוֹלָם.

2. In blessings related to eating, smelling, or the performance of a mitzvah, the blessing is recited first followed by the specific action. However, in the case of Sabbath candles, light them first and then say the blessing (with your eyes covered).

Key words and phrases:

Beracha בְּרָכָה. Blessing (plural, *berachot* בְּרָכוֹת)

Birchot hamitzvot בִּרְכוֹת הַמִּצְווֹת. Blessings said prior to the performance of a mitzvah.

9

Birchot hanehenin בִּרְכוֹת הַנֶּהֱנִין. Blessings said prior to eating, drinking, smelling, and so forth.

Birchot hashachar בִּרְכוֹת הַשַּׁחַר. Blessings of the morning (literally, "at dawn").

Birchot hodaah בִּרְכוֹת הוֹדָאָה. Blessings that speak of praise of God and thanks to God, or that ask God for specific things.

If you want to know more:

Steven M. Brown, *Higher and Higher* (New York, 1979).

Hayim Donin, *To Pray as a Jew* (New York, 1980).

Joel Grishaver, *Basic Berachot* (Los Angeles, 1988).

Isaac Klein, *A Guide to Jewish Religious Practice* (New York, 1979).

Richard Siegel, Michael Strassfeld, and Sharon Strassfeld, *The First Jewish Catalogue* (Philadelphia, 1973).

The Rubrics of Prayer
תְּפִילָה

The source:

"As for me, let my prayer be for You, God, in an acceptable time" (Ps. 69:14).

The beginnings of the order of prayer are found in the second part of the talmudic tractate *Berachot*, which is a compilation from the period of the first *geonim*.

What you need to know:

OUTLINE OF DAILY MORNING SERVICE

Early Morning Blessings בִּרְכוֹת הַשַּׁחַר

Hymns and psalms to prepare us for prayer	*Baruch She'amar* בָּרוּךְ שֶׁאָמַר
	Selected Psalms תְּהִלִּים
	Yishtabach יִשְׁתַּבַּח
	Barechu בָּרְכוּ (Call to Prayer)
שְׁמַע יִשְׂרָאֵל *Shema Yisrael* and its blessings	First blessing before *Shema* שְׁמַע—*Yotzer Or* יוֹצֵר אוֹר (God creates light every day anew)
	Second blessing before *Shema* שְׁמַע—*Ahava Rabba* אַהֲבָה רַבָּה (God gives us the Torah and shows us love)

   Shema שְׁמַע

Three paragraphs	Deut. 6:4–9
	Deut. 11:13–21
	Num. 15:37–41

Blessing after *Shema* שְׁמַע–*Ga'al Yisrael* גָּאַל יִשְׂרָאֵל (God redeems Israel)

Amida עֲמִידָה, also known as the *Shemoneh Esray* שְׁמוֹנֶה עֶשְׂרֵה or *Hatefillah* הַתְּפִילָה

Torah reading קְרִיאַת הַתּוֹרָה (Monday and Thursday)

11

Full *Kaddish* קַדִּישׁ שָׁלֵם
Aleynu עָלֵינוּ
Mourner's *Kaddish* קַדִּישׁ יָתוֹם

Prayer Choreography

When (i.e, during which prayer)	What to do	How to do it	Why
In general	Shuckling	Swaying back and forth on your feet	To involve all of your heart and soul in prayer
Barechu	Bowing	Bow from the waist on the word *barechu*	Like bowing before a sovereign
Shema Yisrael Adonai Elohaynu Adonai Echad	Closing your eyes	Cover your eyes with your right hand	To keep away from distraction and concentrate on God's Oneness
Third paragraph of the *Shema* (i.e., *Vayomer Adonai*)	Kissing *tzitzit* (fringes)	Gather *tzitzit* and kiss them at each mention of *tzitzit* in third paragraph of *Shema*	To symbolically embrace God's *mitzvot*
Adonai sifatai tiftach ufi yagid tihilatecha (verse before the *Amida*)	Approaching God	Walk back three steps and then forward three steps	To symbolically approach the Sovereign
Baruch atah Adonai elohaynu vaylohay avotaynu (beginning of *Amida*)	Bowing	Bend knees at *baruch*, bend over your waist at *atah*, and straighten up at *Adonai* (see fig. 1)	To bow before God the Sovereign

Baruch atah Adonai magen Avraham (second blessing in *Amida*)	Bowing	Same as above	Same as above
Kedusha on words *Kadosh, kadosh, kadosh*	Rise on tiptoes at each mention of the word *kadosh*		To symbolically reach toward heaven
Modim anachnu lach (in *Amida*)	Bowing	Same as first blessing of *Amida*	Same as for bowing
Baruch atah Adonai hatov shimcha ulecha na'eh lehodot (in *Amida*)	Bowing	Same as above	Same as above
Oseh shalom bimromav hu yaaseh shalom alenu ve'al kol Yisrael veimru amen	Taking leave of God	Take three steps backward: at *shalom bimromav* bend your head and shoulders to the left; at *hu yaaseh shalom* bend your head and shoulders to the right; at *alenu ve'al kol Yisrael* bend your head and shoulders forward; at *veimru* stand erect.	This is the reverse of the approach to God at beginning of *Amida*. Here we take leave of God.
Alenu, on words *va'anachnu korim umishtachavim umodim*	Bow	Bend knees at *va'anachnu korim*; bow at *umishtachavim*, stand erect at *lifnay melech* (see fig. below)	We show humility to God, the Sovereign of all Sovereigns

Key words and phrases:

Birchot hashachar בִּרְכוֹת הַשַּׁחַר. Blessings of the morning.

Matbe'ah shel tefillah מַטְבֵּעַ שֶׁל תְּפִילָה. Sacred order of the prayer service.

Pesukai d'zimra פְּסוּקֵי דְזִמְרָה. Prayers in the Preliminary Service.

Tehillim תְּהִלִּים. Psalms.

If you want to know more:

Philip Arian and Azriel Eisenberg, *The Story of the Prayer Book* (Bridgeport, Conn., 1968).

Steven Brown, *Higher and Higher: Making Jewish Prayer Part of Us* (New York, 1979).

Hayim Donin, *To Pray as a Jew* (New York, 1980).

Harvey Fields, *Bechol Levavcha: With All Your Heart* (New York, 1976).

Isaac Klein, *A Guide to Jewish Religious Practice* (New York, 1979).

More particulars:

1. Correct way to bow for *Baruch atah Adonai* בָּרוּךְ אַתָּה ה'. When one bends the knees it is at *baruch* בָּרוּךְ (blessed); and when one straightens up it is at God's name (*Shulchan Aruch, Orach Chayim* 113:7).

Baruch   Ata   Adonai

2. Correct way to bow for *Aleynu* עָלֵינוּ

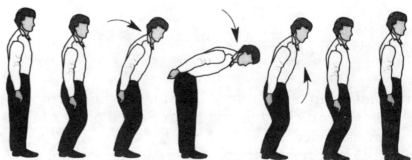

Vanachnu   Korim   Umishtachavim   Umodim   Lifnay Melech   Malchay Hamlachim   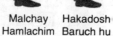Hakadosh Baruch hu

How to Make Aliyah to the Torah
עֲלִיָּה לַתּוֹרָה

The source:

Code of Jewish Law (*Shulchan Aruch, Orach Chayim*
    139–141); Babylonian Talmud, Megillah 31b–32a.

What you need to know:

1. After your name has been called, go up to the Torah,
   to the left side of the reader. After the *baal koreh*
   (Torah reader) has shown you the place about to be
   read, touch it with the *tzitzit* (fringes) of your *tallit* (or
   with the spine of your *siddur*). The scroll will next be
   rolled together. Stand behind the Torah scroll and
   say the following blessing:

   בָּרְכוּ אֶת יְיָ הַמְבֹרָךְ:

   Barechu et Adonai hamevorach.

   Praise Adonai, to whom our praise is due!

   בָּרוּךְ יְיָ הַמְבֹרָךְ לְעוֹלָם וָעֶד:

   Baruch Adonai ha'mevorach le-olam va'ed.

   Praised be Adonai, to whom our praise is due, now
   and forever!

   בָּרוּךְ אַתָּה יְיָ אֱלֹהֵינוּ מֶלֶךְ הָעוֹלָם אֲשֶׁר בָּחַר בָּנוּ מִכָּל הָעַמִּים
   וְנָתַן לָנוּ אֶת תּוֹרָתוֹ: בָּרוּךְ אַתָּה יְיָ נוֹתֵן הַתּוֹרָה:

   *Baruch atah Adonai elohaynu melech ha'olam asher
   bachar banu mikol ha'amim ve'natan lanu et torahto
   Baruch atah Adonai notayn ha-Torah.*

   Praised is Adonai our God, Sovereign of the Universe,
   who has chosen us from all peoples by giving us
   Torah. Praised is Adonai, Giver of the Torah.

   Then move to the right of the *baal koreh* so the Torah can
   be read.

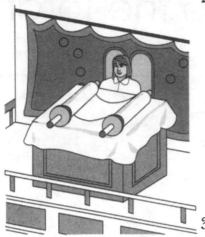

2. After the reading, recite the following:

בָּרוּךְ אַתָּה יְיָ אֱלֹהֵינוּ מֶלֶךְ הָעוֹלָם אֲשֶׁר נָתַן לָנוּ תּוֹרַת אֱמֶת וְחַיֵּי עוֹלָם נָטַע בְּתוֹכֵנוּ: בָּרוּךְ אַתָּה יְיָ נוֹתֵן הַתּוֹרָה:

Baruch atah Adonai elohaynu melech ha'olam asher natan lanu torat emet ve'chayai olam nata bitochaynu. Baruch atah Adonai notayn ha-Torah.

Praised is Adonai our God, Sovereign of the Universe, who has given us a Torah of truth, implanting within us eternal life. Praised is Adonai, Giver of the Torah.

3. Then stay on the left side of the reader during the next *aliyah.*

יַשֵׁר כֹּחַ
בָּרוּךְ תִּהְיֶה

4. Following the next *aliyah,* you may go back to your seat. People will say to you *yasher koach* "May you be strengthened." You should respond *baruch tihyeh,* "May it be blessed."

Things to remember:

בֵּן
בַּת

1. In order to be called to the Torah, the rabbi will want to know your Hebrew name (___ son/daughter of ___and ___).

2. In many synagogues, people are called in order of their priestly legacy (Cohen, Levi, and Israelite). In their quest for equality, Reform synagogues, Reconstructionist and some Conservative ones have generally discontinued this distinction.

בִּרְכַּת הַגּוֹמֵל
מִי שֶׁבֵּרַךְ

3. Following your *aliyah,* one says *Birkat Ha-gomel* if appropriate (see below, p. 45). Blessings for health, recovery and the like (*mi sheberach*) are said at this time also.

בִּימָה

4. Some people descend the *bimah* backwards so as not to turn their back on the Ark—like exiting from an audience with a king.

עֵץ חַיִּים
תּוֹרָתוֹ

5. Some people hold the *etz chaim* while reciting the blessing and actually raise the scroll slightly on the word *Torahto.*

6. Here is the music to help you remember how the blessings for an *aliyah* are to be sung.

First Blessing.

Bar-chu   et   A-do-nai   ham-vo-rach.   Ba-ruch   A-do-nai   ham-vo-rach   li-o-lam   va-ed.   Ba-ruch   a-ta   A-do-nai   e-lo-he-nu   me-lech ha-o-lam   a-sher ba-char   ba-nu   mi-kol   ha-a-mim,   vi-na-tan   la-nu   et   To-ra-to   Ba-ruch   a-ta   A-do-nai   no-ten   ha-To-rah.—

Second Blessing.

Ba-ruch   a-ta   A-do-nai   e-lo-he-nu   me-lech ha-o-lam   a-sher na-tan   la-nu   To-rat   e-met   v-cha-yay   o-lam   na-ta   bi-to-chay-nu.   Ba-ruch   a-ta   A-do-nai   no-ten   ha-To-rah

Key words and phrases:

Aliyah עֲלִיָה. Going up to the Torah, a Torah honor (also means emigrating to Israel).

Baal koreh בַּעַל קוֹרֵא. Torah reader.

Etz chaim עֵץ חַיִים. Torah roller.

Gabbai גַבָּאי. The person in a synagogue who makes things run smoothly during the services by assigning *aliyot* (plural of *aliyah*) and corrects the mistakes of the person reading the Torah.

If you want to know more:

Encyclopaedia Judaica (Jerusalem, 1971) 15:1253–1254.

Hayim Donin, *To Pray as a Jew* (New York, 1980).

Rose Goldstein, *A Time to Pray* (Bridgeport, Conn., 1972).

Isaac Klein, *A Guide to Jewish Religious Practice* (New York, 1979).

Putting on Tefillin
תְּפִלִּין

The sources:

וְהָיָה לְךָ לְאוֹת עַל־יָדְךָ וּלְזִכָּרוֹן בֵּין עֵינֶיךָ לְמַעַן תִּהְיֶה תּוֹרַת יְהֹוָה בְּפִיךָ כִּי בְּיָד חֲזָקָה הוֹצִאֲךָ יְהֹוָה מִמִּצְרָיִם:

"And it shall serve you as a sign on your hand and as a reminder on your forehead—in order that the teachings of Adonai may be in your mouth—that with a mighty hand Adonai freed you from Egypt" (Exod. 13:9).

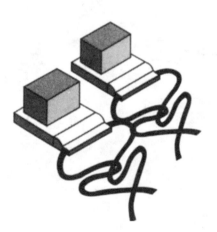

וְהָיָה לְאוֹת עַל־יָדְכָה וּלְטוֹטָפֹת בֵּין עֵינֶיךָ כִּי בְּחֹזֶק יָד הוֹצִיאָנוּ יְהֹוָה מִמִּצְרָיִם:

"And so it shall be as a sign upon your hand and as a symbol on your forehead that with a mighty hand Adonai freed us from Egypt" (Exod. 13:16).

וּקְשַׁרְתָּם לְאוֹת עַל־יָדֶךָ וְהָיוּ לְטֹטָפֹת בֵּין עֵינֶיךָ: וּכְתַבְתָּם עַל־מְזוּזוֹת בֵּיתֶךָ וּבִשְׁעָרֶיךָ:

"Bind them as a sign on your hand and let them serve as a symbol on your forehead" (Deut. 6:8).

וְשַׂמְתֶּם אֶת־דְּבָרַי אֵלֶּה עַל־לְבַבְכֶם וְעַל־נַפְשְׁכֶם וּקְשַׁרְתֶּם אֹתָם לְאוֹת עַל־יֶדְכֶם וְהָיוּ לְטוֹטָפֹת בֵּין עֵינֵיכֶם:

"Therefore impress these My words upon your very heart: bind them as a sign on your hand and let them serve as a symbol on your forehead" (Deut. 11:18).

What you need to know:

1. To begin, roll up the sleeve (if you have one) of your weaker arm (the one you don't write with) to above your biceps muscle. Take off any jewelry (watches, rings) which you can put on your other hand.

18

2. Unwrap the straps of the hand *tefillin* (*tefillin shel yad*). Place the *tefillin* box (*bayit*) on the biceps of your upper arm, with the leather piece (*maabarta*) that sticks out on the side closest to your shoulder. The knot (*kesher*) should be placed on the top of your biceps muscle on the side closest to your body. When everything is in place, say this blessing:

תְּפִלִּין שֶׁל יָד
בַּיִת
מַעֲבַּרְתָּא
קֶשֶׁר

בָּרוּךְ אַתָּה יְיָ אֱלֹהֵינוּ מֶלֶךְ הָעוֹלָם אֲשֶׁר קִדְּשָׁנוּ בְּמִצְוֹתָיו וְצִוָּנוּ לְהָנִיחַ תְּפִלִּין:

Baruch atah Adonai elohaynu melech ha'olam asher kid shanu bemitzvotav vetzivanu lehani'ach tefillin.

Praised are You, Adonai our God, Sovereign of the Universe, who has made us holy with mitzvot and instructed us to wear *tefillin*.

3. Pull on the strap (*retzua*) until the *tefillin* are tightly bound to your arm. Practice makes perfect; eventually you will learn how to keep everything from slipping. Don't let the knot loosen while you wind the rest of the strap.

רְצוּעָה

4. You may want to wind the strap once around your upper arm to keep the *bayit* in place.

בַּיִת

5. Next, wind the strap seven times around your arm between your elbow and wrist. Some rabbis say that the seven times should remind us of the seven Hebrew words in the verse in Psalms, "You open Your hand and satisfy all living creatures" (145:16). Ashkenazic Jews wind the strap counterclockwise (toward their bodies), while Sephardic Jews wind it clockwise (away from their bodies). The black side of the strap should always face outward.

6. After the seventh wind, bring the strap around the outside of your hand to your palm and wrap the rest of it around the middle of your palm (i.e., the space between your thumb and index finger). Tuck the end of the strap underneath this middle coil.

תְּפִלִּין שֶׁל רֹאשׁ 7. Unwrap the head *tefillin* (*tefillin shel rosh*). Hold the *bayit* and place it on the top of your head above your forehead, centered between your eyes. The knot should be on the back of your head, near the nape, and the straps should be brought forward to hang down over your chest with the black side outwards. Say this blessing:

בָּרוּךְ אַתָּה יְיָ אֱלֹהֵינוּ מֶלֶךְ הָעוֹלָם אֲשֶׁר קִדְּשָׁנוּ בְּמִצְוֹתָיו וְצִוָּנוּ עַל מִצְוַת תְּפִלִּין:

Baruch atah Adonai elohaynu melech ha'olam asher kidshanu bemitzvotav vetzivanu al mitzvat tefillin.

Praised are You, Adonai our God, Sovereign of the Universe, who has made us holy with mitzvot and instructed us concerning the precept of *tefillin.*

ד 8. Unwind the part of the strap coiled around the middle
שַׁדַּי   of your palm. According to Ashkenazic custom, wrap the strap three times around your middle finger, once around the lower part of that finger, and once around its middle, and one joining the two strap loops. This forms the Hebrew letter "dalet", the second letter of *Shaddai* (Almighty God). Then quote this verse:

וְאֵרַשְׂתִּיךְ לִי לְעוֹלָם. וְאֵרַשְׂתִּיךְ לִי בְּצֶדֶק וּבְמִשְׁפָּט וּבְחֶסֶד וּבְרַחֲמִים: וְאֵרַשְׂתִּיךְ לִי בֶּאֱמוּנָה, וְיָדַעַתְּ אֶת־יְיָ:

Ve'ayrastich lee l'olam ve'ayrastich lee betzedek u'vmishpat u'vchesed u'vrachamim ve'ayrastich lee be'emunah veyada'at et Adonai.

I will betroth you to Me forever. I will betroth you to Me with righteousness, with justice, with kindness, and with compassion. I will betroth you to Me with faithfulness, and you shall know God (Hosea 2:21).

שׁ 9. Bring the remainder of the strap under your ring finger and over the outside of the hand, forming a "V". Then wind the strap once again around the middle of the palm, forming the Hebrew letter "shin" which is the first letter of *Shaddai* (Almighty God).

10. To take the *tefillin* off, reverse the order. First, take ד
    off the *dalet* and *shin* on your hand. Next, take off the ש
    shel rosh and wrap its straps. Unwind the strap of the
    shel yad and wrap the straps. There is no single way
    of wrapping the *tefillin*. Just try to neatly wrap the
    straps around the *bayit* of the *shel yad* and *shel rosh*.

Things to remember:

1. *Tefillin* are only worn during the *Shacharit* (morning)
   service. Traditionally, only boys who reach the age of
   Bar Mitzvah wear *tefillin*. Some girls who reach the
   age of Bat Mitzvah also choose to wear *tefillin*.

2. *Tefillin* are not worn on Shabbat or major festivals,
   since holidays themselves are a sign of a person's
   relationship with God. *Tefillin* have become a sign of
   one's connection with God on ordinary days.

3. The *tallit* is always put on before *tefillin*, because it is
   worn every day of the year while *tefillin* are worn only
   on ordinary days.

4. Some people follow the custom of touching the *batim*
   (plural of *bayit*) with their fingers and bringing their
   fingers to their lips as a kiss when they say, "bind
   them for a sign" during the *Shema Yisrael* prayer in
   the morning.

Key words and phrases:

Bayit בַּיִת. The box of the *tefillin* containing the parchment.
Giddin גִּידִין. Thread made from the fibers of the hip
   muscles of kosher animals; used for sewing closed
   the *bayit*.
Kesher קֶשֶׁר. *Tefillin* knot.
Maabarta מַעֲבָּרְתָּא. Leather piece that protrudes from the
   back of the *bayit* through which the strap is passed.
Phylacteries תְּפִלִּין. From the Greek word meaning an
   amulet; the common English name for *tefillin*.
Retzua רְצוּעָה. Leather strap.

Shaddai שַׁדַי. Ancient name for God. The *tefillin* straps wound around the arm and fingers form the Hebrew letters *shin* ש and *dalet* ד. The *kesher* (knot) next to the *bayit* of the hand *tefillin* represents the Hebrew letter *yod* י. When, combined, the *shin* ש, *dalet* ד, and *yod* י spell out the word *Shaddai,* שַׁדַי one of God's oldest names.

Shin ש (Hebrew letter). Two letter *shins,* one with three branches (   ) and the other with four (   ) are on the *tefillin shel rosh*. Some say that the three-branched *shin* symbolizes the three patriarchs, Abraham, Isaac, and Jacob. The four-branched *shin* is a reminder of the four matriarchs Sarah, Rebecca, Rachel, and Leah. The mystics say that the meaning of the four-branched *shin* will only be revealed to us when the Messiah comes.

Tefillah תְּפִלָּה. Singular of *tefillin*.

Tefillah shel rosh תְּפִלָּה שֶׁל רֹאשׁ. The *tefillin* placed on the head.

Tefillah shel yad תְּפִלָּה שֶׁל יָד. The *tefillin* placed on the upper arm and wound around the hand.

Titura תִּיתוֹרָא. The square base of the *bayit*.

If you want to know more:

Encyclopaedia Judaica (Jerusalem, 1973) 15:898–903.
Aryeh Kaplan, *Tefillin* (New York, 1975).
Richard Siegel, Michael Strassfeld, and Sharon Strassfeld. *The First Jewish Catalogue* (Philadelphia, 1973).

More particulars:

I. *Adjusting the tefillin knot*
    If your *tefillin* headband is too large for you, and you want to make it smaller, here is what you do.
1. Notice that the knot has four quarters. Take hold of the lower left quarter and pull it out.
2. Now you have a loop hanging down.
3. Take hold of the upper right quarter and loosen it a little. Pull it from the back, taking in the lower left loop you had before. Keep pulling until the lower loop disappears.

4. Now you have a loop left on top. To make this loop disappear, just pull down on the trailing portion of the right *retzua*.

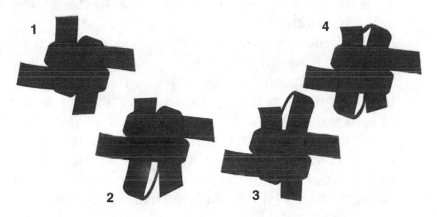

If your headband is too small and you wish to make it larger, here is what you do:

1. Notice that the *kesher* (knot) has four quarters. Each quarter is really a tight loop.

2. Take hold of the upper right quarter and pull it out into a loose loop.

3. Now pull out the lower left quarter of the knot until you get a loop.

4. Now to make the lower loop disappear, simply pull on the portion of the strap which extends upward.

Now your *kesher* is back to normal again, and your headband is enlarged. Readjust the knot so that it is in the center of the loop which goes around your head.

II. *Two Kinds of Tefillin:* Rashi *Tefillin*/Rabbenu Tam *Tefillin.*

There are two kinds of *tefillin:* Rashi *tefillin* and Rabbenu Tam *tefillin*. Most Jews use Rashi *tefillin*. Some put both on at different times of the morning prayers, usually putting on Rabbenu Tam *tefillin* after *Shemoneh Esray* and reciting *Shema* a second time. The two differ only in the order of the passages on the parchment in the *tefillin shel rosh*. Rashi's order follows the order in which the paragraphs appear in the Bible: Exodus 13:1–10, 13:11–16; Deuteronomy 6:4–9, 11:13–21. Rabbenu Tam (Rashi's grandson), reorders the place of the last two paragraphs, placing Deuteronomy 11:13–21 before Deuteronomy 6:4–9.

וידבר יהוה אל משה לאמר קדש לי כל בכור פטר כל רחם בבני ישראל באדם ובבהמה לי הוא ויאמר משה אל העם זכור את היום הזה אשר יצאתם ממצרים מבית עבדים כי בחזק יד הוציא יהוה אתכם מזה ולא יאכל חמץ היום אתם יצאים בחדש האביב והיה כי יביאך יהוה אל ארץ הכנעני והחתי והאמרי והחוי והיבוסי אשר נשבע לאבתיך לתת לך ארץ זבת חלב ודבש ועבדת את העבדה הזאת בחדש הזה שבעת ימים תאכל מצת וביום השביעי חג ליהוה מצות יאכל את שבעת הימים ולא יראה לך חמץ ולא יראה לך שאר בכל גבלך והגדת לבנך ביום ההוא לאמר בעבור זה עשה יהוה לי בצאתי ממצרים והיה לך לאות על ידך ולזכרון בין עיניך למען תהיה תורת יהוה בפיך כי ביד חזקה הוצאך יהוה ממצרים ושמרת את החקה הזאת למועדה מימים ימימה

והיה כי יבאך יהוה אל ארץ הכנעני כאשר נשבע לך ולאבתיך ונתנה לך והעברת כל פטר רחם ליהוה וכל פטר שגר בהמה אשר יהיה לך הזכרים ליהוה וכל פטר חמר תפדה בשה ואם לא תפדה וערפתו וכל בכור אדם בבניך תפדה והיה כי ישאלך בנך מחר לאמר מה זאת ואמרת אליו בחזק יד הוציאנו יהוה ממצרים מבית עבדים ויהי כי הקשה פרעה לשלחנו ויהרג יהוה כל בכור בארץ מצרים מבכר אדם ועד בכור בהמה על כן אני זבח ליהוה כל פטר רחם הזכרים וכל בכור בני אפדה והיה לאות על ידכה ולטוטפת בין עיניך כי בחזק יד הוציאנו יהוה ממצרים

שמע ישראל יהוה אלהינו יהוה אחד ואהבת את יהוה אלהיך בכל לבבך ובכל נפשך ובכל מאדך והיו הדברים האלה אשר אנכי מצוך היום על לבבך ושננתם לבניך ודברת בם בשבתך בביתך ובלכתך בדרך ובשכבך ובקומך וקשרתם לאות על ידך והיו לטטפת בין עיניך וכתבתם על מזוזות ביתך ובשעריך

והיה אם שמע תשמעו אל מצותי אשר אנכי מצוה אתכם היום לאהבה את יהוה אלהיכם ולעבדו בכל לבבכם ובכל נפשכם ונתתי מטר ארצכם בעתו יורה ומלקוש ואספת דגנך ותירשך ויצהרך ונתתי עשב בשדך לבהמתך ואכלת ושבעת השמרו לכם פן יפתה לבבכם וסרתם ועבדתם אלהים אחרים והשתחויתם להם וחרה אף יהוה בכם ועצר את השמים ולא יהיה מטר והאדמה לא תתן את יבולה ואבדתם מהרה מעל הארץ הטבה אשר יהוה נתן לכם ושמתם את דברי אלה על לבבכם ועל נפשכם וקשרתם אתם לאות על ידכם והיו לטוטפת בין עיניכם ולמדתם אתם את בניכם לדבר בם בשבתך בביתך ובלכתך בדרך ובשכבך ובקומך וכתבתם על מזוזות ביתך ובשעריך למען ירבו ימיכם וימי בניכם על האדמה אשר נשבע יהוה לאבתיכם לתת להם כימי השמים על הארץ

Putting on a Tallit
טַלִּית

The source:

וַיֹּאמֶר יְיָ אֶל־מֹשֶׁה לֵּאמֹר: דַּבֵּר אֶל־בְּנֵי יִשְׂרָאֵל וְאָמַרְתָּ אֲלֵהֶם
וְעָשׂוּ לָהֶם צִיצִת עַל־כַּנְפֵי בִגְדֵיהֶם לְדֹרֹתָם וְנָתְנוּ עַל־צִיצִת
הַכָּנָף פְּתִיל תְּכֵלֶת: וְהָיָה לָכֶם לְצִיצִת וּרְאִיתֶם אֹתוֹ וּזְכַרְתֶּם
אֶת־כָּל־מִצְוֹת יְיָ וַעֲשִׂיתֶם אֹתָם וְלֹא תָתוּרוּ אַחֲרֵי לְבַבְכֶם
וְאַחֲרֵי עֵינֵיכֶם אֲשֶׁר־אַתֶּם זֹנִים אַחֲרֵיהֶם: לְמַעַן תִּזְכְּרוּ וַעֲ־
שִׂיתֶם אֶת־כָּל־מִצְוֹתָי וִהְיִיתֶם קְדֹשִׁים לֵאלֹהֵיכֶם: אֲנִי יְיָ אֱלֹ־
הֵיכֶם אֲשֶׁר הוֹצֵאתִי אֶתְכֶם מֵאֶרֶץ מִצְרַיִם לִהְיוֹת לָכֶם לֵאלֹ־
הִים אֲנִי יְיָ אֱלֹהֵיכֶם:

"And God said to Moses: Instruct the people of Israel
that in every generation they shall put fringes on the
corners of their garments and bind a thread of blue
to the fringe of each corner. Looking upon it, you
will always be reminded of all the mitzvot of God and
fulfill them and not be led astray by your eyes. Then
you will remember and observe all of My mitzvot and
be holy before your God. I am Adonai your God, who
brought you out of the land of Egypt to be your God.
I, Adonai, am your God" (Num. 15:37–41).

What you need to know:

1. Before putting on the *tallit,* inspect the *tzitzit* (fringes)
   to be sure that they are intact and correct. Some
   people then say these verses from the Book of Psalms,
   to heighten their desire to put on a *tallit:* "Bless my
   soul, Adonai. You are very great, clothed in glory and
   majesty, wrapped in a robe of light. You spread the
   heavens like a tent cloth" (Ps. 104:1–2).

2. Next, hold the *tallit* and spread it open with the *atara*
   (neckpiece) facing you. Say this *beracha:*

בָּרוּךְ אַתָּה יְיָ אֱלֹהֵינוּ מֶלֶךְ הָעוֹלָם אֲשֶׁר קִדְּשָׁנוּ בְּמִצְוֹתָיו
וְצִוָּנוּ לְהִתְעַטֵּף בַּצִּיצִית:

Baruch atah Adonai elohaynu melech ha'olam asher kid-shanu bemitzvotav vetzivanu l'hitatef ba'tzitzit.

Praised are You, Adonai our God, Sovereign of the Universe, who has made us holy with mitzvot and instructed us to wrap ourselves with *tzitzit.*

Some now have the custom of kissing each end of the neckpiece, after the blessing before putting on the *tallit.* Others wrap their head briefly with the *tallit* for a moment of meditation.

3. Then bring the *tallit* around behind you and have it rest on your shoulders.

Things to remember:

1. The *tallit* is worn during the *Shacharit* (morning) service. (The exception to this is on Yom Kippur. At the *Kol Nidre* service, a *tallit* is worn in the evening and all day on Yom Kippur. Also, on Tisha B'av, it is worn only in the afternoon.) Traditionally, only boys who reach the age of Bar Mitzvah, or married men, wear a *tallit.* Some girls who reach the age of Bat Mitzvah also choose to wear a *tallit.*

2. A *tallit* is always put on before *tefillin,* because it is worn every day of the year while *tefillin* are not worn on Shabbat and holidays.

3. Most traditional boys and men wear a *tallit katan* (a small *tallit*) under their shirts all day and a large *tallit* just for morning prayers.

4. Many people follow the custom of bringing the *tzitzit* to their lips and kissing them each time the word *tzitzit* is mentioned when reading the third paragraph of the *Shema* (Num. 15:37–41).

Key words and phrases:

Atara עֲטָרָה. The crown or neckpiece of the *tallit*.
Shamash שַׁמָּשׁ. The longer strand in a *tzitzit* making kit used for the winding.
Tallit katan טַלִּית קָטָן. Small *tallit* worn under the clothing during the day.
Techelet תְּכֵלֶת. The original blue color which was used in the making of *tzitzit*.
Tzitzit צִיצִית. Fringes on the four corners of the *tallit*.

If you want to know more:

Encyclopaedia Judaica (Jerusalem, 1971) 15:743.
Alfred J. Kolatch, *The Jewish Home Advisor* (Middle Village, N.Y., 1990).
Richard Siegel, Michael Strassfeld, and Sharon Strassfeld, *The First Jewish Catalogue* (Philadelphia, 1973).

More particulars:

I. *Tying the tzitzit*

1. Buy a *tzitzit*—making kit at your local Judaica store. There are sixteen strands in the pack. Separate them into four groups with one long strand and three short in each.

2. Even up the four strands at one end and push the group through one of the corners of the *tallit*.

3. Even up seven of the eight strands (the original four were doubled) and leave the extra length of the *shamash* (the longest strand) hanging to one side.

4. With four strands in one hand and four in the other, make a double knot near the edge of the material. Take the *shamash* and wind it around the other seven strands in a spiral seven times. Make another double knot.

5. Next, spiral the *shamash* eight times around and make another knot.

6. Spiral the *shamash* eleven times around and make a double knot.

7. Finally, spiral the *shamash* thirteen times around and make one final double knot.

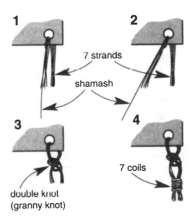

II. *Symbolism of the tzitzit*

   1. In *gematria,* (Jewish numerology) the Hebrew word *tzitzit* (צִיצִית) has the number value of 600. In addition, there are eight strands plus five double knots for each *tzitzit.* This totals 613, which is the exact number of commandments in the Torah.

   2. The wound spirals in each *tzitzit* are seven, eight, eleven, and thirteen. Seven plus eight equals fifteen, which in *gematria* is equal to the letters *yod* י and *hey* ה—the first two letters of God's name. Eleven is the equivalent of the Hebrew letters *vav* ו and *hey* ה—the last two letters of God's name. The combined total of twenty-six is representative of the four-letter name of God יהוה. Thirteen is the number value of the Hebrew word *echad* (אֶחָד), which means One. Thus, to look at the *tzitzit* is to always be reminded that God is One (יהוה אֶחָד).

III. *How to put on a Tallit*

   (1) A *tallit* worn fully over back and shoulders. (2) Folding the *tallit* over the shoulders. (3) A *tallit* folded back over the shoulders—a side view. (4) A front view.

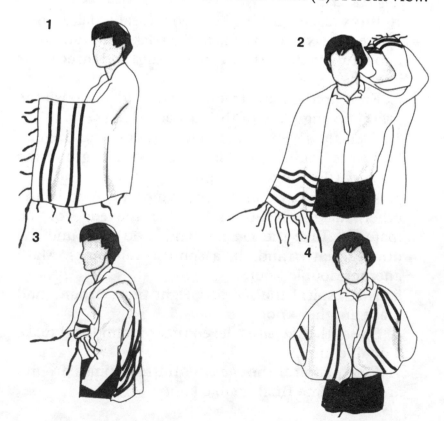

Baking and Braiding a Challah for Shabbat
חַלָּה

The source:

Taking challah is from Numbers 15:19–21, Mishnah Challah 1:1. Braids are mystical; they are from the hair of the Sabbath bride.

What you need to know:

1. Dissolve 2 packages granulated yeast in 2 cups tepid water. Add 1/2 cup sugar. Set aside.

2. Mix together 7 cups flour and 2 teaspoons salt. Add 1/3 cup oil, 2 lightly beaten eggs, and the yeast mixture. Combine well.

3. Knead on a floured board until smooth and silky. Add 1/2 cup golden raisins. Place in well-oiled bowl; cover and allow to rise in a warm, draft-free place until double in size, about 2 hours.

4. Punch down and allow to rise again, about 1 hour.

5. Divide dough and braid into 2 loaves. Place on cookie sheet and allow to rise 2 hours.
   While you are preparing the challah dough, separate a small piece and toss it into the oven. This is a symbol of contemporary sacrifice and also a reminder of the part of the challah that was given to the priests in the ancient Temple. When you do this, recite the following blessing:

בָּרוּךְ אַתָּה יְיָ אֱלֹהֵינוּ מֶלֶךְ הָעוֹלָם אֲשֶׁר קִדְּשָׁנוּ בְּמִצְוֹתָיו
וְצִוָּנוּ לְהַפְרִישׁ חַלָּה.

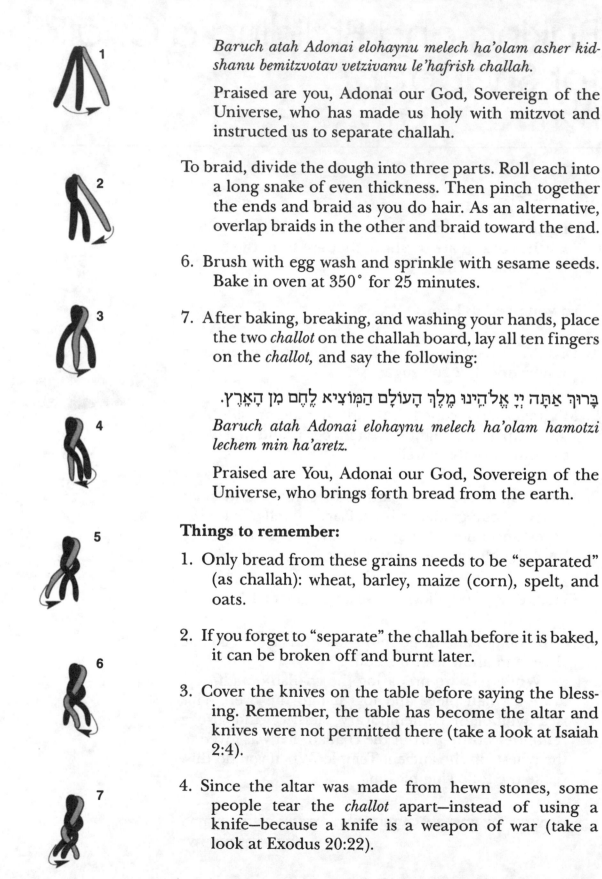

Baruch atah Adonai elohaynu melech ha'olam asher kidshanu bemitzvotav vetzivanu le'hafrish challah.

Praised are you, Adonai our God, Sovereign of the Universe, who has made us holy with mitzvot and instructed us to separate challah.

To braid, divide the dough into three parts. Roll each into a long snake of even thickness. Then pinch together the ends and braid as you do hair. As an alternative, overlap braids in the other and braid toward the end.

6. Brush with egg wash and sprinkle with sesame seeds. Bake in oven at 350° for 25 minutes.

7. After baking, breaking, and washing your hands, place the two *challot* on the challah board, lay all ten fingers on the *challot,* and say the following:

בָּרוּךְ אַתָּה יְיָ אֱלֹהֵינוּ מֶלֶךְ הָעוֹלָם הַמּוֹצִיא לֶחֶם מִן הָאָרֶץ.

Baruch atah Adonai elohaynu melech ha'olam hamotzi lechem min ha'aretz.

Praised are You, Adonai our God, Sovereign of the Universe, who brings forth bread from the earth.

Things to remember:

1. Only bread from these grains needs to be "separated" (as challah): wheat, barley, maize (corn), spelt, and oats.

2. If you forget to "separate" the challah before it is baked, it can be broken off and burnt later.

3. Cover the knives on the table before saying the blessing. Remember, the table has become the altar and knives were not permitted there (take a look at Isaiah 2:4).

4. Since the altar was made from hewn stones, some people tear the *challot* apart—instead of using a knife—because a knife is a weapon of war (take a look at Exodus 20:22).

5. After the blessing, before eating the challah, salt the bread (just a little) as a reminder of the sacrifice at the Temple. This also reveals that "by the sweat of your brow shall you get bread to eat" (Gen. 3:19).

6. Braided *challot* are used on Shabbat. Round *challot* are used on festivals, especially Rosh Hashana. Some communities serve *challot* shaped like birds on Rosh Hashana to show that God's mercy extends even to little birds.

7. The poppy or sesame seeds represent the manna which fell in the desert.

Key words and phrases:

Challah חַלָה (plural, *challot* חַלוֹת). Dough.

If you want to know more:

Freda Reider, *The Hallah Book* (Hobokcn, N.J. 1988).

Lifting and Tying a Torah
הַגְבָּהָה וּגְלִילָה

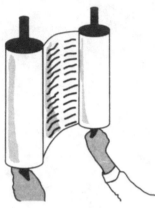

The source:

1. Babylonian Talmud, Sofrim 14:14.
2. Orach Chayim 134:2.

What you need to know:

עֲלִיּוֹת   Generally, both of these *aliyot* (Torah honors, from the word which means "to go up") are called at the same time following the reading of the Torah.

הַגְבָּהָה   1. For *hagbahah* (lifting), unroll the Torah scroll to a width of three columns.

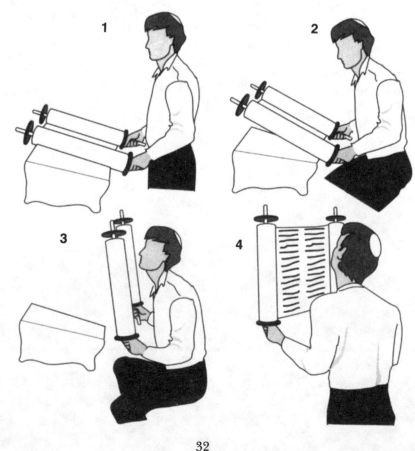

2. Slide the Torah scroll down the reading table so that the bottom rollers are off the table.

3. Hold the rollers tightly. Using the table for leverage, bend your knees and push down on the bottom ends of the rollers.

4. Lift the scroll high above your head. Be careful.

5. Turn around so that the inside of the scroll—the writing—can be seen by the congregation.

6. After the congregation has chanted *Vezot ha-Torah*, sit down in the chair provided for you. Here, the one doing *gelilah* takes over. Just help.

וְזֹאת הַתּוֹרָה
גְּלִילָה

1. For *gelilah* (rolling and tying the Torah), hold the top of the Torah rollers and roll the scroll together (with the steady help of the person who did *hagbahah*).

2. When it is together, put the Genesis side (your left side) of the roller over the other side.

3. Take the *avnet* or wimpel (binder) and fasten it around the front of the Torah.

אַבְנֵט

4. A sash is tied in a bow. A wimpel is tucked at the end, after it has been wrapped.

5. Cover the Torah with its mantle/cover, making sure the decoration faces front.

6. Then put the breastplate and pointer back on. (Some synagogues wait to finish until after the Haftarah is read.)

Now the *gelilah* person sits down in his/her seat, after shaking hands. The *hagbahah* person will remain and hold the Torah in his/her lap until the rest of the folks are ready to return it to the ark.

Things to remember:

יַשֶׁר כֹּחַ
בָּרוּךְ תִּהְיֶה

1. Shake hands with everyone on the *bimah* after you have finished your aliyah. People will say, *yeshar koach*. Remember to respond, *baruch tihyeh*.

Key words and phrases:

Avnet אַבְנֵט. *Torah binder, sometimes called a wimpel.*

Choshen חוֹשֶׁן. Silver shield breastplate over the front of the Torah which remind us of the High Priest's breastplate in the Temple.

Me'il מְעִיל. Torah mantle/cover.

Rimmon(im) רִימוֹן. From the Hebrew word for pomegranates, which were used to adorn Torah scrolls, generally silver objects with bells that are placed on top of each of the Torah rollers.

Yad יָד. Pointer used to point to words in the Torah during reading.

If you want to know more:

Hayim Donin, *To Pray as a Jew* (New York, 1980).

Chanting the Haftarah Blessings and Haftarah Trope
בִּרְכוֹת הַהַפְטָרָה וְטַעֲמֵי הַמִּקְרָא

The source:

The Levites used hand-signs which represented specific
melodies when they were teaching the Torah in public. These were eventually adapted for the Haftarah
as well.

What you need to know:

1. The Haftarah (a section from one of the books of the
   Prophets) is chanted in synagogues on Shabbat and
   festivals.

הַפְטָרָה

2. Each Haftarah consists of Hebrew words with musical
   notations, known as *trop* or *ta'amei hamikra* in Hebrew. These signs tell us how to sing the words and
   phrases in the Haftarah.

טַעֲמֵי הַמִּקְרָא

3. There is a blessing before every Haftarah that is
   chanted, and several blessings after every Haftarah
   that are also chanted.

4. Here are the blessings before and after the Haftarah
   with the accompanying music (used, with permission,
   from Samuel Rosenbaum's *Guide to Haftarah Chanting*
   [KTAV Publishing House, 1973]).

Blessing before the Haftarah

בָּרוּךְ אַתָּה יְיָ, אֱלֹהֵינוּ מֶלֶךְ הָעוֹלָם, אֲשֶׁר בָּחַר בִּנְבִיאִים
טוֹבִים, וְרָצָה בְדִבְרֵיהֶם, הַנֶּאֱמָרִים בֶּאֱמֶת: בָּרוּךְ אַתָּה יְיָ,
הַבּוֹחֵר בַּתּוֹרָה, וּבְמֹשֶׁה עַבְדּוֹ, וּבְיִשְׂרָאֵל עַמּוֹ, וּבִנְבִיאֵי הָאֱמֶת
וָצֶדֶק:

The blessings which follow the Haftarah are chanted, not according to *trop* markings (none are given), but to a traditional tune. This tune may vary from community to community, but, generally speaking, the version notated below is well-known in most American congregations.

Blessings after concluding the Haftarah

בָּרוּךְ אַתָּה יְיָ, אֱלֹהֵינוּ מֶלֶךְ הָעוֹלָם, צוּר כָּל הָעוֹלָמִים, צַדִּיק
בְּכָל־הַדּוֹרוֹת, הָאֵל הַנֶּאֱמָן, הָאוֹמֵר וְעוֹשֶׂה, הַמְדַבֵּר וּמְקַיֵּם,
שֶׁכָּל דְּבָרָיו אֱמֶת וָצֶדֶק:

נֶאֱמָן אַתָּה הוּא יְיָ אֱלֹהֵינוּ, וְנֶאֱמָנִים דְּבָרֶיךָ, וְדָבָר אֶחָד
מִדְּבָרֶיךָ, אָחוֹר לֹא־יָשׁוּב רֵיקָם, כִּי אֵל מֶלֶךְ נֶאֱמָן וְרַחֲמָן
אָתָּה: בָּרוּךְ אַתָּה יְיָ, הָאֵל הַנֶּאֱמָן בְּכָל־דְּבָרָיו:

רַחֵם עַל־צִיּוֹן כִּי הִיא בֵּית חַיֵּינוּ, וְלַעֲלוּבַת נֶפֶשׁ תּוֹשִׁיעַ בִּמְהֵרָה
בְיָמֵינוּ: בָּרוּךְ אַתָּה יְיָ, מְשַׂמֵּחַ צִיּוֹן בְּבָנֶיהָ:

36

(1)
Ba - ruch _____ a - ta A - do - nai _____ e - lo - he - nu me - lech
ha - o - lam _____ tzur kol ha - o - la - mim, _____ tza - dik b - chol ha - do -
rot, _____ ha - el ha - ne - e - man, ha - o - mer vi - o - seh, _____ ha - mi - da - ber
u - mi - ka - yem, _____ she - kol di - va - rav _____ e - met va - tze - dek.

(2)
Ne - e - man _____ a - ta hu Adonai e - lo - he - nu vi -
ne - e - ma - nim de - va - re - cha, vi - da - var e - chad mid va - re - cha a -
chor lo ya - shuv ray - kam _____ ki el me - lech ne - e - man vi - ra - cha - man a - ta.

Ba - ruch a - ta Adonai ha - el ha - ne - e - man _____ b - chol di - va - rav. _____

(3)
Ra - chem _____ al Tzi - yon _____ ki hi vet cha - ya - nu vi - la -
a - lu - vat ne - fesh to - shi - ah bi - mi - hay - rah vi - ya - may - nu. Ba - ruch
a - ta A - do - nai mi - sa - may - ach Tzi - yon _____ bi - va - neh - ha.

שַׂמְּחֵנוּ יְיָ אֱלֹהֵינוּ, בְּאֵלִיָּהוּ הַנָּבִיא עַבְדֶּךָ, וּבְמַלְכוּת בֵּית דָּוִד
מְשִׁיחֶךָ, בִּמְהֵרָה יָבֹא וְיָגֵל לִבֵּנוּ, עַל כִּסְאוֹ לֹא יֵשֶׁב זָר, וְלֹא
יִנְחֲלוּ עוֹד אֲחֵרִים אֶת כְּבוֹדוֹ, כִּי בְשֵׁם קָדְשְׁךָ נִשְׁבַּעְתָּ לּוֹ,
שֶׁלֹּא יִכְבֶּה נֵרוֹ לְעוֹלָם וָעֶד: בָּרוּךְ אַתָּה יְיָ, מָגֵן דָּוִד:
עַל הַתּוֹרָה, וְעַל הָעֲבוֹדָה, וְעַל הַנְּבִיאִים, וְעַל יוֹם הַשַּׁבָּת הַזֶּה,
שֶׁנָּתַתָּ לָּנוּ יְיָ אֱלֹהֵינוּ לִקְדֻשָּׁה וְלִמְנוּחָה לְכָבוֹד וּלְתִפְאָרֶת:

37

עַל־הַכֹּל יְיָ אֱלֹהֵינוּ, אֲנַחְנוּ מוֹדִים לָךְ וּמְבָרְכִים אוֹתָךְ, יִתְבָּרַךְ
שִׁמְךָ בְּפִי כָּל־חַי תָּמִיד לְעוֹלָם וָעֶד: בָּרוּךְ אַתָּה יְיָ, מְקַדֵּשׁ
הַשַּׁבָּת:

* On Sabbath Chol Hamoed Pesach the same *berachot*
are chanted as on an ordinary Sabbath.

(6) Al ha-kol ___ A-do-nai e-lo-he-nu a- nach-nu mo-dim lach ___ u-mi-var-chim o-tach, ___ yit-ba-rech shim-cha ___ be-fee ___ kol chai ta-mid li-o-lam va- ed. Ba-ruch a-ta A-do-nai m-ka-desh ha-sha-bat.

Haftarah *Trop*

Mer-cha ___ tip-cha mu-nach et-nach-ta ___

Ma-pach ___ pash-ta ___ mu-nach ___ ka-ton ___

Dar-gah ___ t'-vir ___

Ger-sha-yim ___ [mu-nach] r'-vi-i ___

Kad-ma az-lah ___ [*only when followed by an azlah]

T'li-sha g'do-lah ___ t'li-sha k'ta-nah ___

Pa-zer ___ [mu-nach] zar-kah ___ [mu-nach] se-gol ___

39

Key words and phrases:

Haftarah הַפְטָרָה. From the Hebrew word meaning "conclusion," specifically refers to the section from the Prophets read on Shabbat and festivals.

Ta'amei hamikra טַעֲמֵי הַמִּקְרָא. Musical signs for the reading of the Torah, Hebrew *trop*; from the Yiddish for "musical sign," cantillation marks.

If you want to know more:

Richard Neumann, *The Roots of Biblical Chants* (New York, 1982).

Samuel Rosenbaum, *A Guide to Haftarah Chanting* (New York, 1973).

Chanting the Torah
טַעֲמֵי הַמִקְרָא

The source:

The Levites used hand-signs which represented specific
   melodies when they were teaching the Torah in public.

What you need to know:

1. The Torah (the Five Books of Moses written on parch-
    ment) is chanted in the synagogue on Mondays,
    Thursdays, Shabbat festivals and fast days.

2. The chanting of the Hebrew words in the Torah are
    practised using a book called a *Tikkun*. This book
    contains the printed text with vowels and musical
    notations known as *trop* or *ta'amei hamikra* in Hebrew.
    This appears alongside the text of the Torah. The
    musical signs tell how to sing the words and phrases
    in the Torah.

3. The chanter of the Torah uses a Torah pointer, called
    a *yad* (in the shape of a hand) with which to follow
    the words.

4. There are no vowels, *trop* or punctuation marks in
    the Torah. The reader must have a good memory in
    addition to some singing skills.

Hand Signs for Torah Reading

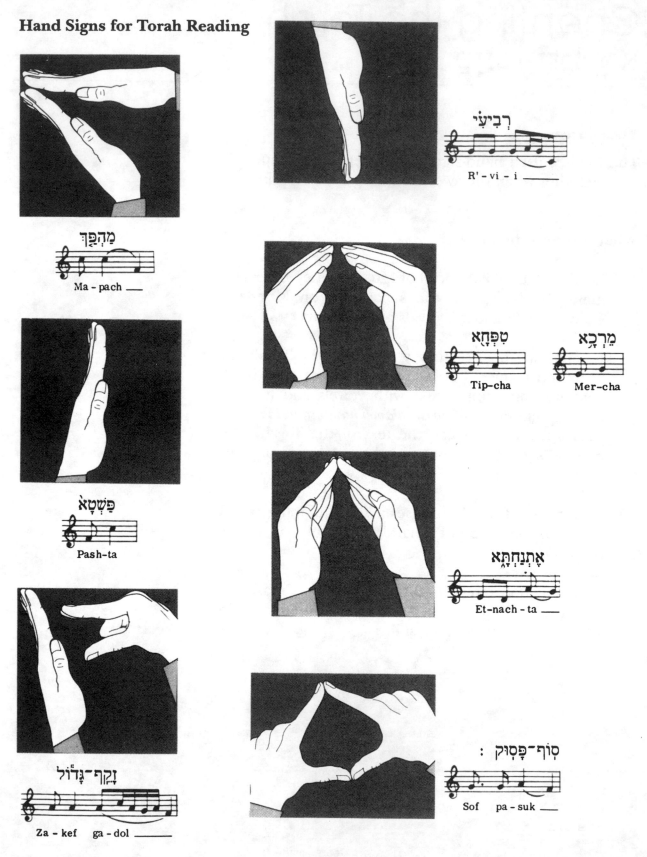

מַהְפַּךְ
Ma – pach

רְבִיעִי
R' – vi – i

פַּשְׁטָא
Pash – ta

טִפְחָא
Tip-cha

מֶרְכָא
Mer-cha

אֶתְנַחְתָּא
Et-nach – ta

זָקֵף־גָּדוֹל
Za – kef   ga – dol

סוֹף־פָּסוּק :
Sof   pa – suk

42

Table of Torah Trop Melodies

Key words and phrases:

Tikkun תִּקּוּן. A special book used to prepare for the reading of the Torah because it contains the printed text with vowels parallel to the text without vowels.

Yad יָד. A pointer used for the reading of the Torah so that one does not touch the Torah scroll itself.

If you want to know more:

Richard Neumann, *The Roots of Biblical Chants* (New York, 1982).

Samuel Rosenbaum, *A Guide to Torah Reading* (New York, 1983).

Samuel Rosenbaum, *To Live as a Jew* (New York, 1969).

Birkat Ha-Gomel
בִּרְכַּת הַגּוֹמֵל

The source:

Psalm 107; Babylonian Talmud, Berachot 54b.

What you need to know:

Just say the following, after an *aliyah* in a public Torah reading:

בָּרוּךְ אַתָּה יְיָ אֱלֹהֵינוּ מֶלֶךְ הָעוֹלָם הַגּוֹמֵל לְחַיָּבִים טוֹבוֹת שֶׁגְּמָלַנִי כָּל טוֹב:

Baruch atah Adonai elohaynu melech ha'olam hagomel lechayavim tovot she'gemalani kol tov.

Praised are You, Adonai our God, Sovereign of the Universe, who bestows favor on those who do not deserve it, just as You have bestowed favor on me.

Things to remember:

1. Say *Birkat Ha-Gomel* after you have returned home from a long trip, recovered from a serious illness, escaped disaster (including an automobile accident), or been released from an imprisonment! Women say it after having a baby too.

2. After you recite your blessing, the congregation will respond:

מִי שֶׁגְּמָלְךָ כָּל טוֹב הוּא יִגְמָלְךָ כָּל טוֹב סֶלָה:

Mi shegemalcha kol tov hu yegemalcha kol tov selah.

May the One who has shown you every kindness continue to deal kindly with you.

Key words and phrases:

Gomel גּוֹמֵל. A person who has been "given a break" and saved from a life—threatening situation.

If you want to know more:

Isaac Klein, *A Guide to Jewish Religious Practice* (New York, 1979).
Richard Siegel, Michael Strassfeld, and Sharon Strassfeld, *The First Jewish Catalogue* (Philadelphia, 1973).

Night Prayer—
Keriat Shema Al Hameeta
קְרִיאַת שְׁמַע עַל הַמִּטָה

The source:

וְשִׁנַּנְתָּם לְבָנֶיךָ וְדִבַּרְתָּ בָּם בְּשִׁבְתְּךָ בְּבֵיתֶךָ וּבְלֶכְתְּךָ בַדֶּרֶךְ וּבְשָׁכְבְּךָ וּבְקוּמֶךָ:

"And you shall speak of them when you are sitting in your home, when you go on a journey, when you lie down" (Deut. 6:7).

Also see Babylonian Talmud, Berachot 60b.

What you need to know:

1. Recited before retiring:

בָּרוּךְ אַתָּה יְיָ אֱלֹהֵינוּ מֶלֶךְ הָעוֹלָם הַמַּפִּיל חֶבְלֵי שֵׁנָה עַל עֵינַי וּתְנוּמָה עַל עַפְעַפָּי: וִיהִי רָצוֹן מִלְפָנֶיךָ יְיָ אֱלֹהַי וֵאלֹהֵי אֲבוֹתַי שֶׁתַּשְׁכִּיבֵנִי לְשָׁלוֹם וְתַעֲמִידֵנִי לְשָׁלוֹם וְאַל יְבַהֲלוּנִי רַעְיוֹנַי וַחֲלוֹמוֹת רָעִים וְהִרְהוּרִים רָעִים וּתְהִי מִטָּתִי שְׁלֵמָה לְפָנֶיךָ: וְהָאֵר עֵינַי פֶּן אִישַׁן הַמָּוֶת, כִּי אַתָּה הַמֵּאִיר לְאִישׁוֹן בַּת עָיִן: בָּרוּךְ אַתָּה יְיָ הַמֵּאִיר לָעוֹלָם כֻּלוֹ בִּכְבוֹדוֹ:

Blessed are You, Adonai, Sovereign of the Universe, who closes my eyes in sleep and my eyelids in slumber. May it be Your desire, God of my ancestors, to grant that I lie down in peace and that I rise up in peace. Let my thoughts not upset me nor evil dreams. May my family be perfect in Your sight. Grant me light, lest I sleep the sleep of death. It is You that gives light to the eyes. Praised are You, God, whose majesty gives light to the entire world.

שְׁמַע יִשְׂרָאֵל יְיָ אֱלֹהֵינוּ יְיָ אֶחָד:

Shema Yisrael Adonai elohaynu Adonai echad.

בָּרוּךְ שֵׁם כְּבוֹד מַלְכוּתוֹ לְעוֹלָם וָעֶד:

Baruch shem kevod malchuto le'olam va'ed.

47

2.

וְאָהַבְתָּ אֵת יְיָ אֱלֹהֶיךָ בְּכָל־לְבָבְךָ וּבְכָל־נַפְשְׁךָ וּבְכָל־מְאֹדֶךָ: וְהָיוּ הַדְּבָרִים הָאֵלֶּה אֲשֶׁר אָנֹכִי מְצַוְּךָ הַיּוֹם עַל־לְבָבֶךָ: וְשִׁנַּנְתָּם לְבָנֶיךָ וְדִבַּרְתָּ בָּם בְּשִׁבְתְּךָ בְּבֵיתֶךָ וּבְלֶכְתְּךָ בַדֶּרֶךְ וּבְשָׁכְבְּךָ וּבְקוּמֶךָ: וּקְשַׁרְתָּם לְאוֹת עַל־יָדֶךָ וְהָיוּ לְטֹטָפֹת בֵּין עֵינֶיךָ: וּכְתַבְתָּם עַל־מְזֻזוֹת בֵּיתֶךָ וּבִשְׁעָרֶיךָ:

Hear, O Israel, Adonai is our God, Adonai is One. Praised be God's majestic reputation forever and ever. Love Adonai your God with all your heart, soul, and might. And these words which I command you today shall be in your heart. Teach them carefully to your children, and speak of them when you sit in your home, when you go on a journey, when you lie down, and when you arise. Bind them as a sign on your hand and they shall be for frontlets between your eyes. Inscribe them on the doorposts of your house and on your gates (Deut. 4:6–9).

Things to remember:

Don't forget to say the Shema each night before going to bed, the last thing you do.

Key words and phrases:

Ayin עַיִן. (plural, *anayim* עֵינַיִם). Eye.
Sheynah שֵׁינָה. Sleep.

If you want to know more:

Haim Donin, *To Pray as a Jew* (New York, 1980).
Isaac Klein, *A Guide to Jewish Religious Practice* (New York, 1979).
Meir Zlotowitz and Nosson Scherman, *Shema Yisrael* (New York, 1982).

Key words and phrases:

Hadlakat nerot הַדְלָקַת נֵרוֹת. The lighting of candles.
Ner נֵר. (plural, *nerot* נֵרוֹת,) candle.

If you want to know more:

Malka Drucker, *Shabbat, a Peaceful Island* (New York, 1983).
Ronald H. Isaacs, *Shabbat Delight* (Hoboken, N.J., 1987).

How to Light
the Sabbath Candles
הַדְלָקַת נֵרוֹת

The sources:

Exodus 20:8; Deuteronomy 5:12.

זָכוֹר (שָׁמוֹר) אֶת יוֹם הַשַּׁבָּת לְקַדְשׁוֹ.

Remember (observe) the Sabbath day to keep it holy.

What you need to know:

1. Candles are lit at between 1 1/2 hours and 18 minutes prior to sunset (according to halacha).

2. Light the candles.

3. Draw your hands around the candles and toward your face from one to seven times (three times is most common).

4. Cover your eyes with your hands and say the following blessing at the same time:

בָּרוּךְ אַתָּה יְיָ אֱלֹהֵינוּ מֶלֶךְ הָעוֹלָם אֲשֶׁר קִדְּשָׁנוּ בְּמִצְוֹתָיו
וְצִוָּנוּ לְהַדְלִיק נֵר שֶׁל שַׁבָּת:

Baruch atah Adonai elohaynu melech ha'olam asher kid-shanu bemitzvotav vetzivanu l'hadlik ner shel Shabbat.

Praised are You, Adonai our God, Sovereign of the Universe, who makes us holy with mitzvot and instructs us to kindle the lights of Shabbat.

The blessing for Yom Tov is:

בָּרוּךְ אַתָּה יְיָ אֱלֹהֵינוּ מֶלֶךְ הָעוֹלָם אֲשֶׁר קִדְּשָׁנוּ בְּמִצְוֹתָיו
וְצִוָּנוּ לְהַדְלִיק נֵר שֶׁל (שַׁבָּת וְשֶׁל) יוֹם טוֹב:

49

Baruch atah Adonai elohaynu melech ha'olam asher kid-shanu bemitzvotav vetzivanu l'hadlik ner shel (Shabbat v'shel) Yom Tov.

Praised are You, Adonai our God, Sovereign of the Universe, who makes us holy with mitzvot and instructs us to kindle the lights of (Shabbat and) Yom Tov.

The blessing for Yom Kippur is:

בָּרוּךְ אַתָּה יְיָ אֱלֹהֵינוּ מֶלֶךְ הָעוֹלָם אֲשֶׁר קִדְּשָׁנוּ בְּמִצְוֹתָיו וְצִוָּנוּ לְהַדְלִיק נֵר שֶׁל (שַׁבָּת וְשֶׁל) יוֹם הַכִּפּוּרִים:

Baruch atah Adonai elohaynu melech ha'olam asher kid-shanu bemitzvotav vetzivanu l'hadlik ner shel (Shabbat v'shel) Yom ha-Kippurim.

Praised are You, Adonai our God, Sovereign of the Universe, who makes us holy with mitzvot and instructs us to kindle the lights of (Shabbat and) the Day of Atonement.

Things to remember:

1. Candles are lit for the sake of *shalom bayit* and *oneg Shabbat.*

2. Traditionally, women light the candles, but men are encouraged to do so.

3. While you are required to light two candles, it is permitted to light more. Families of Eastern European heritage often light more, often one for each child. This is an interpretation of the verse "God blessed the Sabbath day." How? With light. Once you have established a pattern, continue to light that number each week.

4. If there are no candles available, you may say the blessing over electric or gas lights.

Key words and phrases:

Hadlakat nerot הַדְלָקַת נֵרוֹת. The lighting of candles.
Ner נֵר. (plural, *nerot* נֵרוֹת,) candle.

If you want to know more:

Malka Drucker, *Shabbat, a Peaceful Island* (New York, 1983).

Ronald H. Isaacs, *Shabbat Delight* (Hoboken, N.J., 1987).

Isaac Klein, *A Guide to Jewish Religious Practice* (New York, 1979).

Abraham Milgram, *The Shabbat Anthology* (Philadelphia, 1944).

Mark Dov Shapiro, *Gates of Shabbat* (New York, 1991).

How to Make Shabbat Evening Kiddush
קִדּוּש לְשַׁבָּת

The source:

There are various sources, including Exodus 20:8.

זָכוֹר אֶת־יוֹם הַשַּׁבָּת לְקַדְּשׁוֹ:

Remember the Sabbath Day to keep it holy.

What you need to know:

1. Raise the cup by holding it in your hand, cupped at the bottom.

2. Say the following:

וַיְכֻלּוּ הַשָּׁמַיִם וְהָאָרֶץ וְכָל־צְבָאָם: וַיְכַל אֱלֹהִים בַּיּוֹם הַשְּׁבִיעִי
מְלַאכְתּוֹ אֲשֶׁר עָשָׂה. וַיִּשְׁבֹּת בַּיּוֹם הַשְּׁבִיעִי מִכָּל־מְלַאכְתּוֹ
אֲשֶׁר עָשָׂה: וַיְבָרֶךְ אֱלֹהִים אֶת־יוֹם הַשְּׁבִיעִי וַיְקַדֵּשׁ אֹתוֹ. כִּי
בוֹ שָׁבַת מִכָּל־מְלַאכְתּוֹ אֲשֶׁר־בָּרָא אֱלֹהִים לַעֲשׂוֹת:

*Vayechulu hashamayim ve'ha-aretz vechol tzeva'am
vayechal Elohim bayom ha-shevi'i melachto asher asah.
Vayishbot bayom hashevi'i mikol melachto asher asah
vayevarech Elohim et yom hashevi'i vayekadesh oto ki
vo shavat mikol melachto asher bara Elohim la'asot.*

Now the whole universe—sky, earth, and all their
array—was completed. With the seventh day God
ended the work of Creation; on the seventh day God
rested with all the Divine work completed. Then God
blessed the seventh day and called it holy, for with
this day God had completed the work of Creation.

בָּרוּךְ אַתָּה יְיָ אֱלֹהֵינוּ מֶלֶךְ הָעוֹלָם בּוֹרֵא פְּרִי הַגָּפֶן:

Baruch atah Adonai elohaynu melech ha'olam boray pri ha-gafen.

Praised are You, Adonai our God, Sovereign of the Universe, who creates the fruit of the vine.

בָּרוּךְ אַתָּה יְיָ אֱלֹהֵינוּ מֶלֶךְ הָעוֹלָם אֲשֶׁר קִדְּשָׁנוּ בְּמִצְוֹתָיו וְרָצָה בָנוּ וְשַׁבַּת קָדְשׁוֹ בְּאַהֲבָה וּבְרָצוֹן הִנְחִילָנוּ זִכָּרוֹן לְמַעֲשֵׂה בְרֵאשִׁית. כִּי הוּא יוֹם תְּחִלָּה לְמִקְרָאֵי קֹדֶשׁ זֵכֶר לִיצִיאַת מִצְרָיִם: כִּי בָנוּ בָחַרְתָּ וְאוֹתָנוּ קִדַּשְׁתָּ מִכָּל הָעַמִּים. וְשַׁבַּת קָדְשְׁךָ בְּאַהֲבָה וּבְרָצוֹן הִנְחַלְתָּנוּ: בָּרוּךְ אַתָּה יְיָ מְקַדֵּשׁ הַשַּׁבָּת:

Baruch atah Adonai elohaynu melech ha'olam asher kidshanu bemitzvotav veratza vanu veshabbat kod- sho be'ahavah u'vratzon hinchilanu zikaron le'ma'asay vereshit ki hu yom techilah lemikra'ay kodesh zecher l'tziyat mitzrayim. Ki vanu vacharta ve'otanu kidashta mikol ha'amim veshabbat kodshecha be'ahava u'vratzon hinchaltanu. Baruch atah Adonai mikadesh ha-Shabbat.

Praised are You, Adonai our God, Sovereign of the Universe, who makes us holy with mitzvot and takes delight in us. In love and favor You have made the holy Sabbath our heritage, as a reminder of the work of Creation. It is first among our sacred days, and a remembrance of the Exodus from Egypt. O God, You have chosen us and set us apart from all the peoples and in love and favor have given us the Sabbath Day in your love and favor. Praised are You Adonai for the Sabbath and its holiness.

3. Then drink the wine.

Things to remember:

1. On Shabbat morning, sing *Veshamru,* then say only the modified blessing (over wine, not over the day).

וְשָׁמְרוּ בְנֵי־יִשְׂרָאֵל אֶת־הַשַּׁבָּת, לַעֲשׂוֹת אֶת־הַשַּׁבָּת לְדֹרוֹתָם בְּרִית עוֹלָם: בֵּינִי וּבֵין בְּנֵי יִשְׂרָאֵל אוֹת הִיא לְעֹלָם, כִּי־שֵׁשֶׁת יָמִים עָשָׂה יְיָ אֶת־הַשָּׁמַיִם וְאֶת־הָאָרֶץ, וּבַיּוֹם הַשְּׁבִיעִי שָׁבַת וַיִּנָּפַשׁ:

Veshamru venay Yisrael et ha-Shabbat la'asot et ha-Shabbat ledorotam berit olam baynee u'vayn b'nai Yisrael ot hee le'olam ki sheshet yamim asah Adonai et hashamayim ve'et ha-aretz u'vayom hashevi'i shavat vayinafash.

עַל כֵּן בֵּרַךְ יְיָ אֶת־יוֹם הַשַּׁבָּת וַיְקַדְּשֵׁהוּ:

Al ken berach Adonai et yom ha-Shabbat vayekadeshayu.

בָּרוּךְ אַתָּה יְיָ אֱלֹהֵינוּ מֶלֶךְ הָעוֹלָם בּוֹרֵא פְּרִי הַגָּפֶן:

Baruch atah Adonai elohaynu melech ha'olam boray pri hagafen.

2. Remember to drink the wine (before talking) after the blessing.

3. On Yom Tov, the same blessing is replaced with the following:

בָּרוּךְ אַתָּה יְיָ אֱלֹהֵינוּ מֶלֶךְ הָעוֹלָם אֲשֶׁר בָּחַר בָּנוּ מִכָּל־עָם וְרוֹמְמָנוּ מִכָּל לָשׁוֹן, וְקִדְּשָׁנוּ בְּמִצְוֹתָיו.

Baruch atah Adonai elohaynu melech ha'olam asher bachar banu mikol am ve'romimanu mikol lashon vekidshanu bemitzvatav.

Praised is Adonai our God, Sovereign of the Universe, who has chosen us from all the peoples, exalting us by making us holy with mitzvot.

וַתִּתֶּן לָנוּ יְיָ אֱלֹהֵינוּ בְּאַהֲבָה, (שַׁבָּתוֹת לִמְנוּחָה וּ) מוֹעֲדִים לְשִׂמְחָה, חַגִּים וּזְמַנִּים לְשָׂשׂוֹן, אֶת יוֹם (הַשַּׁבָּת הַזֶּה וְאֶת יוֹם)

Vatitayn lanu Adonai elohaynu b'ahavah (Shabbatot limenucha) moadim lesimcha chagim u'zmanim le'sason et yom (ha-Shabbat hazeh ve'et yom)

In Your love, Adonai our God, You have given us (Sabbaths of rest), feasts of gladness, and seasons of joy: this (Sabbath Day and this) festival of

חַג הַמַּצוֹת הַזֶּה, זְמַן חֵרוּתֵנוּ

chag hamatzot hazeh zeman cherutaynu

Pesach—season of our freedom

חַג הַשָׁבוּעוֹת הַזֶּה, זְמַן מַתַּן תּוֹרָתֵנוּ

chag hashavuot hazeh zeman matan torahtenu

Shavuot—season of revelation

חַג הַסֻכּוֹת הַזֶּה, זְמַן שִׂמְחָתֵנוּ

chag hasukkot hazeh zeman simchatenu

Sukkot—season of thanksgiving

הַשְׁמִינִי חַג הָעֲצֶרֶת הַזֶּה, זְמַן שִׂמְחָתֵנוּ

hashemini chag ha'atzeret hazeh–zeman simchatenu

Shemini Atzeret Simchat Torah—season of our gladness

מִקְרָא קֹדֶשׁ זֵכֶר לִיצִיאַת מִצְרָיִם.

mikra kodesh zecher litziyat mitzrayim.

to unite in prayer and recall the Exodus from Egypt.

כִּי בָנוּ בָחַרְתָּ וְאוֹתָנוּ קִדַּשְׁתָּ מִכָּל־הָעַמִּים, (וְשַׁבָּת) וּמוֹעֲדֵי קָדְשֶׁךָ (בְּאַהֲבָה וּבְרָצוֹן) בְּשִׂמְחָה וּבְשָׂשׂוֹן הִנְחַלְתָּנוּ: בָּרוּךְ אַתָּה יְיָ מְקַדֵּשׁ (הַשַׁבָּת וְ) יִשְׂרָאֵל וְהַזְּמַנִּים:

ki vanu vacharta ve'otanu kidashta mikol ha'amim (ve-Shabbat) u'mo'aday kodshecha (be'ahavah u'vratzon) besimcha u'vesason hinchaltanu. Baruch atah Adonai mikadesh (ha-Shabbat v') Yisrael vehazemanim.

For You have chosen us from all peoples, consecrating us to Your service and giving us (the Sabbath a sign of Your love and favor, and) the Festivals, a time of gladness and joy. Praised are You, Adonai, who makes holy (the Sabbath,) the House of Israel and the Festivals.

Key words and phrases:

Kiddush קִדּוּשׁ. From the Hebrew meaning "holy" or "separate," a prayer said to sanctify time and place.

55

Kos כּוֹס. Cup.
Yayin יַיִן. Wine.

If you want to know more:

Malka Drucker, *Shabbat, a Peaceful Island* (New York, 1983).
Ronald H. Isaacs, *Shabbat Delight* (Hoboken, N.J., 1987).
Abraham Milgram, *The Shabbat Anthology* (Philadelphia, 1944).
Mark Dov Shapiro, *Gates of Shabbat* (New York, 1991).

How to Make Havdalah
הַבְדָּלָה

The source:

Various talmudic sources, including Pesachim 103b; also
Shulchan Aruch, Orach Chayim 196:1.

What you need to know:

1. Raise the wine cup and say:

הִנֵּה אֵל יְשׁוּעָתִי, אֶבְטַח וְלֹא אֶפְחָד. כִּי עָזִּי וְזִמְרָת יָהּ יְיָ,
וַיְהִי לִי לִישׁוּעָה. וּשְׁאַבְתֶּם מַיִם בְּשָׂשׂוֹן מִמַּעַיְנֵי הַיְשׁוּעָה. לַיְיָ
הַיְשׁוּעָה עַל עַמְּךָ בִרְכָתֶךָ סֶּלָה. יְיָ צְבָאוֹת עִמֶּנוּ, מִשְׂגָּב לָנוּ
אֱלֹהֵי יַעֲקֹב, סֶלָה.

Behold, God is my deliverer. I trust in You and
am not afraid. For Adonai is my strength and my
stronghold, the source of my deliverance. With joy
we draw water from the wells of salvation. Adonai
brings deliverance, blessings to the people. Selah.
Adonai is a powerful God: the God of Jacob is our
stronghold.

לַיְּהוּדִים הָיְתָה אוֹרָה וְשִׂמְחָה וְשָׂשׂוֹן וִיקָר. כֵּן תִּהְיֶה לָנוּ. כּוֹס
יְשׁוּעוֹת אֶשָּׂא וּבְשֵׁם יְיָ אֶקְרָא.

Give us light and joy, gladness and honor, as in the
happiest days of Israel's past. I lift up the cup of my
salvation and call out the name of Adonai.

בָּרוּךְ אַתָּה יְיָ אֱלֹהֵינוּ מֶלֶךְ הָעוֹלָם בּוֹרֵא פְּרִי הַגָּפֶן:

*Baruch atah Adonai elohaynu melech ha'olam boray pri
ha-gafen.*

57

Praise are You, Adonai our God, Sovereign of the Universe, who creates the fruit of the vine.

2. Next, lift the spice box and say:

בָּרוּךְ אַתָּה יְיָ אֱלֹהֵינוּ מֶלֶךְ הָעוֹלָם בּוֹרֵא מִינֵי בְשָׂמִים:

Baruch atah Adonai elohaynu melech ha'olam boray minay vesamim.

Praised are You, Adonai our God, Sovereign of the Universe, who creates all kinds of spices.

Sniff the spices and pass the spice box around for everyone to sniff.

3. Now recite the blessing over the Havdalah candle:

בָּרוּךְ אַתָּה יְיָ אֱלֹהֵינוּ מֶלֶךְ הָעוֹלָם בּוֹרֵא מְאוֹרֵי הָאֵשׁ:

Baruch atah Adonai elohaynu melech ha'olam boray me'oray ha'aysh.

Praised are You, Adonai our God, Sovereign of the Universe, who creates the lights of the fire.

While the blessing is recited, family members hold out their hands with palms up, cup their hands, and look at the reflection of the flame on their fingernails.

4. Finally recite the final prayer:

בָּרוּךְ אַתָּה יְיָ אֱלֹהֵינוּ מֶלֶךְ הָעוֹלָם הַמַּבְדִיל בֵּין קֹדֶשׁ לְחוֹל
בֵּין אוֹר לְחֹשֶׁךְ בֵּין יִשְׂרָאֵל לָעַמִּים, בֵּין יוֹם הַשְּׁבִיעִי לְשֵׁשֶׁת
יְמֵי הַמַּעֲשֶׂה: בָּרוּךְ אַתָּה יְיָ הַמַּבְדִיל בֵּין קֹדֶשׁ לְחוֹל:

Baruch atah Adonai elohaynu melech ha'olam hamavdil bayn kodesh lechol bayn or lechoshech bayn Yisrael la'amim bayn yom hashevi'i le'sheshet yemay ha-ma'aseh. Baruch atah Adonai hamavdil bayn kodesh le-chol.

Praised are You, Adonai our God, Sovereign of the Universe, who makes a distinction between sacred and secular, light and darkness, Israel and other peoples, the seventh day and the six days of labor. Praised are You, Adonai, who makes a distinction between sacred and secular.

5. Many families conclude the service with the singing of Eliyahu ha-Navi ("Elijah the Prophet").

אֵלִיָהוּ הַנָּבִיא, אֵלִיָהוּ הַתִּשְׁבִּי
אֵלִיָהוּ, אֵלִיָהוּ, אֵלִיָהוּ הַגִּלְעָדִי.
בִּמְהֵרָה בְּיָמֵינוּ יָבֹא אֵלֵינוּ
עִם מָשִׁיחַ בֶּן דָּוִד.

Eliyahu ha-Navi Eliyahu ha-Tishbi
Eliyahu Eliyahu Eliyahu ha-Giladi.
Bimhera beyamaynu yavo aleynu
Im Mashiach ben David.

Elijah the Prophet
Elijah the Tishbite
Elijah the Gileadite.
May Elijah come quickly in our time
Along with the Messiah, the son of David.

6. Everyone takes a sip of the wine. Then pour some of   שָׁבוּעַ טוֹב
the remaining wine onto a plate (or directly over the flame) and put out the flame of the Havdalah candle. Shabbat is over, and everyone proclaims *shavua tov*, "a good week!" Often, people sing, *shavua tov, shavua tov, shavua tov, shavua tov,* "A good week, a week of peace. May gladness reign and joy increase."

Things to remember:

1. Havdalah is said about an hour after sunset on Saturday night, when three stars appear in the sky.

2. What you need:
   A Havdalah candle
   Cup of wine
   Spice box and spices

Key words and phrases:

Besamim בְּשָׂמִים. Spices.

Melaveh Malkah מְלַוֶּה מַלְכָּה. Meaning escorting the queen, it's a small meal or party held on Saturday evenings after Havdalah in some traditional Jewish communities.

Ner Havdalah נֵר הַבְדָּלָה. Twisted Havdalah candle.

If you want to know more:

Ron Isaacs. *Shabbat Delight: A Celebration in Stories, Songs and Games.* (Hoboken, 1987).

Ron Wolfson: *The Art of Jewish Living: The Shabbat Seder.* (Los Angeles, 1985).

Blowing a Shofar
תְּקִיעַת הַשּׁוֹפָר

The source:

וְהַעֲבַרְתָּ שׁוֹפַר תְּרוּעָה בַּחֹדֶשׁ הַשְּׁבִיעִי בֶּעָשׂוֹר לַחֹדֶשׁ בְּיוֹם הַכִּפֻּרִים תַּעֲבִירוּ שׁוֹפָר בְּכָל־אַרְצְכֶם:

"Then you shall sound the horn loud; in the seventh month, on the tenth day of the month—the Day of Atonement—you shall have the horn sounded throughout your land" (Lev. 25:9).

בַּחֹדֶשׁ הַשְּׁבִיעִי בְּאֶחָד לַחֹדֶשׁ יִהְיֶה לָכֶם שַׁבָּתוֹן זִכְרוֹן תְּרוּעָה מִקְרָא־קֹדֶשׁ:

"In the seventh month, on the first day of the month, you shall observe complete rest, a sacred occasion commemorated with loud blasts" (Lev. 23:24).

What you need to know:

A ram's horn is used because of its connection to the near sacrifice of Isaac which is read on the second day of Rosh Hashanah from Genesis 22. Prior to the beginning of the shofar service, the listener says the following blessing:

בָּרוּךְ אַתָּה יְיָ אֱלֹהֵינוּ מֶלֶךְ הָעוֹלָם אֲשֶׁר קִדְּשָׁנוּ בְּמִצְוֹתָיו וְצִוָּנוּ לִשְׁמוֹעַ קוֹל שׁוֹפָר:

Baruch atah Adonai elohaynu melech ha'olam asher kidshanu bemitzvotav vetzivanu lishmo'ah kol shofar.

Praised are You, Adonai our God, Sovereign of the Universe, who has made us holy with mitzvot and has instructed us to hear the call of the shofar.

בָּרוּךְ אַתָּה יְיָ אֱלֹהֵינוּ מֶלֶךְ הָעוֹלָם, שֶׁהֶחֱיָנוּ וְקִיְּמָנוּ וְהִגִּיעָנוּ לַזְּמַן הַזֶּה:

Baruch atah Adonai elohaynu melech ha'olam she-he-cheyanu ve-kimanu vehigiyanu lazman hazeh.

Praised are You, Adonai our God, Sovereign of the Universe, who has given us life, sustained us, and helped us reach this day.

Take out the shofar and blow the notes according to the order established by the caller.

תְּקִיעָה 1. *Tekiah:* lit. "blast," one long blast with a clean, consistent tone.

שְׁבָרִים 2. *Shevarim:* lit. "broken sound," three short calls together as long as *tekiah.*

תְּרוּעָה 3. *Teruah:* lit. "alarm," a rapid series of very short notes, generally three series of three that together total one *tekiah.*

תְּקִיעָה גְדוֹלָה 4. *Tekiah gedolah:* lit. "the great *tekiah*," a single blast that is held as long as you can do it.

On Rosh Hashanah, after the Torah and Haftarah have been read, the shofar service begins. Specific verses from Psalms are read. Then the shofar blower makes two *berachot* (blessings).

Things to remember:

תְּקִיעָה
שְׁבָרִים
תְּרוּעָה
תְּקִיעָה
1. Beginning with the first day of the month of Elul (the month before Rosh Hashanah), it is a custom to blow the shofar. Some sound the entire *tekiah*. Do it every day (except Shabbat) except for the day before Rosh Hashanah.

2. Some keep the shofar concealed in the folds of the *tallit* until the caller (the one who calls the notes) is prepared to call the notes.

3. In shofar blowing, hearing and blowing so that other people can hear are considered equal *mitzvot.*

4. Each cycle has three repetitions. On the last, the *tekiah gedolah* is added.

Key words and phrases:

Akedat Yitzchak עֲקֵידַת יִצְחָק. The binding of Isaac.
Baal Tekiah בַּעַל תְּקִיעָה. Master blaster.
Seder tekiat shofar סֵדֶר תְּקִיעַת שׁוֹפָר. The order of the blowing of the shofar.

If you want to know more:

S. Y. Agnon, *Days of Awe* (New York, 1965).
Isaac Klein, *A Guide to Jewish Religious Practice* (New York, 1979).
Joel Grishaver, *Rosh Hashanah and Yom Kippur* (Los Angeles, 1987).

Tossing Tashlich
תַּשְׁלִיךְ

The source:

וְתַשְׁלִיךְ בִּמְצוּלוֹת יָם כָּל חַטֹּאתָם:

"You will cast all your sins into the depths of the sea" (Micah 7:19).

What you need to know:

1. On the afternoon of the first day of Rosh Hashanah, walk to a river or spring (preferably one with fish in it) and recite special prayers called penitential prayers. Here is the essence of them: Micah 7:18–20, Psalms 118:5–9; 33;130.

2. After you have said the prayers, empty your pockets (or throw bread crumbs which you have brought with you) into the water.

Things to remember:

1. Tossing the bread crumbs is symbolic of casting away our sins and starting over again in a new year.

2. If the first day of Rosh Hashanah falls on Shabbat, then *tashlich* is traditionally done on the second day.

Key words and phrases:

Avon עָוֹן. Intentional sin.
Chet חֵטְא. Missing the mark, mistaken sin.
Pesha פֶּשַׁע. The worst sin, done with malice.

If you want to know more:

Philip Goodman, *The Rosh Hashanah Anthology* (Philadelphia, 1970).

Building a Sukkah
סוּכָּה

The source:

בַּסֻּכֹּת תֵּשְׁבוּ שִׁבְעַת יָמִים

"You shall live in booths for seven days" (Lev. 23:42).

What you need to know:

1. A *sukkah* must have four walls. (One of the walls can be a wall of your own house.)

2. Start building the *sukkah* as soon after Yom Kippur as possible!

3. One possible *sukkah* building recipe is as follows:

a. Use the back wall of your house or garage as one of the four walls.
b. Stack two cement blocks in each corner and insert two-by-fours (seven or eight feet long) into the blocks. Connect the two-by-fours with one-by-twos across the middle and the top.
c. Stretch burlap cloth or plastic, or nail some thin plywood over the frame. (Note: one wall can serve as the entrance if it is covered with burlap cloth.)
d. Put one-by-ones running in both directions on the roof and cover with bamboo, twigs, corn husks, or other organic material. Remember to let the stars shine through!
e. Decorate the inside of the *sukkah* with fruit hangings, Rosh Hashanah greeting cards, posters, paper chains, and the like.
f. Hang an electric light fixture in the *sukkah* for dining in the evening. (Be careful!)
g. If you do not want to build your *sukkah* from scratch there are prefabricated ones for sale at your local Judaica store or through your synagogue.

Sukkah diagram

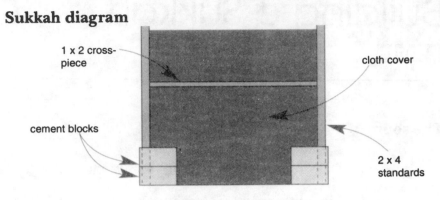

1 x 2 cross-piece

cloth cover

cement blocks

2 x 4 standards

SIDE VIEW OF END WALL

Key words and phrases:

Schach סְכַךְ. Organic material that is used to form the roof of a *sukkah*.

Ushpizin אוּשְׁפִּיזִין. Custom of inviting Jewish biblical ancestors into the *sukkah* as invisible guests.

If you want to know more:

Philip Goodman, *Sukkot and Simhat Torah Anthology* (Philadelphia, 1973).

The Four Species: Assembling the Lulav
אַרְבַּע מִינִים

The source:

וּלְקַחְתֶּם לָכֶם בַּיּוֹם הָרִאשׁוֹן פְּרִי עֵץ הָדָר כַּפֹּת תְּמָרִים וַעֲנַף עֵץ־עָבֹת וְעַרְבֵי־נָחַל וּשְׂמַחְתֶּם לִפְנֵי יְיָ אֱלֹהֵיכֶם שִׁבְעַת יָמִים:

"On the first day, you shall take the product of the beautiful trees, branches of palm trees, boughs of leafy trees, and willows of the brook, and you shall rejoice before Adonai your God for seven days" (Lev. 23:40).

What you need to know:

What to look for in the four species:

1. The four species consists of the *lulav* (palm), the *etrog* (citrus), the *hadas* (myrtle), and the *arava* (willow). לוּלָב אֶתְרוֹג הֲדַס עֲרָבָה

2. The *etrog* should taper upward on the top. Its face should be rough, and its shape symmetrical so that the tip is directly above the stem. There should be no blotches or spots on the skin and the color should be yellow.

3. The *lulav* should be fresh and straight. The leaves should not spread out nor should the tip be broken off. The minimum length is sixteen inches.

4. The myrtle and the willow should be green, fresh, with the leaves intact. The preferred length is approximately twelve inches.

To assemble the *lulav*:

1. Place the *lulav* in the Y-shaped holder.

2. Carefully place three myrtle leaves on the right and two willow twigs in the left part of the Y-shaped holder with the spine of the *lulav* facing you as the *lulav* is placed in the central part of the holder.

3. Take several leaves off of the *lulav* and tie them in a bow in three places along the length of the lulav.

Key words and phrases:

Arava עֲרָבָה. Willow leaves.
Etrog אֶתְרוֹג. Citron.
Hadas הֲדָס. Myrtle leaves.
Lulav לוּלָב. Palm branch.
Okez עוֹקֶץ. The stem of the *etrog*.

Pittam פִּיטָם. The end of the *etrog* that produces the flower.

If you want to know more:

Encyclopaedia Judaica (Jerusalem, 1971) 6:1448–1449.
Morris Epstein, *All About Jewish Holidays and Customs* (New York, 1970).

More particulars:

1. After the festival of Sukkot is over, use the myrtle to make spices for your Havdalah spice box.

2. Use the *lulav* in the search–for–*chametz* ceremony (instead of a spoon). Then burn the *lulav* with your *chametz* at Passover, but be careful, dried *lulavim* can cut and pierce.

3. Stick a whole clove into your *etrog*. Cover it with powdered cinammon and let it dry for a few weeks. Then use it as a spice essence for Havdalah.

4. Or make *etrog* jelly with your used *etrog*!

Waving the Lulav
לוּלָב

The source:

וּלְקַחְתֶּם לָכֶם בַּיּוֹם הָרִאשׁוֹן פְּרִי עֵץ הָדָר כַּפֹּת תְּמָרִים וַעֲנַף עֵץ־עָבֹת וְעַרְבֵי־נָחַל וּשְׂמַחְתֶּם לִפְנֵי יְיָ אֱלֹהֵיכֶם שִׁבְעַת יָמִים:

"On the first day, you shall take the product of the beautiful trees, branches of palm trees, boughs of leafy trees, and willows of the brook, and you shall rejoice before Adonai your God for seven days" (Lev. 23:40).

What you need to know:

שַׁחֲרִית
הַלֵּל

Wave the *lulav* each morning of Sukkot either before the morning service (*Shacharit*) or during the service just before *Hallel*.

Hold the entire *lulav* in your right hand (with the spine facing you, two willows on left, three myrtles on right), the *etrog* in the left. Both should touch each other. Before the blessing, hold the *etrog* with the *pittam* down. After the blessing (and during the waving), hold the *etrog* with the *pittam* up. Always stand facing east to Jerusalem.

After the meditation found in the *siddur* (prayerbook), recite this blessing:

בָּרוּךְ אַתָּה יְיָ אֱלֹהֵנוּ מֶלֶךְ הָעוֹלָם אֲשֶׁר קִדְּשָׁנוּ בְּמִצְוֹתָיו וְצִוָּנוּ עַל נְטִילַת לוּלָב:

Baruch atah Adonai elohaynu melech ha'olam asher kid-shanu bemitzvotav vetzivanu al netilat lulav.

Praised are You, Adonai our God, Sovereign of the Universe, who has made us holy by *mitzvot* and has instructed us to take hold of the *lulav*.

And on the first day:

בָּרוּךְ אַתָּה יְיָ אֱלֹהֵינוּ מֶלֶךְ הָעוֹלָם שֶׁהֶחֱיָנוּ וְקִיְמָנוּ וְהִגִּיעָנוּ לַזְּמַן הַזֶּה:

Baruch atah Adonai elohaynu melech ha'olam she-he-cheyanu vekimanu vehigiyanu lazman hazeh.

Praised are You, Adonai our God, Sovereign of the Universe, who has given us life, sustained us, and helped us to reach this day.

Shake the *lulav* in a motion of reaching out and reaching in, straightening your arms opposite your chest and folding them against your chest. Do this three times in front of you (east), then to the right (south), then back behind you over your shoulder (west), then out to the left (north), then above you (to heaven) and below you (to earth). Do it slowly and deliberately.

Also do it when these verses occur during *Hallel* (Psalms 113–118):

Hodu הוֹדוּ (front) *l'Adonai* לַיְהֹוָה *kee* כִּי (right) *tov* טוֹב (back) *Kee* כִּי (left) *l'olam* לְעֹלָם (up) *chasdo* חַסְדוֹ (down)

Yomar יֹאמַר (front) *na* נָא (right) *Yisrael* יִשְׂרָאֵל (back) *Kee* כִּי (left) *l'olam* לְעוֹלָם (up) *chasdo* חַסְדוֹ (down)

Ana אָנָּא (front, right) *Adonai,* יְהֹוָה *hoshiah* הוֹשִׁיעָה (back, left, up) *na* נָא (down)
Ana אָנָּא (front, right) *Adonai,* יְהֹוָה, *hoshiah* הוֹשִׁיעָה (back, left, up) *na* נָא (down).

Things to remember:

1. Traditional Jews don't shake it on Shabbat.

2. Don't let the *pittam* get broken.

Key words and phrases:

Aravot עֲרָבוֹת. Willows.

Arba minim אַרְבַּע מִינִים. Four species (*etrog*/citron, palm, myrtle, willow).

Hadas הֲדַס. Leafy myrtle.

Hoshana הוֹשַׁע נָא. From the words *hoshiah na,* a fervent plea to God for help.

Lulav לוּלָב. Palm branch, used to name the combined branches because it is the largest.

Pittam פִּטָּם. Not the stem, the protrusion on the bottom of the *etrog*.

If you want to know more:

Encyclopaedia Judaica (Jerusalem, 1971) 15:495–502.

Philip Goodman, *The Sukkot and Simhat Torah Anthology* (Philadelphia, 1973).

Isaac Klein, *A Guide to Jewish Religious Practice* (New York, 1979).

Richard Siegel and Michael Strassfeld and Sharon Strassfeld, *The First Jewish Catalogue* (Philadelphia, 1973).

Lighting a Chanukiyah
הַדְלָקַת חֲנֻכִּיָּה

The source:

"The rabbis taught: The laws of Chanukah require one
light for a person and household; those who want to
be more careful may use one light for each member
of the household. For those who want to be even
more careful, the school of Shammai suggested that
on the first day of the festival, eight candles are to
be lit and we light one fewer each progressive night.
Hillel suggested that on the first day, one candle is
lit and one candle is added each night. Shammai
reasoned that the number of candles corresponds to
the number of days to come; Hillel reasoned that the
number of candles corresponds to the days already
passed" (Babylonian Talmud, Shabbat 21b).

What you need to know:

Place one new candle in the *chanukiyah* for each night of
Chanukah, increasing one candle per night (plus the
shamash). Olive oil may be used. Candles should be
placed from right to left. Light the *shamash* first and
use it to light from the *left*.

חֲנֻכִּיָּה
שַׁמָּשׁ

Then say the blessings:
(on each night)

בָּרוּךְ אַתָּה יְיָ אֱלֹהֵנוּ מֶלֶךְ הָעוֹלָם אֲשֶׁר קִדְּשָׁנוּ בְּמִצְוֹתָיו וְצִוָּנוּ
לְהַדְלִיק נֵר שֶׁל חֲנֻכָּה:

*Baruch atah Adonai elohaynu melech ha'olam asher kid-
shanu bemitzvotav vetzivanu lehadlik ner shel Chanukah.*

Praised are You, Adonai our God, Sovereign of the
Universe, who has made us holy by mitzvot and instructed us to light the Chanukah candles.

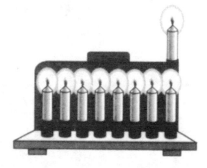

(on each night)

בָּרוּךְ אַתָּה יְיָ אֱלֹהֵינוּ מֶלֶךְ הָעוֹלָם שֶׁעָשָׂה נִסִּים לַאֲבוֹתֵינוּ
בַּיָּמִים הָהֵם בַּזְּמַן הַזֶּה:

Baruch atah Adonai elohaynu melech ha'olam she'asah nisim lavotaynu bayamim hahaym bazman hazeh.

Praised are You, Adonai our God, Sovereign of the Universe, who performed miracles for our ancestors at this season in ancient days.

(on first night only)

בָּרוּךְ אַתָּה יְיָ אֱלֹהֵינוּ מֶלֶךְ הָעוֹלָם שֶׁהֶחֱיָנוּ וְקִיְּמָנוּ וְהִגִּיעָנוּ
לַזְּמַן הַזֶּה:

Baruch atah Adonai elohaynu melech ha'olam she-he-cheyanu vekimanu vehigiyanu lazman hazeh.

Praised are You, Adonai our God, Sovereign of the Universe, who has given us life, sustained us, and helped us to reach this day.

Using the *shamash*, light the candles, one for each night, beginning with the current night first, from left to right. While some communities blow out the *shamash* each night and use it for the duration of the festival, most people let it burn down each night and use a new *shamash* for succeeding nights.

הַנֵּרוֹת הַלָּלוּ   After you have lit the candles, read the following prayer called *Hanerot Hallalu.*

הַנֵּרוֹת הַלָּלוּ אֲנַחְנוּ מַדְלִיקִין עַל הַנִּסִּים וְעַל הַנִּפְלָאוֹת וְעַל
הַתְּשׁוּעוֹת וְעַל הַמִּלְחָמוֹת שֶׁעָשִׂיתָ לַאֲבוֹתֵינוּ בַּיָּמִים הָהֵם
בַּזְּמַן הַזֶּה עַל יְדֵי כֹּהֲנֶיךָ הַקְּדוֹשִׁים. וְכָל־שְׁמוֹנַת יְמֵי חֲנֻכָּה
הַנֵּרוֹת הַלָּלוּ קֹדֶשׁ הֵם, וְאֵין לָנוּ רְשׁוּת לְהִשְׁתַּמֵּשׁ בָּהֶם אֶלָּא
לִרְאוֹתָם בִּלְבָד, כְּדֵי לְהוֹדוֹת וּלְהַלֵּל לְשִׁמְךָ הַגָּדוֹל, עַל נִסֶּיךָ
וְעַל נִפְלְאוֹתֶיךָ וְעַל יְשׁוּעָתֶךָ:

In order to recall the miracles and wonders that You performed for our ancestors through the agency of

74

holy priests, we kindle these lights. We hold these flames sacred throughout the eight-day Chanukah period; we shall not make any profane use of them. Instead, we will simply look at them so that we may recall Your reputation as a God who makes miracles, does wonders, and delivers our people.

Things to remember:

1. Load from the right; light from the left.

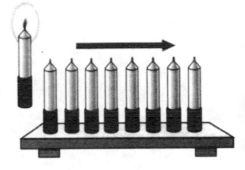

2. Place your *chanukiyah* in the window nearest the street so that all can see.

3. Candle holders in traditional *chanukiyot* are all on the same level, with a higher or separate *shamash*.

4. On Shabbat Chanukah, light the Chanukah candles before you light the Shabbat candles.

5. Light your candles after nightfall but early enough so that people can see them.

6. At the end of Shabbat Chanukah, do Havdalah and then light the Chanukah candles.

7. Don't use the lights of Chanukah for practical purposes, like reading.

Key words and phrases:

Ner נֵר. Candle.
Or אוֹר. Light.
Shemen שֶׁמֶן. Oil.

If you want to know more:

Elias Bickerman, *The Maccabees* (New York, 1947).
Encyclopaedia Judaica (Jerusalem, 1973) 7:1280–1315.

Philip Goodman, *The Hanukkah Anthology* (Philadelphia, 1976).

Mae Shafter Rockland, *The Hanukkah Book* (New York, 1975).

David Rosenberg, *A Blazing Fountain* (New York, 1978).

Sol Scharfstein, *Hanukah: Who? Why? When?* (Hoboken, N.J., 1991).

How to Play the Dreidel Game
דְרֵיידְל

The source:

Probably derived from an old German gambling game.

What you need to know:

1. Each person should start with ten or fifteen pennies, nuts, or raisins.

2. Each player puts a coin or raisin or nut into the middle (what card players call the pot).

3. Taking turns, one person spins at a time. Winning or losing is determined by which side of the dreidel is facing up when it falls.

4. a. *Nun* stands for "nothing" (*nisht* in Yiddish), so the נ player does nothing.
   b. *Gimmel* stands for "all" (*gantz* in Yiddish), so the ג player takes everything in the pot.
   c. *Heh* stands for "half," (*halb* in Yiddish), so the player ה takes half of what is in the pot.
   d. *Shin* stands for "put in" (*shtel* in Yiddish), so the ש player puts one in the pot.

5. After a *gimmel* has been spun, each player adds one. When an odd number of coins are in the pot, the player spinning *heh* takes half plus one. When one player has won everything, the game is over.

Things to remember:

1. Dreidels in Israel read *nes gadol hayah poh,* "a great miracle happened here" (instead of "there").

Key words and phrases:

Chanukah gelt. Coins used in dreidel game (often foil-wrapped chocolate).
Dreidel (Yiddish). Spinning top. *Sevivon* (Hebrew). Spinning top.

If you want to know more:

Philip Goodman, *The Hanukkah Anthology* (Philadelphia, 1976).
Sol Scharfstein, *Hanukah: Who? Why? When?* (Hoboken, N.J., 1991).

The Search for Chametz
בְּדִיקַת חָמֵץ

The source:

מַצּוֹת יֵאָכֵל אֵת שִׁבְעַת הַיָּמִים וְלֹא־יֵרָאֶה לְךָ חָמֵץ וְלֹא־יֵרָאֶה
לְךָ שְׂאֹר בְּכָל־גְּבֻלֶךָ:

"Unleavened bread shall be eaten throughout the seven days; and there shall be no leavened bread or leavening seen with you, in all of your borders" (Exod. 13:7).

What you need to know:

1. The search for *chametz* begins on the evening following the thirteenth of Nisan. (If the first day of Passover is on Sunday, then the search is conducted on the evening following the twelfth of Nisan.)

2. To conduct the search for *chametz*, you will need a candle, a feather, and a wooden spoon.

3. To make sure that the search for *chametz* is successful, several pieces of bread are scattered throughout various parts of the house to be collected during the search.

4. Before the actual search begins, light a candle and recite this blessing:

בָּרוּךְ אַתָּה יְיָ אֱלֹהֵנוּ מֶלֶךְ הָעוֹלָם אֲשֶׁר קִדְּשָׁנוּ בְּמִצְוֹתָיו וְצִוָּנוּ
עַל בִּעוּר־חָמֵץ:

Baruch atah Adonai elohaynu melech ha'olam asher kid-shanu bemitzvotav vetzivanu al bi'ur chametz.

Praised are You, Adonai our God, Sovereign of the Universe, who has made us holy with mitzvot and instructed us to remove the leaven.

5. The search begins. When a piece of bread is discovered, sweep it onto the wooden spoon using the feather. Then place it into a bag for disposal.

6. After all of the pieces of bread have been gathered and placed into the bag, say the following:

כָּל־חֲמִירָא וַחֲמִיעָא, דְּאִכָּא בִרְשׁוּתִי, דְּלָא חֲמִיתֵּהּ וּדְלָא בַעֲרָתֵּהּ, וּדְלָא יָדַעְנָא לֵהּ, לִבְטַל וְלֶהֱוֵי הֶפְקֵר, כְּעַפְרָא דְאַרְעָא:

Kol chamira vechamiya de'ikah virshuti dela chamitay u'dela vay'artei udela yadana lay libtayl ve'lehevay hefker ke'afra de'ara.

Any leaven that may still be in the house, which I have not seen or have not removed, shall be as if it does not exist, and as the dust of the earth.

7. The next day (on the fourteenth of Nisan), at about ten o'clock in the morning, take all the leaven still remaining in the house together with the leaven collected during the search the previous night and burn it. When the leaven is burned, again recite the following:

כָּל־חֲמִירָא וַחֲמִיעָא, דְּאִכָּא בִּרְשׁוּתִי, דַּחֲמִיתֵּהּ וּדְלָא חֲמִיתֵּהּ, דְּבַעֲרָתֵּהּ וּדְ֗לָא בַעֲרָתֵּהּ, לִבְטַל וְלֶהֱוֵי הֶפְקֵר, כְּעַפְרָא דְאַרְעָא:

Kol chamira vachamiya de'ika birshuti (dechamitay) u'dela chamitay devayartay u'dela vayartay libtayl ve'lehavay hefker ke'afra de'ara.

Any leaven that may still be in the house (which I have seen and not seen, which I have or have not removed,) shall be as if it does not exist, and as the dust of the earth.

Things to remember:

1. Leaven (*chametz* in Hebrew) is fermented dough made from the flour of wheat, rye, barley, spelt, or oats. According to Jewish law, eating *chametz* or even having it in your possession is forbidden during the festival of Passover.

2. Before Passover begins, all traces of leaven must be removed from the house. All utensils and cookware must also be free from *chametz*.

3. Some people use the *lulav* from the preceding Sukkot as fuel to burn the *chametz*.

4. Leaven in rabbinic literature has often symbolized the evil impulse in a person. When you remove the leaven from your home prior to Passover, you are also symbolically removing evilness from your heart.

Key words and phrases:

Biur chametz בְּעוּר חָמֵץ. Burning the leaven.
Chametz חָמֵץ. Leaven.

If you want to know more:

Philip Goodman, *The Passover Anthology* (Philadelphia, 1962).
Morris Epstein, *All About Jewish Holidays and Customs* (New York, 1970).
Ron Wolfson, *The Art of Jewish Living* (New York, 1988).

Making Matzah
מַצָּה

The source:

בְּרִאשֹׁן בְּאַרְבָּעָה עָשָׂר יוֹם לַחֹדֶשׁ בָּעֶרֶב תֹּאכְלוּ מַצֹּת עַד יוֹם הָאֶחָד וְעֶשְׂרִים לַחֹדֶשׁ בָּעָרֶב:

"In the first month, on the fourteenth day of the month in the evening, you shall eat unleavened bread, until the twenty-first of the month in the evening" (Exod. 12:18).

What you need to know:

1. Mix Passover flour and water and knead to make the dough.

2. Using a rolling pin, roll the dough into a flat sheet.

3. Perforate the dough to remove all air bubbles.

4. Bake in oven at 500° for no more than eighteen minutes.

Things to remember:

1. For flour to be Passover flour, it has to be supervised as soon as the wheat is milled.

Key words and phrases:

Egg matzah. Matzah that is enriched and more easily digested, eaten only by very young children and people who have specific health needs.
Derlanger. Person putting matzah dough onto rolling pin.
Matzah brei. An omelette made with eggs and matzah that is fried in a pan.
Matzah shemurah. Hand–made matzah.

Mehl mester. Person who measures amount of flour required by the matzah kneader.

Redel. Sharp–toothed wheel used to make perforations in matzah dough.

Redler. Person who makes the matzah perforations.

Shiber. Person responsible for placing matzah dough into oven.

Treger. Person who carries finished matzah to the plate where it was to be packed.

Uggot matzah. Matzah that is round in shape.

Vasser-gisser. Person that pours cold water into the dough as the matzah kneader requires.

If you want to know more:

Encyclopaedia Judaica (Jerusalem, 1973) 11:1155.
Philip Goodman, *The Passover Anthology* (Philadelphia, 1961).

More particulars:

1. Matzah was first baked to serve unexpected visitors. When the angels visited Lot in Sodom, Lot offered them hospitality and baked unleavened bread for them (Gen. 19:3).

2. In Talmudic times some *matzot* were made with designs on them, including figures of fish and doves.

3. In the Middle Ages *matzot* were made one inch thick!

4. Until the nineteenth century *matzot* were usually round in shape.

5. Until the middle of the nineteenth century all *matzot* were baked by hand.

6. In 1857 the first matzah–baking machine was invented in Austria.

7. In the middle of the nineteenth century the growth of Jewish communities was often measured by the amount of matzah that community consumed.

Setting the Seder Table
שֻׁלְחַן הַסֵּדֶר

The source:

Mishnah and Talmud, tractate Pesachim.

What you need to know:

1. Make sure you have a Haggadah for each person.

2. Your Seder plate should look like this:

Make sure you remember to include a hard-boiled egg,
a roasted lamb bone (chicken neck), greens, bitter
herbs, salt water, and *charoset.*

3. Provide salt water for dipping for everyone.

4. Cut up enough greens—parsley or celery—for all.

5. You can use horseradish or romaine lettuce as a bitter
herb, but make sure you have enough for everyone.

6. Be sure to include *charoset*. (There are lots of different recipes depending on the community.) It usually contains apples, nuts, cinnamon, and a little wine.

7. Place three *matzot* on a plate or in a three-layer *matzot* cover if you have one.

8. Provide enough wine–four cups for each person.

9. Place a pillow on each chair for reclining.

10. Don't forget a cup for Elijah and holiday candles. Flowers are nice too.

11. You will want to provide a cup, basin, and towel for washing, as well.

Things to remember:

1. Try to have matching *Haggadot* for everyone at the table.

2. If you have a large gathering for the Seder, you may want to set two Seder plates, one at each end of the table.

Key words and phrases:

Haggadah הַגָּדָה. Story/prayerbook for the Passover Seder.

If you want to know more:

Philip Goodman, *The Passover Anthology* (Philadelphia, 1961).
Kerry Olitzky and Ron Isaacs, *The Discovery Haggadah* (Hoboken, N.J., 1992).

Leading the Seder
סֵדֶר

The sources:

Exodus 12:3–11, 26–11, 26–27; Exodus 13:8, 13:14; Deuteronomy 6:20–21.

What you need to know:

The Order of the Seder

קַדֵּשׁ 1. *Kadesh:* Kiddush (sanctification) over the first cup (of four) of wine. Drink it in a comfortable position.

וּרְחַץ 2. *Urchatz:* Wash your hands—but without the usual blessing. It is an old custom to wash before dipping foods in a liquid or sauce.

כַּרְפַּס 3. *Karpas:* Eat the greens dipped in salt water. Green symbolizes spring; salt water reminds us of the salty tears of our ancestors who endured slavery.

יַחַץ 4. *Yachatz:* Break the middle of the matzah. Half of it is for the afikoman.

מַגִּיד 5. *Maggid:* Tell the story of Passover. This is really what the Haggadah is all about. It includes the Four Questions, the Four Sons (and we add daughters), and the Ten Plagues. This section ends with the second cup of wine. Make sure you drink it in a comfortable position.

רָחְצָה 6. *Rachtzah:* With the proper blessing, wash your hands before you begin the meal.

מוֹצִיא מַצָּה 7–8. *Motzi-Matzah:* This is a double blessing said over the matzah (as unleavened bread and as a bread substitute) just prior to eating the meal. Eat the matzah (the top and half of the middle of the three) in a comfortable position.

9. *Maror:* After saying the appropriate blessing, eat the horseradish. מָרוֹר

10. *Korech:* Called the Hillel sandwich; eat a sandwich made of matzah, horseradish, and *charoset.* Use the bottom matzah. כּוֹרֵךְ

11. *Shulchan Orech:* Now is the time to eat all those good things on the table. Don't forget to keep on singing! שׁוּלְחָן עוֹרֵךְ

12. *Tzafun:* Dessert time—but begin with eating the hidden *afikoman* (once it is found or ransomed). צָפוּן

13. *Barech: Birkat Hamazon,* grace after the meal. Say it over the third cup of wine while you are in a comfortable position. בָּרֵךְ

14. *Hallel:* Say the *Hallel* psalms. After you are finished, drink the fourth cup of wine. Don't forget to stay comfortable. Then pour Elijah's cup and have someone open the door for him. הַלֵּל

15. *Nirtzah:* This concludes the meal. נִרְצָה

Remember to say, "Next year in Jerusalem." Beginning with the second night of Passover, count the *Omer.*

Things to remember:

1. Give participants a chance to participate.

2. Don't just rely on the Haggadah text. Encourage discussion and questioning.

Key words and phrases:

Maimuna. A feast held by Moroccan Jews the day after Passover to make the holiday last longer.

If you want to know more:

Nahum N. Glatzer, *The Passover Haggadah* (New York, 1967).

Kerry Olitzky and Ronald Isaacs, *The Discovery Haggadah* (Hoboken, N.J., 1992).

Haim Raphael, *A Feast of History* (New York, 1972).

Counting the Omer
סְפִירַת הָעוֹמֶר

The source:

וּסְפַרְתֶּם לָכֶם מִמָּחֳרַת הַשַּׁבָּת מִיּוֹם הֲבִיאֲכֶם אֶת־עֹמֶר הַתְּ־
נוּפָה שֶׁבַע שַׁבָּתוֹת תְּמִימֹת תִּהְיֶינָה:

"And from the day on which you bring the sheaf of wave offering—the day after the Sabbath(–first day of Passover)—you shall count off seven weeks. They must be complete" (Lev. 23:15).

What you need to know:

1. Beginning with the second night of Pesach, and ending with Shavuot, recite the following meditation and *kavanah* (available in most complete prayerbooks).

הִנְנִי מְקַיֵּם מִצְוַת עֲשֵׂה שֶׁל סְפִירַת הָעוֹמֶר כְּמוֹ שֶׁכָּתוּב בַּתּוֹרָה.
וּסְפַרְתֶּם לָכֶם מִמָּחֳרַת הַשַּׁבָּת מִיּוֹם הֲבִיאֲכֶם אֶת־עֹמֶר הַתְּ־
נוּפָה שֶׁבַע שַׁבָּתוֹת תְּמִימֹת תִּהְיֶינָה עַד מִמָּחֳרַת הַשַּׁבָּת
הַשְּׁבִיעִית תִּסְפְּרוּ חֲמִשִּׁים יוֹם:

I am now prepared to fulfill the positive mitzvah of counting the *omer* just as it is written in the Torah. And from the day on which you bring the sheaf of wave offering—the day after the day of rest—you shall count off seven weeks. They must be complete. Until the day after the seventh week you should count fifty days.

2. Recite the following blessing:

בָּרוּךְ אַתָּה יְיָ אֱלֹהֵנוּ מֶלֶךְ הָעוֹלָם אֲשֶׁר קִדְּשָׁנוּ בְּמִצְוֹתָיו וְצִוָּנוּ
עַל סְפִירַת הָעוֹמֶר:

Baruch atah Adonai elohaynu melech ha'olam asher kid-shanu bemitzvotav vetzivanu al s'firat ha-omer.

Praised are You, Adonai our God, Sovereign of the Universe, who makes us holy with mitzvot and instructed us to count the *omer*.

3. Using the following formula, count each day. Today is the ___ day, which is ___ weeks and ___ in the *omer*.

הַיּוֹם ___ יוֹם שֶׁהֵם ___ שָׁבוּעוֹת וְ___ יָמִים לָעוֹמֶר

4. Then read the following Psalm (57) and the prayer following:

We beseech You to release Your captive nation by the mighty strength of Your right hand. Accept the joyous chant of Your people. Lift us and purify us, O revered God. O mighty One, guard them that meditate on Your unity. Bless them. Purify them. Have mercy on them. Bestow Your charity on them. O peaceful and holy Being, in Your abundant goodness, lead Your congregation. You who are the only and exalted God, turn to Your people who are mindful of Your holiness. Accept our prayer and hearken to our cry, for You know all secrets. Praised be Your name, whose great Sovereignty is forever and ever.

5. And now, this prayer:

Master of the Universe, through Moses Your servant You have instructed us to count the days of the *omer* in order to help us keep ourselves free from enveloping uncleanness. Therefore, You ordained in Your Torah: "From the morrow after the day of rest, from the day of your bringing the sheaf (*omer*) of the wave–offering you shall count for yourselves seven weeks; complete they shall be, until the fiftieth day," so that Your people Israel might keep themselves free from contamination. Therefore may it be Your will, Adonai our God and God of our ancestors, that the counting of the *omer* which I have done this day may help complete my counting until now, and make me feel clean and made holy through Your divine holiness. May its influence be felt in all spheres of life. May it strengthen my soul and my spirit against all corruption, helping purify me, and inspire me through Your supreme sanctity. Amen. Selah.

Things to remember:

1. *Omer* links the Exodus with the giving of Torah. We count the days of our freedom in anticipation of our people's encounter with God.

2. In Psalm 67:5, the line has forty-nine letters, one for each day.

3. Do the counting while standing, in the evening after three stars come out. Some people also say it in the morning (without the blessing).

4. Since the period of the counting is a semi-mourning period, weddings and certain other events don't take place, except on the 33rd day—Lag Ba-Omer (Iyar 18). There are actually two primary customs for this mourning period. One is from Passover until Lag Ba-Omer; the other is from Rosh Chodesh Iyar until three days before Shavuot.

5. In this context, Sabbath, the day of rest, refers to the first day of Pesach.

Key words and phrases:

Sefirat Ha-omer סְפִירַת הָעֹמֶר. Counting of the *omer*.
Omer עוֹמֶר. Grain measurement.
Wave offering. Barley, the first to ripen of the grains sown in winter, it was solemnly cut in the field and brought to the Temple in thanksgiving.

If you want to know more:

Michael Strassfeld, *The Jewish Holidays* (New York, 1985).
Isaac Klein, *A Guide to Jewish Religious Practice* (New York, 1979).
Arthur Waskow, *Seasons of Our Joy* (New York, 1982).

Leading Birkat Hamazon
בִּרְכַּת הַמָּזוֹן

The source:

וְאָכַלְתָּ וְשָׂבָעְתָּ וּבֵרַכְתָּ אֶת־יְיָ אֱלֹהֶיךָ עַל־הָאָרֶץ הַטֹּבָה אֲשֶׁר נָתַן־לָךְ:

"When you have eaten your fill, give thanks to God for the good land which God has given you" (Deut. 8:10).

What you need to know:

בִּרְכַּת הַמָּזוֹן
הַמּוֹצִיא

1. *Birkat Hamazon* (grace/blessing after the meal) is recited after any meal which began with the blessing over bread (*hamotzi*).

מְזוּמָן
רַבּוֹתַי נְבָרֵךְ

2. When at least three people eat together, they constitute a *mezuman*. One of the three is asked to call the others to say *Birkat Hamazon* through an introductory formula which begins, *Rabbotai nevarech* ("let us say grace").

3. It is the custom to give the honor of leading *Birkat Hamazon* to a guest.

4. Before *Birkat Hamazon*, some have the custom of removing all utensils (especially knives) from the table, and leaving a piece of bread (or crumbs) on the table. Knives were used as weapons of war, and the table is considered an altar of peace and tranquility.

בְּרָכָה
אַחֲרוֹנָה

5. After eating food consisting of cake, wine, and so forth (without bread), there is a special blessing called a *beracha acharona* which is recited. This is a sort of abridged version of *Birkat Hamazon*.

When three or more adults have eaten together, one of them formally invites the others to join in these blessings. (When ten or more are present add the words in parentheses.)

רַבּוֹתַי נְבָרֵךְ:

Rabotai nevaraych

Friends, let us give thanks.

The others respond, and the leader repeats:

יְהִי שֵׁם יְיָ מְבֹרָךְ מֵעַתָּה וְעַד עוֹלָם:

Yehi shem Adonai mevorach may'atah ve'ad olam.

May God be praised now and forever.

The leader continues:

בִּרְשׁוּת רַבּוֹתַי, נְבָרֵךְ (אֱלֹהֵינוּ) שֶׁאָכַלְנוּ מִשֶּׁלוֹ:

Bireshut rabotai, nevaraych (elohaynu) she'achalnu mi-shelo.

With your consent, friends, let us praise (our God) the One of whose food we have partaken.

The others respond, and the leader repeats:

בָּרוּךְ (אֱלֹהֵינוּ) שֶׁאָכַלְנוּ מִשֶּׁלוֹ וּבְטוּבוֹ חָיִינוּ:

Baruch (elohaynu) she'achalnu mishelo uvetuvo cha'yinu.

Praised be (our God) the One whose food we have partaken and by whose goodness we live.

Leaders and others:

בָּרוּךְ הוּא וּבָרוּךְ שְׁמוֹ:

Baruch hu uvaruch shemo.

Praised be God and praised be God's name.

93

בָּרוּךְ אַתָּה יְיָ אֱלֹהֵינוּ מֶלֶךְ הָעוֹלָם, הַזָּן אֶת הָעוֹלָם כֻּלּוֹ בְּטוּבוֹ, בְּחֵן בְּחֶסֶד וּבְרַחֲמִים. הוּא נוֹתֵן לֶחֶם לְכָל־בָּשָׂר כִּי לְעוֹלָם חַסְדּוֹ. וּבְטוּבוֹ הַגָּדוֹל תָּמִיד לֹא חָסַר לָנוּ וְאַל יֶחְסַר לָנוּ מָזוֹן לְעוֹלָם וָעֶד בַּעֲבוּר שְׁמוֹ הַגָּדוֹל, כִּי הוּא אֵל זָן וּמְפַרְנֵס לַכֹּל וּמֵטִיב לַכֹּל וּמֵכִין מָזוֹן לְכָל־בְּרִיּוֹתָיו אֲשֶׁר בָּרָא: בָּרוּךְ אַתָּה יְיָ, הַזָּן אֶת־הַכֹּל:

Baruch atah Adonai, elohaynu melech ha'olam, hazan et ha'olam kulo betuvo, bechayn, bechesed, uverachamim. Hu notayn lechem lechol basar, ki le'olam chasdo. Uvetuvo hagadol, tamid lo chasar lanu, ve'al yechsar lanu mazon le'olam va'ed ba'avur shemo hagadol, ki hu El zan umefarnays lakol, umaytiv lakol, umaychin mazon lechol beriyotav asher bara. Baruch atah Adonai, hazan et hakol.

Praised are You, our God, Sovereign of the Universe, who sustains the whole word with kindness and compassion. God provides food for every creature, for God's love endures forever. God's great goodness has never failed us. God's great glory assures us nourishment. All life is God's creation and God's good to all, providing every creature with food and sustenance. Praised are You, God, who sustains all life.

נוֹדֶה לְּךָ יְיָ אֱלֹהֵינוּ עַל שֶׁהִנְחַלְתָּ לַאֲבוֹתֵינוּ אֶרֶץ חֶמְדָּה טוֹבָה וּרְחָבָה, בְּרִית וְתוֹרָה, חַיִּים וּמָזוֹן. יִתְבָּרַךְ שִׁמְךָ בְּפִי כָל־חַי תָּמִיד לְעוֹלָם וָעֶד, כַּכָּתוּב וְאָכַלְתָּ וְשָׂבָעְתָּ וּבֵרַכְתָּ אֶת־יְיָ אֱלֹהֶיךָ עַל־הָאָרֶץ הַטּוֹבָה אֲשֶׁר נָתַן לָךְ. בָּרוּךְ אַתָּה יְיָ, עַל הָאָרֶץ וְעַל הַמָּזוֹן:

Nodeh lecha Adonai elohaynu al shehinchalta la'avotaynu eretz chemdah, tovah urechavah, brit vetorah, cha'yim umazon. Yitbarach shimcha befi kol chai tamid le'olam va'ed. Kakatuv ve'achalta vesavata uvayrachta et Adonai Elohecha al ha'aretz hatovah asher natan lach. Baruch atah Adonai, al ha'aretz ve'al hamazon.

We thank you, God, for the pleasing, ample, desirable land which You gave to our ancestors, for the covenant and Torah, for life and sustenance. May You forever be praised by all who live, as it is written in the Torah: "When you have eaten and are satisfied, you shall praise God for the good land which God has given you." Praised are You, God, for the land and for sustenance.

וּבְנֵה יְרוּשָׁלַיִם עִיר הַקֹּדֶשׁ בִּמְהֵרָה בְיָמֵינוּ. בָּרוּךְ אַתָּה יְיָ בּוֹנֵה בְּרַחֲמָיו יְרוּשָׁלָיִם. אָמֵן:

Uvenay Yerushala'yim ir hakodesh bimhayrah ve'ya-maynu. Baruch atah Adonai, boneh verachamav Yerusha-la'yim. Amen.

Fully rebuild Jerusalem, the holy city, soon, in our time. Praised are You, God, who in mercy rebuilds Jerusalem. Amen.

בָּרוּךְ אַתָּה יְיָ אֱלֹהֵינוּ מֶלֶךְ הָעוֹלָם, הַמֶּלֶךְ הַטוֹב וְהַמֵּטִיב לַכֹּל. הוּא הֵטִיב הוּא מֵטִיב, הוּא יֵיטִיב לָנוּ, הוּא גְמָלָנוּ, הוּא גוֹמְלֵנוּ, הוּא יִגְמְלֵנוּ לָעַד חֵן וָחֶסֶד וְרַחֲמִים וִיזַכֵּנוּ לִימוֹת הַמָּשִׁיחַ:

Barukh atah Adonai, elohaynu melech ha'olam, hamelech hatov vehamaytiv lakol. Hu haytiv, hu maytiv, hu yay-tiv lanu. Hu gemalanu, hu gomlaynu, hu yigmileynu la'ad chayn vechesed verachamim, viyzakaynu liymot hamashiach.

Praised are You, God, Sovereign of the Universe, who are good to all, whose goodness is constant through all time. Favor us with kindness and compassion now and in the future as in the past. May we be worthy of the days of the Messiah.

הָרַחֲמָן, הוּא יַנְחִילֵנוּ יוֹם שֶׁכֻּלּוֹ שַׁבָּת וּמְנוּחָה לְחַיֵּי הָעוֹלָמִים:

Harachaman hu yanchilaynu yom shekulo Shabbat umenucha lecha'yay ha'olamim.

May the Merciful grant us a day of true Shabbat rest, reflecting the life of eternity.

וְנִשָּׂא בְרָכָה מֵאֵת יְיָ וּצְדָקָה מֵאֱלֹהֵי יִשְׁעֵנוּ, וְנִמְצָא חֵן וְשֵׂכֶל טוֹב בְּעֵינֵי אֱלֹהִים וְאָדָם. עֹשֶׂה שָׁלוֹם בִּמְרוֹמָיו, הוּא יַעֲשֶׂה שָׁלוֹם, עָלֵינוּ וְעַל כָּל יִשְׂרָאֵל, וְאִמְרוּ אָמֵן:

Venisa verachah may'ayt Adonai utzedakah may'elohay yishaynu. Venimtza chayn vesaychel tov be'aynay elohim ve'adam. Oseh shalom bimromav hu ya'aseh shalom alaynu ve'al kol Yisra'el. Ve'imru Amen.

May we receive blessings from God, loving–kindness from the God of our deliverance. May we find grace and good favor before God and all people. May God who brings peace to the universe bring peace to us and to all the people Israel. And let us say: Amen.

Key words and phrases:

Hamezamen הַמְזַמֵן. The leader who leads *Birkat Hamazon.*
Mezuman מְזוּמָן. Unit consisting of a minimum of three adult Jews which as a group recites *Birkat Hamazon* aloud.

If you want to know more:

Hayim Donin, *To Pray as a Jew* (New York, 1980).
Isaac Klein, *A Guide to Jewish Religious Practice* (New York, 1979).
Joel Grishaver, *Basic Berachot* (Los Angeles, 1988).

Lighting the Memorial Candle
נֵר זִכָּרוֹן

The source:

נֵר יְהֹוָה נִשְׁמַת אָדָם

Many sources for this custom have been suggested including Proverbs 20:27, "The soul of the human being is the lamp of Adonai."

What you need to know:

1. While there are no specific rituals for lighting a memorial candle, the lighting should take place in a sacred context. Therefore, we recommend that you say the following before lighting the candle. If you prefer, as an alternative, simply speak from the heart.

   O God, grant us strength as we mourn the loss of ___. We will always have cherished memories of him/her. Bless our family with light and peace. May ___'s memory continue to serve as a blessing and an inspiration to all who knew and loved him/her.

2. Light the candle.

3. Then say the following:

זִכְרוֹנוֹ (זִכְרוֹנָהּ) לִבְרָכָה

   Zichrono (*Zichrona*) *liveracha.* His (her) memory is a blessing.

4. *Kaddish* and/or *El Malei Rachamim* (a prayer for resting souls) is also often recited at this time.

יִתְגַּדַּל וְיִתְקַדַּשׁ שְׁמֵהּ רַבָּא בְּעָלְמָא דִּי בְרָא כִרְעוּתֵהּ וְיַמְלִיךְ
מַלְכוּתֵהּ בְּחַיֵּיכוֹן וּבְיוֹמֵיכוֹן וּבְחַיֵּי דְכָל בֵּית יִשְׂרָאֵל, בַּעֲגָלָא
וּבִזְמַן קָרִיב וְאִמְרוּ אָמֵן: יְהֵא שְׁמֵהּ רַבָּא מְבָרַךְ לְעָלַם וּלְעָלְמֵי
עָלְמַיָּא: יִתְבָּרַךְ וְיִשְׁתַּבַּח וְיִתְפָּאַר וְיִתְרוֹמַם וְיִתְנַשֵּׂא וְיִתְהַדָּר
וְיִתְעַלֶּה וְיִתְהַלָּל שְׁמֵהּ דְּקוּדְשָׁא, בְּרִיךְ הוּא לְעֵלָּא (בעשי״ת
וּלְעֵלָּא מִכָּל) מִן כָּל בִּרְכָתָא וְשִׁירָתָא, תֻּשְׁבְּחָתָא וְנֶחֱמָתָא,
דַּאֲמִירָן בְּעָלְמָא, וְאִמְרוּ אָמֵן: יְהֵא שְׁלָמָא רַבָּא מִן שְׁמַיָּא וְחַיִּים
עָלֵינוּ וְעַל כָּל יִשְׂרָאֵל וְאִמְרוּ אָמֵן: עוֹשֶׂה שָׁלוֹם בִּמְרוֹמָיו הוּא
יַעֲשֶׂה שָׁלוֹם עָלֵינוּ וְעַל כָּל יִשְׂרָאֵל וְאִמְרוּ אָמֵן:

Yit-ga-dal ve-yit-ka-dash she-mei ra-ba be-al-ma di-ve-ra chi-re-u-tei, ve-yam-lich mal-chutei be-cha-yei-chon u-ve-yo-mei-chon u-ve-cha-yei de-chol beit Yis-ra-el, ba-a-ga-la u-vi-ze-man ka-riv, ve-i-me-ru: a-mein. Ye-hei she-mei ra-ba me-va-rach le-a-lam u-le-al-mei al-ma-ya. Yit-ba-rach ve-yish-ta-bach, ve-yit-pa-ar ve-yit-ro-mam ve-yit-na-sei, ve-yit-ha-dar ve-yit-a-leh ve-yit-ha-lal she-mei de-ku-de-sha, be-rich hu, le-ei-la min kol bi-re-cha-ta ve-shi-ra-ta, tush-becha-ta ve-ne-che-ma-ta, da-a mi-ran be-al-ma, ve-i-me-ru; a-mein. Ye-hei she-la-ma ra-ba min she-ma-ya ve-cha-yim a-lei-nu ve-al kol Yis-ra-eil, ve-i-me-ru: a-mein. O-seh sha-lom bi-me-ro-mav, hu ya-a-seh sha-lom a-lei-nu ve-al kol Yis-ra-eil, ve-i-me-ru: a-mein.

Let the glory of God be extolled, let God's great name be hallowed, in the world whose creation God willed. May God's sovereignty soon prevail, in our own day, our own lives, and the life of all Israel, and let us say Amen. Let God's great name be blessed for ever and ever. Let the name of God be glorified, exalted, and honored, though God is beyond all the praises, songs, and adorations that we can utter, and let us say Amen. For us and for all Israel, may the blessing of peace and the promise of life come true, and let us say Amen. May God who causes peace to reign in the high heavens, let peace descend on us, on all Israel and all the world, and let us say: Amen.

אֵל מָלֵא רַחֲמִים
Eil Malei Rachamim

For male

אֵל מָלֵא רַחֲמִים, שׁוֹכֵן בַּמְּרוֹמִים, הַמְצֵא מְנוּחָה נְכוֹנָה
תַּחַת כַּנְפֵי הַשְּׁכִינָה, בְּמַעֲלוֹת קְדוֹשִׁים וּטְהוֹרִים כְּזֹהַר הָרָקִיעַ
מַזְהִירִים, אֶת־נִשְׁמַת __ בֶּן __ שֶׁהָלַךְ לְעוֹלָמוֹ, בְּגַן עֵדֶן
תְּהֵא מְנוּחָתוֹ. אָנָּא, בַּעַל הָרַחֲמִים הַסְתִּירֵהוּ בְּסֵתֶר כְּנָפֶיךָ
לְעוֹלָמִים, וּצְרוֹר בִּצְרוֹר הַחַיִּים אֶת־נִשְׁמָתוֹ, יְיָ הוּא נַחֲלָתוֹ,
וְיָנוּחַ בְּשָׁלוֹם עַל מִשְׁכָּבוֹ, וְנֹאמַר אָמֵן:

*Eil malei rachamim sho-chein bam'romim, ham-tzei
m'nuchah n'chonah tachat kanfei ha-sh'chinah, b'ma-alot
k'doshim u-t'horim k'zohar ha-rakiya maz-hirim et nish-
mat ___ ben ___ she-halach l'olamo, b'gan eiden t'hei
menuchato. Ana, ba-al ha-rachamim, hastireihu b'seiter
k'nafecha l'olamim, u-tzror bi-tzror ha-chayim et nishmato,
Adonai hu nachalato, v'yanu'ach b'shalom al mishkavo,
v'nomar amen.*

God of compassion, grant perfect peace in Your
sheltering Presence, among the holy and the pure
who shine in the brightness of the firmament, to the
soul of our dear ___ who has gone to his eternal
rest. God of compassion, remember all his worthy
deeds in the land of the living. May his soul be bound
up in the bond of everlasting life. May God be his
inheritance. May he rest in peace. And let us answer:
Amen.

For female

אֵל מָלֵא רַחֲמִים, שׁוֹכֵן בַּמְּרוֹמִים, הַמְצֵא מְנוּחָה נְכוֹנָה
תַּחַת כַּנְפֵי הַשְּׁכִינָה, בְּמַעֲלוֹת קְדוֹשִׁים וּטְהוֹרִים כְּזֹהַר הָרָקִיעַ
מַזְהִירִים, אֶת־נִשְׁמַת __ בַּת __ שֶׁהָלְכָה לְעוֹלָמָהּ, בְּגַן עֵדֶן
תְּהֵא מְנוּחָתָהּ. אָנָּא, בַּעַל הָרַחֲמִים הַסְתִּירֶהָ בְּסֵתֶר כְּנָפֶיךָ
לְעוֹלָמִים, וּצְרוֹר בִּצְרוֹר הַחַיִּים אֶת־נִשְׁמָתָהּ, יְיָ הוּא נַחֲלָתָהּ,
וְתָנוּחַ בְּשָׁלוֹם עַל מִשְׁכָּבָהּ, וְנֹאמַר אָמֵן:

99

Eil malei rachamim sho-chein bam'romim, ham-tzei m'nuchah n'chonah tachat kanfei ha-sh'chinah, b'ma-alot k'doshim u-t'horim k'zohar ha'rakiya maz-hirim et nish-mat ___ bat ___ she-halchah l'olamah, b'gan eiden t'hei menuchatah. Ana, ba-al ha-rachamim, hastireha b'seiter k'nafecha l'olamim, u-tzror bi-tzror hachayim et nishmatah, Adonai hu nachalatah, v'tanu-ach b'shalom al mishkavah, v'nomar amen.

God of compassion, grant perfect peace in Your sheltering Presence, among the holy and the pure who shine in the brightness of the firmament, to the soul of our dear ___ who has gone to her eternal rest. God of compassion, remember all her worthy deeds in the land of the living. May her soul be bound up in the bond of everlasting life. May God be her inheritance. May she rest in peace. And let us answer: Amen.

Things to remember:

1. Light the candle in the evening at sunset at the *Yahrtzeit* and on *Yizkor* days of holidays. Make sure it is a twenty-four-hour candle.

2. Even if the candle burns longer than twenty-four, let it burn. Do not extinguish it.

3. If you forget to light it in the evening, do so in the morning.

4. If you forgot to light the candle entirely, make a contribution to *tzedakah*.

Key words and phrases:

Yahrtzeit יָארְצִיט. Yiddish name for anniversary of one's death, known as *anos* among Sephardic Jews.

Yizkor יִזְכֹּר. Literally "May God remember," refers to service of memorial.

If you want to know more:

Ron Isaacs and Kerry Olitzky, *The Jewish Mourner's Handbook* (Hoboken, N.J., 1991).

How to Read a Tombstone
מַצֵּבָה

The source:

וַיַּצֵּב יַעֲקֹב מַצֵּבָה עַל־קְבֻרָתָהּ הִוא מַצֶּבֶת קְבֻרַת־רָחֵל עַד־הַיּוֹם:

"Over her grave Jacob set up a pillar. It is the pillar at Rachel's grave to this day" (Gen. 35:20).

What you need to know:

1. It is customary to erect a tombstone on the grave of the deceased.

2. There is no uniform practice with regard to the inscription on a stone. The stone today will often include the deceased's name in both Hebrew and English. In addition, it might also include dates of birth and death, sometimes in English and Hebrew as well.

3. The Ashkenazic practice is to place the Hebrew letters
   פ״נ, which stands for *po nitman*, meaning "here lies,"
   in front of the Hebrew name of a deceased individual.
   The Sephardic custom is to place the Hebrew letters
   מ״ק, which stands for *matzevet kevurat,* meaning "the
   tombstone of the grave."

   פֹּה נִטְמַן
   מַצֶּבֶת
   קְבוּרַת

101

4. Many tombstones have the Hebrew letters ת"נ"צ"ב"ה. This stands for *tehe nishmato tzerurah bitzror hachayim*, which means, "may his soul be bound in the bond of eternal life."

5. Some tombstones have pictorial Jewish symbols on them. Here are eight of the more common ones:

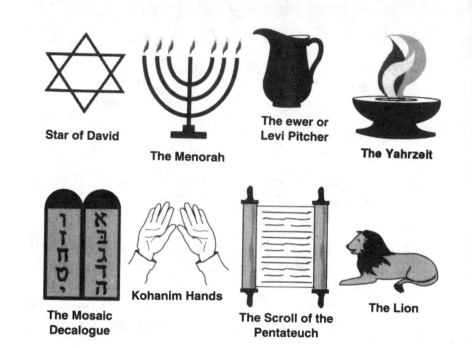

Star of David

The Menorah

The ewer or Levi Pitcher

The Yahrzeit

The Mosaic Decalogue

Kohanim Hands

The Scroll of the Pentateuch

The Lion

Things to remember:

1. A cemetery is a sacred environment. Respect it . . . and the memory of those who are buried there.

2. While a cemetery is like a park, it is no playground.

Key words and phrases:

Bet chaim בֵּית חַיִּים. Euphemism for "cemetery," literally "house of life."

Bet kevarot בֵּית קְבָרוֹת. Hebrew word for "cemetery"; alternatively, *bet chaim*, "house of life."

Matzevah מַצֵּיבָה. Hebrew word for "gravestone."

Unveiling. Consecration of a tombstone, usually occurring within a calendar year of a person's death.

If you want to know more:

Ron H. Isaacs and Kerry Olitzky, *The Jewish Mourner's Handbook* (Hoboken, N.J., 1991).

Isaac Klein, *A Guide to Jewish Religious Practice* (New York, 1979).

Isaac Klein, *A Time to be Born, a Time to Die* (New York, 1977).

Putting up a Mezuzah
מְזוּזָה

The source:

וּכְתַבְתָּם עַל־מְזֻזוֹת בֵּיתֶךָ וּבִשְׁעָרֶיךָ:

"Inscribe them on the doorposts of your house and on your gates" (Deut. 6:9, 11:20).

What you need to know:

1. Roll the parchment from the end to the beginning so that the word *Shema* is on top.

2. Place it in the *mezuzah* case.

3. Say the following blessings:

בָּרוּךְ אַתָּה יְיָ אֱלֹהֵינוּ מֶלֶךְ הָעוֹלָם אֲשֶׁר קִדְּשָׁנוּ בְּמִצְוֹתָיו וְצִוָּנוּ לִקְבּוֹעַ מְזוּזָה:

Baruch atah Adonai elohaynu melech ha'olam asher kidshanu bemitzvotav vetzivanu likboah mezuzah.

Praised are You, Adonai our God, Sovereign of the Universe, who has made us holy with mitzvot and instructed us to affix the *mezuzah*.

בָּרוּךְ אַתָּה יְיָ אֱלֹהֵינוּ מֶלֶךְ הָעוֹלָם שֶׁהֶחֱיָנוּ וְקִיְּמָנוּ וְהִגִּיעָנוּ לַזְּמַן הַזֶּה:

Baruch atah Adonai elohaynu melech ha'olam she-hecheyanu vekimanu vehigiyanu lazman hazeh.

Praised are You, Adonai our God, Sovereign of the Universe, who has kept us alive, sustained us, and helped us to reach this moment.

Things to remember:

1. The *mezuzah* literally means "doorpost" but is normally taken to refer to the case which holds the parchment and then is affixed to the doorpost.

2. A *mezuzah* should be placed on every doorpost in the house except for the bathrooms.

3. The *mezuzah* should be affixed to the upper third of the right-hand doorpost (as you enter) but no less than one handbreadth (the width of your hand) from the top.

4. On the parchment is written the *Shema Yisrael* and Deut 6:4–9, 11:13–31.

5. *Mezuzah* parchments should be checked twice every seven years.

6. When moving to a new home, leave your *mezuzot* for the new family—if it is Jewish. If not, take the *mezuzot* with you.

Key words and phrases:

Klaf קְלָף. The parchment inside the *mezuzah*.

If you want to know more:

Alfred Kolatch, *The Jewish Home Advisor* (Middle Village, N.Y., 1990).

More particulars:

Secret code on back of *mezuzah* parchment: *kuzo bemuchsaz kuzo,* which stands for *Adonai Elohenu Adonai.*

כּוּזוּ בְּמוּכְסָז כּוּזוּ
יְהֹוָה אֱלֹהֵנוּ יְהֹוָה

Shaddai: "Almighty God" and an acronym for *Shomer Daltot Yisrael,* meaning "protector of Israelite doors."

שַׁדַּי
שׁוֹמֵר דַּלְתוֹת
יִשְׂרָאֵל

How to Dance the Hora
הוֹרָה

The source:

חֲלוּצִים

The early Jewish settlers in Israel, known as the *Chalutzim* (pioneers), brought the dance known as the hora from Eastern Europe.

What you need to know:

During the dance the participants form a circle and put their hands on each other's shoulders or hold each other's hands.

| 1 | 2 | 3 |
| Step right with right foot | Place left foot behind right foot | Step right with right foot |

| 4 | 5 | 6 |
| Hop on right foot | Step left with left foot | Hop on left foot |

Things to remember:

1. The hora is probably Judaism's most well-known circle dance.

Key words and phrases:

Rikud רִקּוּד. Dance.

If you want to know more:

Fred Berk, *Ha-Rikud: The Jewish Dance* (New York, 1972).

Making a Jewish Family Tree
מִשְׁפָּחָה

The source:

זֶה סֵפֶר תּוֹלְדֹת אָדָם:

"This is the book of the family record of humankind" (Gen. 5:1).

What you need to know:

1. Look at family photograph albums with your parents and ask them to identify pictures of your relatives. Find out where and when they lived and how you are related to them.

2. Ask your grandparents, aunts, uncles, and cousins to tell you about your close relatives. Then ask them for this information about each person:
   a. Name
   b. Date of birth
   c. Place of birth
   d. Date of marriage
   e. Place of marriage
   f. Date of death
   g. Place of death

3. Once you have all of this information you can proceed to draw your family tree. Here is a sample chart that starts with you and traces your line back through your parents, grandparents, great-grandparents, and so on.

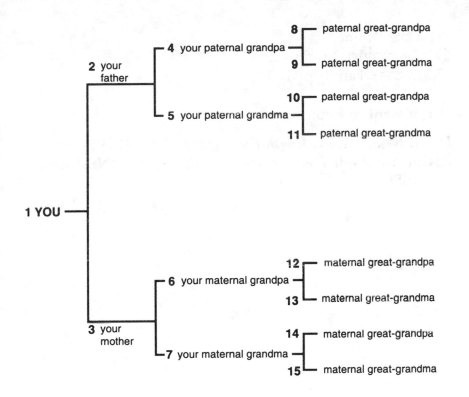

Who's who:

1. You
2. Father
3. Mother
4. Paternal grandfather
5. Paternal grandmother (family name)
6. Maternal grandfather
7. Maternal grandmother (family name)
8–11. Paternal great-grandparents
12–15. Maternal great-grandparents

Things to remember:

If you don't record your family history now, those who
hold the key to family memory may be gone later on,
when you want to know about your ancestors.

Key words and phrases:

L'dor vador לְדוֹר וָדוֹר. "From generation to generation."
Mishpacha מִשְׁפָּחָה. (Yiddish, *mishpacha*). Family.

Shem שֵׁם. Name.
Toledot תּוֹלְדוֹת. Family line.
Yichus יִחוּס. Family pedigree.

If you want to know more:

David Kranzler, *My Jewish Roots* (New York, 1979).
Arthur Kurzweil, *From Generation to Generation* (New York, 1980).

How to Visit the Sick
בִּקוּר חוֹלִים

The source:

"These are the deeds which yield immediate fruit and continue to yield fruit in time to come: honoring parents, doing deeds of kindness, attending the house of study, visiting the sick . . . " (Babylonian Talmud Shabbat 127a).

What you need to know:

(based on *Shulchan Aruch, Yoreh Deah* 335):

1. It is a mitzvah to visit the sick. Feel free to visit even those who are not your relatives or friends.

2. Do not overdo your stay; lengthy visits often tire the patient.

3. Relatives and friends should visit as soon as the person becomes ill. More distant acquaintances may want to wait several days.

4. When visiting, always try to enter cheerfully.

5. Try not to speak about sad things to persons that you visit.

Things to remember:

1. Psalms which can be recited for someone who is ill: Psalms 6, 9, 13, 16, 17, 22, 23, 25, 30, 31, 32, 33, 37, 49, 55, 86, 88, 90, 91, 102, 103, 104, 118, 119, 142, 143.

2. Many synagogues and Jewish communities have *bikkur cholim* societies (or caring committees), which visit hospitals and nursing homes on a regular basis. If you have one, become an active member!

Key words and phrases:

Bikkur cholim בִּקּוּר חוֹלִים. The mitzvah of visiting the sick.
Bet cholim בֵּית חוֹלִים. Hebrew word for "hospital."
Mi sheberach מִי שֶׁבֵּרַךְ. Prayer for the sick, often recited in synagogue on behalf of person who is ill.
Vidui וִדּוּי. Confessional prayer often said by traditional Jew suffering from life-threatening illness.

If you want to know more:

Sharon and Michael Strassfeld, *The Third Jewish Catalogue* (Philadelphia, 1980).
Barbara Fortgang Summers, *Community Responsibility in the Jewish Tradition* (New York, 1978).

Tzedakah and Doing Deeds of Kindness
צְדָקָה וּמַעֲשִׂים טוֹבִים

The sources:

עַל שְׁלשָׁה דְבָרִים הָעוֹלָם עוֹמֵד—עַל הַתּוֹרָה, וְעַל הָעֲבוֹדָה,
וְעַל גְּמִילוּת חֲסָדִים:

"The world rests on three things: Torah, worship and the performance of good deeds" (Pirke Avot 1:2).

צֶדֶק צֶדֶק תִּרְדּוֹף:

"Charity, charity, shall you pursue" (Deut. 16:20).

"These are things for which no measure is prescribed: gleanings of the field, first fruits, festival offerings, loving deeds of kindness, and the study of Torah. These are things whose fruit a person enjoys in this world and whose reward is stirred up in the World-to-Come: honoring parents, doing deeds of kindness, making peace, but the study of Torah is equal to them all [because it leads to them]" (Peah 1:1).

What you need to know:

1. *Tzedakah,* often translated "charity," is derived from the Hebrew root *tzedek,* meaning "righteous" and "just." Giving *tzedakah* is the just and right thing to do.   צְדָקָה   צֶדֶק

2. *Gemilut chasadim* is the Hebrew term for "loving acts of kindness." Included in these acts are giving clothing to the needy, visiting the sick, comforting the mourner, and burying the dead.   גְּמִילוּת חֲסָדִים

113

3. When you give to someone or help someone, you should do it cheerfully and graciously.

4. It is considered best to help someone without the recipient knowing from whom the help is coming.

5. The highest form of a deed of kindness is to help a person to be self-supporting.

Key words and phrases:

Hachnasat orchim הַכְנָסַת אוֹרְחִים. "hospitality to strangers," an important act of kindness.
Pushke. (Yiddish). A charity box.
Tithe מַעֲשֵׂר. The giving of one tenth of your earnings to *tzedakah*.

If you want to know more:

Joseph Feinstein, *I Am My Brother's Keeper* (New York, 1970).
Jacob Neusner, *Tzedakah* (New York, 1982).
Danny Siegel, *Gym Shoes and Irises (Personalized Tzedakah).* (New York, 1982).

Finding the Meaning of Your Hebrew Name
שֵׁם עִבְרִי

The source:

נִבְחָר שֵׁם מֵעשֶׁר רָב:

"A good name is rather. to be chosen than great riches" (Prov. 22:1).

What you need to know:

1. There are 2,800 personal names in the Bible, some of which are used to name children today. All Hebrew names have meanings.

2. Hebrew names with the prefix or suffix *el, eli, ya,* and *yahu* all refer to God.

   אֵל, אֵלִי
   יָה, יָהוּ

3. Many Hebrew names are nature names, such as Deborah (bee) or Jonah (dove).

   דְּבוֹרָה
   יוֹנָה

4. The usual American custom is to give a child both a secular and a Hebrew name. Sometimes the name may be the same in both Hebrew and English (like David, Leora, Shirah).

   דָּוִד
   לִיאוֹרָה
   שִׁירָה

5. If you want some advice about your particular Hebrew name you can ask a rabbi or cantor, or review one of the Hebrew-Name dictionaries listed in the "If you want to know more" section.

Some Biblical Names Commonly Used in English

אַהֲרֹן	Aaron	"singing" or "teaching"
אַבְרָהָם	Abraham	"father of a mighty nation"

אָדָם	Adam	"red earth"
עָמוֹס	Amos	"burdened"
בִּנְיָמִין	Benjamin	"son of my right hand"
דָנִיֵּאל	Daniel	"God is my judge"
דְּבוֹרָה	Deborah	"bee"
דִּינָה	Dinah	"judgment"
עִמָּנוּאֵל	Emanuel	"God is with us"
אֶסְתֵּר	Esther	"a star"
חַנָה	Hannah	"merciful"
יַעֲקֹב	Jacob	"held by the heel"
יוֹנָתָן	Jonathan	"gift of God"
יוֹאֵל	Joel	"God is willing"
יוֹסֵף	Joseph	"He will increase"
יְהוּדִית	Judith	"praise"
מִיכָאֵל	Michael	"who is like God?"
מִרְיָם	Miriam	"bitter waters"
רָחֵל	Rachel	"ewe"
רִבְקָה	Rebekkah	"to bind"
רוּת	Ruth	"friendship"
שְׁמוּאֵל	Samuel	"God has listened"
שָׂרָה	Sarah	"princess"

Things to remember:

1. Most naming customs are just customs without a great deal of logic to them. There are no rules.

2. Different communities have different naming customs. For example, Ashkenazic Jews generally do not name their children in honor of a living person (only in memory of someone who is dead) but Sephardic Jews have a system (beginning with the paternal grandfather) of honoring living people by naming babies in their honor.

Key words and phrases:
Shem שֵׁם (plural, *shemot* שְׁמוֹת). Name.

116

If you want to know more:

Anita Diamant, *The Jewish Baby Book* (New York, 1988).

Heinrich and Eva Guggenheimer, *Jewish Family Names and Their Origins: An Etymological Dictionary* (Hoboken, N.J., 1992).

Benzion C. Kaganoff, *A Dictionary of Jewish Names and Their History* (New York, 1977).

Alfred J. Kolatch, *The Name Dictionary* (New York, 1967).

Sample entry from
*Jewish Family Names and Their Origins:
An Etymological Dictionary*

Schif, Schiff, Shief, Shieff, Shif, Shiff, שיף, "ship" (M.H.G., G.), transl. Hung. *hajó* (Hajos), Pol. *okręt* (Okrent), Russ. судно *sudno* (Sudnovsky); G. synonym Nauen. In Frankfurt/Main priestly family, descendants of Aberle Schiff ("ship", G.), son of Benedict Kahn ("boat", G.). Otherwise matr. from Shifke, Ashk. כ for Bibl. n. Shifra ("the beautiful", *Ex.* 1:15). Comp. Schiffeldrim, Shiffeldrim;bf (cf. M.H.G. *schipfe* "shovel, digging stick", *drum* "splinter, end piece"), Schiffenbauer (G. *Schiffbauer* "shipbuilder"), Schifer, Schiffer ("skipper" G.), Shifer, Shiffer, Schiffman, Schiffmann, Schifman ["skipper" M.H.G., cf. Sternik (Pol.), Steuerman (G.), Sturman (Russ.)], Shiffman, Shifman, Schifter, Shifter. Matr. of Shifra: Schifrin, Shifrin, Shifrine, Schifris, Shifris, Shifriss.

Synagogue Geography
בֵּית כְּנֶסֶת

The source:

There is no exact source regarding the synagogue as a building for Jewish public prayer. It is widely believed to have originated among the Babylonian exiles as a substitute for the Temple, but probably coexisted with the ancient Temple in an early form.

What you need to know:

1. There should be an ark in the east wall of the synagogue to contain the Torah scrolls.

2. There should be a *bimah* (platform) in the center from which the Torah is read.

3. The synagogue should have windows. (This requirement comes from Daniel 6:11, which describes how Daniel prayed by windows facing toward Jerusalem.)

Key words and phrases:

Aron hakodesh אֲרוֹן הַקֹּדֶשׁ. Holy ark, the receptacle on the eastern wall that holds the Torah scrolls. It is located there so that worshippers face Jerusalem when they pray.

Bimah בִּימָה. Elevated platform from which the Torah is read. In some synagogues it is placed in the center of the sanctuary.

Ner tamid נֵר תָּמִיד. Eternal light, the light above the *aron hakodesh* that is kept on daily throughout the year. Its source is the *menorah* מְנוֹרָה (candelabrum) in the ancient Tabernacle whose light burned continuously (Exod. 27:20–21).

Parochet פָּרוֹכֶת. Curtain that covers the *aron hakodesh.*

Torah תּוֹרָה. The scroll of the Five Books of Moses, written on parchment in Hebrew by a scribe. The parchment is placed on wooden handles known as *atzay chaim* (trees of life).

Who's who in the synagogue:

Rabbi רַב. Literally "teacher"; the rabbi gives the sermons, announces pages, gives the benediction, and many other things.

Chazzan חַזָן. The cantor; chants and sings the prayers, acting as *shaliach tzibbur,* or messenger/spokesperson of the congregation.

Gabbai גַבַּאי and *shamash.* Coordinates activities during the service, gives out the honors, assists the Torah reader, among other things.

Baal Koreh בַּעַל קוֹרֵא. Torah reader; reads from the Torah on the Sabbath, holidays, and Monday and Thursday mornings. This person is often the same as the *gabbai* or *shamash.*

Ushers. Persons who assist in keeping the decorum during a service. They will often give out prayer books and Bibles to the guests.

If you want to know more:

Encyclopaedia Judaica (Jerusalem, 1973) 15:579–627.
Richard Siegel, Michael Strassfeld, and Sharon Strassfeld, *The First Jewish Catalogue* (Philadelphia, 1973).

Thirty-Nine Labors Traditionally Prohibited on Shabbat
ל״ט מְלָאכוֹת

The source:

Babylonian Talmud, Shabbat 106a.

baking
bleaching
building
carrying in a public place
combing raw material
cutting to shape
demolishing
dyeing
erasing
extinguishing a fire
grinding
inserting thread in a loom
kindling a fire
kneading
marking out
plowing
reaping
removing the finished article
scraping
selecting
separating into threads
sewing
sheaf-making
sheep-shearing
sifting
skinning or flaying
slaughtering

sowing
spinning
tanning
tearing
the final hammer blow
threshing
trapping
tying a knot
untying a knot
weaving
winnowing
writing

Things to remember:

1. The Conservative, Reconstructionist, and Reform movements have different perspectives on these labors and their individual understanding of what is prohibited on Shabbat.

Key words and phrases:

Melacha מְלָאכָה. Form of work prohibited on the Sabbath.
Muktzeh מוּקְצֶה. Precautionary measure by traditional Jews to not handle anything on the Sabbath pertaining to work, like tools or money.

If you want to know more:

I. Grunfeld. *The Sabbath* (New York, 1959).

What to Avoid at Pesach
פֶּסַח

The sources:

שִׁבְעַת יָמִים מַצּוֹת תֹּאכֵלוּ אַךְ בַּיּוֹם הָרִאשׁוֹן תַּשְׁבִּיתוּ שְּׂאֹר
מִבָּתֵּיכֶם כִּי כָּל־אֹכֵל חָמֵץ וְנִכְרְתָה הַנֶּפֶשׁ הַהִוא מִיִּשְׂרָאֵל׃

"For seven days, you shall eat unleavened bread . . . for seven days, there shall be no leavened products in your home for whoever eats *chametz* shall be cut off from the congregation" (Exod. 12:15, 19).

What you need to know:

חָמֵץ   1. *Chametz* is the leavened product that results when wheat, rye, barley, oats, or spelt (the "five grains") comes into contact with water for more than eighteen minutes. Therefore, all breads, pastries, cakes, cookies, and dry cereal are considered pure *chametz.*

2. In addition to these five grains, Askenazic Jews do not eat rice, corn, beans, peas, and peanuts on Pesach. Since flour can be made of these grains and baked into bread, it may lead to confusion, say the rabbis.

Things to remember:

1. When matzah is made from flour and water, it is carefully watched so that no water touches the flour prior to mixing for dough. Then it is mixed and baked in less than eighteen minutes.

Key words and phrases:

Chametz חָמֵץ. Unleavened products.
Matzah מַצָּה. Unleavened bread.

If you want to know more:

Isaac Klein, *A Guide to Jewish Religious Practice* (New York, 1979).

Morris Golumb, *Know Your Festivals and Enjoy Them* (New York, 1976).

Philip Goodman, *The Passover Anthology* (Philadelphia, 1961).

Prohibited/Permitted Foods

כָּשֵׁר—טְרֵפָה

The sources:

Leviticus 11:1–43; Exodus 23:19, 34:26; Deuteronomy 14:21.

Fowl

Prohibited	*Permitted*
bat	capon
cuckoo	chicken
eagle	dove
hawk	duck
heron	geese
kite	pigeon
lapwing	turkey
ostrich	
owl	
pelican	
stork	
swan	
vulture	

Fish and Seafood

Prohibited	*Permitted*
catfish	anchovy
eel	bluefish
porpoise	butterfish
shark	carp
whale	cod
clam	flounder

crab	fluke
frog	haddock
lobster	halibut
octopus	herring
oyster	mackerel
scallop	pike
shrimp	porgy
snail	red snapper
	salmon
	sardine
	seabass
	shad
	smelt
	sole
	trout
	tuna
	weakfish
	whitefish

Meat

1. All animals which chew their cud and have a split hoof are kosher. This includes cattle, sheep, goats, and deer. It excludes horses, donkeys, camels, and pigs.

2. Meat must be killed according to the laws of *shechitah*.

3. Once the beast has been slaughtered, it must be properly salted (to remove excess blood).

Eggs

1. Eggs from non-kosher birds are not kosher.

2. Eggs with bloodspots are not kosher.

Things to remember:

1. Kashrut refers to
   a. proper
   b. foods that can be eaten
   c. separation of milk and meat

2. Because of the nature of liver, its kashrut is extra difficult to determine. See your rabbi.

3. There are lots of new fish being sold in the market today. If you are unsure whether something is kosher, consult your rabbi.

Key words and phrases:

Asur אָסוּר. Prohibited.
Mutar מוּתָּר. Permitted.
Shehitah שְׁחִיטָה. Process of ritual slaughter.
Shochet שׁוֹחֵט. The one who does the ritual slaughter.
Treif טְרֵפָה. Unfit.

If you want to know more:

Seymour Freedman, *The Book of Kashruth* (New York, 1970).
Isaac Klein, *A Guide to Jewish Religious Practice* (New York, 1979).

Instant Information
Rules for Kashrut
חוּקֵי כַּשְׁרוּת

The sources:

לֹא־תְבַשֵּׁל גְּדִי בַּחֲלֵב אִמּוֹ:

a. "You shall not cook a kid in its mother's milk" (Exod. 23:19).

וְהִבְדַּלְתֶּם בֵּין־הַבְּהֵמָה הַטְּהֹרָה לַטְּמֵאָה:

b. "You shall set apart the (ritually) clean beast from the unclean" (Lev. 20:25).

וּבָשָׂר בַּשָּׂדֶה טְרֵפָה לֹא תֹאכֵלוּ לַכֶּלֶב תַּשְׁלִכוּן אֹתוֹ:

c. "You must not eat flesh torn by beasts" (Exod. 22:30).

לֹא תֹאכְלוּ כָל־נְבֵלָה:

d. "You shall not eat anything that died a natural death" (Deut. 14:21).

What you need to know:

1. The basic requirements for a kosher kitchen are:
    a. There should be nothing non-kosher in it.
    b. Meat and dairy products and utensils need to be separated.

2. Permitted foods include the following:
    a. All fresh fruits and vegetables are kosher.
    b. All unprocessed grains and cereals are kosher.
    c. All milk and most dairy products, including hard cheese, are kosher according to the Rabbinical Assembly of America, an organization of Conservative rabbis.

127

d. Eggs from kosher fowl are kosher.

e. Fish that have fins and scales are kosher.

f. For an animal to be kosher, it must have split hooves, chew its cud, and be slaughtered in a kosher slaughtering house.

g. Most domestic fowl are kosher.

h. According to the Rabbinical Assembly of America, all machine-made wines are kosher.

3. Conservative Jews and some Reform Jews wait three or six hours after eating meat before eating dairy things.

Things to remember:

1. Kosher symbols: identifying symbols placed on various food products by the manufacturer identifying the product as certified kosher.

   Sample symbols include the following:

   Union of Orthodox Jewish Congregations

   Kosher Supervision Service

   Organized Kashrus Laboratories

Key words and phrases:

Chalaf חַלָף. Razor-sharp knife used by *shochet* שׁוֹחֵט in slaughtering animals.

Chalav Yisrael חָלָב יִשְׂרָאֵל. Literally "Israelite milk," refers to milk that has been under careful supervision by a Jew from the moment of milking to the time of bottling.

Fleishig (Yiddish). A product deriving from meat (*besari* in Hebrew).

Glatt kosher גְלַאט כָּשֵׁר. Literally "smooth," refers to animals whose lungs are smooth with no punctures. Generally, this refers to meat that was inspected to be kosher on slaughtering and does not require further inspection.

Kasher כָּשֵׁר. Fit and proper to eat.

Kashering. The process of making utensils kosher for use.

Kashrut כַּשְׁרוּת. The system of the Jewish dietary laws.

128

Milchig (Yiddish). A dairy-based food (*chalavi* חֲלָבִי in Hebrew).

Nevelah נְבֵלָה. Refers to an animal that dies by itself. Such an animal is non-kosher.

Pareve פַּרְוֶע. Something neutral, neither meat nor dairy. (All fish, eggs, fruits, vegetables, and grains are pareve.)

Tref טְרֵפָה. The opposite of kosher. Non-kosher food that is forbidden to be eaten by those who observe the laws of kashrut.

If you want to know more:

Samuel H. Dresner and Seymour Siegel, *The Jewish Dietary Laws* (New York, 1982).

James M. Lebeau, *The Jewish Dietary Laws: Sanctify Life* (New York, 1983).

Instant Information
Books of the Bible
סִפְרֵי הַתַּנַ"ךְ

What you need to know:

	Hebrew Name	*English Name*
	TORAH	**TORAH**
בְּרֵאשִׁית	Bereishit	Genesis
שְׁמוֹת	Shemot	Exodus
וַיִּקְרָא	Vayikra	Leviticus
בְּמִדְבָּר	Bamidbar	Numbers
דְּבָרִים	Devarim	Deuteronomy
	NEVI'IM	**PROPHETS**
יְהוֹשֻׁעַ	Yehoshua	Joshua
שׁוֹפְטִים	Shofetim	Judges
שְׁמוּאֵל א'	Shmuel Aleph	I Samuel
שְׁמוּאֵל ב'	Shmuel Bet	II Samuel
מְלָכִים א'	Melachim Aleph	I Kings
מְלָכִים ב'	Melachim Bet	II Kings
יְשַׁעְיָה	Yeshayah	Isaiah
יִרְמְיָה	Yermiyah	Jeremiah
יְחֶזְקֵאל	Yechezkel	Ezekiel
הוֹשֵׁעַ	Hoshaya	Hosea
יוֹאֵל	Yoel	Joel
עָמוֹס	Amos	Amos
עוֹבַדְיָה	Ovadyah	Obadiah
יוֹנָה	Yonah	Jonah
מִיכָה	Michah	Micah
נַחוּם	Nachum	Nahum
חֲבַקּוּק	Chabakkuk	Habakkuk
צְפַנְיָה	Tzephanyah	Zephaniah

חַגַּי	Chaggai	Haggai
זְכַרְיָה	Zecharyah	Zecharyah
מַלְאָכִי	Malachi	Malachi
KETUVIM		**WRITINGS**
תְּהִלִּים	Tehillim	Psalms
מִשְׁלֵי	Mishlei	Proverbs
אִיּוֹב	Eeyov	Job
שִׁיר הַשִּׁירִים	Shir Ha-shirim	Song of Songs
רוּת	Root	Ruth
אֵיכָה	Eicha	Lamentations
קֹהֶלֶת	Kohelet	Ecclesiastes
אֶסְתֵּר	Ester	Esther
דָּנִיֵּאל	Daniel	Daniel
עֶזְרָה	Ezra	Ezra
נְחֶמְיָה	Nechemyah	Nehemiah
דִּבְרֵי הַיָּמִים א׳	Divrey Hayamim Aleph	I Chronicles
דִּבְרֵי הַיָּמִים ב׳	Divrey Hayamim Bet	II Chronicles

Things to remember:

1. English names usually communicate themes. Hebrew names usually refer to the first large words in the opening section of the particular book.

Key words and phrases:

Chumash חוּמָשׁ. From the word for "five," *chamesh* חָמֵשׁ; the first five books of the Bible.

Tanach תַּנַּ״ךְ. Hebrew name for entire Bible, acronym derived from the names of the Bible's three divisions: Torah תּוֹרָה, Nevi'im נְבִיאִים (Prophets), and Ketuvim כְּתוּבִים (Writings).

If you want to know more:

Azriel Eisenberg, *The Book of Books* (New York, 1976).
Sylvan Schwartzman and Jack Spiro, *The Living Bible* (New York, 1966).

More particulars:

Masoretic text. Authoritative Hebrew text of the Bible produced by the scribes called the Masoretes.

Instant Information
Parashat Hashavuah:
Weekly Torah/Haftarah Readings
פָּרָשַׁת הַשָׁבוּעַ

The source:

Babylonian Talmud, Megilla 29b.

What you need to know:

Name		Torah Text	Prophetic Reading
Bereishit	Genesis	1:1-6:8	Isaiah 42:5-43:11 (42:5-21)
Noach		6:9-11:32	Isaiah 54:1-55:5 (54:1-10)
Lech Lecha		12:1-17:27	Isaiah 40:27-41:16
Vayera		18:1-22:24	II Kings 4:1-37 (4:1-23)
Chayei Sarah		23:1-25:18	I Kings 1:1-31
Toledot		25:19-28:9	Malachi 1:1-2:7
Vayetzei		28:10-32:3	Hosea 12:12-14:10
			(11:7-12:12)
Vayishlach		32:4-36:43	Hosea 11:17-12:12
			(Obadiah 1:1-21)
Vayeshev		37:1-40:23	Amos 2:6-3:8
Miketz		41:1-44:17	I Kings 3:15-4:1
Vayigash		44:18-47:27	Ezekiel 37:15-25
Vayechi		47:28-50:26	I Kings 2:1-12
Shemot	Exodus	1:1-6:1	Isaiah 27:6-28:13; 29:22-23
			(Jeremiah 1:1-2:3)
Vaeyra		6:2-9:35	Ezekiel 28:25-29:21
Bo		10:1-13:16	Jeremiah 46:13-28

Beshallach		13:17-17:16	Judges 4:4-5:31 (5:1-31)
Yitro		18:1-20:23	Isaiah 6:1-7:6; 9:5-6
			(6:1-13)
Mishpatim		21:1-24:18	Jeremiah 34:8-22; 33:25-26
Terumah		25:1-27:19	I Kings 5:26-6:13
Tetzaveh		27:20-30:10	Ezekiel 43:10-27
Ki Tisa		30:11-34:35	I Kings 18:1-39
			(18:20-39)
Vayakhel		35:1-38:20	I Kings 7:40-50 (7:13:26)
Pekudei		38:21-40:38	I Kings 7:51-8:21
			(7:40-50)
Vayikra	Leviticus	1:1-5:26	Isaiah 43:21-44:23
Tzav		6:1-8:36	Jeremiah 7:21-8:3; 9:22-23
Shemini		9:1-11:47	II Samuel 6:1-7:17
			(6:1-19)
Tazria		12:1-13:59	II Kings 4:42-5:19
Metzora		14:1-15:33	II Kings 7:3-20
Acharei Mot		16:1-18:30	Ezekiel 22:1-19 (22:1-16)
Kedoshim		19:1-20:27	Amos 9:7-15
			(Ezekiel 20:2-20)
Emor		21:1-24:23	Ezekiel 44:15-31
Behar		25:1-26:2	Jeremiah 32:6-27
Bechukotai		26:3-27:34	Jeremiah 16:19-17:14
Bemidbar	Numbers	1:1-4:20	Hosea 2:1-22
Naso		4:21-7:89	Judges 13:2-25
Behaalotecha		8:1-12:16	Zechariah 2:14-4:7
Shelach		13:1-15:41	Joshua 2:1-24
Korach		16:1-18:32	I Samuel 11:14-12:22
Chukat		19:1-22:1	Judges 11:1-33
Balak		22:2-25:9	Micah 5:6-6:8
Pinchas		25:10-30:1	I Kings 18:46-19:21
Mattot		30:2-32:42	Jeremiah 1:1-2:3
Masey		33:1-36:13	Jeremiah 2:4-28; 3:4
			(2:4-28; 4:1-2)
Devarim	Deuteronomy	1:1-3:22	Isaiah 1:1-27
Va-etchanan		3:23-7:11	Isaiah 40:1-26

Ekev	7:12-11:25	Isaiah 49:14-51:3
Re'eh	11:26-16:17	Isaiah 54:11-55:5
Shofetim	16:18-21:9	Isaiah 51:12-52:12
Ki Tetze	21:10-25:19	Isaiah 54:1-10
Ki Tavo	26:1-29:8	Isaiah 60:1-22
Nitzavim	29:9-30:20	Isaiah 61:10-63:9
Vayelech	31:1-30	Isaiah 55:6-56:8
Haazinu	32:1-52	II Samuel 22:1-51
Vezot Ha-berachah	33:1-34:12	Joshua 1:1-18 (1:1-9)

Note: parentheses indicate Sephardic ritual

Special Readings

Rosh Hashanah	1st Day	Genesis 21:1-34;	I Samuel 1:1-2:10
		Numbers 29:1-6	
	2nd Day	Genesis 22:1-24;	Jeremiah 31:2-20
		Numbers 29:1-6	
Shabbat Shuvah		Weekly portion	Hosea 14:2-10;
			Micah 7:18-20 or
			Hosea 14:2-10;
			(Hosea 14:2-10;
			Micah 7:18-20)
Yom Kippur	Morning	Leviticus 16:1-34;	Isaiah 57:14-58:14
		Numbers 29:7-11	
Sukkot	1st Day	Leviticus 22:26-23:44;	Zechariah 14:1-21
		Numbers 29:12-16	
	2nd Day	Leviticus 22:26-23:44;	I Kings 8:2-21
		Numbers 29:12-16	
Shabbat Chol Hamoed Sukkot		Exodus 33:12-34:26;	Ezekiel 38:18-39:16
		Daily portion from Numbers 29	
	8th Day	Deuteronomy 14:22-16:17;	I Kings 8:56-66
		Numbers 29:35-30:1	
Simchat Torah		Deuteronomy 33:1-34:12;	Joshua 1:1-18

		Genesis 1:1-2:3	(1:1-9)
		Numbers 29:35-30:1	
1st Shabbat Chanukah		Weekly and Chanukah portions	Zechariah 2:14-4:7
2nd Shabbat Chanukah		Weekly and Chanukah portions	I Kings 7:40-50
Shabbat Shekalim		Weekly portion;	II Kings 12:1-17
		Exodus 30:11-16	(11:17-12:17)
Shabbat Zachor		Weekly portion;	I Samuel 15:2-34
		Deuteronomy 25:17-19	(15:1-34)
Shabbat Parah		Weekly portion;	Ezekiel 36:16-38
		Numbers 19:1-22	(36:16-36)
Shabbat Hachodesh		Weekly portion;	Ezekiel 45:16-46:18
		Exodus 12:1-20	(45:18-46:15)
Shabbat Hagadol		Weekly portion	Malachi 3:4-24
Pesach	1st Day	Exodus 12:21-51;	Joshua 3:5-7; 5:2-6:1;
		Numbers 28:16-25	6:27 (5:2-6:1)
	2nd Day	Leviticus 22:26-23:44;	II Kings 23:1-9; 21-25
		Numbers 28:16-25	
Shabbat Pesach		Exodus 33:12-34:26;	Ezekiel 36:37-37:14
		Numbers 28:19-25	(37:1-14)
	7th Day	Exodus 13:17-15:26;	II Samuel 22:1-51
		Numbers 28:19-25	
	8th Day	Deut. 15:19-16:17;	Isaiah 10:32-12:6
		(on Shabbat 14:22-16:17)	
		Numbers 28:19-25	
Shavuot	1st Day	Exodus 19:11-:23	Ezekiel 1:1-28; 3:12
		Numbers 28:26-31	

	2nd Day	Deut. 15:19-16:17	Habakkuk 3:1-19
		(on Shabbat 14:22-6:17)	(2:20-3:19)
		Numbers 28:26-31	
Tisha B'av	Morning	Deut. 4:25-40	Jeremiah 8:13-9:23
	Afternoon	Exodus 32:11-14 34:1-10	Isaiah 55:6-56:8
Shabbat Rosh Chodesh		Weekly portion	Isaiah 66:1-24
Shabbat immediately preceding Rosh Chodesh		Weekly portion	I Samuel 20:18-42

Things to remember:

1. Number of *aliyot*
   Weekdays: three
   Rosh Chodesh/Chol Hamoed: four
   Holidays: five
   Yom Kippur: six
   Shabbat: seven

2. In some cases, the Reform movement has adjusted the cycle of Torah/Haftarah readings especially for the High Holidays.

Key words and phrases:

Derasha דְּרָשָׁה. Torah commentary or sermon.
Devar Torah דְּבַר תּוֹרָה. Torah lesson.
Parashat hashavuah פָּרָשַׁת הַשָּׁבוּעַ. Weekly Torah reading.
Sidrah סִדְרָה. Generally used today interchangeably with *parashat hashavuah,* the Torah portion read any particular week.

If you want to know more:

Azriel Eisenberg, *The Book of Books* (New York, 1976).
Sylvan Schwartzman and Jack Spiro, *The Living Bible* (New York, 1966).

Instant Information
The Hebrew (Luni-Solar) Calendar
לוּחַ עִבְרִי

The source:

הַחֹדֶשׁ הַזֶּה לָכֶם רֹאשׁ חֳדָשִׁים.

This month should be the first of months for you (Exodus 12:1).

What you need to know:

Months of the Year

נִיסָן	**Nisan**
אִיָּיר	**Iyar**
סִיוָן	**Sivan**
תַּמּוּז	**Tammuz**
אָב	**Av**
אֱלוּל	**Elul**
תִּשְׁרֵי	**Tishri**
חֶשְׁוָן (מַר)	**(Mar) Cheshvan**
כִּסְלֵו	**Kislev**
טֵבֵת	**Tevet**
שְׁבָט	**Shevat**
אֲדָר	**Adar**

Holidays/Festivals

רֹאשׁ הַשָׁנָה	**Rosh Hashanah**	**1 Tishri**
יוֹם כִּפּוּר	**Yom Kippur**	**10 Tishri**

סוכות	Sukkot	15 Tishri
שְׁמִינִי עֲצֶרֶת/	Shemini Atzeret/	22/23 Tishri
שְׂמְחַת תּוֹרָה	Simchat Torah	
חֲנוּכָּה	Chanukah	25 Kislev-2/3 Tevet
ט״ו בִּשְׁבָט	Tu Bishevat	15 Shevat
פּוּרִים	Purim	14 Adar
פֶּסַח	Pesach	15 Nisan-23 Nisan
יוֹם הַשּׁוֹאָה	Yom Hashoah	27 Nisan
יוֹם הָעַצְמָאוּת	Yom Ha-atzmaut	5 Iyar
שָׁבוּעוֹת	Shavuot	6 Sivan
תִּשְׁעָה בְּאָב	Tisha B'av	9 Av

Things to remember:

1. Since the Reform movement accepts the precision of the mathematical formula used to anticipate holidays in advance, the three pilgrimage festivals are celebrated for one day less, as is Rosh Hashanah. Thus, Simchat Torah may be celebrated one day earlier in Reform congregations.

2. During leap year, a full month (Adar II) is added.　　אֲדָר ב׳

3. Cheshvan is sometimes called Marcheshvan.

Key words and phrases:

Luach לוּחַ. Calendar.
Shana me-uberet שָׁנָה מְעוּבֶּרֶת. Hebrew leap year.

If you want to know more:

Raymond Zwerin, *The Jewish Calendar* (Denver, 1975).

More particulars:

Symbols of the Jewish zodiac.

Nisan—lamb;　Iyar—ox;　Sivan—twins;　Tammuz—crab; Av—lion;　　Elul—young maiden;　　Tishri—scale; Cheshvan—scorpion;　Kislev—rainbow;　Tevet—goat; Shevat—vessel filled with water;　　Adar—fish.

Phases of the Moon

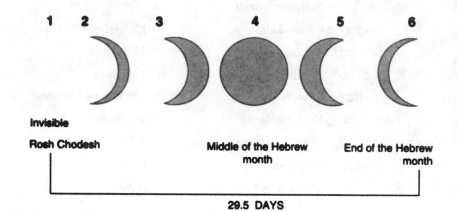

Instant Information
Alef-bet
א-ב

What you need to know:

Name	Print	Script	Sound	Numerical Value
Aleph	א	lc	silent	1
Bet	בּ	ว	B	2
(Vet)	ב	ว	(V)	(2)
Gimel	ג	८	G	3
Dalet	ד	२	D	4
Heh	ה	ๆ	H	5
Vav	ו	/	V	6
Zayin	ז	১	Z	7
Chet	ח	ŋ	CH	8
Tet	ט	๖	T	9
Yod	י	'	Y	10
Kaf	כּ	១	K	20
(Chaf)	כ	১	(CH)	(20)
(Final Chaf)	ך	೯	(CH)	(20)
Lamed	ל	∫	L	30
Mem	מ	N	M	40
(Final Mem)	ם	ಕ	(M)	(40)
Nun	נ	⅃	N	50
(Final Nun)	ן	|	(N)	(50)
Samech	ס	O	S	60
Ayin	ע	४	silent (guttural)	70
Peh	פּ	⊘	P	80
(Feh)	פ	⊘	(F)	(80)
(Final Feh)	ף	၄	(F)	(80)
Tzadee	צ	3	TZ	90
(Final Tzadee)	ץ	၄	(TZ)	(90)
Kuf	ק	ၣ	K	100

Resh	ר	⟩	R	200
Shin	שׁ	℮˙	SH	300
(Sin)	שׂ	℮	S	(300)
Tav	ת	ת	T	400

Vowels

Name	Block/Script	Sound
kametz	ָ	ah
patach	ַ	ah
tzere	ֵ	ay
segol	ֶ	eh
shooruk	וּ	oo
kubutz	ֻ	oo
cholem	וֹ	o
chiriq	ִ	ee
sheva	ְ	ih/silent

Things to remember:

1. When a *patach* is under a *chet* ח at the end of a word, the vowel is sounded before the letter.

2. When a *sheva* is added to a vowel, the word *chataf* is added to the vowel name.

Key words and phrases:

Sofer סוֹפֵר. Scribe.

Tagin תָּגִין. (singular, *tag*). Aramaic word for special designs resembling crowns used by scribes on selected letters (שעטנזגץ).

If you want to know more:

Lawrence Kushner, *The Book of Letters, the Mystical Alef Bet* (Woodstock, Vt. 1990).

David Diringer, *The Story of the Aleph Bet* (New York, 1960).

Instant Information

Basic Modern Hebrew Vocabulary
עִבְרִית מוֹדֶרְנִית

What you need to know:

English	Hebrew	Transliteration
father	אַבָּא	abba
mother	אִמָא	ima
grandfather	סַבָּא	saba
grandmother	סַבְתָּא	savta
uncle	דוֹד	dod
aunt	דוֹדָה	doda
brother	אָח	ach
sister	אָחוֹת	achot
boy	יֶלֶד	yeled
girl	יַלְדָה	yalda
family	מִשְׁפָּחָה	mishpacha
house	בַּיִת	bayit
synagogue	בֵּית כְּנֶסֶת	bet knesset
store	חָנוּת	chanut
car	מְכוֹנִית	mechonit
school	בֵּית סֵפֶר	bet sefer
teacher	מוֹרָה (m)(f)	moreh (m) morah (f)
restaurant	מִסְעָדָה	misada

Hebrew Phrases

hello, goodbye, peace unto you	שָׁלוֹם	shalom

143

how are you (m)	מַה שְׁלוֹמְךָ	mah shlomcha
how are you (f)	מַה שְׁלוֹמֵךְ	mah shlomech
what's your name (m)	מַה שִׁמְךָ	ma shimcha
what's your name (f)	מַה שְׁמֵךְ	ma shmech
all is okay	הַכֹּל בְּסֵדֶר	hakol b'seder
good morning	בֹּקֶר טוֹב	boker tov
good evening	עֶרֶב טוֹב	erev tov
good night	לַיְלָה טוֹב	liala tov
please	בְּבַקָשָׁה	bevakasha
thank you	תּוֹדָה	todah
really!	בֶּאֱמֶת	be'emet
what time is it	מַה הַשָׁעָה	mah ha-shaah
too bad	חֲבָל	chaval
so so	כָּכָה כָּכָה	kacha kacha
excuse me	סְלַח לִי	slach lee
right	יְמִינָה	yemina
left	שְׂמֹאלָה	smolah
up	לְמַעְלָה	lemalah
down	לְמַטָה	lemata
quiet	שֶׁקֶט	sheket
see you again	לְהִתְרָאוֹת	l'hitraot
yes	כֵּן	ken
no	לֹא	lo

If you want to know more:

Reuven Alcalay, *The Complete Hebrew-English English-Hebrew Dictionary*, 2 vol. (Jerusalem, 1981).

Instant Information
Greetings for Shabbat, Holiday and Everyday

Shabbat

Shabbat Shalom שַׁבָּת שָׁלוֹם. Sabbath greetings.
Gut Shabbos (Yiddish). Good Sabbath.

After Havdalah

Shavuah tov שָׁבוּעַ טוֹב. Good week.
A gut voch (Yiddish). A good week.

General Holiday

Gut yontif (from *yom tov*) (Yiddish). Happy holiday.
Chag sameach חַג שָׂמֵחַ. Happy holiday.

Rosh Hashanah

Shanah tovah שָׁנָה טוֹבָה. A good year.
Shanah tovah u'metukah שָׁנָה טוֹבָה וּמְתוּקָה. A good sweet
   year.
Le'shanah tovah tikatayvu לְשָׁנָה טוֹבָה תִּכָּתֵבוּ. May you be
   inscribed [in the book of life] for a good year.
Gut yohr (Yiddish). Good year.

Between Rosh Hashanah and Yom Kippur

G'mar chatimah tovah גְּמַר חֲתִימָה טוֹבָה. (shortened to *G'mar
   tov* גְּמַר טוֹב). May your inscription [in the book of life]
   be concluded.
Tzom kal צוֹם קַל. An easy fast (said prior to Yom Kippur
   after Rosh Hashanah).

Yom Kippur

Le'shanah tovah tikatayvu ve'techataymu לְשָׁנָה טוֹבָה תִּכָּתֵבוּ וְתֵחָתֵמוּ. May you be inscribed and sealed [in the book of life] for a good year.

Sukkot, Pesach, Shavuot

Moadim lesimcha מוֹעֲדִים לְשִׂמְחָה. Happy holiday. (Response: *Chagim uzmanim lesasson* חַגִים וּזְמַנִים לְשָׂשׂוֹן, may your holiday be a happy one.)

Daily Greetings

Boker tov בֹּקֶר טוֹב. Good morning (response: *boker or* בֹּקֶר אוֹר "the morning light").
Erev tov עֶרֶב טוֹב. Good evening.
Laila tov לַיְלָה טוֹב. Good night.
Lihitraot לְהִתְרָאוֹת. See you later.
Shalom שָׁלוֹם. Hello, goodbye, may you be at peace.

Things to remember:

1. Don't tell people *shanah tovah tikatayvu* after Rosh Hashanah. It's sort of an insult which implies that they were not inscribed in the book of life during Rosh Hashanah.

2. On somber fast days like Yom Kippur, greetings are generally not exchanged.

3. After you have had an *aliyah* or addressed the congregation, people may say *yasher koach*, "May your strength increase."
   (response *Baruch tiheyeh*: May it blessedly come to be.)

4. Upon leaving the cemetery, friends form two parallel columns to say the following to the mourner: *Hamakom yinachem etchem betoch shear avelai tziyon Verushalayim:* May God comfort you among the other mourners for Zion and Jerusalem.

Instant Information
The Ten Commandments
עֲשֶׂרֶת הַדִּבְּרוֹת

The sources:

Exodus 20:1–17; Deuteronomy 5:1–18.

What you need to know:

1. I am Adonai your God, who brought you out of the land of Egypt, out of the house of bondage.

2. You shall have no other gods in place of Me, nor make for yourself any idols.

3. You shall not speak God's name for no purpose.

4. Remember the Sabbath Day and keep it holy.

5. Honor your father and mother.

6. Do not murder.

7. Do not commit adultery.

8. Do not steal.

9. Do not bear false witness against your neighbor.

10. Do not covet anything that your neighbor owns.

Things to remember:

1. The Ten Commandments are repeated in a slightly different way in Exodus and Deuteronomy.

2. When the Ten Commandments are read in the synagogue, the entire congregation stands.

Key words and phrases:

Aseret hadibrot עֲשֶׂרֶת הַדִּבְּרוֹת. Literally, ten spoken words.
Luchot habrit לוּחוֹת הַבְּרִית. Literally, tablets of the covenant.

If you want to know more:

Abraham Chaim Feuer, *Aseres Hadibros* (New York, 1981).
Isaac Klein, *The Ten Commandments in a Changing World* (Jerusalem, 1965).

Instant Information
Thirteen Principles of Faith
שְׁלֹשׁ עֶשְׂרֵה עִקָּרֵי אֱמוּנָה

The source:

Maimonides' Commentary on the Mishnah.

What you need to know:

1. I believe with perfect faith that the Creator, blessed be Your name, is the Author and Guide of everything that has been created, and that God alone has made, does make, and will make all things.

2. I believe with perfect faith that the Creator, blessed be Your name, is a Unity, and that there is no unity in any manner like unto You, and that You alone are our God, who was, is, and will be.

3. I believe with perfect faith that the Creator, blessed be Your name, is not a body, and that You are free from all the accidents of matter, and that You have not any form whatsoever.

4. I believe with perfect faith that the Creator, blessed be Your name, is the first and the last.

5. I believe with perfect faith that to the Creator, blessed be Your name, and to You alone, it is right to pray, and that it is not right to pray to any being besides You.

6. I believe with perfect faith that all the words of the prophets are true.

7. I believe with perfect faith that the prophecy of Moses

149

our teacher, peace be unto him, was true, and that he was the chief of the prophets, both of those that preceded and of those that followed him.

8. I believe with perfect faith that the whole Torah, now in our possession, is the same that was given to Moses our teacher, peace be unto him.

9. I believe with perfect faith that this Torah will not be changed, and that there will never be any other law from the Creator, blessed be Your name.

10. I believe with perfect faith that the Creator, blessed be Your name, knows every deed of the human race and all of their thoughts, as it is said, "It is You who fashions the hearts of them all, that give heed to all their deeds."

11. I believe with perfect faith that the Creator, blessed be Your name, rewards those that keep Your *mitzvot,* and punishes those who transgress them.

12. I believe with perfect faith in the coming of the Messiah, and, though Messiah tarry, I will wait daily for the coming of the Messiah.

13. I believe with perfect faith that there will be a resurrection of the dead at the time when it shall please the Creator blessed be Your name, and exalted be the remembrance of You forever and ever.

Things to remember:

1. This is one man's attempt at getting to the essential system of Judaism, but there is no basic creed or dogma in Judaism.

יִגְדַּל

2. The *Yigdal* hymn is based on these thirteen principles. It was written as a mnemonic (memory) device to help people remember them by singing them.

150

3. Moses Maimondes (or Moses ben Maimon, also known by the acronym RaMBaM) was among the greatest Jewish philosophers. He lived 1135–1204 in Spain and later Egypt. His major works include the *Guide for the Perplexed* (*Moreh Nevuchim*) and *Mishneh Torah.*

Key words and phrases:

Ani maamin אֲנִי מַאֲמִין. I believe.
Emunah אֱמוּנָה. Faith.

If you want to know more:

Aryeh Kaplan, *Maimonides' Principles* (New York, 1975).

Instant Information
Maimonides'
Eight Degrees of Tzedakah
צְדָקָה

The source:

Mishneh Torah of Moses Maimonides.

What you need to know:

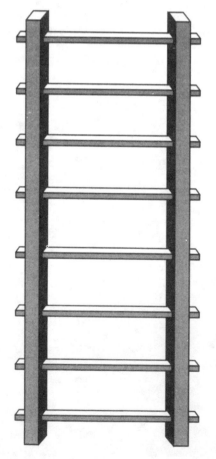

1. The person who gives reluctantly and with regret.

2. The person who gives graciously, but less than one should.

3. The person who gives what one should, but only after being asked.

4. The person who gives before being asked.

5. The person who gives without knowing to whom one gives, although the recipient knows the identity of the donor.

6. The person who gives without making one's identity known.

7. The person who gives without knowing to whom one gives. The recipient does not know from whom he receives.

8. The person who helps another to support oneself by a gift or a loan or by finding employment for that person, thus helping that person to become self-supporting.

Things to remember:

1. The dignity of the poor must always be respected.

2. Helping people to help themselves is the greatest form of *tzedakah*.

Key words and phrases:

Tzedakah צְדָקָה. Righteous giving, charity.

If you want to know more:

Joseph Feinstein, *I Am My Brother's Keeper* (New York, 1970).

Joel Grishaver and Beth Huppin, *Tzedakah, Gemilut Chasadim and Ahavah* (Denver, 1983).

Jacob Neusner, *Tzedakah* (Chappaqua, N.Y., 1982).

Instant Information
Singing Hatikvah
הַתִּקְוָה

The source:

The text was written by poet Naphtali Herz Imber, probably in Jassy, Romania, in 1878, and was inspired by the founder of Petach Tikvah (near Tel Aviv). The music, prepared by Samuel Cohen, is based on a Romanian folk song.

What you need to know:

כָּל־עוֹד בַּלֵּבָב פְּנִימָה
נֶפֶשׁ יְהוּדִי הוֹמִיָּה
וּלְפַאֲתֵי מִזְרָח קָדִימָה
עַיִן לְצִיּוֹן צוֹפִיָּה.
עוֹד לֹא אָבְדָה תִּקְוָתֵנוּ
הַתִּקְוָה בַּת שְׁנוֹת אַלְפַּיִם
לִהְיוֹת עַם חָפְשִׁי בְּאַרְצֵנוּ
אֶרֶץ צִיּוֹן וִירוּשָׁלָיִם.

Kol od ba-levav pnimah
Nefesh Yehudi homiyyah
U-lefa'atei mizrach kadimah
Ayin le-Tziyyon tzofiyah

Od lo avdah tikvatenu
Ha-tikvah bat shenot alpayim
Lihyot am chofshi be-artzenu
Eretz Tziyyon viY-rushalayim

As long as deep in the heart
The soul of a Jew yearns
And towards the East
An eye looks to Zion

Our hope is not yet lost
The hope of two thousand years
To be a free people in our land
The land of Zion and Jerusalem

Things to remember:

1. Always stand when Hatikvah is played or sung.

2. In religious Zionist families, there is a tradition of singing Psalm 126 during *zemirot* (Sabbath table songs) to the melody of Hatikvah.

Key words and phrases:

Hatikvah הַתִּקְוָה. The hope.

If you want to know more:

Encyclopaedia Judaica (Jerusalem, 1973) 7:1470–1472.

Instant Information
How To Locate Twelve Important Places in Israel
אֶרֶץ יִשְׂרָאֵל

The source:

סֹבּוּ צִיּוֹן וְהַקִּיפוּהָ׃

"Walk around Zion, circle it" (Ps. 48:13).

What you need to know:

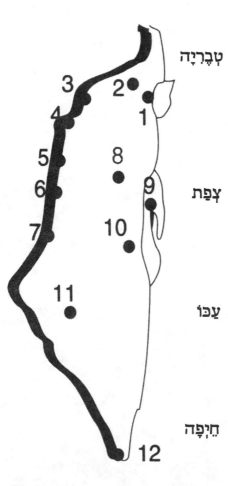

טְבֶרְיָה

1. Tiberias (*Teverya*): A popular holiday resort, it is located in the north on the west shore of the Kinneret (Sea of Galilee). One of the four holy cities of the Jewish people, Tiberias is rich in historical and religious interest. A main attraction is the synagogue, which was built in the third century.

צְפַת

2. Safed (*Tzefat*): Located in the upper Galil (Galilean mountains), twenty-two miles from Tiberias. One of the four holy cities of the Jewish people and the center of the mystics, its attractions today include several old synagogues and the artists colony.

עַכּוֹ

3. Acre (*Akko*): From ancient times until the nineteenth century, Acre was the most important seaport in Palestine. Today its attractions include the remainder of a Crusader city. It is located fourteen miles north of Haifa on the Mediterranean Sea.

חֵיפָה

4. Haifa (*Chaifa*): Haifa is Israel's chief port, lying on the northern slopes of Mount Carmel. Its attractions today include the Bahai Shrine and Garden, the Haifa

156

Museum, the Maritime Museum, and the Carmelit (Israel's only subway).

5. Caesarea (*Kaysaria*): This ancient city lies half-way between Tel Aviv and Haifa. Its archaeological ruins include a Roman theater which offers musical concerts in the summer. Its golf course is another popular attraction.

קֵיסָרְיָה

6. Tel Aviv: Located some forty miles northwest of Jerusalem on the Mediterranean Sea, Tel Aviv is the hub of Israel's commerce. Among its many places of interest are the Diaspora Museum, the Great Synagogue, the Israel National Museum, the Carmel Market, the Tel Aviv Museum, and the beaches.

תֵּל אָבִיב

7. Ashkelon: Located thirty-five miles south of Tel Aviv on the Mediterranean Sea, its history goes back to the days of the Canaanites and Philistines. Its archaeological sites are popular tourist attractions along with its extensive bathing beach.

אַשְׁקְלוֹן

8. Jerusalem (*Yerushalayim*): The capital of Israel, Jerusalem is undoubtedly Israel's most historic city. It is one of the four holy cities of Judaism. Among its many sights are the Bezalel Art School, the Biblical Zoo, Hebrew University, the Israel Museum, the Kennedy Memorial, the Knesset (Israel's Parliament), the Western Wall, the Yad VaShem Holocaust Museum, and Hadassah Hospital with its Chagall Windows.

יְרוּשָׁלַיִם

9. Dead Sea (*Yam Hamelech*): This is the lowest place on the earth's surface, forty-seven miles long and ten miles wide. At Ein Gedi, located on the west shore, one can float in the Dead Sea and visit the hot springs.

יָם הַמֶּלַח

10. Masada (*Metzada*): Located on the Dead Sea and rising 1,424 feet above sea level, Masada is most noted as the place where the Zealots managed to hold out against the Romans for three years after the

מְצָדָה

fall of Jerusalem. Its sights include the archaeological remains of the stronghold, including the ancient synagogue where many American tourists celebrate a Bar or Bat Mitzvah.

בְּאֵר שֶׁבַע 11. Beersheba (*Bersheva*): Known as the city of the patriarchs because of its many references in the Five Books of Moses, today Beersheba has become the "capital" of the south. Among its many attractions are the Desert Research Institute and Ben-Gurion University.

אֵילַת 12. Eilat: The southernmost town of Israel, it is situated on the northern end of the Red Sea. It is a popular tourist attraction with its dry hot climate and excellent coral beaches.

Things to remember:

1. One always makes *aliyah* (going up) to Israel and specifically to Jerusalem. When you leave, it is always a *yerida* (going down).

Key words and phrases:

Tel Aviv תֵּל אָבִיב. Literally, mound of spring.
Yam Hamelach יָם הַמֶּלַח. Dead Sea (literally salty sea).

If you want to know more:

David Bamberger, *A Young Person's History of Israel* (New York, 1985).
Encyclopaedia Judaica (Jerusalem, 1975) 9:107 ff.
Zev Vilnay, *Guide to Israel* (Jerusalem, 1978).

Instant Information
Psalm for Pilgrimage to Jerusalem
עֲלִיָּה לָרֶגֶל

The source:

עׇמְדוֹת הָיוּ רַגְלֵינוּ בִּשְׁעָרַיִךְ יְרוּשָׁלָ͏ִם: יְרוּשָׁלַ͏ִם הַבְּנוּיָה כְּעִיר שֶׁחֻבְּרָה־לָּהּ יַחְדָּו:

Psalm 122:2–3.

What you need to know:

Our feet are standing at your gates, Jerusalem. Jerusalem, built as a city bound firmly together, where tribes once went up to give thanks unto Adonai, where thrones of justice were once set, thrones of the house of David. Pray for the peace of Jerusalem; may those who love her prosper. May peace be in her walls, tranquility in her towers. May Adonai bless us from Zion and let us see the good of Jerusalem. Let us see our children's children and peace upon Israel.

Adapted from Psalm 122
for use at Hebrew Union College
–Jewish Institute of Religion, Jerusalem

Things to remember:

1. Jews used to make three annual pilgrimages to Jerusalem (for the three major festivals of Sukkot, Pesach, and Shavuot). There they sang the Psalms of Ascent.

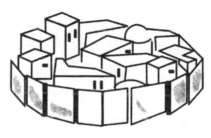

2. When you take a trip to Israel, remember to say this psalm when you arrive in Jerusalem.

3. One always goes up to Jerusalem, physically and spiritually.

Key words and phrases:

Shir hamaalot שִׁיר הַמַּעֲלוֹת. Song of ascending to Jerusalem.

If you want to know more:

Chaya Burstein, *A Kid's Catalogue of Israel* (Philadelphia, 1988).

Barbara Sofer, *Kids Love Israel, Israel Loves Kids* (Rockville, Md., 1981).

Instant Information
Tefillat Haderech
(Prayer said on traveling or taking a trip)
תְּפִלַת הַדֶּרֶךְ

The source:

יְהִי רָצוֹן מִלְפָנֶיךָ, יְיָ אֱלֹהֵינוּ וֵאלֹהֵי אֲבוֹתֵינוּ, שֶׁתּוֹלִיכֵנוּ
לְשָׁלוֹם וְתַצְעִידֵנוּ לְשָׁלוֹם, וְתַגִּיעֵנוּ אֶל מְחוֹז חֶפְצֵנוּ לְחַיִּים
וּלְשִׂמְחָה וּלְשָׁלוֹם. וְתַצִּילֵנוּ מִכַּף כָּל אוֹיֵב וְאוֹרֵב וְאָסוֹן בַּדֶּרֶךְ,
וְתִתְּנֵנוּ לְחֵן וּלְחֶסֶד וּלְרַחֲמִים בְּעֵינֶיךָ וּבְעֵינֵי כָל רוֹאֵינוּ.
וְתִשְׁמַע קוֹל תַּחֲנוּנֵינוּ, כִּי אֵל שׁוֹמֵעַ תְּפִלָּה וְתַחֲנוּן אָתָּה.
בָּרוּךְ אַתָּה, יְיָ, שׁוֹמֵעַ תְּפִלָּה:

Babylonian Talmud, Berachot 29b.

What you need to know:

May it be Your will, Adonai, my God and God of my
ancestors, to lead me, to direct my steps, and to support
me along the way. Lead me throughout my life, tranquil
and serene, until I arrive at where I am going. Deliver
me from every enemy, conflict, and hurt that I might
encounter along the way, and from all painful afflictions
that trouble the world.

Bless all that I do. Let me receive Your divine grace and
mercy. Let me also be the recipient of the loving acts of
kindness of all those I meet. Listen to the voice of my
appeal, for You are a God who responds to pleas and
prayers. Praised are You, Adonai, who hearkens to prayer.
Amen.

Things to remember:

1. In some communities, additional scriptural verses are
   read, as well as Psalms 91 and 121.

161

Key words and phrases:

Haderech הַדֶּרֶךְ. The road or way.
Nesiah tovah נְסִיעָה טוֹבָה. Have a nice trip (a way of saying goodbye).
Tefillah תְּפִילָה. Prayer.

If you want to know more:

Steven M. Brown, *Higher and Higher* (New York, 1979).

Instant Information
Kaddish Derabbanan
קַדִּישׁ דְּרַבָּנָן

The sources:

1) Babylonian Talmud Sotah 49a.
   2) Seder Eliyahu Rabba, chapter 5.

What you need to know:

יִתְגַּדַּל וְיִתְקַדַּשׁ שְׁמֵהּ רַבָּא. בְּעָלְמָא דִּי בְרָא כִרְעוּתֵהּ וְיַמְלִיךְ
מַלְכוּתֵהּ, בְּחַיֵּיכוֹן וּבְיוֹמֵיכוֹן וּבְחַיֵּי דְכָל בֵּית יִשְׂרָאֵל, בַּעֲגָלָא
וּבִזְמַן קָרִיב, וְאִמְרוּ אָמֵן:
יְהֵא שְׁמֵהּ רַבָּא מְבָרַךְ לְעָלַם וּלְעָלְמֵי עָלְמַיָּא:
יִתְבָּרַךְ וְיִשְׁתַּבַּח וְיִתְפָּאַר וְיִתְרוֹמַם וְיִתְנַשֵּׂא וְיִתְהַדָּר וְיִתְעַלֶּה
וְיִתְהַלָּל שְׁמֵהּ דְּקוּדְשָׁא, בְּרִיךְ הוּא. לְעֵלָּא (בעשי״ת לְעֵלָּא
מִכָּל) מִן כָּל בִּרְכָתָא וְשִׁירָתָא, תֻּשְׁבְּחָתָא וְנֶחֱמָתָא, דַּאֲמִירָן
בְּעָלְמָא, וְאִמְרוּ אָמֵן:
עַל יִשְׂרָאֵל וְעַל רַבָּנָן וְעַל תַּלְמִידֵיהוֹן וְעַל כָּל תַּלְמִידֵי
תַלְמִידֵיהוֹן, וְעַל כָּל מָאן דְּעָסְקִין בְּאוֹרַיְתָא, דִּי בְאַתְרָא הָדֵין
וְדִי בְכָל אֲתַר וַאֲתַר, יְהֵא לְהוֹן וּלְכוֹן שְׁלָמָא רַבָּא חִנָּא וְחִסְדָּא
וְרַחֲמִין וְחַיִּין אֲרִיכִין וּמְזוֹנָא רְוִיחֵי וּפוּרְקָנָא מִן קֳדָם אֲבוּהוֹן
דְּבִשְׁמַיָּא וְאַרְעָא וְאִמְרוּ אָמֵן:
יְהֵא שְׁלָמָא רַבָּא מִן שְׁמַיָּא וְחַיִּים טוֹבִים עָלֵינוּ וְעַל כָּל יִשְׂרָאֵל
וְאִמְרוּ אָמֵן:
עוֹשֶׂה שָׁלוֹם בִּמְרוֹמָיו הוּא בְּרַחֲמָיו יַעֲשֶׂה שָׁלוֹם עָלֵינוּ וְעַל
כָּל יִשְׂרָאֵל וְאִמְרוּ אָמֵן:

Yitgadal v'yitkadash sh'mei raba b'alma di v'ra chir'utei,
v'yamlich malchutei b'chayeichon u-v'yomeichon u-vchayei
d'chol beit yisrael, ba-agala u-vi-z'man kariv, v'imru amen.
Y'hei sh'mei raba m'varach l'alam u'l'almei almaya.
Yitbarach v'yishtabach v'yitpa'ar v'yitromam v'yitnasei,
v'yit'hadar v'yit'aleh v'yit-halal sh'mei d'kudsha, b'rich hu
l'eila (l'eila mi-kol) min kol birchata v'shirata, tushbechata
v'nechemata da-amiran b'alma, v'imru amen.
Al yisrael v'al rabbanan v'al talmideihon, v'al kol talmidei

talmideihon, v'al kol man d'askin b'oraita, di v'atra ha-
dein v'di b'chol atar v'atar, y'hei l'hon u-l'chon sh'lama
raba, china v'chisda v'rachamin, v'chayin arichin u-
mzona r'vichei, u-furkana min kodam avuhon di vi-
sh'maya v'ar'a, v'imru amen.
Y'hei sh'lama raba min sh'maya ve'chayim tovim aleinu
v'al kol yisrael, v'imru amen.
Oseh shalom bi-m'romav, hu b'rachamav ya'aseh shalom
aleinu v'al kol yisrael, v'imru amen.

Exalted and hallowed be God's great name. In this world of Your creation. May Your will be fulfilled and Your Sovereignty revealed. In the days of your lifetime and the life of the whole house of Israel speedily and soon, and say, Amen.

Be Your great name blessed forever, indeed, to all eternity.

Be the name of the most Holy Blessed One praised and honored, extolled and glorified, adored and exalted supremely. Beyond all blessings and hymns, praises and consolations that may be uttered in this world, and say, Amen.

May we of Israel and our rabbis, their disciples, and all their pupils, and all who engage in the study of Torah here and everywhere, find abundant peace, gracious favor and mercy, long life, ample sustenance and liberation through their Parent in heaven, and say, Amen.

May peace abundant descend from Heaven with a good life for us and for all Israel, and say, Amen.

May You Who creates the harmony of the spheres create peace in Your tender love for us and for all Israel, and say, Amen.

Things to remember:

1. *Kaddish Derabbanan* is said after public study of sacred literature.

2. Often a small section of Mishna is read at the conclusion of a regular service in order to provide people with an opportunity to recite this *Kaddish*.

164

3. Since the Holocaust, it is a practice in some synagogues to routinely recite this *Kaddish* in memory of all of the martyred teachers who perished.

4. *Kaddish Derabbanan,* like the other *Kaddish* prayers, is written in Aramaic (a sister language to Hebrew).

5. *Kaddish* prayers are used both to affirm belief in God and to separate different sections of the liturgy. (They function like special commas and periods.)

6. *Kaddish Derabbanan* is said while standing.

7. Out of respect for our teachers, it is a custom to actually read the words each time you say *Kaddish* even if you know the prayer by memory.

Key words and phrases

Kaddish derabbanan קַדִּישׁ דְּרַבָּנָן (Aramaic). Literally, the Rabbis' *Kaddish.*

If you want to know more:

Steven M. Brown, *Higher and Higher* (New York, 1979).

The Second
How-To Handbook
for
Jewish Living

Giving a *Devar Torah*
דְּבַר תּוֹרָה

The source:

Understood in general terms as a short sermon, the precise origin of the *devar Torah* (literally "a word of Torah") is not clear. It is probably a very old form of exposition which dates back to the *targum,* the translation of the Torah into the vernacular Aramaic. Remember: all translation is interpretation.

What you need to know:

1. Since a *devar Torah* reflects your understanding of a particular text or selection from the Bible, begin there. Review the text in context in order to understand what it meant for the biblical writer.

2. Review the classical commentary of Rashi, available in various editions in English, as a means of accessing the tradition's clear understanding of the portion of text. Rashi is encyclopedic (and pre–CD ROM!) in his approach to the history of Jewish tradition.

3. Now enter the text on your own. Grapple with the struggle of the character in the Bible. Ask yourself, "How do his or her issues of faith impact on my own?" This is where Torah offers ultimate meaning to you as an individual.

4. Now you can write down your thoughts. Don't try to tell the listeners everything you know about Torah and Judaism. There will be plenty of other times for that. Just tell them what you want them to know. Be brief. Like any good composition, make sure there is a logical flow from the introduction through the conclusion. Remember that oral presentations require a different style than written presentations.

5. If you are comfortable in doing so, use the *devar Torah* as a way of engaging the community in dialogue.

6. When speaking to young children, try to be concrete. Avoid abstractions. Feel free to use props, puppets, and visual aids.

Things to remember:

1. While the modern synagogue has championed freedom of the pulpit, do not use the pulpit as a vehicle to force your political views on others.

2. Speak slowly, clearly, and emphatically. Make good eye contact with your listeners.

3. Study. The more you learn, the more you will have to say.

4. Listen. The more you hear others offer *divrei Torah,* the more comfortable you will be delivering your own. Remember: don't compare yourself to others. Develop your own unique style.

5. Remember whatever you have to say: Jewish tradition teaches us that words from the heart enter the heart.

Key words and phrases:

Darshan דַּרְשָׁן. Preacher.
Drash דְּרָשׁ. Central idea in the explanation of the sacred text under discussion.
Drasha דְּרָשָׁה. Sermon. May be used almost interchangeably with *devar Torah.*
Maggid מַגִּיד. Person who tells stories/parables in order to teach lessons from the biblical text.
Musar מוּסָר. Ethical lesson derived from the text.
Vort (Yiddish) וואָרט. Literally, "a word"; reflects the same sense as *devar Torah.*

If you want to know more:

The American Rabbi (periodical).
Bradley Shavit Artson, "Delivering the Classical D'var Torah." In *Proceedings of the 1993 Convention, The Rabbinical Assembly* (New York, 1993).
Israel Bettan, *Studies in Jewish Preaching* (Cincinnati, 1939).
Solomon Freehof, *Modern Jewish Preaching* (Cincinnati, 1941).

Richard Israel, *The Kosher Pig* (Los Angeles, 1993). (See chapter "How to Give a Devar Torah.")

Bruce Kadden and Barbara Kadden, *Teaching Tefillah: Insights and Activities on Prayer* (Denver, 1994).

Joel Rosenberg, "Giving a Devar Torah." In *The Second Jewish Catalog,* edited by Sharon Strassfeld and Michael Strassfeld (Philadelphia, 1976).

Arranging *Aliyot* or, How to Be a *Gabbai*
עֲלִיּוֹת

The source:

Traditionally the *gabbai* was a lay communal official charged with a variety of duties, including the collection of *tzedakah*. In many instances the *gabbai* performed administrative duties in the synagogue comparable to those of the ritual director in the modern Jewish house of worship. Nowadays the *gabbai* is most active during the Torah-reading service, making sure that everything runs smoothly, attending to such matters as covering and uncovering the Torah scroll at the appropriate moment, and most especially arranging the *aliyot* and calling individuals to the Torah when it is their turn.

What you need to know:

1. The *gabbai* uncovers the Torah scroll by removing its mantle, breastplate, and crown (or *rimmonim*) when it is brought to the *bimah* after being carried through the congregation in procession.

2. The *gabbai* invites individual worshippers to the Torah honor in accordance with the synagogue's customary practice. In traditional synagogues, a *kohen* (priestly descendant) is invited first, followed by a Levite (assistant priest), and then come the ordinary Israelites. In liberal synagogues, where all worshippers are considered equal, Torah honors are distributed without regard to ancestry.

3. On Shabbat there should be at least seven *aliyot* for the reading, the *maftir*, as well as the honor of lifting the Torah scroll (*hagbahah*) and dressing the Torah scroll (*gelilah*). Make sure that you get the Hebrew names of the individuals to be honored, so that you can call them to the Torah by their Hebrew given names followed by the patronymic "son or daughter of mother/father." If

a Levite is not available, a *kohen* may be called for the second *aliyah*, but a *kohen* may not be called for any of the Israelite *aliyot*.

4. The Torah reader shows the individual called for an *aliyah* the place where the next reading begins. Make sure that the reader moves over slightly so that the *aliyah* honoree can grasp the handles of the Torah scroll and stand in front of it while reciting the blessing.

5. Generally, the *gabbai* covers the Torah scroll with its mantle after the blessing is recited following the reading of the Torah while the next person is called for an *aliyah*. The scroll is also covered during any discussion and during the recitation of a *Misheberach* or any other particular blessing.

6. While at the Torah, hold the *etz chayim* so that the Torah scroll does not move around.

7. Help the reader to roll the Torah scroll at the end of the reading of each column.

8. Follow the reading in the *tikkun* to watch out for mistakes.

9. Assist the persons doing *hagbahah* and *gelilah*.

Things to remember:

1. While some believe that every error in reading the Torah should be corrected, the Torah reading should only be corrected when the reading mistake changes the meaning of the text. In that case the word should be repeated.

2. Whether you use the annual or the triennial cycle for reading, most *Chumashim* will indicate each *aliyah*. At least three verses should be read for each *aliyah*, but the entire reading should not end on an unfavorable topic. This is especially important when you add more honors than the required *aliyot*.

3. While most synagogues have regular routes for reaching the reading table, one is supposed to take the shortest route possible, depending on where the individual is

seated in the synagogue. If the person is equidistant, ascend to the reader's right and descend from the reader's left. Often, out of respect, honorees descend from the pulpit, or leave the reading table, backwards—not wanting to turn their backs on the Torah or the ark.

4. The congregation should stand when the following sections are read: Song of Moses (Exodus 15:1–21); Ten Commandments (Exodus 20:1–14 and Deuteronomy 5:6–18). It is also considered an honor to read these portions before the congregation.

5. The following portions should be read softly, since they reflect the backsliding of our people and God's rebuke: Exodus 32:1–33:6; Leviticus 26:14–43; Numbers 11; and Deuteronomy 28:15–68.

6. While different communities have their own traditions for the musical cantillation of the Torah and Haftarah (which of course are different from each other in all communities), there are also special cantillations for the *megillot* of Esther, Lamentations, Ruth, Ecclesiastes, and Song of Songs. A person who does not read the proper system of cantillations is said to violate the verse, "You shall not move your neighbor's landmarks set up by previous generations" (Deuteronomy 19:14).

7. Traditionally, the third and sixth *aliyot* are reserved for those of great learning and piety, as is the *aliyah* that concludes each of the five books of the Torah.

8. According to Jewish tradition, all those called to the Torah are legal witnesses to the Sinai experience, which we are reenacting by reading the Torah publicly, and therefore the laws concerning witnesses are in force. Thus a father and son may not be called consecutively, nor may two brothers (and we would add sisters). Perhaps this custom is a leftover from the superstition of the evil eye. (*Note:* This tradition is often relaxed in many Reform, Conservative, and Reconstructionist synagogues.)

9. If there are many honors to be given, here is the list of priorities according to Jewish tradition:

  a. Bridegroom (and bride)

b. Bar (and Bat) Mitzvah
c. Baby naming
d. A person commemorating a *Yahrtzeit*
c. A person rising from *shivah*

10. Some congregations have reintroduced the triennial reading of the Torah, whereby only a third of each weekly Torah portion is actually read each year. In this case the *maftir* remains the same each year regardless of what is being read.

11. When in doubt, check with the rabbi or cantor. Some communities, particularly Sephardic ones, have different traditions. For example, there are synagogues where family members rise in deference to the father (or mother) if that individual is given a Torah honor.

12. When calling a rabbi to the honor of the Torah, use the phrase *morenu harav* or *moratenu harav,* "our teacher and rabbi," before the individual's name.

13. When there are more than seven *aliyot* plus the *maftir,* traditionally one pauses before continuing with the next *aliyah.*

Key words and phrases:

Aliyah (plural, *aliyot*) עֲלִיָּה. Literally "going up"; a Torah honor.

Baal koreh בַּעַל-קוֹרֵא. Torah reader.

Hosafot הוֹסָפוֹת. Additional *aliyot* beyond the Shabbat seven plus one (*maftir*).

Maftir מַפְטִיר. Concluding reading, repeating the last few verses of the Torah portion; *aliyah* given to the person who is to read the Haftarah so that he or she does not feel less honored than the Torah reader.

Minyan מִנְיָן. Prayer quorum. Traditionally, ten adult males are required for a *minyan.* In many Conservative congregations, women are included in the *minyan* requirement. Reconstructionist and Reform congregations are egalitarian; the Reform movement does not require a *minyan* for the recitation of any prayer.

Mi she-yirtzah מִי שֶׁיִּרְצֶה. Volunteer, especially one willing to act as *baal koreh* and read the verses of backsliding and rebuke.

Segan סְגָן. The person who stands next to the Torah reader to ensure that no mistakes are made and in addition acts as assistant *gabbai,* handling things at the reading desk. In most synagogues today, no distinction is made between the *gabbai* and the *segan.*

Shliach tzeebur שְׁלִיחַ צִבּוּר. Literally, "messenger of the congregation"; the one who leads the congregation in worship, often the cantor or rabbi.

If you want to know more:

Hayim Halevy Donin, *To Pray as a Jew* (New York, 1980).

"The Geography of the Synagogue," in *The Second Jewish Catalog,* edited by Sharon Strassfeld and Michael Strassfeld (Philadelphia, 1976).

Bruce Kadden and Barbara Kadden. *Teaching Tefillah: Insights and Activities on Prayer* (Denver, 1994).

Earl Klein, *Jewish Prayer: Concepts and Customs* (Columbus, OH, 1986).

Alfred Kolatch, *The Jewish Home Advisor* (New York, 1990).

More particulars:

1. We are taught in the Talmud to rise before those of great learning (Babylonian Talmud, Kiddushin 33b). Since the Torah represents the pinnacle of learning, we rise in its presence. Thus we rise as the Torah scroll is taken from the ark and carried around the sanctuary prior to and following its reading.

2. There are three *aliyot* on normal Torah-reading days (Monday and Thursday) and at the *minchah* (afternoon) service on Shabbat. On new moons and the intermediate days of Passover and Sukkot, there are four *aliyot.* On holidays there are five *aliyot.* On Yom Kippur there are six.

3. The reason the Torah is read at the weekday services on Monday and Thursday as well as on Shabbat is to ensure that we do not go three days in a row without reading the Torah.

How to Tell If a Torah Is Kosher, *Tallit* and *Tefillin* Too!

תּוֹרָה, טַלִּית וּתְפִלִּין

The source:

"Everyone should write his [or her] own Torah scroll" (Babylonian Talmud, Sanhedrin 21b). Since that is not really possible, we invite a scribe (*sofer*) to prepare a scroll on our behalf, sometimes even filling in the letters prepared for us to simulate the writing of a Torah. The word *sofer* comes from the Hebrew root meaning "to count." *Soferim* (plural) learned their trade in families, much like the guilds in ancient Israelite society.

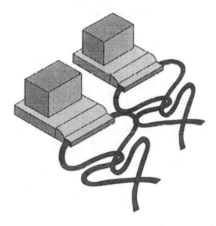

What you need to know:

This is only a guide to help you. For real guidance, consult a trained and skilled *sofer* in your community. If in doubt, contact your local rabbi for help in finding a *sofer*.

1. A Torah scroll is *pasul* (unfit for use) when it contains errors, has faded letters, or the stitching of the pieces of parchment has come undone. In most cases, these things can be repaired by a competent scribe. If the scroll (or *tefillin* or *mezuzah*) cannot be fixed, it must be placed in a *genizah* to be eventually buried properly.

2. The parchment in a *mezuzah* should be examined regularly—twice every seven years.

3. While *tefillin* straps (*retzua, retzuot*) can be easily replaced, the stitching must be removed from the *tefillin* boxes (*batim*), the *bayit shel rosh* (for the head) and the *bayit shel yad* (for the arm), in order for it to be checked properly.

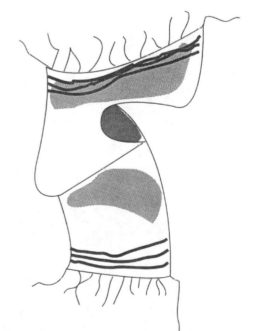

Things to remember:

1. Scribes work on Torah scrolls, *tefillin, mezuzot,* and bills of divorce (*gittin*). Other documents may be handled by a

calligrapher. Therefore, do not make corrections in these things; allow a scribe to do so.

2. Scribes use a feather quill and indelible ink, working in straight lines on specially prepared parchment. Everything they use of animal origin must be kosher.

3. A scribe must properly prepare for the job of writing sacred objects. Traditionally, the scribe goes to a *mikvah* (ritual bath) before starting such holy work.

Key words and phrases:

Get (plural, *gittin*) גֵּט. Bill of divorce.

Sofer סוֹפֵר. Scribe.

Sofer stam סוֹפֵר סְתַּ"ם. Acronym from the words *Sefer Torah*, *tefillin*, *mezuzot*. Refers to a traditional Scribe.

Tikkun soferim תִּקּוּן סוֹפְרִים. A *sofer*'s copybook, a professional compendium or guide that contains the traditional Torah text (for purposes of writing and correcting Torah scrolls), as well as rules for spacing and flourishes (*tagin*) like crowns. There are also rules which instruct the scribe how to start a column which begins with the Hebrew letter *vav*.

If you want to know more:

J. Simcha Cohen, *The 613th Commandment: An Analysis of the Mitzvah to Write a Sefer Torah* (New York, 1983).

Paul Cowan, *A Torah Is Written* (Philadelphia, 1986).

Alfred Kolatch, *The Jewish Home Advisor* (New York, 1990).

Moses Maimonides, *Hilchot Tefillin Umezuzah V'sefer Torah: The Laws Governing Tefillin, Mezuzah, and Torah* and *Hilchot Tzitzit: The Laws of Tzitzit*. Translated by Eliyahu Touger (Brooklyn, 1990).

Eric Ray, *Sofer: The Story of a Torah Scroll* (Los Angeles, 1986).

Finding Dates on a Hebrew (Soli-Lunar) Calendar
לוּחַ עִבְרִי

The source:

"This month shall be the beginning of the months, the very first of the months" (Exodus 12:2). The Jewish people's march toward freedom at Passover became the beginning point for Israel's calendar. When you are on a journey, keeping track of time is important. In the year 350 C.E., Hillel II helped to establish a permanent calendar for the Jewish people that coordinated the lunar and solar years with each other.

What you need to know:

1. There are twelve months in the Hebrew calendar. Based on the moon's cycle around the earth, each of them has either 29 or 30 days. Thus, the lunar year is 354 days long.

2. A solar year is 365 days long. In order for the Hebrew lunar months to keep in sync with the earth's annual circuit around the sun, so that the seasons come out at the right time of year, an extra month (Adar II) is added to the Jewish year approximately once every three years.

3. Most people think that the Hebrew calendar numbers the years from the date of the world's creation as determined by Jewish tradition. It's not quite that simple. We recognize the age of the world. However, in ancient times it was customary for events to be dated according to the year of the king's reign. Since we proclaim God as Ruler, we symbolically organize the calendar the same way, reckoning God's "reign" to have begun at the beginning of consciously recorded time.

4. The secular solar calendar counts years from the birth of Jesus, using the abbreviation A.D. (*anno domini*), meaning "in the year of our lord." Thus, 1996 means 1996 years

after the birth of Jesus. Dates before the birth of Jesus are followed by the abbreviation B.C.

5. When citing dates in the civil calendar, many Jewish people use the abbreviation C.E. ("common era") instead of A.D., and B.C.E. ("before the common era") instead of B.C.

6. To find a particular date on a Hebrew calendar simply locate the English date. Most likely, the Hebrew date will appear at the bottom of the box in which the English date appears. For example, the Hebrew date for July 6, 1994, is 27 Tammuz 5754 (see Fig. 2).

7. If you need to find a Hebrew date of many years ago, or if you are interested in learning the Hebrew date of a future year, you can purchase a comprehensive or perpetual Hebrew calendar (see Fig. 1.) There are also Hebrew calendar programs for the computer with which you can project almost any past or future secular date equivalent.

Things to remember:

1. There are twelve lunar months in the Hebrew calendar. Each of them has either 29 or 30 days.

2. The names of the Hebrew months, beginning with the spring month, are Nisan, Iyar, Sivan, Tammuz, Av, Elul, Tishri, Cheshvan, Kislev, Tevet, Shevat, Adar, and, in a leap year, Adar II.

3. There is one leap year (in which an entire month is added) approximately every three years in the Hebrew calendar.

4. The middle of every Hebrew month is a full moon.

5. The Hebrew calendar day begins at sunset.

Key words and phrases:

Adar II אֲדָר ב. Extra month added during leap year in Hebrew calendar.
Chodesh חֹדֶשׁ. Month.
Luach לוּחַ. Calendar.

Rosh Chodesh רֹאשׁ חֹדֶשׁ. New moon, generally the first day of the Hebrew month.

Shanah me'uberet שָׁנָה מְעוּבֶּרֶת. Literally "pregnant year"; a leap year in the Hebrew calendar.

If you want to know more:

Ronald H. Isaacs and Kerry M. Olitzky, *Sacred Celebrations: A Jewish Holiday Handbook* (Hoboken, NJ, 1994).

Arthur Spier, *The Comprehensive Hebrew Calendar* (New York, 1952).

CIVIL CALENDAR   HEBREW CALENDAR

	SUN	MON	TUE	WED	THU	FRI	SAT		SUN	MON	TUE	WED	THU	FRI	SAT	SABBATH	
APRIL	8	9	10	11	12	13	14	⟷	15 Pesah	16 Pesah	17 Hol Hamoed	18 Hol Hamoed	19 Hol Hamoed	20 Hol Hamoed	21 Pesah	Pesah VII	**NISAN**
	15	16	17	18	19	20	21	⟷	22 Pesah	23	24	25	26	27	28	Shemini*	
	22	23	24	25	26	27	28	⟷	29	30	1	2	3	4	5	Tazria Metzora (0)	**IYAR**
	29	30	1	2	3	4	5	⟷	6	7	8	9	10	11	12	Ahare Kedoshim (8)	
MAY	6	7	8	9	10	11	12	⟷	13	14	15	16	17	18 Lag Baomer	19	Emor	
	13	14	15	16	17	18	19	⟷	20	21	22	23	24	25	26	Behar* Behukkotài (0)	
	20	21	22	23	24	25	26	⟷	27	28	29	1	2	3	4	Bemidbar	**SIVAN**
	27	28	29	30	31	1	2	⟷	5	6 Shavuoth	7 Shavuoth	8	9	10	11	Naso	
JUNE	3	4	5	6	7	8	9	⟷	12	13	14	15	16	17	18	Behaalot'cha	
	10	11	12	13	14	15	16	⟷	19	20	21	22	23	24	25	Shelah L'cha*	
	17	18	19	20	21	22	23	⟷	26	27	28	29	30	1	2	Korah	**TAMMUZ**
	24	25	26	27	28	29	30	⟷	3	4	5	6	7	8	9	Hukkath	
	1	2	3	4	5	6	7	⟷	10	11	12	13	14	15	16	Balak	
JULY	8	9	10	11	12	13	14	⟷	17 Fast Tammuz	18	19	20	21	22	23	Pin'has* (10)	
	15	16	17	18	19	20	21	⟷	24	25	26	27	28	29	1	Mattoth Mase (11, 3)	**AB**
	22	23	24	25	26	27	28	⟷	2	3	4	5	6	7	8	Devarim Hazon	
	29	30	31	1	2	3	4	⟷	9 Fast Ab	10	11	12	13	14	15	Vaethanan Nahamu	
AUGUST	5	6	7	8	9	10	11	⟷	16	17	18	19	20	21	22	Ekev	
	12	13	14	15	16	17	18	⟷	23	24	25	26	27	28	29	Reeh* (4)	
	19	20	21	22	23	24	25	⟷	30	1	2	3	4	5	6	Shof'tim	
	26	27	28	29	30	31	1	⟷	7	8	9	10	11	12	13	Ki Tetze	**ELLUL**
SEP	2	3	4	5	6	7	8	⟷	14	15	16	17	18	19	20	Ki Tavo	
	9	10	11	12	13	14	15	⟷	21	22	23	24	25	26	27	Nitzavim	

Reprinted by permission from **The Comprehensive Hebrew Calendar** by Arthur Spier, © 1986. Published by Feldheim Publishers.

Symbols: (0) indicates Haphtarah to be recited. (1) through (12) indicate special Haphtaroth. Light numerals without designation indicate the days of the New Moon (Rosh Hodesh). *Proclamation of the New Moon (Mevar'chim Hahodesh).

OCTOBER 1995

Tishrei–Cheshvan 5756   תשרי–חשון תשנ"ו

ראשון SUNDAY	שני MONDAY	שלישי TUESDAY	רביעי WEDNESDAY	חמישי THURSDAY	שישי FRIDAY	שבת SATURDAY
1 ז' · 7	**2** ח · 8	**3** Kol Nidre Yom Kippur Eve Candles: 6:17 ערב יום כפור כל נדרי · ט · 9	**4** Yizkor Yom Kippur Ends: 7:14 יום כפור יזכר · י · 10	**5** 9:50 סזק"ש יא · 11	**6** Candles: 6:13 יב · 12	**7** Ends: 7:14 יג · 13
8 Erev Sukkos 14 Candles: 6:09 ערב סוכות יד	**9** Columbus Day 1st Day Sukkos 15 Candles: 7:11 א' סוכות טו	**10** 2nd Day Sukkos 16 Ends: 7:09 ב' סוכות טז	**11** 1st Day Chol Hamoed 17 א' חוה"מ יז	**12** 2nd Day Chol Hamoed 18 9:51 סזק"ש ב' חוה"מ · יח	**13** 3rd Day Chol Hamoed 19 Candles: 6:01 ג' חוה"מ יט	**14** 4th Day Chol Hamoed 20 Ends: 7:03 ד' חוה"מ כ
15 Hoshanah Rabbah 21 Candles: 5:58 הושענא רבה כא	**16** Shemini Atzeres 22 Candles: 7:00 שמיני עצרת יזכר · כב	**17** Simchas Torah 23 Ends: 6:59 שמחת תורה כג	**18** 24 אסרו חג כד	**19** 25 9:54 סזק"ש כה	**20** Candles: 5:51 26 כו	**21** Ends: 6:53 27 כז
22 28 כח	**23** 29 כט	**24** 1st Day Rosh Chodesh 30 א' ראש חדש ל	**25** 2nd Day Rosh Chodesh Cheshvan 1 ב' ראש חדש חשון · א	**26** 2 9:58 סזק"ש ב	**27** Candles: 5:41 3 ג	**28** Ends: 6:44 4 ד
29 Move Back Clock 5 2 a.m. ה	**30** 6 ו	**31** 9:02 סזק"ש 7 ז				

Light Candles 18 Minutes Before Sunset

Candle Lighting Time is for New York City Only

Daylight Savings Time

When to Say Amen and Mean It
אָמֵן

The source:

The word *amen* (meaning "may it be so") is found in the Torah as an affirmation used in the form of a response. In Deuteronomy 27:15–26, the people respond "Amen" to a series of statements by the Levites. The First Book of Chronicles (16:36), describing an incident during King David's reign (ca. 1000 B.C.E.), reports that the people responded "Amen" when they heard the blessing "Praised be Adonai, God of Israel, from now to all eternity."

What you need to know:

1. When a person says "Amen," he or she is publicly agreeing with what has just been said or endorsing it. It is an affirmation of one's belief.

2. Rabbi Chanina, a talmudic sage, stated that *amen* (אָמֵן) is an acronym for the three Hebrew words *El Melech Ne'eman* (אֵל מֶלֶךְ נֶאֱמָן), meaning "God, Faithful Ruler" (Babylonian Talmud, Shabbat 119b). As such, saying "Amen" acknowledges God as Ruler.

3. Jewish law instructs us to respond "Amen" after we hear another person recite a blessing (Code of Jewish Law, Orach Chayim 215:2 and 124:6).

Things to remember:

1. One never responds "Amen" to a blessing that one says oneself. Amen is only said as a response to a blessing by someone else. Often, this Amen functions as if you had said the blessing and thereby releases you from the obligation of saying it. That's prayer logic.

2. If you are in the midst of saying a prayer that cannot be interrupted, you may not stop even to say "Amen."

3. Never say "Amen" to a blessing that takes God's name in vain.

4. When saying "Amen," say it distinctly and in a loud voice (Code of Jewish Law, Orach Chayyim 124:8).

5. Do not say "Amen" for a blessing that you do not actually hear.

Key words and phrases:

Amen אָמֵן. So may it be.

Baruch hu u'varuch shemo בָּרוּךְ הוּא וּבָרוּךְ שְׁמוֹ. Blessed be God and blessed be God's Name (i.e., God's reputation).

Kein yehi ratzon כֵּן יְהִי רָצוֹן. So may it be God's will.

If you want to know more:

Hayim Halevy Donin, *To Pray as a Jew* (New York, 1980).
Sholom Yehuda Gross, *The Amen Response* (New York, 1981).

More particulars:

1. Another prayer response is *Baruch hu u'varuch shemo,* "Blessed be God, and blessed be God's Name." This is the correct response when hearing the (personal) name of God (that is, Adonai), as in the opening part of a blessing, *Baruch atah Adonai* (Code of Jewish Law, Orach Chayyim 124:5).

2. The response to the call to praise God, *Barchu et Adonai hamevorach,* "Praised are You, Source of blessings," is *Baruch Adonai hamevorach l'olam va-ed,* "Praised be Adonai, Source of blessings, throughout all time."

3. The response to each line of the three-sentence Priestly Benediction blessing in the repetition of the *Amidah* prayer is *Kein yehi ratzon,* "So may it be God's will."

4. According to the Babylonian Talmud (Shabbat 119b), the "Amen" response was introduced because some people could not read and therefore could not recite the blessings on their own.

Announcing the New Month
בִּרְכַּת הַחֹדֶשׁ

The source:

During the Rabbinic period, a new month was announced when two independent witnesses reported to the Sanhedrin (rabbinical court) that the crescent of a new moon had appeared. Then an official announcement would be made.

What you need to know:

1. Recite this blessing on the Shabbat before Rosh Chodesh:

יְהִי רָצוֹן מִלְּפָנֶיךָ יהוה אֱלֹהֵינוּ וֵאלֹהֵי אֲבוֹתֵינוּ, שֶׁתְּחַדֵּשׁ
עָלֵינוּ אֶת־הַחֹדֶשׁ הַבָּא לְטוֹבָה וְלִבְרָכָה. וְתִתֶּן לָנוּ חַיִּים אֲרֻ-
כִּים, חַיִּים שֶׁל שָׁלוֹם, חַיִּים שֶׁל טוֹבָה, חַיִּים שֶׁל בְּרָכָה, חַיִּים
שֶׁל פַּרְנָסָה, חַיִּים שֶׁל חִלּוּץ עֲצָמוֹת, חַיִּים שֶׁיֵּשׁ בָּהֶם יִרְאַת
שָׁמַיִם וְיִרְאַת חֵטְא, חַיִּים שֶׁאֵין בָּהֶם בּוּשָׁה וּכְלִמָּה, חַיִּים שֶׁל
עֹשֶׁר וְכָבוֹד, חַיִּים שֶׁתְּהֵא בָנוּ אַהֲבַת תּוֹרָה וְיִרְאַת שָׁמַיִם,
חַיִּים שֶׁיִּמָּלְאוּ מִשְׁאֲלוֹת לִבֵּנוּ לְטוֹבָה, אָמֵן סֶלָה.

May it be Your will, Adonai our God and God of our ancestors, to renew our lives in the coming month. Grant us a long life, a peaceful life filled with goodness and blessing, sustenance and physical vitality, a life informed by purity and piety, a life free from shame and reproach, a life of abundance and honor, a life encompassing sanctity and love of Torah, a life in which our heart's aspirations for goodness will be fulfilled.

2. Continue with this blessing while holding the Sefer Torah:

מִי שֶׁעָשָׂה נִסִּים לַאֲבוֹתֵינוּ וְגָאַל אוֹתָם מֵעַבְדוּת לְחֵרוּת,
הוּא יִגְאַל אוֹתָנוּ בְּקָרוֹב וִיקַבֵּץ נִדָּחֵינוּ מֵאַרְבַּע כַּנְפוֹת הָאָרֶץ,
חֲבֵרִים כָּל יִשְׂרָאֵל, וְנֹאמַר אָמֵן.

May the One who brought miracles for our ancestors, moving them from slavery to freedom, redeem us soon and gather our dispersed from the four corners of the earth in the community of the entire people of Israel. And let us say: Amen.

3. While still holding the Sefer Torah, announce the month:

רֹאשׁ חֹדֶשׁ _____ יִהְיֶה בְּיוֹם _____ הַבָּא עָלֵינוּ וְעַל כָּל־יִשְׂרָאֵל לְטוֹבָה.

The new month _____ will begin on _____.
May it hold blessings for us and for all the people of Israel.

4. Ask the congregation to repeat the preceding announcement and then continue with its own prayer:

יְחַדְּשֵׁהוּ הַקָּדוֹשׁ בָּרוּךְ הוּא עָלֵינוּ וְעַל כָּל־עַמּוֹ בֵּית יִשְׂרָאֵל לְחַיִּים וּלְשָׁלוֹם, לְשָׂשׂוֹן וּלְשִׂמְחָה, לִישׁוּעָה וּלְנֶחָמָה, וְנֹאמַר אָמֵן.

May the Holy One bless the new month for us and for all Your people, the House of Israel, with life and peace, joy and gladness, deliverance and consolation. And let us say: Amen.

5. Then repeat the prayer just said by the congregation.

Things to remember:

While we are able to calculate the arrival of a new moon (and therefore the Reform movement only marks one day of Rosh Chodesh), we still announce the coming of the new month in the synagogue on the Shabbat before it begins.

1. This procedure for announcing the month is followed for each month, except for Tishri. Because Rosh Hashanah begins on the first of Tishri, it is unnecessary to do so.

Key words and phrases:

Rosh Chodesh רֹאשׁ חֹדֶשׁ. New month.
Shabbat Mevarchim שַׁבָּת מְבָרְכִים. Shabbat on which the prayer for the new moon is recited.

If you want to know more:

Hayim Halevy Donin, *To Pray as a Jew* (New York, 1980).
Chaim Lipschutz, *Kiddush Levono: The Monthly Blessing of the Moon* (Brooklyn, 1987).
Abraham Millgram, *Jewish Worship* (Philadelphia, 1971).

More particulars:

1. The cycle of the moon is approximately 29 days. However, some months in the Hebrew calendar are 30 days. Therefore, Rosh Chodesh is often celebrated on two days, once on the 29th day of the cycle (which may be marked as the 30th day of a particular month) and on the first day of the month whether it coincides with the cycle or is simply the first day of the month.

2. When announcing the new month, some cantors will use a melody that somehow reflects the month about to be celebrated. For example, when announcing the new month of Kislev in which Chanukkah is celebrated, many cantors use the melody for "Maoz Tzur."

Blessing the Sun
בְּרְכַּת הַחַמָּה

The source:

Our rabbis taught that a person who sees the sun at its turning point, the moon in its power, the planets in their orbits, or the signs of the zodiac in their order should say: "Praised are You who makes the work of creation." When does this occur? Abaye said, "Every twenty-eight years, when the cycle begins again and the spring equinox falls in Saturn on the evening of Tuesday, going into Wednesday" (Babylonian Talmud, Berachot 59b).

What you need to know:

1. The blessing of the sun is a prayer service in which the sun is blessed in thanksgiving for its creation and its being set into motion in the firmament on the fourth day of creation (see Genesis 1:16–19).

2. The ceremony of the blessing of the sun takes place once every twenty-eight years. It takes place after the morning service, when the sun is about 90 degrees above the eastern horizon, on the first Wednesday of the month of Nisan (late March–early April).

3. When you see the sun on the morning following the vernal equinox, begin your service by reciting Psalms 84:12, 72:5; 75:2, Malachi 3:20, Psalm 97:6, and Psalm 148. Then recite this blessing:

בָּרוּךְ אַתָּה יהוה אֱלֹהֵינוּ מֶלֶךְ הָעוֹלָם, עוֹשֶׂה מַעֲשֶׂה בְרֵאשִׁית.

Baruch atah Adonai elohaynu melech ha'olam oseh ma'asey v'reshit.

Praised are You, Adonai our God, Sovereign of the Universe, Source of creation.

Next read Psalms 19 and 121, the hymn *El Adon,* and the Talmud passage quoted above. The ritual ends with a thanksgiving prayer in which the community says thank you to God for sustaining it.

Things to remember:

1. Although it is preferable to recite the blessing in the midst of a community (minimally with a *minyan*), even traditional Jewish law does not require this.

2. The blessing of the sun should be recited while standing. It should be pronounced as early in the day as possible.

3. The blessing is usually not recited if the sun is obscured by clouds.

Key words and phrases:

Chamah חַמָּה. Sun.

If you want to know more:

Encyclopaedia Judaica (Jerusalem, 1971), 15:518.
J. David Bleich, *Bircas HaChammah* (New York, 1980).

More particulars:

During the latter half of the twentieth century, the community blessed the sun on April 8, 1953 and March 18, 1981. The blessing of the sun will next occur on April 7, 2009.

Blessing the Moon
קִדוּש לְבָנָה

The source:

The blessing of the moon originated in the time of the Second Temple. The basic text for blessing the moon is presented in the Talmud (Sanhedrin 42a and Soferim 2:1). However, you will find many subsequent additions in the blessing used today.

What you need to know:

1. The blessing of the moon, known in Hebrew as *birkat ha'levanah* or *kiddush levanah* (sanctification of the moon), is a prayer of thanksgiving recited at the periodical reappearance of the moon's crescent.

2. The prayer can be recited from the third evening after the appearance of the new moon until the fifteenth of the lunar month. After that day, the moon begins to diminish.

3. We suggest that you recite the blessing of the moon on Saturday night, following the departure of the Sabbath, when you are still in a festive mood and dressed in your festive clothes.

4. We recite the blessing of the new moon because we understand the moon as a symbol of the renewal of nature as well as of Israel's renewal and redemption. Here is the basic text for blessing the new moon:

אָמַר רַבִּי יוֹחָנָן: כָּל־הַמְבָרֵךְ אֶת־הַחֹדֶשׁ בִּזְמַנּוֹ כְּאִלּוּ מְקַבֵּל פְּנֵי הַשְּׁכִינָה:
הַלְלוּיָהּ הַלְלוּ אֶת־יהוה מִן הַשָּׁמַיִם הַלְלוּהוּ בַּמְּרוֹמִים: הַלְלוּהוּ כָל־מַלְאָכָיו הַלְלוּהוּ כָּל־צְבָאָיו: הַלְלוּהוּ שֶׁמֶשׁ וְיָרֵחַ הַלְלוּהוּ כָּל־כּוֹכְבֵי אוֹר: הַלְלוּהוּ שְׁמֵי הַשָּׁמַיִם וְהַמַּיִם אֲשֶׁר מֵעַל הַשָּׁמָיִם: יְהַלְלוּ אֶת־שֵׁם יהוה כִּי הוּא צִוָּה וְנִבְרָאוּ: וַיַּעֲמִידֵם לָעַד לְעוֹלָם חָק־נָתַן וְלֹא יַעֲבוֹר:
בָּרוּךְ אַתָּה יהוה אֱלֹהֵינוּ מֶלֶךְ הָעוֹלָם אֲשֶׁר בְּמַאֲמָרוֹ בָּרָא שְׁחָקִים וּבְרוּחַ פִּיו כָּל־צְבָאָם. חֹק וּזְמַן נָתַן לָהֶם שֶׁלֹּא יְשַׁנּוּ

191

אֶת־תַּפְקִידָם. שָׂשִׂים וּשְׂמֵחִים לַעֲשׂוֹת רְצוֹן קוֹנָם. פּוֹעֵל אֱמֶת שֶׁפְּעֻלָּתוֹ אֱמֶת. וְלַלְּבָנָה אָמַר שֶׁתִּתְחַדֵּשׁ עֲטֶרֶת תִּפְאֶרֶת לַעֲ־ מוּסֵי בָטֶן. שֶׁהֵם עֲתִידִים לְהִתְחַדֵּשׁ כְּמוֹתָהּ וּלְפָאֵר לְיוֹצְרָם עַל שֵׁם כְּבוֹד מַלְכוּתוֹ: בָּרוּךְ אַתָּה יהוה, מְחַדֵּשׁ חֳדָשִׁים:

Rabbi Yochanan said: "Whoever blesses the new moon at the proper time is considered as having welcomed the presence of the *Shechinah*."

Halleluyah. Praise Adonai from the heavens. Praise God, angels on High. Praise God, sun and moon and shining stars. Praise God, highest heavens. Let them praise the glory of Adonai at whose command they were created, at whose command they endure forever, and by whose laws nature abides. (Psalm 148:1–6)

Praised are You, Adonai our God, Sovereign of the Universe, whose word created the heavens, whose breath created all that they contain. God set statutes and seasons for them, that they should not deviate from their assigned task. Happily they do the will of their Creator, whose work is dependable. God spoke to the moon: renew yourself, crown of glory for those who were borne in the womb, who also are destined to be renewed and to extol their Creator for God's glorious sovereignty. Praised are You, Adonai, who renews the months.

דָּוִד מֶלֶךְ יִשְׂרָאֵל חַי וְקַיָּם:

King David of Israel lives and endures.
Greetings are exchanged:

Shalom Aleichem	שָׁלוֹם עֲלֵיכֶם
Aleichem Shalom	עֲלֵיכֶם שָׁלוֹם

סִמָּן טוֹב וּמַזָּל טוֹב יִהְיֶה לָנוּ וּלְכָל יִשְׂרָאֵל. אָמֵן:

May good fortune be ours and blessing for the entire House of Israel. Amen.

Things to remember:

1. It is preferable to recite the blessing of the new moon with a *minyan* (prayer quorum of ten persons).

2. The blessing of the new moon is recited only if the moon is clearly visible (in other words, not hidden by clouds). It should preferably be said outdoors in open space.

3. In some communities, the blessing of the new moon in the month of Av is delayed until after Tisha B'Av, in Tishri until after the Day of Atonement, and in Tevet until after the fast of the Tenth of Tevet.

4. A mourner should not recite the blessing for the moon until after *shivah* (the week of mourning) is concluded.

5. The blessing of the new moon is traditionally not recited on Sabbath evenings because of the traditional prohibition against carrying prayer books outside the house or synagogue.

Key words and phrases:

Birkat Levanah בְּרְכַּת לְבָנָה. Blessing of the new moon.

Kiddush Levanah קִדּוּשׁ לְבָנָה. Sanctification of the new moon, another way of saying: blessing of the new moon.

Shalom Aleichem שָׁלוֹם עֲלֵיכֶם. Traditional form of greeting, literally, "Peace be unto you."

Siman tov u'mazel tov סִמָן טוֹב וּמַזָּל טוֹב. May you have good fortune and good luck.

If you want to know more:

Philip Birnbaum, *A Book of Jewish Concepts* (New York, 1964).

Joseph Hertz, *Daily Prayer Book* (New York, 1961).

Elie Munk, *The World of Prayer* (New York, 1963), vol. 2, pp. 94–101.

More particulars:

1. The expression "Long live King David of Israel" refers to Psalm 89:38, which says that David's dynasty shall "like the moon be established forever." The numerical value of *David melech yisrael chai vekayam* (819) is equal to the numerical equivalent of *rosh chodesh* (new month). As a

result, the phrase *rosh chodesh* became the password of Bar Kochba's army!

2. According to mystical tradition, a worshipper who says *siman tov* should perform three dancing gestures in the direction of the moon while saying three times: "Just as I cannot touch you, may my enemies never be able to harm me."

Entertaining Bride and Groom
מְשַׂמֵּחַ חָתָן וְכַלָּה

The source:

In the *Mishneh Torah* of Maimonides (Avelim 14:1), the rabbis instruct us to rejoice with the bride and groom at a wedding.

What you need to know:

1. In ancient times the betrothal and the marriage were separate ceremonies often weeks or months apart. Since the modern wedding combines the betrothal with the marriage, two cups of wine are used in the ceremony.

2. Witnesses may sign the *ketubah* (marriage document) in private before the ceremony but must be present during the ceremony. They must not be blood relatives of the bride or groom or of one another.

3. Following the reading of the *ketubah,* the officiant reads or chants these seven blessings:

בָּרוּךְ אַתָּה יהוה אֱלֹהֵינוּ מֶלֶךְ הָעוֹלָם, בּוֹרֵא פְּרִי הַגָּפֶן:

בָּרוּךְ אַתָּה יהוה אֱלֹהֵינוּ מֶלֶךְ הָעוֹלָם, שֶׁהַכֹּל בָּרָא לִכְבוֹדוֹ:

בָּרוּךְ אַתָּה יהוה אֱלֹהֵינוּ מֶלֶךְ הָעוֹלָם, יוֹצֵר הָאָדָם:

בָּרוּךְ אַתָּה יהוה אֱלֹהֵינוּ מֶלֶךְ הָעוֹלָם, אֲשֶׁר יָצַר אֶת הָאָדָם בְּצַלְמוֹ, בְּצֶלֶם דְּמוּת תַּבְנִיתוֹ, וְהִתְקִין לוֹ מִמֶּנּוּ בִּנְיַן עֲדֵי עַד, בָּרוּךְ אַתָּה יהוה, יוֹצֵר הָאָדָם:

שׂוֹשׂ תָּשִׂישׂ וְתָגֵל הָעֲקָרָה, בְּקִבּוּץ בָּנֶיהָ לְתוֹכָהּ בְּשִׂמְחָה, בָּרוּךְ אַתָּה יהוה, מְשַׂמֵּחַ צִיּוֹן בְּבָנֶיהָ:

שַׂמֵּחַ תְּשַׂמַּח רֵעִים הָאֲהוּבִים, כְּשַׂמֵּחֲךָ יְצִירְךָ בְּגַן עֵדֶן מִקֶּדֶם, בָּרוּךְ אַתָּה יהוה, מְשַׂמֵּחַ חָתָן וְכַלָּה:

בָּרוּךְ אַתָּה יהוה אֱלֹהֵינוּ מֶלֶךְ הָעוֹלָם, אֲשֶׁר בָּרָא שָׂשׂוֹן וְשִׂמְחָה, חָתָן וְכַלָּה, גִּילָה רִנָּה, דִּיצָה וְחֶדְוָה, אַהֲבָה וְאַחֲוָה, וְשָׁלוֹם וְרֵעוּת, מְהֵרָה יהוה אֱלֹהֵינוּ יִשָּׁמַע בְּעָרֵי יְהוּדָה וּבְחוּ־צוֹת יְרוּשָׁלָיִם, קוֹל שָׂשׂוֹן, וְקוֹל שִׂמְחָה, קוֹל חָתָן וְקוֹל כַּלָּה, קוֹל מִצְהֲלוֹת חֲתָנִים מֵחֻפָּתָם, וּנְעָרִים מִמִּשְׁתֵּה נְגִינָתָם, בָּרוּךְ אַתָּה יהוה, מְשַׂמֵּחַ חָתָן עִם הַכַּלָּה:

Praised are You, Adonai our God, Sovereign of the Universe, who creates the fruit of the vine.

Praised are You, Adonai our God, Sovereign of the Universe, who has created all things to Your glory.

Praised are You, Adonai our God, Sovereign of the Universe, who has made the human species.

Praised are You, Adonai our God, Sovereign of the Universe, who has made the human in Your image, after Your likeness, and has prepared for each human a perpetual fabric out of his/her essential self. Praised are You, Adonai, Creator of the human species.

May Zion who was barren be exceptionally glad and rejoice when her children joyfully gather around her. Praised are You, Adonai, who makes Zion joyful through her children.

Oh make these loving companions rejoice greatly, just as You gladdened the creatures in the Garden of Eden. Praised are You, who makes brides and grooms rejoice.

Praised are You, Adonai our God, Sovereign of the Universe, who has created joy and gladness, bride and groom, mirth and exultation, pleasure and delight, harmony, peace, and fellowship. Soon may there be heard in the cities of Judah, and in the streets of Jerusalem, the voice of joy and gladness, the voice of the groom and the bride, the jubilant voice of lovers from their *chuppot*, and youth from their feasts of song. Praised are You, Adonai our God, who causes brides and grooms to rejoice.

4. Now the groom breaks the glass and everyone shouts, *Mazel tov!*

Things to remember:

1. According to Jewish law, marital status can be attained through one of three acts: (1) before witnesses (i.e., a marriage ceremony); (2) through cohabitation before witnesses (technically legal but considered immoral); (3) through the delivery of a written document [betrothed] from a man to a woman or the presentation of a valuable article [wedding] by the man to the woman. Today's wedding represents the ceremonial enactment of these three

actions, combining the betrothal and wedding together in one formal ceremony.

2. According to tradition, "Even the study of Torah may be suspended to rejoice with bride and groom" (Babylonian Talmud, Ketuvot 17b).

3. The bride always stands to the right of the groom (see Psalm 45:10 for the textual reference).

4. Traditionally, marriages are celebrated for seven days. The *shevah berachot* are recited each day at a festive meal.

5. If their parents are dead, the bride and groom should visit their graves before the wedding to recite *El Maleh Rachamin* and pray for happiness in their marriage.

6. The preparations for a marriage often include a visit to the *mikvah* (ritual bath).

Key words and phrases:

Aufruf (Yiddish) אָפְרוּף. Literally "calling up"; refers to the Torah *aliyah* prior to one's wedding.

Badeken (Yiddish) בַּאדֶעקֶן. The ceremonial covering of the bride's face before the marriage ceremony, derived from Rebecca's covering herself with a veil before meeting Isaac (see Genesis 24:65).

Chuppah חוּפָּה. Marriage canopy, from "to cover with garlands."

Hachnasat kallah הַכְנָסַת כַּלָה. Bringing in the bride.

Ketubah כְּתֻבָּה. Marriage contract.

Kiddushin קִדּוּשִׁין. Literally "holy and separate," referring to marriage, alternatively called *nissuin* נְשׂוּאִין.

Kinyan sudor קִנְיָן סוּדָר. Agreement by handkerchief.

Nissuin נְשׂוּאִין. Wedding or marriage, alternatively called *kiddushin*.

Shadchan שַׁדְכָן. Matchmaker.

Sheva berachot שֶׁבַע בְּרָכוֹת. Seven wedding blessings.

Shidduch שִׁדּוּךְ. Literally "connection"; refers to establishing a connection between people for the purpose of marriage.

Tenaim תְּנָאִים. Conditions for the marriage.

Yichud יְחוּד. Act of consummation (i.e., unchaperoned togetherness).

If you want to know more:

Anita Diament, *The New Jewish Wedding* (New York, 1985).

Philip and Hanna Goodman, *The Jewish Marriage Anthology* (Philadelphia, 1965).

Ronald H. Isaacs, *The Bride and Groom Handbook* (West Orange, NJ, 1987).

——– and Leora W. Isaacs, *Loving Companions: Our Jewish Wedding Album* (Northvale, NJ, 1991).

More particulars:

1. It is the custom not to marry a woman bearing the same first name as one's mother.

2. Biblically, *kohanim* (priestly descendants) are not permitted to marry divorced women or converts. Reform rabbis and many Conservative and Reconstructionist rabbis reject this prohibition.

3. Bride and groom are often showered with nuts by the wedding guests since the alphanumerical equivalent of *egoz* ("nuts") is equal to *tov* ("good") in gematria. Another custom includes the throwing of raisins and candies. Rice and nuts are symbols of fertility.

4. Often, a bride will present a groom with a *tallit* prior to the wedding because the verse in Torah which refers to *tzitzit* comes right before the verse about a man and woman marrying (Deuteronomy 12:12).

5. Tuesday is a favorite day for weddings because the Torah uses the phrase *ki tov,* "And it was good," twice in its account of the third day of creation.

6. There are several periods in the calendar during which time marriages are traditionally prohibited. Check with the local rabbi for the custom of the community. In particular, weddings do not take place between Pesach and Lag B'omer or between Rosh Chodesh Iyar and Shavuot. Likewise, they are not scheduled for the three weeks prior to Tisha B'Av. Some Reform and Reconstructionist rabbis interpret these prohibitions more liberally. While there is no prohibition against marrying between Rosh Hashanah and Yom Kippur, people tend to avoid having weddings during this intense period of introspection.

7. Traditionally, bride and groom fast on their wedding day in order to ask forgiveness as they enter upon their new life together. The Talmud assures the couple that the act of getting married provides atonement for previous transgressions.

8. The groom's *tallit* is often used as a *chuppah* because it represents the commitment of one to protect the other.

Doing Gematria
גִּימַטְרִיָה

The source:

Gematria, or numerology, is a device used to interpret the Torah. It is one of the thirty-two methods of interpreting the Bible permitted by the rabbis.

What you need to know:

1. Gematria is a method used to discover the hidden meaning of Torah texts and other texts by manipulating the numerical equivalents of the Hebrew letters in particular words.

2. At times, gematria is used as a playful number game. Mystical literature has made much use of speculations based on the numerical values of the Hebrew letters. For example, since the word *torah* (תּוֹרָה) has the numerical value of 611, it refers to the 611 commandments transmitted to Israel through Moses, which together with the first two commandments of the Ten Commandments given directly to Israel by God on Mount Sinai make up the 613 positive and negative precepts.

Another example: The numerical value of the word אֶחָד (one) is the same as that of אַהֲבָה (love). This teaches us that the highest goal we should try to attain is love for God, who is One.

3. There are a variety of systems of gematria. *Atbash* refers to the one wherein the last letter of the alphabet, ת (*tav*), is substituted for the first letter, א (*alef*); the next-to-last, ש (*shin*), is substituted for the second, (*bet*); and so forth. This method is quite ancient, as shown by its use in Jeremiah 51:1.

Things to remember:

1. When doing gematria you will need to know the numerical values of the Hebrew letters. Here is a handy reference for you to use:

100	ק	40	מ	7	ז	1	א
200	ר	50	נ	8	ח	2	ב
300	שׁ	60	ס	9	ט	3	ג
400	ת	70	ע	10	י	4	ד
		80	פ	20	כ	5	ה
		90	צ	30	ל	6	ו

2. Gematria has little significance in Jewish law, but occupies an important place in the rich treasury of rabbinic literature interpreting the Bible.

3. One of the most well-known numbers in gematria is 18, which is equivalent to the Hebrew word *chai* (חַי), meaning "life." When giving *tzedakah*, it is customary to give amounts in multiples of 18, such as 36, 72, and so forth.

Key words and phrases:

Atbash אַתְבַּשׁ. System of gematria which consists of substituting the last letter of the Hebrew alphabet ת for the first א, and so forth.

If you want to know more:

Philip Birnbaum, *A Jewish Book of Concepts* (New York, 1964).
Encyclopaedia Judaica (Jerusalem, 1973), 7:369–374.

More particulars:

While this system is rarely used, there is a method of gematria in which the letters of the words are calculated according to their squared numerical value. Thus, for example, יהוה (Adonai), a name of God, = $10^2 + 5^2 + 6^2 + 5^2 = 186 =$ מָקוֹם ("Place"), another name for God.

Making a *Misheberach*
מִי שֶׁבֵּרַךְ

The source:

Misheberach is a collapsed form (that's a technical term) of the two words *Mi sheberach,* "the One who blesses," namely God. Thus, when we speak of "making a *misheberach,*" we are referring to a prayer asking God to bless a particular person or persons with well-being, especially in the case of prayers for healing or celebration (such as a Bar/Bat Mitzvah).

What you need to know:

1. While *Misheberach* prayers can be said at any time for nearly any purpose, they are generally said in public, during the Torah service, following a concluding Torah blessing.

2. Anyone can say a *Misheberach* blessing; you don't have to be a rabbi or a cantor, just a Jew who believes in the efficacy of prayer.

3. These blessings generally are said to bless the congregation, individuals who are ill, those called up for Torah honors, those celebrating a Bar or Bat Mitzvah, and people preparing for marriage.

4. Here is the basic text for one who is called to the Torah:

מִי שֶׁבֵּרַךְ אֲבוֹתֵינוּ אַבְרָהָם יִצְחָק וְיַעֲקֹב, הוּא יְבָרֵךְ אֶת (פלוני בן פלוני) בַּעֲבוּר שֶׁעָלָה לִכְבוֹד הַמָּקוֹם, לִכְבוֹד הַתּוֹרָה, (בשבת לִכְבוֹד הַשַּׁבָּת,) (ביום טוב לִכְבוֹד הָרֶגֶל,) בִּשְׂכַר זֶה, הַקָּדוֹשׁ בָּרוּךְ הוּא יִשְׁמְרֵהוּ וְיַצִּילֵהוּ מִכָּל צָרָה וְצוּקָה, וּמִכָּל נֶגַע וּמַחֲלָה, וְיִשְׁלַח בְּרָכָה וְהַצְלָחָה בְּכָל מַעֲשֵׂה יָדָיו, (בְּיוֹם טוֹב וְיִזְכֶּה לַעֲלוֹת לָרֶגֶל,) עִם כָּל יִשְׂרָאֵל אֶחָיו, וְנֹאמַר אָמֵן:

May the One who blessed our ancestors Abraham, Isaac, and Jacob, Sarah, Rebecca, Leah, and Rachel, bless _____ who has come for an *aliyah* with reverence for God and respect for the Torah. May the Holy One bless him/her and his/her family and cause to succeed all that he/she does, together with the deeds of fellow Jews everywhere. And let us say: Amen.

5. Here is the basic text for one who is ill:

מִי שֶׁבֵּרַךְ אֲבוֹתֵֽינוּ אַבְרָהָם יִצְחָק וְיַעֲקֹב, מֹשֶׁה אַהֲרֹן דָּוִד וּשְׁלֹמֹה, הוּא יְבָרֵךְ וִירַפֵּא אֶת הַחוֹלֶה (פלוני בן פלונית) בַּעֲבוּר שֶׁ(פלוני בן פלוני) יִתֵּן לִצְדָקָה בַּעֲבוּרוֹ. בִּשְׂכַר זֶה, הַקָּדוֹשׁ בָּרוּךְ הוּא יִמָּלֵא רַחֲמִים עָלָיו, לְהַחֲלִימוֹ וּלְרַפֹּאתוֹ וּלְהַחֲזִיקוֹ וּלְהַחֲיוֹתוֹ, וְיִשְׁלַח לוֹ מְהֵרָה רְפוּאָה שְׁלֵמָה מִן הַשָּׁמַֽיִם, לִרְמַ"ח אֵבָרָיו, וּשְׁסָ"ה גִּידָיו, בְּתוֹךְ שְׁאָר חוֹלֵי יִשְׂרָאֵל, רְפוּאַת הַנֶּֽפֶשׁ, וּרְפוּאַת הַגּוּף, (בשבת שַׁבָּת הִיא מִלִּזְעֹק, וּרְפוּאָה קְרוֹבָה לָבֹא,) (ביום טוב יוֹם טוֹב הוּא מִלִּזְעֹק, וּרְפוּאָה קְרוֹבָה לָבֹא,) הַשְׁתָּא, בַּעֲגָלָא וּבִזְמַן קָרִיב, וְנֹאמַר אָמֵן:

May the One who blessed our ancestors Abraham, Isaac, and Jacob, Sarah, Rebecca, Leah, and Rachel, bless and heal _____. May the Holy One in mercy strengthen him/her and heal him/her soon, body and soul, together with all others who suffer from illness. And let us say: Amen.

Things to remember:

1. In some congregations, collective prayers for healing are offered. In other synagogues, entire services are devoted to prayers of healing.

2. If the Torah scroll is still open on the reader's desk, as it should be, while the *Misheberach* is being said, place the Torah mantle (*me'il*) over the Torah during the prayer. (Don't re-dress the Torah.) Some congregations have an additional cover to be used for this purpose.

3. When using a person's Hebrew name, there are two different customs regarding the *Misheberach* prayer. If it is a prayer to honor someone, then the person is called in the name of his or her father. When the prayer is for healing, the individual is called in the name of his or her mother. In this age of political correctness, decide for

yourself, but remember to check on the *minhag ha'makom* (the custom of the place).

Key words and phrases:

Aliyah עֲלִיָּה. Literally, "going up" or "ascending"; a Torah honor.
Berachah בְּרָכָה. Blessing.

If you want to know more:

Jules Harlow, *A Rabbi's Manual* (New York, 1965).
David Polish, *Rabbi's Manual* (New York, 1988).

A Parent's Prayer for Bar/Bat Mitzvah
בַּר/בַּת מִצְוָה

The source:

"At thirteen, one is ready for *mitzvot*" (Avot 5:2).

What you need to know:

1. When the parents of a Bar/Bat Mitzvah child are called to the Torah to recite the Torah blessing, they traditionally add, *Baruch she-petarani me'ansho shel zeh,* "Praised is the One who has freed me from the responsibility for this child's actions." Traditionally this was spoken by the father of the Bar Mitzvah as the son concluded reciting the Torah blessings.

2. As an alternative, try this blessing (or, better yet, just speak from the heart):
Into our hands, O God, You have placed Your Torah, to be held high by parents and children, and taught by one generation to the next. Whatever has befallen us, our people have remained steadfast in loyalty to the Torah. It was carried into exile in the arms of parents that their children might not be deprived of their birthright. And now I pray that you, my child, will always be worthy of this inheritance. Take its teaching into your heart, and in turn, pass it on to your children and those who come after you. May you be a faithful Jew, searching for wisdom and truth, working justice and peace. Thus will you be among those who labor to bring nearer the day when Adonai shall be One and God's name shall be One.
—Adapted from *Gates of Prayer*

Things to remember:

1. A Bar or Bat Mitzvah may take place on any day when the Torah is read at services, including Mondays, Thursdays, and Rosh Chodesh (the first day/days of the month).

2. When one becomes a Bar/Bat Mitzvah and from that day forward, one takes personal responsibility for one's religious conduct.

3. Whether the occasion is marked with a ceremony or not, a child becomes Bar or Bat Mitzvah (i.e., personally responsible from the standpoint of Jewish law) at thirteen (some maintain the traditional age for girls of twelve years plus one day).

Key words and phrases:

Grammen גְּרָאמֶן. Rhymed lyrics about the Bar or Bat Mitzvah child.

If you want to know more:

Jeffrey Salkin, *Putting God on the Guest List: How to Reclaim the Spiritual Meaning of Your Child's Bar or Bat Mitzvah* (Woodstock, VT, 1992).

More particulars:

1. Some parents follow the custom of taking the *tallit* from their own shoulders and placing it on the shoulders of their child prior to reading the Torah blessings.

2. Often these blessings are preceded by what has come to be known as the Torah transmission ceremony in which an elder of the family hands the Torah scroll to the Bar/Bat Mitzvah, thereby symbolically passing the Torah from one generation to the next.

3. The Torah transmission ceremony sometimes takes place when the Torah scroll is taken from the ark, the elder removing it and handing it on to the youngster.

4. The parental blessing is sometimes concluded by reciting the *Shehecheyanu.* In some congregations, the Torah transmission ceremony replaces the parental blessing.

How to Make a Blessing or Say a Prayer
בְּרָכָה

The source:

Babylonian Talmud, Tractate Berachot.

What you need to know:

1. Blessings are simple. Begin with the traditional formula. It is probably well known to you. Here is the phrase that begins most blessings: *Baruch atah Adonai elohaynu melech ha'olam,* "Praised are You, Adonai our God, Sovereign of the Universe."

2. Then continue with the subject of your blessing, whatever is on your mind: peace, love, health, your children.

3. Prayers are just a little more complex. Here's how they work.
There are three simple sections to any prayer:

> a. The introductory *berachah,* which establishes the theme of the prayer.
> b. The middle part of the prayer, which gives the details.
> c. The closing *berachah,* which recaps the theme of the prayer.

Things to remember:

1. Anyone can offer a blessing. You don't have to be a rabbi.

2. Making blessings is serious business. By making a blessing, you are inviting God's presence—and God's power—into your midst.

3. We use traditional formulas for blessings because they ensure that our prayer statements are in harmony with the principles of the Judaic heritage. Often we feel unpoetic and turn to the tradition for spiritual insight, especially

207

on designated occasions of blessing. However, feel free to transcend the traditional parameters and offer your own prayer.

Key words and phrases:

Berachah בְּרָכָה. Blessing.

Iyyun tefillah עִיּוּן תְּפִלָּה. Transcending the words of the prayer by capturing its spiritual essence.

Kavannah כַּוָּנָה. The intention or attitude with which one prays, one's spiritual posture.

Kevah קֶבַע. Fixed prayer.

Klalah קְלָלָה. Opposite of blessing; curse.

M'ayrah מְאֵרָה. Opposite of blessing; curse.

Tefillah תְּפִלָּה. Prayer.

If you want to know more:

Joel Lurie Grishaver, *And You Shall Be a Blessing: An Unfolding of the Six Words That Begin Every Brakhah* (Northvale, NJ, 1993).

More particulars:

1. Some people are uncomfortable with the traditional language of blessing and prefer to change the Hebrew or its English translation. In many instances this is to ensure that the language referring to worshippers, both individual and collectively, and/or to the Jewish people is gender-sensitive or gender-neutral. In addition, some feel that male images of God (like *melech ha'olam*, "King of the World") need to be changed (for example, to *mekor chayim*, "Source of Life"). Do what is comfortable for you and your community.

2. Say the *Shehecheyanu* blessing whenever you experience something new:

בָּרוּךְ אַתָּה יהוה אֱלֹהֵינוּ מֶלֶךְ הָעוֹלָם, שֶׁהֶחֱיָנוּ וְקִיְּמָנוּ וְהִגִּיעָנוּ, לַזְּמַן הַזֶּה׃

Baruch atah Adonai elohaynu melech ha'olam she-hecheyanu ve'keemanu ve'heegeeyanu lazman ha'zeh.

Praised are You, Adonai our God, Sovereign of the Universe, who has kept us alive, sustained us, and enabled us to reach this day.

Saying *Selichot*
סְלִיחוֹת

The source:

"At midnight, I will rise to give thanks to You" (Psalm 119:62).

What you need to know:

Selichot services are held at midnight on the Saturday night prior to Rosh Hashanah unless Rosh Hashanah falls shortly thereafter (on Monday or Tuesday). In that case, *Selichot* are held on the preceding Saturday.

Things to remember:

1. Special *Selichot* services are scheduled during fast days, on occasions requesting God's intercession, and during the period between Rosh Hashanah and Yom Kippur.

2. Sephardim begin saying *Selichot* prayers forty days before Rosh Hashanah and continue through Yom Kippur, while Ashkenazim begin on the Saturday night (at midnight) before Rosh Hashanah and continue through Yom Kippur.

3. Originally the *Selichot* prayers were offered after the sixth blessing of the *Amidah*. Generally, they are now offered after the entire *Amidah*.

4. *Selichot* are also said on semi-official fast days—depending on the tradition of the community—like the Monday, Thursday, and Monday after Passover and Sukkot; in leap years on the Thursday before each of the eight Sabbaths when reading the Torah portions *Shemot* through *Tetzaveh;* on Yom Kippur Katan by members of the Chevra Kaddisha; and, according to Jewish tradition, to avert plagues affecting children.

Key words and phrases:

Selichot סְלִיחוֹת (singular, *selichah* סְלִיחָה). The singular form refers to individual *piyutim* (liturgical poems) whose subject is the forgiveness of sins; the plural

209

form designates a special order of service consisting of nonstatutory additional prayers for the forgiveness of sins recited during various penitential periods.

If you want to know more:

Rachel Adler and Yaffa Weisman, *Selihot Service* (Los Angeles, 1991).

Gates of Forgiveness (New York, 1980).

Sidney Greenberg, *Contemporary Prayers and Readings for the High Holidays, Sabbaths and Special Occasions* (Bridgeport, CT, 1974).

Harold Kushner, *New Prayers for the High Holy Days* (Bridgeport, CT, 1973).

Jack Reimer, *The World of the High Holidays: Poems, Parables, Prayers, Stories, Insights and Words of Torah for the Days of Awe* (Miami, FL, 1992).

Starting a Jewish Library at Home
סִפְרִיָּה

The source:

"Talmud Torah is more important than other *mitzvot* [of unlimited quantity] because it leads to them all" (Peah 1:1).

What you need to know:

There are lots of books you can purchase to start a home Jewish library. As Kohelet said, "Of the making of books there is no end" (Ecclesiastes 12:12). Here are some categories to begin with:

1. Bible

> a. A Hebrew Bible with a readable English translation.
> b. A commentary on the weekly Torah portions. Linear commentaries, as they are called, help you to follow the English translation while improving your Hebrew skills at the same time. Remember to get one that fits into the way you view the Jewish world--or the way you would like to view it. Remember to use a *Chumash* so that you can follow the weekly Torah reading. There are many books which offer a specific prism through which to read the weekly portion (like *Sparks Beneath the Surface: A Spiritual Commentary on the Torah* by Lawrence Kushner and Kerry Olitzky).

2. Prayer book

In addition to your own *siddur,* the one you use regularly, keep on hand the standard prayer books of other movements and perhaps a few examples of prayerbooks prepared by congregations for their own use.

3. Encyclopedia

The *Encyclopaedia Judaica* has become the standard. Remember to buy the yearbooks to keep it up to date. However, there are some excellent one-volume reference books. Try *A Glossary of Jewish Life* by Ron Isaacs and

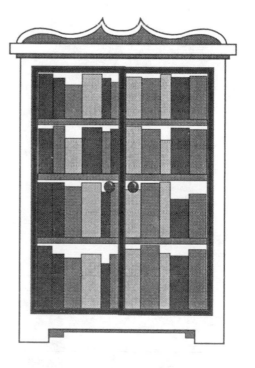

Kerry Olitzky or the new *Oxford Dictionary of Jewish Religion* edited by Geoffrey Wigoder. Other encyclopedias have different emphases. For example, the out-of-print *Universal Jewish Encyclopedia* is excellent for pre-1940 Jewish Americana. Used-book stores are great resources for out-of-print classics like the *UJE*.

4. History

All historians (and therefore all history books) interpret history according to their own understanding of it. Therefore, when you acquire a history book, try to get a sense of the historian's point-of-view ahead of time. Book jackets are great sources for this approach. Some books are written simply in order to present a theoretical construction of Jewish history, like *The Shaping of Jewish History* by Ellis Rivkin. We like to recommend complementary (or synthetic, if you prefer) viewpoints. For example, *A Certain People* by Charles Silberman and *The Jews in America* by Arthur Hertzberg present a balanced look at the current state of the North American Jewish community. Make sure you have a good set of volumes that covers most of Jewish history. Then you will want one on European history (with an emphasis on the Holocaust), one on Israel, and one on America. There are some excellent one-volume histories which read like an outline. Historical novels or histories written by novelists, like *The Jews* by Howard Fast, provide easy access.

5. Guides and Manuals

If you want to "do" Judaism and not just intellectualize about it, there are some excellent guides to the Jewish holidays (see *Sacred Celebrations* by Ron Isaacs and Kerry Olitzky) and how-to handbooks (like the one you are reading).

Things to remember:

1. Subscribe to Jewish newspapers and magazines. And don't forget to read about Israel.

2. Follow the weekly Torah portion. Keep a *Chumash* or a *Tehillim* (Book of Psalms) by your bed.

3. Keep up with the "Jewish" listings on the *New York Times* best seller list.

Key words and phrases:

Am ha'sefer עַם הַסֵּפֶר. People of the book.
Chumash חֻמָשׁ. From the word for "five"; the Torah (Five Books of Moses) arranged by weekly Torah and Haftarah portions.
Sefer סֵפֶר. Book, often referring to a sacred text.
Siddur סִדּוּר. Prayer book.

If you want to know more:

Barry Holtz, *The Schocken Guide to Jewish Books: Where to Start Reading About Jewish History, Literature, Culture, and Religion* (New York, 1992).

Choosing a Religious School
בֵּית סֵפֶר

The source:

"Teach them to your children" (Deuteronomy 11:19). "Train a child in the way to go, and even when old, he or she will not depart from it" (Proverbs 22:6). "The study of Torah is the most basic *mitzvah* of them all" (Babylonian Talmud, Shabbat 127a).

What you need to know:

1. A child's Jewish education should begin at a very early age.

2. Enroll your child in Jewish early-childhood, preschool, and primary programs.

3. Before choosing a school for your children, carefully consider the options in your area. Review the philosophy of education and goals of the school. Consider whether they are in harmony with your own.

4. Ask these questions and review the relevant documents:

    a. Does the school have a well-defined philosophy and mission statement (of purpose)?
    b. Does the school have a written curriculum that reflects its goals?
    c. Does the school have a pleasant atmosphere and a physical plant conducive to learning?
    d. Does the school have a trained educational director and experienced teaching staff?
    e. Does the school have strong community support?
    f. If needed, does the school provide opportunities for students with special learning needs?

Things to remember:

1. Always remember the importance of Jewish education in the home. Children should have opportunities early

in life to experience the sights, sounds, and flavors of Judaism in the home.

2. Raising Jewish children requires parents who lead Jewish lives. The home is the key, and Judaism must become a source of pleasure from the very beginning.

3. Many congregations provide innovative family-oriented educational programming that can assist in providing families with the knowledge and tools to bring Judaism back into their homes. Research the types of family programs that are available in your own area.

Key words and phrases:

Bet ha'sefer בֵּית הַסֵּפֶר (alternatively, *bet ha'midrash* בֵּית הַמִּדְרָשׁ). School.
Mishpachah מִשְׁפָּחָה. Family.

If you want to know more:

Hayim Halevy Donin, *To Raise a Jewish Child* (New York, 1977).
Ronald H. Isaacs, *Vesheenantam Levanekha: A Jewish Parents Handbook* (New York, 1995).
Kerry M. Olitzky et al., *When Your Jewish Child Asks Why: Answers to Tough Questions* (Hoboken, NJ, 1993).

How to Celebrate a *Simchah*
שִׂמְחָה

The source:

"You shall rejoice in your feast" (Deuteronomy 16:13).

What you need to know:

1. Jewish holidays and life-cycle events are cause for rejoicing and celebration. Such an event is called a *simchah,* the ultimate joyous event.

2. The celebration following a Jewish life-cycle event (like a Bar/Bat Mitzvah or a wedding) usually takes the form of a reception where food is served. This meal is called a *seudat mitzvah,* a "*mitzvah* meal." Often it is accompanied by singing and dancing.

3. Since a Jewish celebration is a sacred event, it should include activities of a religious nature. Here are some things that you might want to consider:

> a. Serve kosher food so that all your guests, whether traditionally observant of the dietary laws or not, can enjoy the meal.
> b. Begin the meal with the *Hamotzi* blessing over the bread, and conclude it with the reciting of the *Birkat Hamazon* (blessing after the meal).
> c. Select spirited Jewish and Israeli music for group dancing and rejoicing.
> d. Arrange in advance to give the leftover food to a local food bank.
> e. Give any flowers to a local nursing home or hospital after the *simchah* has concluded.
> f. In addition to giving friends of the Bar/Bat Mitzvah a souvenir "favor," plant a tree in Israel in their honor and give each a tree certificate as a memento. A Jewish book like this one is also a nice souvenir gift.
> g. Ask guests to bring canned food, clothing, or toys to the party for subsequent distribution to the homeless.

h. Give a percentage of the cost of your *simchah* to a Hunger Fund (for example, Mazon, A Jewish Response to Hunger, 2940 West Boulevard, Suite 7, Los Angeles, CA 90064).

Things to remember:

Be certain that your Jewish celebration emphasizes Jewish values. These include compassion, dignity, justice, learning, generosity, humility, and modesty. Plan your celebration around these values.

Key words and phrases:

Seudat mitzvah סְעוּדַת מִצְוָה. Religious meal following Jewish life-cycle event.

Simchah שִׂמְחָה. Joyous celebration, usually a family life-cycle event.

If you want to know more:

Jeffrey K. Salkin, *Putting God on the Guest List* (Woodstock, VT, 1992).

How to Welcome Friends and Neighbors into Your Home (Or: Rules for Jewish Etiquette)
הַכְנָסַת אוֹרְחִים

The source:

"Because you were a stranger in a strange land" (Leviticus 19:34 and Exodus 12:49).

What you need to know:

Hospitality is simple. Make it easy for people to feel welcome in your home. Whatever you have, whether it is a lot or a little, share it with others.

Things to remember:

1. Remember that your ancestors were strangers in Egypt and America.

2. Extend a welcome to newcomers in your synagogue and school. Don't wait for someone to say hello to you. Extend yourself to them. As Rabbi Andy Warmflash, formerly of Congregation B'nai Tikvah in North Brunswick, New Jersey, likes to say each Shabbat, "After we make *Kiddush,* go up to someone whom you don't know or you don't know well and wish them *Shabbat Shalom.*"

3. Welcoming strangers includes helping the hungry and the homeless.

Key words and phrases:

Hachnasat orchim הַכְנָסַת אוֹרְחִים. Welcoming guests or visitors; hospitality

Kol dichfin yeitei ve-yeichol כָּל דִכְפִין יֵיתֵי וְיֵכֹל. "Let all who are hungry come and eat," the phrase which begins the Passover seder.

If you want to know more:

Encyclopaedia Judaica (Jerusalem, 1978), 8:1030–33.

Ronald Isaacs and Kerry Olitzky, *Doing Mitzvot: Mitzvah Projects for Bar/Bat Mitzvah* (Hoboken, NJ, 1994).

Charles Kroloff, *When Elijah Knocks* (West Orange, NJ, 1992).

Barbara Fortgang Summers, *Community Responsibility in the Jewish Tradition* (New York, 1978).

More particulars:

1. In the medieval period, Jewish families used to display flags on their homes that would let travelers know they were welcome as guests.

2. *Ushpizin* is an unusual form of hospitality in which we invite exalted ancestors like Moses to dwell with us in the *sukkah* each year. This tradition comes from the core Jewish mystical text, the *Zohar*.

How to Give *Tzedakah*
צְדָקָה

The source:

"Justice, charity, you shall pursue" (Deuteronomy 16:20).

What you need to know:

1. No matter whether you are rich or poor, you have an obligation to give *tzedakah*. It is our human way of helping God to establish balance in the order of the world.

2. Whatever you are doing, whatever holiday you are celebrating, whatever success you are acknowledging, remember to share your joy—and express your gratitude to God—by giving *tzedakah.*

3. There are many ways to give from the heart. Money is only one of them.

Things to remember:

1. *Tzedakah* is a responsibility of all Jews, regardless of their socio-economic status. There is always someone less fortunate than you with whom you can share. One way we thank God for what we have is by sharing with others.

2. Establish your own pattern for giving, one that works for you and your family. Some people like to wait until they are finished paying bills at the end of the month. Others keep change in their pockets to be distributed while they are walking down the street. Still others keep *pushkes* at home, at work, everywhere—to remind themselves and others. There are those who make "year-end" gifts to fit into the American tax year, and there are those who participate in "planned giving" programs which will ensure that their resources are available for *tzedakah* after they die. In our families, we like to empty the change in our pockets into a *tzedakah* box as we prepare for Shabbat, just before we light the candles and sit down for Shabbat dinner.

3. Every Jewish holiday has a *tzedakah* component. For example, one should set aside *maot chittin* (literally "wheat money") during Pesach so that the poor will be able to buy matzah. Remember: as you celebrate, share.

Key words and phrases:

Gemilut chasadim גְּמִילוּת חַסָדִים. Loving acts of kindness, the giving of self to others.
Pushke (Yiddish) פּוּשְׁקֶע. *Tzedakah* container; for example, the JNF (Jewish National Fund) Blue Box.
Tzedakah צְדָקָה. Often translated as "charity"; we prefer "righteous giving."

If you want to know more:

Joel Lurie Grishaver and Beth Huppin, *Tzedakah, Gemilut Chasadim, and Ahavah: A Manual for World Repair* (Denver, 1983).
Danny Siegel, *Mitzvahs* (Pittsboro, NC, 1990).

More particulars:

Check out Maimonides' ladder of *tzedakah* in *The First How-To Handbook for Jewish Living*.

How to Arrange for a *Brit Milah* (Circumcision)
בְּרִית מִילָה

The source:

"Every male among you shall be circumcised. You shall circumcise the flesh of your foreskin, and that shall be the sign of the covenant between you and Me. At the age of eight days you shall be circumcised" (Genesis 17:10–12).

What you need to know:

1. Traditionally, it is the primary obligation of every Jewish father to circumcise his son. Since few parents have the competence to do this, it has become customary to appoint a *mohel* (ritual circumciser) to do this for them. If it is impossible to locate a *mohel,* a knowledgeable Jewish physician can be used.

2. The *Brit Milah* (circumcision ceremony) is always held on the eighth day after birth, even if it is the Sabbath or a Jewish holiday. (Some Reform rabbis permit the circumcision to take place on another day, under certain circumstances.)

3. Since the *Brit Milah* is a way of initiating a Jewish child into the House of Israel, it is appropriate to notify the entire community. In some communities young children of four or five visit the infant the night before and recite *Kriat Shema* at the baby's crib.

4. In addition to the *mohel,* the following take part in the ceremony:

> a. *Kvater.* The godfather; he brings the baby into the room where the circumcision will be performed.
> b. *Kvaterin.* The godmother; she accompanies the *kvater* in bringing the baby into the room.
> c. *Sandek.* He holds the baby while the circumcision is performed.

5. The Chair of Elijah, named in honor of Elijah the Prophet, is the chair or pillow on which the baby rests during the circumcision ceremony.

6. A festive meal follows the *Brit Milah*.

Things to remember:

1. There is a custom to place two candles in the room where the circumcision ceremony is to take place, as a symbol of God's Light and Presence.

2. Before the ceremony begins, some parents follow the beautiful custom of saying a few words about the meaning and choice of the baby's name.

3. The ceremony begins when the godparents bring the baby into the room where the *Brit Milah* will be performed.

4. The *sandek* holds the baby and the officiant then says this blessing:

בָּרוּךְ אַתָּה יהוה אֱלֹהֵינוּ מֶלֶךְ הָעוֹלָם, אֲשֶׁר קִדְּשָׁנוּ בְּמִצְוֹתָיו וְצִוָּנוּ עַל הַמִּילָה:

Baruch atah Adonai elohaynu melech ha'olam asher kidshanu b'mitzvotav ve'tzivanu al ha'milah.

Praise are You, Adonai our God, Sovereign of the Universe, who made us holy through *mitzvot* and instructed us concerning circumcision.

5. After the circumcision has been performed, the father, and quite often the mother too, recites this blessing:

בָּרוּךְ אַתָּה יהוה אֱלֹהֵינוּ מֶלֶךְ הָעוֹלָם, אֲשֶׁר קִדְּשָׁנוּ בְּמִצְוֹתָיו וְצִוָּנוּ לְהַכְנִיסוֹ בִּבְרִיתוֹ שֶׁל אַבְרָהָם אָבִינוּ:

Baruch atah Adonai elohaynu melech ha'olam asher kidshanu b'mitzvotav ve'tzivanu le'hachniso be'vrito shel Avraham Avinu.

Praised are You, Adonai our God, Sovereign of the Universe, who made us holy through *mitzvot* and instructed us to bring our son into the covenant of Abraham our ancestor.

6. All of those present then respond:

כְּשֵׁם שֶׁנִּכְנַס לַבְּרִית, כֵּן יִכָּנֵס לְתוֹרָה וּלְחֻפָּה וּלְמַעֲשִׂים טוֹבִים:

Keshem she'nichnas labrit ken yikanes le'torah ule'chuppah ule'ma'asim tovim.

As he has entered the covenant, so too may he enter a life of Torah, marriage, and good deeds.

7. The officiant then recites a blessing over a cup of wine and formally gives the baby his Hebrew name.

Key words and phrases:

Brit Milah בְּרִית מִילָה. Circumcision.
Hatafat dam brit הַטָּפַת דַּם בְּרִית. Symbolic circumcision letting out a drop of blood.
Kvater קוואַטער. Godfather.
Kvaterin קוואַטערין. Godmother.
Mohel מוֹהֵל (Mohelet מוֹהֶלֶת). Ritual circumciser.
Sandek סַנְדֵּק. One who holds the child during circumcision.
Shalom zachar שָׁלוֹם זָכָר. Ceremony for welcoming the son.

If you want to know more:

Lewis M. Barth, ed., *Berit Mila in the Reform Context* (New York, 1990).
Ronald H. Isaacs, *Rites of Passage: Guide to the Jewish Life Cycle* (Hoboken, NJ, 1992).

More particulars:

1. Mornings are preferable to afternoons for a circumcision ceremony, so as to show zeal in the performance of this *mitzvah*.

2. Some families hold a *Shalom Zachar,* a sort of welcome ceremony for the new son, on the Friday evening prior to the *Brit Milah,* either in the synagogue or at home. As friends and neighbors gather, the rabbi or the parent speaks words of Torah in honor of the occasion and blesses the child.

3. If a baby cannot be circumcised on the eighth day for reasons of health, the *Brit Milah* may be postponed.

4. If a baby is medically circumcised but the proper blessings are not recited, and the ceremony did not take place on the eighth day, then a symbolic circumcision, called a *hatafat dam brit,* is performed. This ceremony involves a pinprick that lets out a spot of blood on the genital. It must be done either by a *mohel* or a qualified Jewish physician. The symbolic circumcision is also used in the conversion to Judaism of a non-Jewish male child or adult who has been surgically circumcised.

How to Arrange for a *Simchat Bat* (Female Hebrew Naming and Covenant Ceremony)
שִׂמְחַת בַּת

The source:

The custom of naming children after other persons began in approximately the sixth century B.C.E.

What you need to know:

1. Traditionally, a Jewish girl is named in the synagogue, usually on a day when the Torah is read. However, home ceremonies are also nice.

2. Although there is no prescribed time for naming a Jewish girl, we recommend that you do so as soon as possible after birth.

3. You may want to include these elements if you design your own naming ceremony:

a. The baby is carried into the room. Candles are lit. (*Note:* if the ceremony takes place on the Sabbath or a Jewish festival, the candles should be lit at the proper candle-lighting time.) Recently, a blessing to be recited after the lighting of the candles has been suggested:

בָּרוּךְ אַתָּה יהוה אֱלֹהֵינוּ מֶלֶךְ הָעוֹלָם, אֲשֶׁר קִדְּשָׁנוּ בְּמִצְוֹתָיו
וְצִוָּנוּ עַל קִדּוּשׁ הַחַיִּים:

Baruch atah Adonai elohaynu melech ha'olam asher kid-shanu b'mitzvotav vitzivanu al kiddush ha'chayim.

Praised are You, Adonai our God, Sovereign of the Universe, who made us holy through *mitzvot* and instructed us to sanctify life.

226

b. Next, chant this blessing over a cup of wine:

בָּרוּךְ אַתָּה יהוה אֱלֹהֵינוּ מֶלֶךְ הָעוֹלָם, בּוֹרֵא פְּרִי הַגֶּפֶן:

Baruch atah Adonai elohaynu melech ha'olam boray pri ha'gafen.

Praised are You, Adonai our God, Sovereign of the Universe, who creates the fruit of the vine.

c. Next, recite this conventional paragraph of the ceremony:

בָּרוּךְ אַתָּה יהוה אֱלֹהֵינוּ מֶלֶךְ הָעוֹלָם, אֲשֶׁר קִדֵּשׁ יְדִיד מִבֶּטֶן, אֵל חַי חֶלְקֵנוּ צוּרֵנוּ, צַוֵּה לְהַצִּיל יְדִידוּת שְׁאֵרֵנוּ מִשָּׁחַת, לְמַעַן בְּרִיתוֹ. בָּרוּךְ אַתָּה יְיָ, כּוֹרֵת הַבְּרִית:
אֱלוֹהַ כָּל הַבְּרִיאוֹת קַיֵּם אֶת־הַיַּלְדָּה הַזֹּאת לְאָבִיהָ וּלְאִמָּהּ:

You have sanctified Your beloved from the womb and established Your holy covenant throughout the generations. May devotion to the covenant continue to sustain us as a people. Praised are You, God, who has established the covenant.

d. Ask the participants to respond:

כְּשֵׁם שֶׁנִּכְנְסֶת לַבְּרִית, כֵּן תִּכָּנְסִי לְתוֹרָה וּלְחֻפָּה וּלְמַעֲשִׂים טוֹבִים:

K'shem shenichneset la'brit ken tikansi l'torah ul'chuppah ule'ma'asim tovim.

As she has entered the covenant, so may she enter a life devoted to Torah, the marriage canopy, and the accomplishment of good deeds.

e. This is followed by the actual naming, in Hebrew, of the baby girl.

f. Conclude the ceremony by having the parents recite the prayer for the gift of life, called the *Shehecheyanu*:

בָּרוּךְ אַתָּה יהוה אֱלֹהֵינוּ מֶלֶךְ הָעוֹלָם, שֶׁהֶחֱיָנוּ וְקִיְּמָנוּ וְהִגִּיעָנוּ, לַזְּמַן הַזֶּה:

Baruch atah Adonai elohenyu melech ha'olam she-hecheyanu ve'keemanu ve'heegeeyanu lazman ha'zeh.

Praised are You, Adonai our God, Sovereign of the ZUniverse, who has kept us alive and sustained us and enabled us to reach this happy day.

g. A festive meal follows, where the blessing over the bread (*Hamotzi*) and the blessing after the meal (*Birkat Hamazon*) are appropriate.

Key words and phrases:

Brit ha'chayim בְּרִית חַיִּים. Literally "covenant of life"; often refers to naming ceremony for Jewish girls.

Simchat bat שִׂמְחַת בַּת. Literally "joy of the daughter"; another designation of the naming ceremony for girls.

Zeved ha'bat זֶבֶד הַבַּת. Literally "celebration for the gift of a daughter"; Sephardic naming ceremony for girls.

If you want to know more:

Ronald H. Isaacs, *Rites of Passage: Guide to the Jewish Life Cycle* (Hoboken, NJ, 1992).

How to Arrange for a *Pidyon Haben* (Redemption of Firstborn Son)
פִּדְיוֹן הַבֵּן

The source:

"From a month old a child shall be redeemed" (Numbers 18:16).

What you need to know:

1. A *Pidyon Haben* ceremony (i.e., redemption of the firstborn son) takes place thirty days after birth.

2. If the thirty-first day falls on a Sabbath or festival, the redemption ceremony is postponed to the following day.

3. The *Pidyon Haben* ceremony generally takes place in one's home during the daytime.

4. In order to conduct the *Pidyon Haben* ceremony, you need a cup of wine, a *challah* (part of the festive meal), a *Kohen* (priestly descendant), the firstborn male child and his parents, five shekels (silver dollars are often used today, or you can purchase silver coins specially minted for the *Pidyon Haben* ceremony which are often donated to charity afterwards), and the officiant, usually a rabbi or cantor, who helps to facilitate the conducting of the ceremony.

Things to remember:

Please note: Since the Reform movement has removed the class distinctions of *Kohen, Levi,* and Israelite, most Reform rabbis (including one of the authors) do not encourage this ceremony as detailed below. Instead, one should encourage the child who is the focus of the ceremony to serve God in a variety of ways.

1. The following is a sample *Pidyon Haben* ceremony which you may use or adapt in any way you see fit:

a. The father hands his son to the *kohen* and says the following:

זֶה בְּנִי בְכוֹרִי וְהוּא פֶּטֶר רֶחֶם לְאִמּוֹ, וְהַקָּדוֹשׁ בָּרוּךְ הוּא צִוָּה לִפְדּוֹתוֹ, שֶׁנֶּאֱמַר, וּפְדוּיָו מִבֶּן חֹדֶשׁ תִּפְדֶּה בְּעֶרְכְּךָ כֶּסֶף חֲמֵשֶׁת שְׁקָלִים בְּשֶׁקֶל הַקּוֹדֶשׁ עֶשְׂרִים גֵּרָה הוּא. וְנֶאֱמַר, קַדֶּשׁ לִי כָל בְּכוֹר פֶּטֶר כָּל רֶחֶם בִּבְנֵי יִשְׂרָאֵל בָּאָדָם וּבַבְּהֵמָה, לִי הוּא:

This my firstborn is the firstborn of his mother, and God has directed us to redeem him, as it is written in the Torah: "when he is one month old you shall redeem him for five shekels." And it is written: "Sanctify unto Me every firstborn Israelite; he is Mine."

b. Next the father places the five silver shekels before the *kohen* and the *kohen* asks:

מַה בָּעִית טְפֵי לִיתֶּן לִי בִּנְךָ בְּכוֹרֶךָ שֶׁהוּא פֶּטֶר רֶחֶם לְאִמּוֹ, אוֹ בָּעִית לִפְדּוֹתוֹ בְּעַד חָמֵשׁ סְלָעִים כִּדְמְחַיַּבְתָּ מִדְּאוֹרַיְתָא:

What is your preference—to give me your firstborn son or to redeem him for five shekels, as you are commanded to do in the Torah?

c. The father gives the five shekels to the *kohen* and says:

חָפֵץ אֲנִי לִפְדּוֹת אֶת בְּנִי וְהֵילָךְ דְּמֵי פִּדְיוֹנוֹ כִּדְמְחַיַּבְתִּי מִדְּאוֹרַיְתָא:

I want to redeem my son. Here is the equivalent of five shekels, and thus I fulfill my obligation according to the Torah.

d. The *kohen* accepts the redemption money and returns the child to the father, whereupon the father recites:

בָּרוּךְ אַתָּה יהוה אֱלֹהֵינוּ מֶלֶךְ הָעוֹלָם, אֲשֶׁר קִדְּשָׁנוּ בְּמִצְוֹתָיו וְצִוָּנוּ עַל פִּדְיוֹן הַבֵּן:

Baruch atah Adonai elohaynu melech ha'olam asher kid-shanu b'mitzvotav ve'tzivanu al pidyon ha'ben.

Praised are You, Adonai our God, Sovereign of the Universe, who made us holy with your *mitzvot* and instructed us concerning the redemption of the first-born.

e. Father and mother together say the prayer for the gift of life:

בָּרוּךְ אַתָּה יהוה אֱלֹהֵינוּ מֶלֶךְ הָעוֹלָם, שֶׁהֶחֱיָנוּ וְקִיְּמָנוּ וְהִגִּיעָנוּ, לַזְּמַן הַזֶּה:

Baruch atah Adonai elohaynu melech ha'olam she-hecheyanu ve'keemanu ve'heegeeyanu lazman ha'zeh.

Praised are You, Adonai our God, Sovereign of the Universe, who has kept us alive, sustained us, and enabled us to reach this day.

e. The *kohen* then holds the coins and says:

זֶה תַּחַת זֶה זֶה חִלּוּף זֶה זֶה מָחוּל עַל זֶה. וְיִכָּנֵס זֶה הַבֵּן לְחַיִּים, לְתוֹרָה וּלְחֻפָּה וּלְמַעֲשִׂים טוֹבִים, אמן;

I accept the five shekels and hereby declare your son redeemed. May he be granted a complete and full life, live in devotion to the Torah and with reverence for God. As this child has attained redemption, so may it be God's will that he attain the blessings of Torah, marriage, and a life of good deeds.

f. The *kohen* blesses the child with the threefold priestly blessing.

יְשִׂמְךָ אֱלֹהִים כְּאֶפְרַיִם וְכִמְנַשֶּׁה.

Yiseemcha Eloheem k'efrayim v'cheem'nasheh.

May God make you like Ephraim and Manasseh.

יְבָרֶכְךָ יהוה וְיִשְׁמְרֶךָ.

Yevarechecha Adonai v'yishmerecha.

May God bless and keep you.

יָאֵר יהוה פָּנָיו אֵלֶיךָ וִיחֻנֶּךָּ.

Ya'er Adonai panav eylecha veechuneka.

May God's Presence shine on and be good to you.

יִשָּׂא יהוה פָּנָיו אֵלֶיךָ וְיָשֵׂם לְךָ שָׁלוֹם.

Yisa Adonai panav eylecha ve'yasem lecha shalom.

May God's face turn toward you and give you peace.

2. A festive meal concludes the ceremony. It ought to begin with the recitation of the blessing over the bread (*Hamotzi*) before the meal, and should conclude with the blessing after the meal (*Birkat Hamazon*) following it.

Key words and phrases:

Kohen כֹּהֵן. Descendant of the priestly caste.
Pidyon Haben פִּדְיוֹן הַבֵּן. Redemption of the firstborn son.

If you want to know more:

Ronald H. Isaacs, *Rites of Passage: Guide to the Jewish Life Cycle* (Hoboken, NJ, 1992).
Leo Trepp, *The Complete Book of Jewish Observance* (New York, 1980).

More particulars:

1. Traditional Jewish law requires that a *Pidyon Haben* be performed if the child is male and the first "issue" of the mother's womb. If the child's father is a *kohen* or levite, he automatically belongs to the special caste of ministers called *kohanim* and *levi'im* and need not have a *Pidyon Haben*. Also, if the mother of the child is the daughter of a *kohen* or *levi* the rite is not performed.

2. A male child born by Caesarean operation does not have to be redeemed because Jewish law does not consider such a child to have "issued forth" from the womb.

3. A son born of a woman who previously had a miscarriage does not require a *Pidyon Haben*, nor does a son born to a woman who previously had a stillbirth.

4. If a man marries twice, the firstborn son of each wife must be redeemed.

5. In recent years some families have created a personalized ritual for their firstborn daughters. Such ceremonies are known by different names, including *pidyon habat*

(redemption of the firstborn daughter) and *kiddush petter rechem* (sanctification of the one who opens the womb). These ceremonies often include a dialogue between the officiant and the parents related to the importance of consecrating firstborn children, as well as an exchange of coins, which are often donated to charity in honor of the firstborn daughter. Such ceremonies offer an alternative to those uncomfortable with social-class distinctions.

Family Blessings
בִּרְכוֹת הַמִּשְׁפָּחָה

The source:

The first source for the family blessings is Genesis 48:20. In this passage, Jacob blesses his grandchildren Ephraim and Menasseh. The second source for the family blessings is the Book of Numbers 6:23–26. In this section God speaks to Moses who in turn is told to speak to his brother Aaron. God then presents Aaron with the blessing, which has come to be known as the three-fold priestly blessing.

What you need to know:

1. It is customary for parents to bless their children before sitting down to a Sabbath meal. The blessing provides parents with a privileged opportunity to express appreciation for their children.

2. Through the touch of a parent's hands or the sound of a parent's voice, children can feel and respond to the love and affection their family has for them.

3. The blessing for boys invokes the shining examples of Jacob's grandchildren Ephraim and Manasseh, who, although raised in Egypt, did not lose their identity as Jews.

4. The blessing for girls refers to the four matriarchs, Sarah, Rebekah, Rachel and Leah, all of whom were known for their concern and compassion for others.

5. The family blessings conclude with the priestly benediction invoking God's protection and peace.

6. For boys, parents gently place both hands on his head and recite:

יְשִׂמְךָ אֱלֹהִים כְּאֶפְרַיִם וְכִמְנַשֶּׁה.

Yiseemcha Eloheem k'Efraim v'cheemenasseh

234

May God make you like Ephraim and Menasseh. (Genesis 48:20)

For girls, parents approach each daughter and gently place both their hands upon her head and recite:

יְשִׂימֵךְ אֱלֹהִים כְּשָׂרָה, רִבְקָה, רָחֵל, וְלֵאָה,

Yesimech Eloheem k'Sarah, Rivka, Rachel v'Leah

May God make you like Sarah, Rebekah, Rachel and Leah.

For both boys and girls, conclude with the priestly blessing.

יְבָרֶכְךָ יְיָ וְיִשְׁמְרֶךָ,

Yevarechecha Adonai v'yishmerecha

May God bless and keep you.

יָאֵר יְיָ פָּנָיו אֵלֶיךָ וִיחֻנֶּךָּ,

Ya'er Adonai panav eylecha veechuneka

May God's Presence shine and be good to you.

יִשָּׂא יְיָ פָּנָיו אֵלֶיךָ וְיָשֵׂם לְךָ שָׁלוֹם.

Yisa Adonai panav eylecha veyasem lecha shalom.

May God's face turn toward you and give you peace.

Key words and phrases:

Birkat hacohanim בִּרְכַּת הַכֹּהֲנִים Priestly blessing.

If you want to know more:

Ronald H. Isaacs and Kerry M. Olizky, *Sacred Celebrations: A Jewish Holiday Handbook* (Hoboken, 1994).

Preparing for Shabbat
הֲכָנָה לְשַׁבָּת

The source:

"You shall labor for six days and do all your work, but the seventh day is a Sabbath of Adonai your God: You shall not do any work" (Exodus 20:9–10).

What you need to know:

1. In the Jewish mystical tradition, the Sabbath has been portrayed as a bride or queen who visits homes every week of the year. Jewish people are expected to get ready—physically and spiritually—to greet this special guest.

2. Polish the Shabbat candlesticks and *Kiddush* wine cup a few days before the Sabbath begins.

3. Clean your house before the Sabbath actually begins and prepare your Shabbat dinner. Make sure you have the following items: two *challot* to represent the double portion of manna in the desert, saving one for Shabbat lunch, kosher wine, a pretty tablecloth, and a table set with your best dinnerware. Decorating the table with fresh flowers will help to create a *Shabbesdik* ("Shabbat-like") atmosphere. Naturally the meal you serve should be a special one.

4. It is customary to wash oneself and put on fresh clothing for Shabbat, symbolizing readiness to welcome the Sabbath into one's home.

5. To add to the mood of caring and sharing, many families make it a habit to drop some coins in a *pushke* (*tzedakah* box), before lighting the Sabbath candles. When the *tzedakah* box is full, decide as a family to which organization you want to donate the money.

Things to remember:

1. It is a nice gesture to invite friends to your home for the Sabbath meal in keeping with the important Jewish value of *hachnasat orchim* (hospitality).

2. Since singing songs is an important tradition during the Sabbath meal, you may want to obtain (or even prepare yourself) a small booklet with the Shabbat songs that you sing from week to week. Be sure to have enough copies so that everyone can participate. Use English and Hebrew songs, and be creative!

3. Family cooperation is indispensable to the completion of all pre-Shabbat tasks. Give each member of the family something to do so that everyone can help get ready for Shabbat.

4. According to Jewish tradition, we get an extra soul during Shabbat.

5. Invite the angels to accompany you during Shabbat. (That's what *Shalom Aleichem* is all about.)

Key words and phrases:

Hachanah le'shabbat הֲכָנָה לְשַׁבָּת. Preparation for the Sabbath.
Pushke (Yiddish) פּוּשְׁקֶע. *Tzedakah* (charity) box.
Zemirot זְמִירוֹת. Sabbath table songs.

If you want to know more:

Ronald H. Isaacs, *Shabbat Delight: A Celebration in Stories, Games and Songs* (Hoboken, NJ, 1987).
—— and Kerry M. Olitzky, *Sacred Celebrations: A Jewish Holiday Handbook* (Hoboken, NJ, 1994).

Getting Ready for Rosh Hashanah
הֲכָנָה לְרֹאשׁ הַשָּׁנָה

The source:

"In the seventh month, on the first day of the month, shall be a solemn rest for you, a memorial proclaimed with the blast of horns, a holy convocation" (Leviticus: 23:24).

What you need to know:

1. The month of Elul, which immediately precedes Rosh Hashanah (and the month of Tishri), is spent in introspection, what the tradition calls *cheshbon hanefesh*. Thus, the best way to get ready for Rosh Hashanah is by looking deeply into yourself, trying to assess where you have gone so that you can determine where you want to go. This is happy time but a serious soul-searching business, as well.

2. Depending on the tradition of the community, penitential prayers called *Selichot* are said during the month of Elul. These prayers culminate in a *Selichot* service, generally held at midnight on Saturday just prior to Rosh Hashanah. (In some years, the service is held the preceding Saturday night.)

Things to remember:

1. While Rosh Hashanah has become a High Holiday in the modern Jewish community, it is really less significant than Shabbat. It begins the important Ten Days of Awe which culminate in Yom Kippur. Thus, a lot of the rules for Shabbat, but not all of them, also apply on Rosh Hashanah. The major thing to remember is to make sure that what you do is in the spirit of the holiday.

2. Use a round *challah* for Rosh Hashanah to represent the cycle of life, instead of the braided one reserved for Shabbat.

3. Prepare your table (eat in the dining room, not the kitchen) with flowers and your best dinnerware. Remember to invite guests, especially those new to the community who do not have local family to share the holiday together.

4. If you wear a *kittel* (white robe-like garment) during the holidays, make sure you know where it is.

5. Send out holiday cards in advance. Make your holiday calls, especially to those you haven't spoken to in a long time. Use the preholiday period as a time to mend broken bridges with estranged friends and family.

Key words and phrases:

Leshanah tovah tikateivu לְשָׁנָה טוֹבָה תִּכָּתֵבוּ. "May you be inscribed [in the book of life] for the new year"; traditional greeting for Rosh Hashanah.

Rosh Hashanah ראש הַשָּׁנָה. Literally, "head of the year"; new year.

Shofar שׁוֹפָר. Ram's horn used on Rosh Hashanah (and a few other occasions) to call us to the work of *teshuvah* (repentance).

Yom Hazikaron יוֹם הַזִכָּרוֹן. Day of Remembrance, alternative name for Rosh Hashanah.

If you want to know more:

Ronald H. Isaacs and Kerry Olitzky, *Sacred Celebrations: A Jewish Holiday Handbook* (Hoboken, NJ, 1994).

More particulars:

Prepare apples and honey to usher in the sweet year. Hint: sprinkle a little lemon juice on your sliced apples to prevent them from turning brown. After you say *Hamotzi*, say the following (then dip your apples in honey and enjoy!):

יְהִי רָצוֹן מִלְפָנֶיךָ יהוה אֱלֹהֵינוּ וֵאלֹהֵי אֲבוֹתֵינוּ שֶׁתְּחַדֵשׁ
עָלֵינוּ שָׁנָה טוֹבָה וּמְתוּקָה.

Yehi ratzon milfanecha Adonai elohaynu vaylohay avotenu shetechadesh alaynu shanah tovah u'metukah.

239

May it be Your will, Adonai our God, that Your renew
for us a good and sweet year.

בָּרוּךְ אַתָּה יהוה אֱלֹהֵינוּ מֶלֶךְ הָעוֹלָם, בּוֹרֵא פְּרִי הָעֵץ:

*Baruch atah Adonai elohaynu melech ha'olam boray pri
ha'etz.*

Praised are You, Adonai our God, Sovereign of the
Universe, who creates the fruit of the tree.

How to Construct Your Own Theology
תּוֹרַת הַדָּת

The source:

"I am Adonai your God, who brought you out of the land of Egypt, out of the house of bondage" (Exodus 20:1).

What you need to know:

1. While the notion of theology in Judaism is a relatively new phenomenon, don't leave the construction of your theology to theologians. While you should consult the thoughts of others in order to determine whether you agree or disagree, your beliefs are more truly expressed by what you do than by what you say. So don't just say what you believe, express your beliefs in action.

2. To make a statement of your personal theology, begin with the words "I believe . . ." and fill in whatever should come next. That's all you need to get started. Encourage others to do the same. Do not criticize the beliefs of others. You will share many common beliefs with others, but you will disagree as well—even with people with whom you study, pray, and play.

Things to remember:

1. Before you venture out on your own and try constructing your own theology, consult those who have come before you. Consider also the works of contemporary theologians like Eliezer Berkovits, Eugene Borowitz, Emil Fackenheim, Abraham Joshua Heschel, and Mordecai Kaplan. Read and study. Remember, there is more out there than just what appears on the *New York Times* bestseller list. The study of a sacred text—and its implicit theology—will help you form your own.

2. Don't be afraid to reconsider your beliefs, to change your opinions, as you open yourself up to new experiences of Jewish living.

3. Struggle for consistency in your belief system, however difficult it may be to achieve, but don't be so inflexible that you cannot live with contradictions.

4. Think with your heart and your mind.

5. A belief in God is central to Jewish theology.

6. Test out your beliefs in the context of the world in which you live.

If you want to know more:

Eugene B. Borowitz, *Choices in Modern Jewish Thought* (New York, 1983).

Arthur Green, *Seek My Face, Speak My Name: A Contemporary Jewish Theology* (Northvale, NJ, 1992).

Ron Isaacs, *Close Encounters with God* (Northvale, NJ, In Press).

Louis Jacobs, *A Jewish Theology* (New York, 1973).

Nathan Rotenstreich, *Jewish Philosophy in Modern Times* (New York, 1968).

Planning a Jewish Trip
טִיּוּל

The source:

"Jews are an omniterritorial people. They are everywhere. There is never a first Jew in any place. There was always a Jew there before" (Jacob Rader Marcus, historian).

What you need to know:

Bring a pair of portable candlesticks, *siddur*, and anything else you need for personal observance while traveling.

Things to remember:

1. Chabad-Lubavitch is everywhere. While you may not share the Chabad-Lubavitch approach to Judaism, know that you have a friend representing the Jewish community in most places wherever you travel in the world.

2. Many of the larger cities in United States and Canada have prepared books called "A Jewish Guide to _____." When planning a trip, contact the local Jewish Federation or Jewish Community Center at your destination.

3. Before you set out on a journey, don't forget to recite the traveler's prayer (*tefillat ha'derech*), available in most prayer books and in our *First How-To Handbook for Jewish Living*. Small laminated wallet-sized copies of *tefillat ha'derech* are available in most Jewish book stores.

4. Depending on your dietary requirements, check out what may be available ahead of time, then plan accordingly. Some people always travel with a kosher salami in their suitcase, just in case.

Key words and phrases:

Tiyul טִיּוּל. A trip, usually in Israel.

If you want to know more:

Warren Freedman, *The Selective Guide for the Jewish Traveler* (New York, 1972).

Stephen Massil, *The Jewish Travel Guide* (London, published annually).

Bernard Postal and Samuel Abramson, *The Landmarks of a People: A Guide to Jewish Sites in Europe* (New York, 1971).

Bernard Postal and Lionel Kopman, *A Jewish Tourist's Guide to the U.S.* (Philadelphia, 1954).

Richard Siegel, Sharon Strassfeld, and Michael Strassfeld, *The Jewish Catalogue* (Philadelphia, 1973, 1976). See "The Jewish Yellow Pages."

Alan M. Tigay, *The Jewish Traveler* (Northvale, NJ, 1994).

More particulars:

The national or international body of each of the various religious movements generally has a guide to affiliated institutions around the world. Contact these organizations for help in locating synagogues (and other Jewish community resources), especially to find a daily *minyan* and Shabbat services:

Agudath Israel
84 William Street
New York, NY 10038

Chabad-Lubavitch
770 Eastern Parkway
Brooklyn, NY 11213

Federation of Reconstructionist Synagogues and Havurot
15 West 86th Street
New York, NY 10024

Union of American Hebrew Congregations
838 Fifth Avenue
New York, NY 10021

Union of Orthodox Jewish Congregations of America
333 Seventh Avenue
New York, NY 10001

Union of Sephardic Congregations
8 West 70th Street
New York, New York 10023

United Synagogue of Conservative Judaism
115 Fifth Avenue
New York, NY 10010

World Union for Progressive Judaism
838 Fifth Avenue
New York, NY 10021

How to Bury Ritual Objects or Place Them in a *Genizah*

גְּנִיזָה

The source:

Various sources, including Megillah 26b; Hilchot Yesodei Hatorah 6:8.

What you need to know:

While there is no specific ritual for burying ritual objects, people often recite poetic texts about study and the sacredness of Torah in preparation for burying a ritual object or ceremoniously placing something in a *genizah*.

Things to remember:

Sacred objects (like Torah scrolls and *tefillin*) and sacred writings (Bibles, prayer books) should be treated with respect. That's why we don't simply throw them away when they are no longer suitable for use.

Key words and phrases:

Genizah גְּנִיזָה. From the word for "hidden"; usually a closet, room, or hidden place in a synagogue where old prayer books and other sacred books are kept prior to burial.

Sefarim genuzim סְפָרִים גְּנֻזִים. Books to be hidden away.

If you want to know more:

Moses Maimonides, *Mishneh Torah*, Hilchot Yesodei Hatorah.

More particulars:

1. Some things may not require special treatment according to Jewish law yet Jewish sensitivities require that they be handled specially. For example, you may want to

consider using the *lulav* for Sukkot for lighting the fire to burn your *chametz* prior to Pesach. And use your *etrog* for jam (see "Making *Etrog* Jam").

2. While we must be careful about using God's name in vain, it seems to us that photocopy paper with God's name on it should be recycled for further use rather than buried. This is not in accordance with traditional practice, but it seems to us that it makes sense in the contemporary context. While some Orthodox Jews may question this approach, many members of the Reform, Reconstructionist, and Conservative movements will find it appropriate.

3. There is an ancient custom of honoring a dead person by burying sacred books (or Torah scrolls) next to the coffin.

Making a *Shivah* Call
שִׁבְעָה

The source:

"May the Almighty comfort you among the mourners for Zion and Jerusalem" (traditional greeting of comfort to mourners).

What you need to know:

1. If you join the bereaved right after the interment, you should arrange their first meal (called the *seudah ha'havra'ah,* "meal of consolation"). Don't expect to be entertained or served.

2. When you approach the home of the bereaved, especially right after the funeral, there may be a pitcher of water next to the door. If you are comfortable in doing so, wash your hands prior to entering the home. This reflects the ancient custom of ridding oneself of the impurities associated with death. Upon doing so, it is customary to recite these words:

> You will swallow up death forever;
> And Adonai, God will wipe away tears from off all faces; And the reproach of Your people will You take away from off all the earth;
> For Adonai has said it.

> Isaiah 25:8

3. When you enter a *shivah* home, remember that it is a house in which people are mourning. Participate in prayer if you visit during the time in which prayers are being said. Try to comfort the bereaved person by speaking from the heart. Avoid truisms and cliches. And don't feel obliged to fill up the silence. Often, your presence alone is comforting. Indeed, Rabbi Yochanan taught, "Comforters are not permitted to say a word until the mourner begins the conversation" (Babylonian Talmud, Moed Katan 28b).

Things to remember:

1. The term *shivah* is taken from the word for "seven," referring to the seven days of intensive mourning following the death of a loved one. The name *shivah* is generally applied to everything related to mourning during this period. Thus, we speak of the *shivah* house, the *shivah minyan*, and making a *shivah* call.

2. It is customary for a mourner concluding *shivah* to take a walk around the block, "to get up from *shivah*," as a way of symbolically reentering routine life. If you happen to make your call at the end of the *shivah* period, be prepared to take this walk with your bereaved friend or relative.

3. For a variety of reasons which primarily have to do with focusing the attention of the mourners on the process of mourning rather than on themselves, it is customary to cover the mirrors in a *shivah* home. Do not uncover them.

Key words and phrases:

Avelut אֲבֵילוּת. Period of mourning following the interment.

Chesed shel emet חֶסֶד שֶׁל אֱמֶת. True piety, referring to honoring the dead and comforting mourners.

Sheloshim שְׁלוֹשִׁים. Twenty-three-day period of less intensive mourning which follows *shivah*, concluding on the thirtieth day after the funeral.

Shivah שִׁבְעָה. From the word for "seven"; the seven days of intensive mourning following a death.

If you want to know more:

Ronald H. Isaacs and Kerry M. Olitzky, *A Jewish Mourner's Handbook* (Hoboken, NJ, 1991).

Maurice Lamm, *The Jewish Way in Death and Mourning* (New York, 1969).

Sitting *Shivah* and Observing the *Sheloshim*
שִׁבְעָה וּשְׁלוֹשִׁים

The source:

The Bible records various instances of the seven-day mourning ritual (*shivah*). For example, in Genesis 50:10 Jacob dies and Joseph mourns for his father for a period of seven days (see also Amos 8:10).

What you need to know:

1. The traditional period of "sitting *shivah*" (as the seven-day mourning period is called) begins immediately after the funeral and concludes after the morning (*shacharit*) service six days later. (Among some Reform and Reconstructionist Jews, the period of mourning is less than seven days.)

2. The laws of mourning are suspended on the Sabbath that occurs during the *shivah* period, but despite this the Sabbath day counts as one of the seven days for *shivah*.

3. Jewish tradition encourages the ritual washing of hands before entering the house of *shivah* after the funeral as an act of spiritual cleansing.

4. A seven-day *shivah* candle is lit immediately when one returns to the house of *shivah* after the burial.

5. It is customary to cover all mirrors in a house of *shivah* since mourners should not be concerned with issues of vanity.

6. Traditionally, the mourner remains in the house of *shivah* during the entire week. Food is provided by friends, and prayer services are arranged and led by friends in the house of *shivah*.

6. As a sign of mourning, mourners traditionally refrain from wearing leather shoes (specifically, shoes with

leather soles) because they are considered a sign of luxury and vain comfort. In addition, the mourners sit on low stools or benches as a symbol of their lowly state. Traditional mourners do not watch television, study (except the books of Job, Lamentations, and Jeremiah and laws pertaining to mourning), wear new clothes, or make love with their spouses.

7. Mourners during the period of *shivah* may attend synagogue services on Friday evening and Saturday morning and afternoon. Otherwise, prayer should take place at home. When mourners arrive at the synagogue on Shabbat, they enter after *Lecha Dodi* is recited. As they do so, the congregants turn and say, "May God comfort you among the mourners of Zion and Jerusalem."

8. *Shivah* ends on the morning of the seventh day. It is customary for mourners to take a short walk with their family and close friends. The walk symbolizes the return to everyday life.

9. When visiting a house of *shivah* it is customary to bring food (cake, a fruit basket, and the like). Of course making a donation in memory of the deceased is a most appropriate way of paying tribute.

10. During the period of *sheloshim* (the twenty-three days after *shivah* ends) mourners are permitted to return to work and their regular routine. They recite the Mourner's *Kaddish* each day, however (and continue to do so for eleven months), and moderate their leisure-time activities.

Things to remember:

1. During *shivah,* friends and family will often feel uncomfortable and not be exactly sure what to say to the mourner. Searching for words to give the mourner comfort, they may feel inclined not to speak until the mourner speaks to them. In fact, this is the advice that Jewish tradition offers the individual making a *shivah* call.

2. If the holiday of Rosh Hashanah, Yom Kippur, Passover, Shavuot, or Sukkot occurs during the *shivah* period, the *shivah* ends when the holiday begins even if it is not yet

the seventh day. If the interment takes place during *chol hamoed* of Passover or Sukkot, the mourner waits until the conclusion of the festival before sitting *shivah*. One does not sit *shivah* on Purim, but Chanukah has no impact on *shivah*.

Key words and phrases:

Kaddishel קַדִּישֶׁל (Yiddish). "Little *Kaddish*." An affectionate diminutive applied by parents to a child as an expression of their expectation that someday, when they die, he or she will say *Kaddish* for them.

Seudat ha'havra'ah סְעוּדַת הַהַבְרָאָה. Meal of condolence prepared by friends and offered as the first meal after mourners return from the cemetery.

Sheloshim שְׁלוֹשִׁים. Literally "thirty"; the first thirty days of mourning (*shivah* plus the twenty-three days that follow).

Shivah שִׁבְעָה. First seven days of mourning.

If you want to know more:

Ronald H. Isaacs and Kerry M. Olitzky, *A Jewish Mourner's Handbook* (Hoboken, NJ, 1991).

Ron Wolfson, *A Time to Mourn, a Time to Comfort* (New York, 1993).

More particulars:

1. Round-shaped foods (eggs, chickpeas) which reflect the circle of life are often served at the meal of condolence.

2. Traditionally, the mourner is encouraged to lead services in the house of *shivah* (providing he or she is able to do so).

3. In Sephardic homes, it is traditional for mourners to sit on pillows or on the floor in a house of *shivah*. In addition, mourners study the *Zohar* (the primary source for Jewish mysticism) during the week of *shivah*.

4. When counting days of *shivah*, a part of a day counts for a whole day.

How to Write a Condolence Letter
נֶחָמְתָּא

The source:

"After the death of Abraham, God visited and blessed Isaac, his son" (Genesis 25:11). In this verse, God comforts Isaac. As a result, the rabbis teach us that it is our religious obligation to comfort the bereaved.

What you need to know:

1. Comforting the mourner is considered a supreme act of kindness in Judaism.

2. While one makes a short visit to the mourner at the house of shivah, this in not always possible. Thus, writing a letter of condolence is also greatly appreciated by the bereaved.

Here are some suggestions for writing meaningful condolence letters:

a. Express your inner feelings by using words of sympathy that express your sorrow. Avoid cliches and truisms. Speak from the heart.
b. Note your personal memories of the deceased, reflecting the impact that he or she had on your life. Mention any outstanding qualities of him/her that you will always cherish.
c. Remind the mourner that you will always "be there" for them, that they are not alone in their grief.
d. Conclude your letter with some words of love and the traditional greeting to mourners which is "May God comfort you among the other mourners of Zion and Jerusalem."

Key words and phrases:

Hamakom yenachem otcha (m), *otach* (f) *betoch she'ar aveilay tzion ve'yerushalayim:* הַמָּקוֹם יְנַחֵם אוֹתְךָ (אוֹתָךְ) בְּתוֹךְ

שְׁאָר אֲבֵלֵי צִיוֹן וִירוּשָׁלָיִם "May God comfort you among the other mourners of Zion and Jerusalem," traditional greeting to mourners, at the end of an interment and when they return to the synagogue on Shabbat during shiva.

If you want to know more:

Sidney Greenberg, *A Treasury of Comfort.* (Los Angeles, 1960).

Ronald H. Isaacs and Kerry M. Olitzky, *A Jewish Mourner's Handbook.* (Hoboken, NJ, 1991).

Barbara Fortgang Summers, *Community Responsibility in the Jewish Tradition.* (New York, 1978).

How to Prepare an Ethical Will
צַוָּאָה מוּסָרִית

The source:

While there is no specific source for the practice of
writing ethical wills, many examples of parents offering
final words of guidance to their children are available,
such as the deathbed statement of Jacob to his sons in
Genesis 49. Many of the medieval ethical wills use the
Book of Proverbs as a source for practical advice on how
to lead a good life.

What you need to know:

1. The sole aim of the ethical will is to provide the
recipient with guidance for behavior. So don't worry
about a theoretical core. For once, it is unnecessary.

2. You may want to secure your ethical will and ask
that it not be read until after your death. Some people,
however, want to discuss the will's contents with their
children before their death. Whether or not to do so
depends in part on the age of one's children.

3. Some people use milestone events like a significant
birthday or major life challenges like surviving an illness
or the death of an elderly parent to revise their ethical
wills.

4. Feel free to put your ethical will on audiotape or
videotape. As technological advances are made, you may
want to use other means as well.

5. As a beginning, review the major events or accomplish-
ments in your life and what you have learned from them.
Include insights, practical advice, and ethical decisions
you have made.

6. The ethical will may be included in your regular will.
Remember to include *tzedakah*.

Things to remember:

The goal of the ethical will is to provide those who come after you with sound advice based on what you have learned from life. In other words, you want them to be able to learn what you have learned without having to experience some of the challenges you had to face.

Key words and phrases:

Hanhagot הַנְהָגוֹת. Guidance manuals for everyday living from the medieval period.

Musar מוּסָר. Classic form of ethical guidance from Jewish tradition.

Tzava'ah צַוָּאָה. Will, instruction.

If you want to know more:

Israel Abrahams, *Hebrew Ethical Wills* (Philadelphia, 1926).

Jacob Rader Marcus, *This I Believe* (Northvale, NJ, 1991).

Jack Reimer and Nathaniel Stampfer, *So That Your Values Live On: Ethical Wills and How to Prepare Them* (Woodstock, VT, 1991).

More particulars:

In addition to its personal impact on family members, the ethical will had great influence as a literary genre. Thus, major works have been written in the form of a parent writing to a child, for example.

How to Write a Living Will
צַוָּאַת חַיִּים

The sources:

1. "A dying person is considered as a living person in all matters. It is forbidden to touch the person to prevent the hastening of death" (Code of Jewish Law, Yoreh Deah 339:1).

2. "Even if a patient has agonized for a long time, it is forbidden to hasten death by, for instance, closing his eyes or removing a pillow from under his head" (ibid.).

3. "If there is an obstacle which prevents the departure of the soul, such as noise outside or salt present on the dying person's tongue, we may stop the noise or remove the salt in order not to hinder death" (ibid., commentary of Rabbi Moses Isserles).

What you need to know:

1. Jewish law obliges us to care for our bodies in the best way possible, since we are made in the image of God. Similarly, it allows for and permits a person who has a life-threatening illness to prepare for a death with dignity.

2. Directives called living wills tell doctors, hospital staff, or nursing home employees whether you want to be kept alive on artificial life-support systems if you are in a coma beyond all reasonable hope for recovery. Laws concerning advanced directives for health care vary in different states and countries, so inquire about the law in your state when deciding what to do. In addition, each Jewish religious movement has developed its own Jewish medical directive for health care, in accordance with its own interpretation of Jewish laws and values. This directive will guide you and family members in making the appropriate decisions.

3. Jewish living wills should include the following:

   a. Goals of the medical treatment.
   b. Knowledge of the person's medical condition.

c. Appointment of a health care agent.
d. Rabbinic consultation.
e. Modes of feeding if terminally ill.
f. Use of so-called aggressive medical procedures, including mechanical life support.
g. Use of cardiopulmonary resuscitation.
h. Type of pain relief.
i. Choice of hospital or home care.
j. Wishes in case of death, including organ donation and autopsy.

Things to remember:

1. It is advisable to talk over the matter of a living will with your physician and your rabbi so that all of the relevant medical facts and Jewish law can be explained to you.

2. It is advisable to secure a durable power of attorney that names someone to carry out your wishes.

3. Once you have completed a living will, you should give a copy of your document appointing a proxy to the close members of your family. You may also wish to carry a card in your wallet or purse indicating that you have appointed a proxy and telling how that person can be contacted.

Sample Living Will from the Euthanasia Educational Council:

To my family, my physician, my lawyer, my clergyperson,
To any medical facility in whose care I happen to be,
To any individual who may become responsible for my health, welfare, or affairs:

Death is as much a reality as birth, growth, maturity, and old age—it is the one certainty of life. If the time comes when I, _____, can no longer take part in decisions for my own future, let this statement stand as an expression of my wishes, while I am still of sound mind.

If the situation should arise in which there is no reasonable expectation of my recovery from physical or mental disability, I request that I be allowed to die and not be kept alive by artificial means or "heroic measures." I do not fear death itself as much as the indignities of deterioration, dependence, and hopeless pain. I therefore ask that medication be mercifully administered to me to alleviate suffering even though this may hasten the moment of death.

This request is made after careful consideration. I hope you who care for me will feel morally bound to follow its mandate. I recognize that this appears to place a heavy responsibility upon you, but it is with the intention of relieving you of such responsibility and of placing it upon myself in accordance with my strong convictions, that this statement is made.

Signed _____

Date _____

Witness _____

Witness _____

Copies of this request have been given to _____

_____

Sample Durable Power of Attorney for Health Care Appointment of Proxy form:

My name: _____

I am over eighteen years old and of sound mind. Should I become medically unable to make health care decisions for myself, I name _____, my _____, (relationship) as my representative to make medical decisions for me. S/he resides at _____, where the telephone number is _____.

Signature of designated proxy: _____

Notary's seal and signature

Dated: _____

4. A copy of your appointment of proxy should be given to your physician, proxy, and family, and a copy of your living will to your proxy. Two witnesses should sign the document in the presence of a notary.

Key words and phrases:

Living will. Document that tells doctors and hospital staff what medical directives to follow when a person is in a coma beyond any reasonable hope of recovery.

Proxy. Authority or power to act on behalf of another person.

If you want to know more:

Richard Address, *A Time to Prepare: A Practical Guide for Individuals and Families in Extraordinary Medical Treatment and Financial Arrangements* (Philadelphia, 1991).

Elliot N. Dorff, "Choose Life: A Jewish Perspective on Medical Ethics," vol. 4, no. 1 *University Papers.* The University of Judaism (Los Angeles, 1985).

Aaron Mackler, ed., *Jewish Medical Directives for Health Care* (New York, 1994).

James L. Simon, Raymond Zwerin, and Audrey Friedman Marcus, *Bioethics: A Jewish View* (Denver, 1984).

Saying Yizkor
יִזְכּוֹר

The Source:

The custom may date back to the period of the Maccabees (ca. 165 B.C.E.), when Judah and his men prayed for the souls of their fallen companions and brought offerings to the Temple in Jerusalem in order to atone for the sins of the dead.

What you need to know:

1. While there is a traditional three-part framework for the memorial service, the specific texts read may differ in some synagogues. In general, the *Yizkor* service begins with a prayer asking God to remember particular individuals (*Yizkor Elohim,* "May God remember . . ."), framed by biblical passages related to the meaning of life and death. Some congregations expand the material; others limit it. As is the practice in many synagogues today, you may want to add material which reflects the lives of Jewish martyrs and those who perished in the Holocaust. Next, chant *El Malei Rachamim,* in which we ask God to shelter the souls of our loved ones, and end with the *Av Ha'rachamim* prayer before returning the Torah to the ark. In Conservative and Reform synagogues, the Mourner's *Kaddish* is generally recited. Some congregations also read Psalm 23. In Sephardic synagogues, the memorial prayer is recited during the Torah service and said by those individuals who are given Torah honors.

2. As with *Yahrtzeit,* it is customary to light a twenty-four hour candle on the evening preceding *Yizkor.* No special prayer is required. Consult your own *siddur* for suggested readings. Alternatively, you may want to simply speak from the heart with a prayer to God, beginning with something like, "I now remember my dear _____who has gone to his/her eternal resting place. May his/her soul be given life everlasting, and may his/her memory be a source of blessing to those who knew and loved him/her."

261

Mourners often also make a *tzedakah* contribution or pledge some act of *gemilut chasadim* to honor the memory of their loved ones.

Things to remember:

1. Different synagogues (and their representative religious movements) have different traditions about *Yizkor* memorial services.

2. In the Ashkenazic ritual, *Yizkor* is recited after the reading of the Torah during the morning service of the last day of Passover, Shavuot, and Sukkot (Shemini Atzeret) and on Yom Kippur. In the Sephardic ritual, it is also recited on Erev Yom Kippur (Kol Nidre eve) before the *ma'ariv* (evening) service.

Key words and phrases:

Gemilut chasadim גְּמִילוּת חַסָדִים. Loving acts of kindness, often in the form of volunteerism.

Hazkarat Neshamot הַזְכָּרַת נְשָׁמוֹת. Literally, "the mentioning of individual souls"; technical name for the *Yizkor* service.

Tzedakah צְדָקָה. Charitable giving.

Yahrtzeit יָאָרצַייט. Yearly anniversary, on the Hebrew calendar, of the date of death of loved ones.

Yizkor יִזְכּוֹר. Literally "May He remember," referring to God's remembrance of a particular person who has died. Among those who prefer to use gender-neutral theological terminology, this is often rendered as "May You remember" or "May God remember." Since the word *yizkor* is the opening of the principal part of the first memorial prayer recited on Yom Kippur, Shemini Atzeret, Passover, and Shavuot, *Yizkor* has come to be the designation for the entire memorial service.

Yizkor-buch יִזְכּוֹר-בּוּך (Yiddish). Alternatively, *memorbuch* or *kunteres*. Memorial books dating back to medieval times, listing the names of martyrs killed during Crusade-related pogroms in Jewish communities of Western and Central Europe.

262

If you want to know more:

Ronald H. Isaacs and Kerry M. Olitzky, *A Jewish Mourner's Handbook* (Hoboken, NJ, 1991).

More particulars:

1. Some people who have living parents choose not to participate in *Yizkor* services. For some departed, especially the millions killed in the Holocaust, there is no one left to say *Yizkor*.

2. While it is common practice not to recite *Yizkor* on the holiday following a death, one may do so. Consult your rabbi for guidance.

3. Some believe that the deeds of merit of the dead can help atone for the sins of their descendants. However, others oppose this notion and contend that only the individual's deeds count before God.

4. Some Reform congregations say *Yizkor* on the afternoon of Yom Kippur rather than in the morning as part of the Torah service.

How to Take a Dip in the *Mikvah*
מִקְוֶה

The source:

The Torah requires immersion in a *mikvah* (ritual bath) to cleanse the body from impurity resulting from leprosy, discharge of semen, menstruation, childbirth, or contact with a corpse (see Leviticus 12:2, 15:5–13; Numbers 19:19).

What you need to know:

1. From ancient times until the present the *mikvah* has played an important part in maintaining Jewish family purity (*taharat ha'mishpachah*).

2. The water of the *mikvah* has to come from a natural spring or a river, and must be running, not drawn. The *mikvah* must have a minimum of 120 gallons of water.

3. Traditionally the *mikvah* is used by women after their menstrual cycle and in certain groups by both men and women as an aid to spirituality, particularly on the eve of the Sabbath and festivals, especially the Day of Atonement. Converts (Jews by choice) are required to use the *mikvah* as part of the ceremony of conversion. (Some Reform rabbis do not require the use of the *mikvah* for conversion.)

4. The *mikvah* is also used to immerse new vessels and utensils manufactured by non-Jews (in accordance with Numbers 31:22–23).

5. At the *mikvah,* people prepare themselves for the ritual immersion by bathing or showering first and removing all articles from their bodies, such as jewelry, hairpins, and so forth. After immersing completely in the *mikvah,* women recite the following blessing:

בָּרוּךְ אַתָּה יהוה אֱלֹהֵינוּ מֶלֶךְ הָעוֹלָם, אֲשֶׁר קִדְּשָׁנוּ בְּמִצְוֹתָיו וְצִוָּנוּ עַל הַטְּבִילָה:

*Baruch atah Adonai elohaynu melech ha'olam asher kid-
shanu b'mitzvotav ve'tzivanu al ha'tevillah.*

Praised are You, Adonai our God, Sovereign of the
Universe, who has instructed us concerning ritual
immersion.

After the immersion, totally immerse yourself once again.
Note: If you are using the *mikvah* for conversion to Ju-
daism, immerse two additional times. Then recite the
Shehecheyanu blessing:

בָּרוּךְ אַתָּה יהוה אֱלֹהֵינוּ מֶלֶךְ הָעוֹלָם, שֶׁהֶחֱיָנוּ וְקִיְּמָנוּ וְהִגִּיעָנוּ,
לַזְּמַן הַזֶּה:

Praised are You, Adonai our God, Sovereign of the
Universe, who has kept us alive, sustained us, and
enabled us to reach this day.

Things to remember:

1. Generally, women who immerse after their menstrual
period use the *mikvah* after sundown; others do so during
the day.

2. Traditionally, a bride and bridegroom-to-be will immerse themselves in the *mikvah* (separately, of course) in
anticipation of their wedding.

3. Traditional Jewish women immerse themselves in the
mikvah after bearing a child.

Key words and phrases:

Mikvah מִקְוֶה (plural, *mikva'ot* מִקְוָאוֹת). Ritual bath.
Taharat ha'mishpachah טָהֳרַת הַמִּשְׁפָּחָה. Family purity.
Tevillah טְבִילָה. Ritual immersion.

If you want to know more:

Philip Birnbaum, *A Book of Jewish Concepts* (New York,
1964).

Hayim Donin, *To Be a Jew* (New York, 1972).

Encyclopaedia Judaica (Jerusalem, 1971), 11:1534.

Ron Isaacs, *Becoming Jewish: A Handbook for Conversion* (Hoboken, NJ, 1994)

Aryeh Kaplan, *Waters of Eden: The Mystery of the Mikvah* (New York, 1982).

How to Save the Planet
גְּאוּלָה

The source:

"The earth is Adonai's and all it contains" (Psalm 24:1). Alternatively, "Generations come and go, but the earth stands forever" (Kohelet 1:4).

What you need to know:

1. The earth is not ours. We are lent the earth while we are sojourners on it. Just as we received it for our use, we must bequeath it to our children and grandchildren.

2. Judaism forbids the wanton destruction of anything. Hence the charge, "When you besiege a city for a long time, making war against it in order to take it, you shall not destroy (*bal tashchit*) its trees by yielding an axe against them. You shall not cut them down" (Deuteronomy 20:19).

3. The Torah sets aside a sabbatical year—and a jubilee—for the earth to rest. Some form of crop rotation might be a modern take on this practice.

Things to remember:

1. Shabbat helps us to remember our responsibility to the world.

2. Recycle—even when it requires an extra effort or seems more expensive to do so.

3. Whenever possible, don't replace—repair.

4. Be an advocate. When you see people abusing the earth, gently remind them of their responsibility to those who come after us.

5. Famous for its Blue Boxes, the Jewish National Fund helps us to restore and protect the land of Israel. It plants forests, prepares the soil, builds roads through mountains and deserts, and gives land and employment

to new immigrants. JNF is also active in the race to harness solar energy.

Key words and phrases:

Bal tashchit בַּל תַּשְׁחִית. Mitzvah which prohibits the willful and wanton destruction of anything from which someone might benefit, especially living things.

Chag Ha'ilanot חַג הָאִילָנוֹת. Holiday of the trees, Tu Bishevat.

Shmittah שְׁמִיטָה. Sabbatical year.

Yovel יוֹבֵל. Jubilee year, occurring every half-century.

If you want to know more:

Ellen Bernstein and Dan Fink, *Let the Earth Teach You* (Wyncote, PA, 1992).

John Javna, *50 Simple Things Kids Can Do to Save the Earth* (Kansas City, 1990).

Yaakov Kirschen, *Trees, the Green Testament* (New York, 1993).

Mary Ann F. Kohl and Cindy Gainer, *Good Earth Art: Environment Art for Kids* (Bellingham, Wa, 1991).

Lillan Ross, *The Judaic Roots of Ecology* (Miami, 1986).

Jeffrey Schrier, *Judaism and Ecology* (Washington, DC, and Wyncote, PA, 1993).

More particulars:

1. As an excellent Bar/Bat Mitzvah project, we recommend that students commit themselves to three things: (a) a program that feeds the hungry and houses the homeless; (b) an act of *gemilut chasadim* that makes the world a better place to live in, which can include simple things like a litter patrol; and (c) time and *tzedakah* to protect wildlife and endangered animals (as well as those that could possibly be threatened in the future with endangerment).

2. Many people associate Jewish work toward saving the planet as part of an effort to repair a broken world (*tikkun olam*). Others relate it to celebrating the festival of Tu Bishevat, but most Jewish holidays have some explicit connection to the land.

Avoiding the Evil Eye
עֵין הָרָע

The source:

In Pirke Avot, the rabbis teach that a good eye (by which they mean generosity) is the best quality of a person. On the other hand, an "evil eye" is the worst quality. In time, it became a widespread belief that a malevolent glance could actually work evil on the person at whom it was directed. As a result, according to the Babylonian Talmud (Baba Metzia 107b), ninety-nine people out of a hundred died of an evil eye.

What you need to know:

1. Belief in a potentially evil power residing in the eye is widespread in human culture.

2. In early Jewish sources "evil eye" simply denoted envy of the good fortune of another person. For example, "The one who has an evil eye hastens after riches" (Proverbs 28:22).

3. In talmudic times, it was believed that the evil eye could not harm a descendant of Joseph (Babylonian Talmud, Berachot 55b). Hence, we find the following incantation to ward off the evil eye: "Take the thumb of the right hand in the left hand, and the thumb of the left hand in the right hand, and say: 'I, so-and-so, am of the seed of Joseph, over which the evil eye has no power.'"

4. Over the centuries, various amulets (such as the *chamsa*, an amulet that looks like a hand, often containing an eye in its center), charms, and spells to ward off the evil eye have been developed and used. Here are several examples:

 a. Tie a red band around the wrist of a newborn child to avert the spell of the evil eye.
 b. If a woman is childless, she should find an *etrog* after the holiday of Sukkot and bite the tip off it.
 c. Use candles at a wedding ceremony to ward off the evil eye.

269

d. When a husband gives the evil eye to his wife (or vice versa), it will be removed if she opens her hand and says *chamesh* (five).

e. A loud *shofar* blast can be used to drive away the evil eye.

f. To prevent a bad dream, put a prayer book under your pillow.

Things to remember:

1. If someone praises your good health or good fortune, use the Hebrew words *blee ayin hara* ("without a begrudging eye") or the Yiddish phrase *kenanhora* (a collapsed form of "like an evil eye") to ward off the evil spirits.

2. In modern times, the use of paint, generally on building or on the walls of interior rooms, and metal amulets in the form of an open palm of the hand, are popular ways of avoiding the evil eye.

3. Spitting or saying "pooh pooh pooh" is considered a potent means of warding off the evil eye, especially among Eastern European immigrants.

4. Always be sure not to accept a Torah *aliyah* immediately before or after one of your blood relatives. In this way, you will avoid the evil eye.

Key words and phrases:

Blee ayin hara בְּלִי עַיִן הָרָע. Literally, "without a begrudging eye."

Kenanhora קֵיין עַיִן־הָרָע/קֵיינֶען־הָרָע (Yiddish). "Like an evil eye"; as in "Don't give him/her a *kenanhora*."

If you want to know more:

Louis Jacobs, *What Does Judaism Say About . . . ?* (Jerusalem, 1973).

Brenda Z. Rosenbaum, *How to Avoid the Evil Eye* (New York, 1985).

Rivka Ulmer, *The Evil Eye in the Bible and Rabbinic Literature* (Hoboken, NJ, 1994).

Doing *Teshuvah*
תְּשׁוּבָה

The source:

"Repent on the day before you die" (Pirke Avot 2:10).

What you need to know:

1. While *teshuvah* specifically means turning or returning to a life of Torah and *mitzvot*, it refers generally to the process of getting one's life back in order.

2. *Teshuvah* requires constant attention through study, prayer, and good acts. Begin with yourself (through the process of introspection called *cheshbon ha'nefesh*), then focus on your relationships with others. Start by avoiding gossip, going to *shul* regularly, and studying.

Things to remember:

1. It takes only one step to turn and face the other direction in life.

2. *Teshuvah* is an ongoing, lifelong process. You never really finish the process of turning. That's its power and its mystery.

3. Use the opportunities provided to you in the Jewish calendar, such as Yom Kippur, to do *teshuvah*. Use the month of Elul (usually late August–early September) as a period of introspection prior to the High Holy Day period. Recite Psalm 27 each day as a means of directing your thoughts.

Key words and phrases:

Cheshbon ha'nefesh חֶשְׁבּוֹן הַנֶּפֶשׁ. Literally, "accounting of the soul"; life review, introspection.
Teshuvah תְּשׁוּבָה. Literally, "turning" or "returning" to God and a life of goodness; repentance.

If you want to know more:

Leonard S. Kravitz and Kerry M. Olitzky, *The Journey of the Soul: Traditional Sources on Teshuvah* (Northvale, NJ, 1995).

Lawrence S. Kushner, *The Book of Words* (Woodstock, VT, 1994).

_____ and Kerry M. Olitzky, *Sparks Beneath the Surface: A Spiritual Commentary on the Torah* (Northvale, NJ, 1994).

Kerry M. Olitzky, *100 Blessings Every Day* (Woodstock, VT, 1994).

More particulars:

For some, *teshuvah* is part of a process of recovery from addiction or some other compulsive behavior. For others, it is a means of getting their lives back in order. While your soul needs a healthy place to reside, it should be kept "clean" for its own sake. Therefore, stop abusing your body with alcohol and other drugs. Exercise and watch what you eat.

How to Be a *Mentsch*
מֶענְטְש

The source:

"In a place where people do not act like human beings, strive to be one [i.e., strive to be a *mentsch*]" (Pirke Avot 2:6).

What you need to know:

1. Treat others as you would want to be treated. This is the essential ingredient of being a *mentsch*. As Rabbi Hillel said, "What is hateful to you, do not do to someone else." (Babylonian Talmud, Shabbat 31a).

Things to remember:

Martin Buber, the noted theologian, suggested that our relationship with others should mirror our relationship with God.

Key words and phrases:

Mentsch מֶענְטְש (Yiddish). A good person, a "human" person.
Mentschlichkeit מֶענְטְשׁלֶעכְקייט (Yiddish). The quality or state of being a *mentsch*.

If you want to know more:

Neil Kurshan, *How to Be a Mentsch* (New York, 1992).

More particulars:

Being a *mentsch* is indispensable in our struggle to bring the *mashiach* (Messiah) into the world. When we turn strangers into friends, then there is real potential for ultimate peace in the world.

How to Bring the *Mashiach*
מָשִׁיחַ

The source:

According to Jewish tradition, God chose King David and his descendants, when David was at the height of his power, to reign over Israel to the end of time (see II Samuel 7; 23:1–3, 5; 22:44–51). This was the beginning of what has come to be known as the Messiah (*mashiach*) and the messianic era.

What you need to know:

1. Originally the word *mashiach* (meaning "anointed one") referred to anointed kings and high priests. These humans had a special mission from God.

2. After the Babylonian exile (586 B.C.E.) prophets had visions of the universal establishment of God's sovereignty under a scion of King David's house, who would be God's anointed. This individual would bring total and complete peace to the world and spiritual regeneration to all humanity.

3. Jewish tradition described Elijah the Prophet as the forerunner of the Messiah.

4. Jewish tradition contains numerous references to the Messiah. Here are some which suggest ways in which you may hasten the coming of the Messiah:

> a. "The Messiah will come when the entire Jewish people keep two Sabbaths in a row" (Babylonian Talmud, Shabbat 118b). In order to help, you may want to consider increasing your personal Sabbath observance.
> b. "If you are planting a tree and you hear that the Messiah has come, first finish planting the tree and then run to the city gates to greet the Messiah" (Yochanan ben Zakkai in Leviticus Rabbah 25:3). To respond to this text, do what you can to preserve the ecological balance of the world.

c. "In the time of the Messiah, nation shall not lift up sword against nation; neither shall people know war anymore" (Isaiah 2:4). To extend the meaning of this message, do all that you can to promote peace in the world.

d. "On that day God shall be One and God's name shall be One" (Zechariah 14:9). The word "one" (*echad*) is an integral part of the *Shema* prayer. Say the *Shema* every morning and evening, and as you pronounce *echad*, concentrate on the concept of God's Oneness.

e. Rabbi Joshua ben Levi found Elijah the Prophet, disguised as a leper, begging at the gates of Rome. "When will you come to proclaim the Messiah?" he asked. "Today, if you will hear his voice," replied Elijah (Babylonian Talmud, Sanhedrin 98a). Therefore, listen carefully to the Messiah's voice, especially at times when the name of Elijah is invoked (as at a circumcision ceremony, or at the Passover *seder*, and at the *Havdalah* ceremony bidding farewell to the Sabbath on Saturday evenings).

f. "In the days of the Messiah there will be no hunger or war, no jealousy or strife; prosperity will be universal, and the world's predominant occupation will be to know God" (Code of Jewish Law, Melachim 12:2, 5). Therefore, try to do all you can to feed the hungry and not cause strife or jealousy among your family and friends.

Key words and phrases:

Mashiach מָשִׁיחַ. Literally "one who is anointed"; now used specifically in reference to the Messiah.

If you want to know more:

Philip Birnbaum, *A Book of Jewish Concepts* (New York, 1964).
Encyclopaedia Judaica (Jerusalem, 1971), 11:1407–1416.

More particulars:

1. Throughout Jewish history many people have claimed to be the Messiah. They are called "false messiahs." Shab-

batai Tzvi (1626–1676), who proclaimed himself Messiah in 1648, was the most notorious.

2. An alternative Jewish tradition (which surfaces in the midrash) suggests that the messianic line can be traced through Joseph rather than David.

2. Some Jews, generally those affiliated with the Reform and Reconstructionist movements, believe that the messianic era will be ushered in, not by a single individual known as the Messiah, but by the cumulative activities of the entire Jewish people.

Instant Information
Angels and Demons

What you need to know:

In Jewish tradition, God is often considered to delegate power to a messenger or angels directed to perform God's will. Demons are also considered messengers of God, but their role was to bring harm to people. Here is a partial summary of some of the more well known angels and demons in Jewish tradition.

Ashmodai. Destructive angel and king of the demons. His name means "Destroyer."

Beelzebub. Sovereign of the netherworld. His name means "Lord of the Flies."

Cherubim. Angelic sentinels who guarded the Tree of Life in the Garden of Eden. Statues of cherubim adorned the Tabernacle and later the Temple in Jerusalem.

Gabriel. Leader of the archangels; one of the two angels mentioned by name in the Bible (Daniel 8:10).

Lilith. Female demon who reigned at night; often considered the queen of the demons.

Malach ha'mavet. Angel of Death, charged with summoning dying souls from the earth.

Metatron. In mystical literature, the highest figure in the angelic world.

Michael. One of the two angels mentioned by name in the Bible (Daniel 8:10).

Ophanim. Angelic drivers of the holy chariot, as depicted in the Book of Ezekiel; their name means "Wheels."

Raphael. One of seven archangels who brought prayers before God; his name means "God heals."

Raziel. Angel of magic; his name means "Secret of God."

Samael. Prince of the evil demons.

Satan. As in the Book of Job, the accuser who called God's attention to people's sins; his name means "Adversary."

Seraphim. In Isaiah 6:2 these "fiery angels" declare God's holiness.

Uriel. Prince of the archangels; identified by thunder and earthquakes.

If you want to know more:

Morris B. Margolies, *A Gathering of Angels: Angels in Jewish Life and Literature* (New York, 1994).

Instant Information
The Twenty-third Psalm
תְּהִלִּים כ"ג

The source:

Jewish tradition attributes the composition of the Twenty-third Psalm and much of the Book of Psalms to King David.

What you need to know:

מִזְמוֹר לְדָוִד. יהוה רוֹעִי לֹא אֶחְסָר: בִּנְאוֹת דֶּשֶׁא יַרְבִּיצֵנִי. עַל מֵי מְנֻחוֹת יְנַהֲלֵנִי: נַפְשִׁי יְשׁוֹבֵב. יַנְחֵנִי בְמַעְגְּלֵי צֶדֶק לְמַעַן שְׁמוֹ: גַּם כִּי אֵלֵךְ בְּגֵיא צַלְמָוֶת לֹא אִירָא רָע. כִּי אַתָּה עִמָּדִי. שִׁבְטְךָ וּמִשְׁעַנְתֶּךָ הֵמָּה יְנַחֲמֻנִי: תַּעֲרֹךְ לְפָנַי שֻׁלְחָן נֶגֶד צֹרְרָי. דִּשַּׁנְתָּ בַשֶּׁמֶן רֹאשִׁי. כּוֹסִי רְוָיָה: אַךְ טוֹב וָחֶסֶד יִרְדְּפוּנִי כָּל יְמֵי חַיָּי. וְשַׁבְתִּי בְּבֵית יהוה לְאֹרֶךְ יָמִים:

Adonai is my shepherd, I lack nothing.
God gives me my rest near rich pastures.
God leads me beside tranquil waters to revive my spirit.
God guides me on straight paths, for that is God's nature.
Though I walk through the valley of the shadows
I fear no evil, for You are with me.
Your sustaining staff comforts me.
You permit me to eat in the presence of my enemies.
You anoint my head with oil, my cup runs over.
Surely goodness and mercy will accompany me for the rest of my life.
And I will spend my days in God's court forever.

Mizmor L'David
Adonai ro'ee lo echsar
Beenot desheh yarbeetzaynee
Al may menuchot yenahalaynee nafshee yeshovayu
Yancheelaynee vemaglay tzedek le'ma'an shemo

Gam kee aylaych begay tzalmavet
Lo eera rah kee atah eemadee
Sheevticha u'meeshantecha haymah yenachamoonee
Ta'aroch lefanai shulchan neged tzorirai
Deeshanta vashemen roshee kosee revayah
Ach tov va'chesed yeerdefoonee kol yemai chayai
Veshavtee bevayt Adonai le'orech yameem.

Things to remember:

1. The Twenty-third Psalm expresses the most intimate, personal relationship of a person with God. It begins with the comforting metaphor of God as Shepherd, focusing God's concern for the world in the image of a shepherd for the flock.

2. Because of its message of comfort, officiants often read the Twenty-third Psalm aloud at funerals.

3. The Twenty-third Psalm may also be recited when visiting a cemetery.

Key words and phrases:

Kosee revaya. כּוֹסִי רְוָיָה My cup runs over.
Ro'ee. רֹעִי Shepherd.
Tov va-chesed. טוֹב וָחֶסֶד Goodness and mercy.

If you want to know more:

A. Cohen, *The Soncino Book of Psalms* (London, 1962).
Mitchell Dahood, *The Anchor Bible, Psalms 1–50* (New York, 1965).

Instant Information
Mourner's *Kaddish*
קַדִּישׁ יָתוֹם

The source:

Originally, the *Kaddish* was used as a short prayer at the close of sermons. At a later period the *Kaddish* was introduced into the liturgy to mark the conclusion of specific sections of the service. Since the merit of studying Torah was considered very important, the rabbis felt that one might honor the memory of the deceased through Torah study. Hence, such study was assigned to mourners. Study sessions were concluded by the chanting of the *Kaddish* (Soferim 19:12). The first official mention of the custom of the Mourner's *Kaddish* at the end of the service is found in *Or Zarua,* a thirteenth-century work of Jewish law. Rabbi Moses Isserles spoke of the "custom" of reciting the *Kaddish* for a period of eleven months after the death of a father or mother (*Shulchan Aruch,* Yoreh Deah 376:4).

What you need to know:

יִתְגַּדַּל וְיִתְקַדַּשׁ שְׁמֵהּ רַבָּא. בְּעָלְמָא דִּי בְרָא כִרְעוּתֵהּ וְיַמְלִיךְ
מַלְכוּתֵהּ. בְּחַיֵּיכוֹן וּבְיוֹמֵיכוֹן וּבְחַיֵּי דְכָל בֵּית יִשְׂרָאֵל. בַּעֲגָלָא
וּבִזְמַן קָרִיב וְאִמְרוּ אָמֵן:
יְהֵא שְׁמֵהּ רַבָּא מְבָרַךְ לְעָלַם וּלְעָלְמֵי עָלְמַיָּא:
יִתְבָּרַךְ וְיִשְׁתַּבַּח וְיִתְפָּאַר וְיִתְרוֹמַם וְיִתְנַשֵּׂא וְיִתְהַדָּר וְיִתְעַלֶּה
וְיִתְהַלָּל שְׁמֵהּ דְּקוּדְשָׁא. בְּרִיךְ הוּא. לְעֵלָּא (בעשי״ת וּלְעֵלָּא
מִכָּל) מִן כָּל בִּרְכָתָא וְשִׁירָתָא. תֻּשְׁבְּחָתָא וְנֶחֱמָתָא. דַּאֲמִירָן
בְּעָלְמָא. וְאִמְרוּ אָמֵן:
יְהֵא שְׁלָמָא רַבָּא מִן שְׁמַיָּא וְחַיִּים עָלֵינוּ וְעַל כָּל יִשְׂרָאֵל וְאִמְרוּ
אָמֵן. עוֹשֶׂה שָׁלוֹם בִּמְרוֹמָיו הוּא יַעֲשֶׂה שָׁלוֹם עָלֵינוּ וְעַל כָּל
יִשְׂרָאֵל וְאִמְרוּ אָמֵן:

281

Yit-ga-dal ve-yit-ka-dash she-mei ra-ba be-al-ma di-ve-ra chi-re-u-tei, ve-yam-lich mal-chu-tei be-cha-yei-chon u-ve-yo-mei-chon u-ve-cha-yei de-chol beit Yis-ra-eil, ba-a-ga-la u-vi-ze-man ka-riv ve-i-me-ru: a-mein.

Ye-hei she-mai ra-ba me-va-rach le-a-lam u-le-al-mei al-ma-ya.

Yit-ba-rach ve-yish-ta-bach, ve-yit-pa-ar ve-yit-ro-mam ve-yit-na-sei ve-yit-ha-dar ve-yit-a-leh ve-yit-ha-lal she-mei de-ku-de-sha be-rich hu le-ei-la min kol bi-re-cha-ta ve-shi-ra-ta tush-be-cha-ta ve-ne-che-ma-ta da-ami-ran be-al-ma ve-i-me-ru a-mein.

Ye-hei she-la-ma ra-ba min she-ma-ya ve-cha-yim a-lei-nu ve-al kol Yis-ra-eil ve-i-me-ru a-mein.

O-seh sha-lom bi-me-ro-mav hu ya-a-seh sha-lom a-lei-nu ve-al kol Yis-ra-eil ve-i-me-ru a-mein.

Let the glory of God be extolled, let God's great name be hallowed, in the world whose creation God willed. May God's sovereignty soon prevail, in our own day, our own lives, and the life of all Israel, and let us say Amen.

Let God's great name be blessed for ever and ever.

Let the name of God be glorified, exalted, and honored, though God is beyond all the praises, songs, and adorations that we can utter, and let us say Amen. For us and for all Israel, may the blessing of peace and the promise of life come true, and let us say Amen.

May God, who causes peace to reign in the high heavens, let peace descend on us, on all Israel, and all the world, and let us say: Amen.

Things to remember:

1. The *Kaddish* is traditionally said in a *minyan* (prayer quorum) of ten persons. (Reform Judaism does not require a *minyan*.)

2. Traditionally, one is required to say *Kaddish* for deceased parents. The Conservative, Reform, and Reconstructionist movements have come to understand this obligation as binding on daughters as well as on sons.

3. While not required, most communities encourage the recitation of *Kaddish* for other deceased relatives, including brother, sister, son, daughter, husband and wife.

4. The Mourner's *Kaddish* may be recited for anyone, especially close friends, martyrs, Torah scholars, soldiers, and anyone who died for the sanctification of God's name.

5. The Mourner's *Kaddish* is said while standing.

6. The Mourner's *Kaddish* functions differently than the other *Kaddish* prayers (such as the reader's or half-Kaddish, used to designate different parts of the service). *Kaddish* is to be said, during the year of mourning, on Yahrtzeits, and during Yizkor memorial services.

Key words and phrases:

Kaddish Yatom. קַדִּישׁ יָתוֹם (Aramaic). Literally, "Orphan's Sanctification"; the special *Kaddish* said during the year of mourning.

If you want to know more:

Ronald H. Isaacs and Kerry M. Olitzky, *A Jewish Mourner's Handbook* (Hoboken, NJ, 1991).
Maurice Lamm, *The Jewish Way in Death and Mourning* (New York, 1972).

Instant Information
Hallel Psalms
הַלֵּל

The source:

In the Babylonian Talmud (Pesachim 117a), we learn that the prophets told the people to offer hymns of praise to God whenever we celebrate historical events that commemorate the deliverance of our people from dire straits. Today, the *Hallel* psalms of praise (Psalms 113–118) are customarily recited following the morning *Amidah* on the festivals of Passover, Shavuot, Sukkot, Chanukkah, and Rosh Chodesh. They are also often recited on Yom Ha-atzma'ut (Israel Independence Day) and on Yom Yerushalayim (Jerusalem Day).

What you need to know:

Recite the blessing before saying the *Hallel* Psalms:

בָּרוּךְ אַתָּה יהוה אֱלֹהֵינוּ מֶלֶךְ הָעוֹלָם, אֲשֶׁר קִדְּשָׁנוּ בְּמִצְוֹתָיו
וְצִוָּנוּ לִקְרֹא אֶת־הַהַלֵּל.

Baruch atah Adonai elohaynu melech ha'olam asher kidshanu b'mitzvotav v'tzivanu likro et ha-Hallel.

Praised are You, Adonai our God, Sovereign of the Universe, who has made us holy through *mitzvot* and instructed us to read the *Hallel.*

Psalm 113

הַלְלוּיָהּ. הַלְלוּ, עַבְדֵי יהוה, הַלְלוּ אֶת־שֵׁם יהוה.
יְהִי שֵׁם יהוה מְבֹרָךְ מֵעַתָּה וְעַד־עוֹלָם.
מִמִּזְרַח־שֶׁמֶשׁ עַד־מְבוֹאוֹ מְהֻלָּל שֵׁם יהוה.
רָם עַל כָּל־גּוֹיִם יהוה, עַל הַשָּׁמַיִם כְּבוֹדוֹ.
מִי כַּיהוה אֱלֹהֵינוּ, הַמַּגְבִּיהִי לָשָׁבֶת,
הַמַּשְׁפִּילִי לִרְאוֹת בַּשָּׁמַיִם וּבָאָרֶץ.
מְקִימִי מֵעָפָר דָּל, מֵאַשְׁפֹּת יָרִים אֶבְיוֹן,

לְהוֹשִׁיבִי עִם־נְדִיבִים, עִם נְדִיבֵי עַמּוֹ.
מוֹשִׁיבִי עֲקֶרֶת הַבַּיִת, אֵם־הַבָּנִים שְׂמֵחָה.
הַלְלוּיָה.

Halleluyah! Praise Adonai, you who serve Adonai,
praise the name of Adonai.

May Adonai's name be blessed now and forever.

From sunrise to sunset, Adonai's name is praised.
Adonai is above all the nations,
God's glory goes beyond the heavens.

Who is like Adonai our God, who is far above us,
yet bends down to look at the heavens and the earth?
God lifts up the poor from the dust,
The needy from the trash heap,
and seats them with the nobles of God's people.

God makes the childless woman a mother happy
with her children. Halleluyah!

Psalm 114

בְּצֵאת יִשְׂרָאֵל מִמִּצְרָיִם, בֵּית יַעֲקֹב מֵעַם לֹעֵז.
הָיְתָה יְהוּדָה לְקָדְשׁוֹ, יִשְׂרָאֵל מַמְשְׁלוֹתָיו.
הַיָּם רָאָה וַיָּנֹס, הַיַּרְדֵּן יִסֹּב לְאָחוֹר.
הֶהָרִים רָקְדוּ כְאֵילִים, גְּבָעוֹת כִּבְנֵי צֹאן.
מַה לְּךָ הַיָּם כִּי תָנוּס, הַיַּרְדֵּן תִּסֹּב לְאָחוֹר.
הֶהָרִים תִּרְקְדוּ כְאֵילִים, גְּבָעוֹת כִּבְנֵי־צֹאן:
מִלִּפְנֵי אָדוֹן חוּלִי אָרֶץ, מִלִּפְנֵי אֱלוֹהַ יַעֲקֹב,
הַהֹפְכִי הַצּוּר אֲגַם מָיִם, חַלָּמִישׁ לְמַעְיְנוֹ מָיִם.

B'tzayt Yisrael mi-Mitz-ra-yim bayt Ya'akov may-am lo'ez
Hai-y'ta Ye-hu-dah l'kad-sho, Yisrael mam-sh'lo-tav.
Ha-yam ra'ah va-ya-nos, ha-Yar-den yi-sov l'achor.
Heh-ha-reem rak-du ch'ay-leem, g'va'ot kiv'nay tzon.
Ma l'cha ha-yam kee ta-nus, ha-Yar-den ti-sov l'a-chor
Heh-ha-reem tir-k'du ch'ay-leem g'va'ot kiv'nay tzon.
Mi-lif-nay adon chuli a-retz mi-lif-nay Elo-a Ya-akov
Ha-hof-chi ha-tzur a-gam ma-yim cha-la-meesh l'mai-no
ma-yim.

When Israel went out of Egypt,
The House of Jacob from a foreign people.

Judah became God's holy people, Israel became
God's nation.

The sea saw and turned back, the Jordan fled.

The mountains jumped like rams, the hills jumped like lambs.

> What is with you, sea, that you flee;
> Jordan, that you turn back;

Mountains, that you jump like rams; hills like lambs?

Quake, earth, before the Ruler, before the God of Jacob,

> Who turns the rock into a pool of water;
> Who turns flint into fountains.

Psalm 115:1–11

Not because we deserve it, Adonai, but for Your own reasons act gloriously, for the sake of Your lovingkindness and Your truth.

> Why should the nations say, "Where is their God?"
> Our God is in heaven. God does as God pleases.

Their idols are just silver and gold, made by human hands.

They have mouths and can't speak, eyes but cannot see.

> They have ears but can't hear, noses but can't smell.
> Their hands can't feel, their feet can't walk,
> They cannot speak with their throats.

Those who make them shall become like them—all who trust in them.

> Israel, trust in Adonai, our help and shield.
> House of Aaron, trust in Adonai, our help and our shield.

Everyone who respects Adonai, trust in Adonai,

Our help and our shield.

Psalm 115:12–18

יְהוָה זְכָרָנוּ יְבָרֵךְ, יְבָרֵךְ אֶת־בֵּית יִשְׂרָאֵל, יְבָרֵךְ אֶת־בֵּית אַהֲרֹן:
יְבָרֵךְ יִרְאֵי יְהוָה, הַקְּטַנִּים עִם־הַגְּדֹלִים: יֹסֵף יְהוָה עֲלֵיכֶם,
עֲלֵיכֶם וְעַל־בְּנֵיכֶם: בְּרוּכִים אַתֶּם לַיהוָה, עֹשֵׂה שָׁמַיִם וָאָרֶץ:
הַשָּׁמַיִם שָׁמַיִם לַיהוָה, וְהָאָרֶץ נָתַן לִבְנֵי־אָדָם: לֹא־הַמֵּתִים
יְהַלְלוּ־יָהּ, וְלֹא כָּל־יֹרְדֵי דוּמָה: וַאֲנַחְנוּ נְבָרֵךְ יָהּ, מֵעַתָּה וְעַד־
עוֹלָם הַלְלוּיָהּ:

Adonai z'cha-ra-nu y'va-rech, y'va-rech et bayt Yisrael,
y'va-rech et bayt A-ha-ron.
Y'va-rech yir-ay Adonai, hak'ta-neem im ha-g'do-leem.
Yo-sef Adonai a-lay-chem, a-lay-chem v'al b'nay-chem.
B'ru-cheem a-tem l'Adonai, o-seh sha-ma-yim va-a-retz.

Ha-sha-ma-yim sha-ma-yim l'Adonai,
v'ha-a-retz na-tan liv'nay a-dam.
Lo ha-me-teem y'hal'lu Yah, v'lo kol yor-day du-mah.
Va'a-nach-nu n'va-rech Yah, may-a-tah v'ad olam Hal-
leluyah.

God, remember us and bless us;
God, bless the House of Israel.
God, bless the House of Aaron;
God, bless those who respect Adonai, everyone alike.
May Adonai increase you and your children.
You are blessed by Adonai, who made heaven and
earth.
The heavens belong to Adonai,
But the earth was given to human beings.
The dead do not praise God, nor do those that death
silences.
But we will praise God now and forever. Halleluyah!

Psalm 116:12–19

How can I pay Adonai back for all God's gifts to me?
   I will lift up the cup of deliverance, and call out
Adonai's name.
I will keep my promises to Adonai, before the whole
community.
   Thank you, Adonai, for the freedom to serve You,
   for You have released me from bondage.
I will publicly keep my promises to Adonai, in the
courts of Adonai's House, in the center of Jerusalem.
Halleluyah!

Psalm 117

הַלְלוּ אֶת־יְהֹוָה כָּל־גּוֹיִם, שַׁבְּחוּהוּ כָּל־הָאֻמִּים:
כִּי גָבַר עָלֵינוּ חַסְדּוֹ, וֶאֱמֶת־יְהֹוָה לְעוֹלָם, הַלְלוּיָהּ:

Hall'lu et Adonai kol goyeem, shab-chu-hu kol ha-u-meem.
Kee ga-var a-lay-nu chas-do, ve-emet Adonai l'o-lam. Hal-
leluyah!

Praise Adonai, all nations; praise God, all peoples!
God's kindness overwhelms us. Adonai's truth is for-
ever.
Halleluyah!

Psalm 118

הוֹדוּ לַיהוה כִּי טוֹב, כִּי לְעוֹלָם חַסְדּוֹ.
יֹאמַר נָא יִשְׂרָאֵל, כִּי לְעוֹלָם חַסְדּוֹ.
יֹאמְרוּ־נָא בֵית אַהֲרֹן, כִּי לְעוֹלָם חַסְדּוֹ.
יֹאמְרוּ נָא יִרְאֵי יהוה, כִּי לְעוֹלָם חַסְדּוֹ.

Ho-du l'Adonai kee tov, kee l'olam chas-do.
Yo-mar na Yisrael, kee l'o-lam chas-do.
Yom-ru na vayt A-ha-ron, kee l'o-lam chas-do.
Yom-ru na yir-ay Adonai, kee l'o-lam chas-do.

Thank Adonai for being good, God's kindness lasts forever.
Let Israel say: God's kindness lasts forever.
Let the House of Aaron say: God's kindness lasts forever.
Let those who respect Adonai say: God's kindness lasts forever.

עָזִּי וְזִמְרָת יָה, וַיְהִי לִי לִישׁוּעָה.

O'zee v'zimrat Yah, va-y'hee lee li-shu-ah.
God is my strength and might, and has always rescued me.

קוֹל רִנָּה וִישׁוּעָה, בְּאָהֳלֵי צַדִּיקִים,
יְמִין יהוה עֹשָׂה חָיִל.
יְמִין יהוה רוֹמֵמָה, יְמִין יהוה עֹשָׂה חָיִל.

Kol ri-nah viy'shu-ah, b'o-ha-lay tza-dee-keem.
y'meen Adonai o-sah cha-yil.
Y'meen Adonai ro-me-ma, y'meen Adonai o-sah cha-yil.

The sound of joyous songs celebrating God's help is heard in the tents of the good: Adonai's right hand does mightily! Adonai's right hand is lifted up in victory! Adonai's right hand succeeds greatly!

פִּתְחוּ־לִי שַׁעֲרֵי צֶדֶק, אָבֹא בָם, אוֹדֶה יָהּ.
זֶה הַשַּׁעַר לַיהוה, צַדִּיקִים יָבֹאוּ בוֹ.

Pit-chu lee sha'aray tzeh-dek, a-vo'vam o-deh Yah.
Zeh ha-sha'ar l'Adonai, tza-dee-keem ya-vo-u vo.

Open the gates of righteousness for me. I will enter them to thank God. This is Adonai's gate, the righteous shall enter it.

אוֹדְךָ כִּי עֲנִיתָנִי, וַתְּהִי לִי לִישׁוּעָה.
אֶבֶן מָאֲסוּ הַבּוֹנִים, הָיְתָה לְרֹאשׁ פִּנָּה.
מֵאֵת יהוה הָיְתָה זֹּאת, הִיא נִפְלָאת בְּעֵינֵינוּ.
זֶה הַיּוֹם עָשָׂה יהוה, נָגִילָה וְנִשְׂמְחָה בוֹ.

Od'cha kee a-nee-ta-nee, vat'hee lee lee-shuah.
Eh-ven ma'a-su ha-bo-neem, hai'y'ta l'rosh pi-nah.
Me-et Adonai hai'y'tah zot, hee nif-lat b'ay-nay-nu.
Zeh ha-yom a-sah Adonai, na-gee-lah v'nis-m'cha vo.

I thank You for answering me and rescuing me.
The stone which the builders rejected is now the cornerstone.
This is Adonai's doing. It is wonderful in our eyes.
This is the day that Adonai has made,
Let us rejoice and be glad on it.

אָנָּא יהוה, הוֹשִׁיעָה נָּא!
אָנָּא יהוה, הוֹשִׁיעָה נָּא!
אָנָּא יהוה, הַצְלִיחָה נָא!
אָנָּא יהוה, הַצְלִיחָה נָא!

Ana Adonai hoshee'ah na. Ana Adonai hoshee'ah na.
Ana Adonai hatz-lee-cha na. Ana Adonai hatz-lee-cha na.

Please, Adonai, save us. Please, Adonai, cause us to succeed.
May we enjoy many opportunities to thank and praise You, Adonai. It is good to thank You, it is good to praise Your name. You are God forever and ever. Praised are You, Adonai, who is a Ruler praised with songs of praise.

בָּרוּךְ אַתָּה יהוה, מֶלֶךְ מְהֻלָּל בַּתִּשְׁבָּחוֹת.

Baruch atah Adonai, melech m'hu-lal batish-bah-chot.

Praised are You, Adonai O Sovereign who is acclaimed with songs of praise.

Things to remember:

1. The psalms of *Hallel* recall the festival celebrations at the ancient Jerusalem Temple. Through the *Hallel*, we express thanksgiving and joy for God's providence and concern for our people.

2. The *Hallel* psalms are never recited on Rosh Hashanah or Yom Kippur because these holidays were not intended for rejoicing. They are also not customarily said on Purim, a festival which celebrates a miracle that happened in Persia, since the redemption was only partial.

3. The first eleven verses of Psalms 115 and 116 are not recited on the last six days of Passover and on Rosh Chodesh. When *Hallel* is said without these verses, it is called the "Half *Hallel*."

4. *Hallel* is always recited while standing because it reflects our witness to God's wondrous deeds and power.

5. *Hallel* is recited during the morning service in Ashkenazic synagogues. In Sephardic synagogues and in some Israeli congregations it is the custom to recite *Hallel* at the evening service.

6. *Hallel* is recited at the Passover *seder*, part before the meal and part after the meal. We remain seated during the recitation of *Hallel* at the *seder*.

7. Since the *Hallel* refers to the Exodus from Egypt, this series of six psalms is called the Egyptian *Hallel*.

Key words and phrases.

Chatzi Hallel. חֲצִי הַלֵּל Half *Hallel*.
Hallel. הַלֵּל Psalms of praise.
Hallel ha-Mitzri. הַלֵּל הַמִּצְרִי Egyptian *Hallel*.

If you want to know more:

Steven Brown, *Higher and Higher: Making Jewish Prayer Part of Us* (New York, 1979).
Hayim Halevy Donin, *To Pray as a Jew* (New York, 1980).

Instant Information
The Order of the Prayer Service
סֵדֶר הַתְּפִילָה

The source:

Although some form of group prayer service existed by the early days of the Second Temple (400 B.C.E.), it was Rabbi Gamliel II, head of the Sanhedrin in the first century C.E., who first systematized the liturgy. Eight hundred years later, in the eighth century C.E., Rav Amram Gaon arranged a prayer book that is most likely the source for the modern order of worship.

What you need to know:

A general overview of the structure of the major prayer services is presented below.

Evening Service (*Ma'ariv*)

Kabbalat Shabbat. Service for welcoming the Sabbath on Friday evening.

Kol Nidre. Formulaic release of vows on the eve of Yom Kippur.

Barchu. Call to prayer, set in a poetic formula.

Ha'ma'ariv Aravim. First blessing before *Shema;* God is acknowledged as the Creator of the cycles of time and brings on the evening.

Ahavat Olam. Second blessing before *Shema;* God is acknowledged for giving Israel the Torah and showing love for the people of Israel.

Shema. Statement of faith in God as One.

Ga'al Yisrael. First blessing after *Shema;* God is recognized for the redemption of Israel.

Shomer Amo Yisrael La'ad. Second blessing after *Shema;* we ask God to bring us peace and keep us safe at night.

Selection from Bible (On Shabbat: Veshamru; other texts for holidays.)

Chatzi Kaddish. Half *Kaddish.*

Amidah. Also called *Hatefillah,* "the Prayer"; series of blessings whose themes direct worshipper's thoughts during prayer.

Vayechulu and *Magen Avot.* Recited only on Shabbat, these prayers reflect the work of Creation and the Divine instruction to rest.

Kaddish Shalem. Full *Kaddish.*

Kiddush. Blessing over wine (on Sabbath and on holidays).

Aleynu. Adoration of God.

Mourner's *Kaddish.*

Yigdal or *Adon Olam.* Concluding hymn.

Morning Service (*Shacharit*)

Blessings of the Morning.

Baruch She'amar. "God spoke and the world came to be."

Selected Psalms.

Yishtabach. Prayer of praise to God.

Barchu. Call to prayer, set in a poetic formula.

Yotzer Or. First blessing before *Shema*; God is recognized as the Creator of light who renews the work of creation each day.

Ahavah Rabbah. Second blessing before *Shema*; God's love for Israel is expressed in the form of the gift of Torah.

Shema. Statement of faith in God as One.

Ga'al Yisrael. Blessing after *Shema*; God is called the Redeemer of Israel.

Amidah. Also called *Ha'tefillah,* "*the* Prayer"; series of blessings whose themes direct worshipper's thoughts during prayer.

Hallel. Psalms of praise, said on Rosh Chodesh and holidays.

Chatzi Kaddish. Half *Kaddish.*

Reading of Torah Monday, Thursday, Sabbath, Rosh Chodesh, and holidays.

Musaf. Additional service for Sabbath, Rosh Chodesh, and holidays; generally eliminated by Reform movement.

Kaddish Shalem. Full *Kaddish.*

Aleynu. Adoration of God.

Mourner's *Kaddish.*

Afternoon Service (*Minchah*)

Ashray. Psalm 145.
Uvah Letziyon. Sabbath and holidays only; "There comes a redeemer" is the theme.
Chatzi Kaddish. Half *Kaddish*.
Torah reading. Sabbath and fast days only.
Chatzi Kaddish. Half *Kaddish*.
Amidah. Also called *Hatefillah,* "*the* Prayer"; series of blessings whose themes direct worshipper's thoughts during prayer.
Kaddish Shalem. Full *Kaddish*.
Aleynu. Adoration of God.
Mourner's *Kaddish*.

Things to remember:

Although the basic order and structure of the service are the same for all religious streams or movements in Judaism, customs may vary from congregation to congregation. Some prayers may be abbreviated or omitted altogether.

Key words and phrases:

Chatzi Kaddish חֲצִי קַדִּישׁ. Half *Kaddish,* used to divide small subsections of worship service.
Kabbalat Shabbat קַבָּלַת שַׁבָּת. Short service for welcoming the Sabbath which precedes full evening service.
Kaddish Shalem קַדִּישׁ שָׁלֵם. Full *Kaddish,* used to divide major sections of service.
Ma'ariv מַעֲרִיב. Evening service.
Matbe'ah shel tefillah מַטְבֵּעַ שֶׁל תְּפִילָה. Fixed structure of prayer service.
Mincha מִנְחָה. Afternoon service.
Musaf מוּסָף. Additional service on Shabbat and holidays.
Shacharit שַׁחֲרִית. Morning service.

If you want to know more:

Hayim Donin, *To Pray as a Jew* (New York, 1980).
Evelyn Garfiel, *Service of the Heart* (Northvale, NJ, 1989).
Abraham Millgram, *Jewish Worship* (Philadelphia, 1971).

More particulars:

1. In most Reform congregations, the *musaf* service, which reflects the additional sacrifice brought to the ancient Temple for Sabbaths and holidays, has been eliminated. In addition, Reform congregations generally do not use the multiplicity of *Kaddish* prayers to separate the sections of the service (such as the Full *Kaddish* before *Aleynu*).

2. The general themes that run through the worship service are: creation, revelation, redemption.

Instant Information
The Twelve Tribes of Israel
י"ב שְׁבָטִים

The source:

According to the Bible (Genesis 49), Jacob's twelve sons eventually became the twelve tribes of Israel. They were: Reuben, Simeon, Levi, Judah, Issachar, Zebulun, Joseph, Benjamin, Dan, Naphtali, Gad, and Asher. Since Moses conferred the priestly office on the tribe of Levi (without land), he transferred the property rights of Joseph to his children, Ephraim and Manasseh, to maintain the number of tribes receiving territory at twelve (a sacred number).

What you need to know:

Here is a summary of the twelve tribes of Israel, their emblems, banners, and jewels:

Name	Emblem	Banner	Jewel
Benjamin	wolf	multicolored	jasper
Dan	serpent	deep blue	jacinth
Naphtali	deer	wine color	amethyst
Asher	woman and olive tree	pearl color	beryl
Levi	*urim* and *tummim*	white, red, and black	emerald
Judah	lion	sky blue	turquoise
Issachar	donkey	black; sun and moon	sapphire
Zebulun	ship	white	amethyst
Reuben	mandrake	red	carnelian
Simeon	city of Shechem	green	topaz
Gad	encampment	gray	crystal
Ephraim	bullock	jet black	lapis lazul
Manasseh	unicorn	jet black	lapis lazul

Things to remember:

1. The nation was divided into twelve tribes during the time of the judges and the early kings.

2. Each tribe of Israel received a portion of land when the Israelites entered Canaan after the Exodus from Egypt.

295

3. Although each of the tribes was "fathered" by Jacob, they had different "mothers." Leah was the mother of Reuben, Simeon, Levi, Judah, Issachar, and Zebulun. Bilhah (Rachel's maid) was the mother of Dan and Naphtali; Zilpah (Leah's maid) was the mother of Gad and Asher. Finally, Rachel was the mother of Joseph and Benjamin.

4. The tribes slowly lost their distinct identities when Israel became a more consolidated nation.

Key words and phrases:

Degel דֶּגֶל. Banner.
Shevet שֵׁבֶט. Tribe.

If you want to know more:

Nahum M. Sarna, ed., *J.P.S. Torah Commentary: Book of Genesis* (Philadelphia, 1989).

Instant Information
The *Ketubah*
כְּתוּבָה

The source:

Rabbi Shimon ben Shetach, president of the ancient rabbinic court, prepared the earliest form of the Jewish marriage contract, called a *ketubah*.

What you need to know:

1. The *ketubah* is the Jewish marriage contract that traditionally specifies the husband's primary obligations to his spouse. These include honoring his wife and providing her with food, clothing, and sexual satisfaction. The traditional *ketubah* also specifies a husband's financial obligations if the marriage ends in divorce.

2. Couples in the Conservative, Reform, and Reconstructionist movements generally choose *ketubot* that express their love for one another rather than one that legally spells out the seemingly male-biased property transfer and conjugal rights which appear in the traditional document. Yet, in the traditional ketubah the husband has obligations to the wife but the wife has none to him.

3. Originally, *ketubot* were written on parchment and often enhanced by drawings and illumination in bright colors.

3. The officiating rabbi or cantor at a wedding will generally provide the couple with a *ketubah*. Often the rabbi will present several choices, including one with traditional language and one which reflects an egalitarian approach to marriage.

4. Often couples prefer to have a personalized *ketubah* designed especially for them by a calligrapher or artist.

5. Here are two sample *ketubot*.

Traditional *Ketubah:*

בְּאֶחָד (בִּשְׁלִישִׁי) בְּשַׁבַּת, אֶחָד עָשָׂר יוֹם (יָמִים)
לַחֹדֶשׁ _____ שְׁנַת חֲמֵשֶׁת אֲלָפִים וְשֵׁשׁ מֵאוֹת
וְ_____לִבְרִיאַת עוֹלָם לְמִנְיָן שֶׁאָנוּ מוֹנִין כַּאן ק״ק (עיר)
מְדִינַת אֲמֶרִיקָה הַצְּפוֹנִית, אֵיךְ הֶחָתָן ר' _____ בֶּן ר'
_____ אֲמַר לָהּ לַהֲדָא בְּתוּלְתָּא מָרַת _____ בַּת ר'
_____, הֲוִי לִי לְאִנְתּוּ כְּדַת מֹשֶׁה וְיִשְׂרָאֵל, וַאֲנָא אֶפְלַח
וְאוֹקִיר אִיזוֹן וַאֲפַרְנֵס יָתִיכִי (לִיכִי) כְּהִלְכוֹת גּוּבְרִין יְהוּדָאִין
דְּפָלְחִין וּמוֹקְרִין וְזָנִין וּמְפַרְנְסִין לִנְשֵׁיהוֹן בְּקוּשְׁטָא. וְיָהֲבְנָא לֵיכִי
מֹהַר בְּתוּלַיְכִי כְּסַף זוּזֵי מָאתָן דְּחָזֵי לֵיכִי מִדְאוֹרַיְתָא, וּמְזוֹנַיְכִי
וּכְסוּתַיְכִי וְסִפּוּקַיְכִי, וּמֵיעַל לְוָתַיְכִי כְּאוֹרַח כָּל אַרְעָא. וּצְבִיאַת
מָרַת _____ בְּתוּלְתָּא דָא וַהֲוַת לֵהּ לְאִנְתּוּ, וְדֵין נְדוּנְיָא
דְּהַנְעֲלַת לֵהּ מִבֵּי אֲבוּהָ בֵּין בְּכֶסֶף בֵּין בִּדְהַב בֵּין בְּתַכְשִׁיטִין,
בְּמָאנֵי דִלְבוּשָׁא, בְּשִׁמּוּשֵׁי דִירָה וּבְשִׁמּוּשֵׁי דְעַרְסָא, הַכֹּל קִבֵּל
עָלָיו ר' _____ חֲתָן דְּנַן בְּמֵאָה זְקוּקִים כֶּסֶף צָרוּף. וְצָבִי ר'
_____ חֲתָן דְּנַן וְהוֹסִיף לָהּ מִן דִּילֵהּ עוֹד מֵאָה זְקוּקִים כֶּסֶף
צָרוּף אֲחֵרִים כְּנֶגְדָּן, סַךְ הַכֹּל מָאתַיִם זְקוּקִים כֶּסֶף צָרוּף. וְכָךְ אָמַר
ר' _____ חֲתָן דְּנַן, אַחֲרָיוּת שְׁטַר כְּתוּבְתָּא דָא, נְדוּנְיָא דֵן
וְתוֹסֶפְתָּא דָא קַבֵּלִית עֲלַי וְעַל יַרְתַי בַּתְרַאי לְהִתְפָּרַע מִכָּל שְׁפַר
אֲרַג נִכְסִין וְקִנְיָנִין דְּאִית לִי תְּחוֹת כָּל שְׁמַיָּא, דִּקְנָאִי וּדְעָתִיד אֲנָא
לְמִקְנָא, נִכְסִין דְּאִית לְהוֹן אַחֲרָיוּת וּדְלֵית לְהוֹן אַחֲרָיוּת, כֻּלְּהוֹן
יְהוֹן אַחֲרָאִין וְעַרְבָאִין לְפָרוֹעַ מִנְּהוֹן שְׁטַר כְּתוּבְתָּא דָא, נְדוּנְיָא דֵן
וְתוֹסֶפְתָּא דָא מִנָּאי, וַאֲפִילוּ מִן גְּלִימָא דְעַל כַּתְפָּאי, בְּחַיֵּי וּבָתַר
חַיֵּי, מִן יוֹמָא דְּנַן וּלְעָלַם. וְאַחֲרָיוּת שְׁטַר כְּתוּבְתָּא דָא, נְדוּנְיָא דֵן
וְתוֹסֶפְתָּא דָא, קַבֵּל עָלָיו ר' _____ חֲתָן דְּנַן כְּחוֹמֶר כָּל שְׁטָרֵי
כְּתוּבּוֹת וְתוֹסֶפְתוֹת דְּנַהֲגִין בִּבְנוֹת יִשְׂרָאֵל, הָעֲשׂוּיִין כְּתִקּוּן חֲכָמֵינוּ
זִכְרָם לִבְרָכָה, דְּלָא כְּאַסְמַכְתָּא וּדְלָא כְּטוֹפְסֵי דִשְׁטָרֵי. וְקָנִינָא מִן
ר' _____ בֶּן _____ חֲתָן דְּנַן לְמָרַת _____ בַּת
ר' _____ בְּתוּלְתָּא דָא עַל כָּל מַה דִּכְתוּב וּמְפוֹרָשׁ לְעֵיל
בְּמָאנָא דְכָשֵׁר לְמִקְנָא בֵּיהּ, וְהַכֹּל שָׁרִיר וְקַיָּם.

נְאוּם _____ בֶּן _____עֵד.

וּנְאוּם _____ בֶּן _____עֵד.

On the (first) day of the week, the _____day of the
month _____in the year five thousand, six hundred
and _____since the creation of the world, the era
according to which we are accustomed to reckon here in
the city of (name of city, state, and country), how (name of
bridegroom), son of (name of father), surnamed (family

name), said to this virgin (name of bride), daughter of (name of father), surnamed (family name): "Be thou my wife according to the law of Moses and Israel, and I will cherish, honor, support, and maintain thee in accordance with the custom of Jewish husbands who cherish, honor, support, and maintain their wives in truth. And I herewith make for thee the settlement of virgins, two hundred *zuzim*, which belongs to thee, according to the law of Moses and Israel; and I will also give thee thy food, clothing, and necessaries, and live with thee as husband and wife according to universal custom." And Miss (name of bride), this virgin, consented and became his wife. The wedding outfit that she brought unto him from her father's house in silver, gold valuables, wearing apparel, house furniture, and bed clothes, all this (name of bridegroom), the said bridegroom, accepted in the sum of one hundred silver pieces, and (name of bridegroom), the bridegroom, consented to increase this amount from his own property with the sum of one hundred silver pieces, making in all two hundred silver pieces. And thus said (name of bridegroom), the bridegroom: "The responsibility of this marriage contract, of this wedding outfit, and of this additional sum, I take upon myself and my heirs after me, so that they shall be paid from the best part of my property and possession that I have beneath the whole heaven, that which I now possess or may hereafter acquire. All my property, real and personal, even the mantle on my shoulders, shall be mortgaged to secure the payment of this marriage contract, of the wedding outfit, and of the addition made thereto, during my lifetime and after my death, from the present day and forever." (Name of bridegroom), the bridegroom, has taken upon himself the responsibility of this marriage contract, of the wedding outfit and the addition made thereto, according to the restrictive usages of all marriage contracts and the additions thereto made for the daughters of Israel, in accordance with the institution of our sages of blessed memory. It is not to be regarded as a mere forfeiture without consideration or as a mere formula of a document. We have followed the legal formality of symbolical delivery (*kinyan*) between (name of bridegroom), the son of _____, the bridegroom, and (name of bride), the daughter of _____this virgin, and we have used a garment legally fit for the purpose, to strengthen all that is stated above,

And Everything is Valid and Confirmed.

Attested to _____(Witness)

Attested to _____(Witness)

Egalitarian *Ketubah*:

"שבע שמחות את פניך"

_____בשבת_____ימים   לחדש

_____לבריאת   העולם   שנת_____

בעיר _____.

כמנהגי עם ישראל וכדת משה, אנחנו, כן עומדים בנוכחות שפחתנו וחברינו על מנת להיכנס לברית קידושין.

ביום הקידושין שלנו, אנו מקדישים את עצמינו, כרעים אהו־בים, לעולם ועד בכח תלותנו זה בזו, אנו מתחילים פרשה חדשה זו של חיינו כשווים בצלם אלהים שבנו, שואבים עוז ממעיני האהבה שאיפותינו כרוכים אלו באלו אנו מקדישים את עצמינו להקמת משפחה ובית שיהיו בהם אהבה מסירות לב ליהדות, אנו מאמינים שחיינו ביחד כוונים ביד האלהים הם, ואנו מודים לקדוש ברוך הוא.

וקימנו קנין מן החתן ומן הכלה והכל שריר וקים.

נאום_____עד

נאום_____עד

נאום_____עד

נאום_____עד

"In your presence in perfect joy."

On the _____day of the week, the _____day of the month, in the year _____since the creation of the world corresponding to the _____day of _____nineteen hundred _____in the city of _____, as is the custom of the people of Israel and under the laws of Moses, we _____and _____, stand before our family and friends in order to enter the covenant of marriage.

On this, our wedding day, we consecrate ourselves, as beloved companions, forever. Strengthened by our mutual dependence, we begin our future as equals, empowered by each other's love. Our aspirations are entwined. We devote ourselves to creating a family and home inspired by love and commitment to Judaism. We believe that our life together is *bashert,* [destined by fate] and we are thankful to God.

This contract has been legally acquired and accepted by the groom and the bride. And everything is valid and confirmed.

Attested to _____Witness
Attested to _____Witness
Attested to _____Witness
Attested to _____Witness

Things to remember:

1. Two witnesses are required for the signing of the *ketubah.* This is done prior to the actual wedding ceremony. The witnesses cannot be related by blood or marriage to either the bride or the groom. While Orthodox rabbis and some Conservative rabbis will allow only Jewish men to serve as witnesses, Reform and Reconstructionist rabbis also permit women to serve as witnesses.

2. The *ketubah* is generally signed with complete Hebrew names. Therefore, remind your witnesses to make sure they know their Hebrew names (which include their parents' names). In addition, some *ketubot* include a place for both bride and groom to sign.

3. Part or all of the *ketubah* should be read aloud during the marriage ceremony.

Key words and phrases:

Ayd. עֵד. Witness.
Ketubah כְּתוּבָה (plural *ketubot*). Jewish marriage contract.

If you want to know more:

Ronald H. Isaacs, *The Bride and Groom Handbook* (West Orange, NJ, 1990).

_____, *Rites of Passage: A Guide to the Jewish Life Cycle* (Hoboken, NJ, 1992).

Maurice Lamm, *The Jewish Way in Love and Marriage* (New York, 1980).

Instant Information
Jewish Divorce: The *Get*
גֵּט

The source:

"A man takes a wife and possesses her. She fails to please him . . . and he writes her a bill of divorce" (Deuteronomy 24:1-2). An entire talmudic tractate called *Gittin* (Book of Divorce) is devoted to specific details related to the divorce procedure.

What you need to know:

1. According to Jewish law, a *get* (bill of divorce) is required for every Jewish divorce, whether or not there was a religious marriage ceremony. According to traditional law, the only exception is an interfaith marriage: Jew to non-Jew.

2. Originally, the *get* was a document of twelve lines, written in Hebrew and Aramaic in Torah script on parchment. Today heavy white paper is often used instead of parchment.

3. Each *get* contains the following parts:

> a. A statement that the husband divorces his wife without duress.
> b. A statement that the husband and wife may have no further sexual relationship after the *get* has been written and accepted.
> c. The time and place of the writing of the *get.*
> d. Complete Hebrew names of husband and wife.

4. A *get* is usually written by a *sofer,* a qualified Jewish scribe who has specific expertise in this area. You may want to contact your local rabbi or Jewish Federation for a scribe in your area.

5. The entire procedure may take from one to two hours. The *get* itself is retained by the *Bet Din* (rabbinic court)

and kept in a permanent file. Official letters, called a release or *petur*, are given to the couple after the divorce.

6. In an effort to strive for equal rights in marriage, Reform and Reconstructionist rabbis (and some Conservative rabbis too) will prepare *gittin* which reflect equal participation in a divorce.

7. Here is a sample *get*:

בחמישי בשבת בחמשה ועשרים יום לירח תשרי שנת חמשת
אלפים ושבע מאות ועשרים ושתים לבריאת עולם למנין שאנו
מנין כאן בבאסטאן מתא דיתבא על כיף ימא ועל נהר טשא־
רלעם אנא _____ המכונה _____ בן _____ המ־
כונה _____ העומד היום בבאסטאן מתא דיתבא על כיף
ימא ועל נהר טשארלעס צביתי ברעות נפשי בדלא אניסנא ושב־
קית ופטרית ותרוכית יתיכי ליכי אנת אנתתי _____ המ־
כונה _____ בת _____ דמתקרי _____ ומתקרי
_____ העומדת היום בבאסטאן מתא דיתבא על כיף ימא
ועל נהר טשארלעס דהוית אנתתי מן קדמת דנא וכדו פטרית
ושבקית ותרוכית יתיכי ליכי דיתיהוייין רשאה ושלטאהבנפשיכי
למהך להתנסבא לכל גבר די תיצבייין ואנש לא ימחא בידיכי מן
יומא דנן ולעלם והרי את מותרת לכל אדם ודן די יהוי ליבי מנאי
ספר תרוכין ואגרת שבוקין יגט פטורין כדת משה וישראל

On the _____ day of the week, the _____ day of the month of _____ in the year _____ from the creation of the world according to the calendar reckoning we are accustomed to count here, in the city _____ (which is also known as _____) which is located on the river _____ (and on the river _____) and situated near wells of water, I _____ (also known as _____), the son of _____ (also known as _____), who today am present in the city _____ (which is also known as _____) located on the river _____ (and on the river _____) and situated near wells of water, do willingly consent, being under no restraint, to release, to set free, and put aside you, my wife, _____ (also known as _____), daughter of _____ (also known as _____), which is located on the river _____ (and on the river   ) and situated near wells of water, who has been my wife from before. Thus I do set free, release you, and put you aside, in order that you may have permission and the authority over yourself to go and marry any man you may desire. No person may hinder you from this day onward, and you are permitted to every man. This shall be for you from me a bill of dismissal, a letter of release, and a document of freedom, in accordance with the laws of Moses and Israel.

_____the son of _____Witness

_____the son of _____Witness

בחמישי בשבת בחמשה ועשרים יום לירח תשרי שנת חמשת אלפים ושבע מאת ועשרים ושיתים

לבריאת עולם למנין שאנו מנין כאן בבאסמאן מתא דיתבא על כיף ימא ועל נ̇הר̇

טשיארלעס אנא   המכונה   בן   המכונה   דעומד̇

היום בבאסטאן מתא דיתבא על כיף ימא ועל נ̇הר טשיארלעס צביתי ברעות נפשי

בדלא אניסנא ושבקית ופטרית ותרוכית יתיכי ליכי אנ̇ת ענ̇ד̇י

המכונה   בת   דמתקרי   ומתקרי   העומדת

היום בבאסטאן מתא דיתבא על כיף ימא ועל נ̇הר טשיארלעס דהוית אנתתי מן קדמת

דנא וכדו פטרית ושבקית ותרוכית יתיכי ליכי דידיהויין רשאה ושלטאה בנפשיכי

למהך להתנסבא לכל גבר די תיצבייין ואנש לא ימחא בידיכי מן יומא

דן ולעלם ודירי אד̇ מודנריד̇ כלכל אה̇ם

ודן די יהוי ליכי מנאי ספר תרוכין ואגרת שבוקין וגט פטורין

כ̇   משי̇ה̇   וישי̇   אכ̇ל

חיים בן שמעיהו עד
חיים בן נפתלי מרדכי עד

Reprinted with permission from **The Second Jewish Catalogue** by Sharon Strassfeld and Michael Strassfeld © 1976 by the Jewish Publication Society of America.

Things to remember:

1. You will need to have your civil divorce filed before you can obtain a *get*.

2. Sometimes the wife is unable to be present when the *get* is written. In such a case, the husband may appoint an

agent (called a *shaliach*) to deliver the *get* to her. If this is not feasible, the husband may authorize his agent to appoint yet another agent to deliver the *get* to his wife. The wife may also appoint an agent to act on her behalf in receiving the *get* from her husband.

3. While some Reform rabbis are more lenient in this regard, all other rabbis require a *get* before performing a marriage for a divorced person.

4. Traditionally, a divorced woman may not marry a *kohen*, a descendant of the priesthood. However, Reform, Reconstructionist, and some Conservative rabbis permit such marriages.

Key words and phrases:

Bet Din בֵּית דִּין. Literally "house of judgment"; a rabbinic court, the witnesses who sign the *get*.

Get גֵּט. Jewish divorce.

Ptur פְּטוּר. Official letter given to husband and wife to certify that their marriage has been dissolved in accordance with Jewish law.

Shaliach שָׁלִיחַ. Agent appointed for to deliver or receive *get* on behalf of husband or wife.

Sofer סוֹפֵר. Scribe.

If you want to know more:

Ronald H. Isaacs, *Rites of Passage: Guide to the Jewish Life Cycle* (Hoboken, NJ, 1992).

Isaac Klein, *A Guide to Jewish Religious Practice* (New York, 1979).

More particulars:

Here is an outline of the process of the presentation of the *get*.

Husband and wife are both asked a number of routine questions to ascertain their free will and consent in the divorce action. For example, the rabbi will begin by asking the husband: "Do you, _____(name of husband), give this *get* of your own free will without duress or compulsion?" After the give-and-take of questions and answers, the rabbi tells the wife to remove all jewelry from her hands, and to hold her hands together with open palms upward in a position to receive the *get*. The scribe folds the *get* and gives it to the rabbi. The rabbi gives the *get* to the husband, who, holding it in both hands, drops it into the palms of the wife and says: "This be your *get*, and with it you are divorced from me from this time forth so that you may become the wife of any man." The wife then receives the *get*, lifts up her hands, walks with the *get* a short distance, and returns. She then gives the *get* to the rabbi, who again reads it with the witnesses. After the proceedings are completed, a tear is made in the *get* to indicate that it has been used and cannot be used again. The document itself is retained by the *Bet Din* in a permanent file. Official letters, called a *ptur* (release), are given to husband and wife to certify that their marriage has been dissolved according to Jewish law.

Instant Information
Hakafot for Simchat Torah
הַקָּפוֹת לְשִׂמְחַת תּוֹרָה

The source:

Seven circuits are mentioned in the Bible. For example, seven circuits were made around Jericho—once a day for six days, and seven times on the seventh day (Joshua 6:14–15). The Mishnah notes that the *lulav* was carried around the Temple altar during the seven days of Sukkot (Sukkah 3:12).

Happy Simchat Torah!!

What you need to know:

1. Today, a single circuit is made around the sanctuary on each of the first six days of the festival of Sukkot (except for the Sabbath) during the chanting of the *hoshannot* (prayers asking God to save us) at the close of the *musaf* additional service. On Hoshannah Rabbah, the seventh day of Sukkot, the procession around the sanctuary with the *lulav* and *etrog* and the Torah scroll is repeated seven times.

2. All but one of the Torah scrolls are carried around the synagogue in processional circuits during both the evening and morning services on the festival of Simchat Torah. Following the circuits, all the worshippers are given an opportunity to be called up to the Torah for an *aliyah*. Unlike other traditional Torah honors, these *aliyot* are intended for a group. Traditionally a *kohen* (priest) is called first, followed by a Levite and then by ordinary Israelites. Finally come the persons honored with the last *aliyah* in Deuteronomy and the first in Genesis, who stand under a *tallit* (prayer shawl) held up by those on the perimeter. The last *aliyah* is reserved for children.

3. Hasidim also perform these circuits at the conclusion of the evening service on Shemini Atzeret; in Reform congregations they are also performed on Shemini

Atzeret. However, since the Reform movement does not acknowledge the distinction between Israelites, priests, and Levites, different assignments are made.

4. There are texts that are read aloud to accompany each circuit on Simchat Torah. After each one it is customary to dance with and around the Torah scrolls, singing appropriate songs.

Read:

אָנָּא יהוה הוֹשִׁיעָה נָא, אָנָּא יהוה הַצְלִיחָה נָא, אָנָּא יהוה
עֲנֵנוּ בְיוֹם קָרְאֵנוּ:

O God, we beseech You, save us, and cause us to prosper. O God, answer us when we call. *Aneinu v'yom koreinu.*

Read:

אֱלֹהֵי הָרוּחוֹת הוֹשִׁיעָה נָא, בּוֹחֵן לְבָבוֹת הַצְלִיחָה נָא, גּוֹאֵל
חָזָק עֲנֵנוּ בְיוֹם קָרְאֵנוּ:

God of all spirits, save us. Searcher of our hearts, cause us to prosper. Mighty Redeemer, answer us when we call. *Aneinu v'yom koreinu.*

Now march in the first *hakafah.*

Read:

דּוֹבֵר צְדָקוֹת הוֹשִׁיעָה נָא, הָדוּר בִּלְבוּשׁוֹ הַצְלִיחָה נָא, וָתִיק
וְחָסִיד עֲנֵנוּ בְיוֹם קָרְאֵנוּ:

Dispenser of righteousness, save us. God clothed in splendor, cause us to prosper. With everlasting love, answer us when we call. *Aneinu v'yom koreinu.*

Now march in the second *hakafah.*

Read:

זַךְ וְיָשָׁר הוֹשִׁיעָה נָא, חוֹמֵל דַּלִּים הַצְלִיחָה נָא, טוֹב וּמֵטִיב
עֲנֵנוּ בְיוֹם קָרְאֵנוּ:

Pure and Upright One, save us. You who are gracious to the needy, cause us to prosper. Good and benevolent God, answer us when we call. *Aneinu v'yom koreinu.*

Now march in the third *hakafah*.

Read:

יוֹדֵעַ מַחֲשָׁבוֹת הוֹשִׁיעָה נָּא, כַּבִּיר וְנָאוֹר הַצְלִיחָה נָּא, לוֹבֵשׁ צְדָקוֹת עֲנֵנוּ בְיוֹם קָרְאֵנוּ:

You who know our thoughts, save us. Mighty One, cause us to prosper. God robed in righteousness, answer us when we call. *Aneinu v'yom koreinu.*

Now march in the fourth *hakafah*.

Read:

מֶלֶךְ עוֹלָמִים הוֹשִׁיעָה נָּא, נָאוֹר וְאַדִּיר הַצְלִיחָה נָּא, סוֹמֵךְ נוֹפְלִים עֲנֵנוּ בְיוֹם קָרְאֵנוּ:

Eternal Ruler, save us. Source of light and majesty, cause us to prosper. Upholder of the fallen, answer us when we call. *Aneinu v'yom koreinu.*

Now march in the fifth *hakafah*.

Read:

עוֹזֵר דַּלִּים הוֹשִׁיעָה נָּא, פּוֹדֶה וּמַצִּיל הַצְלִיחָה נָּא, צוּר עוֹלָמִים עֲנֵנוּ בְיוֹם קָרְאֵנוּ:

Helper of those in need, save us. Redeemer and Deliverer, cause us to prosper. Everlasting Rock, answer us when we call. *Aneinu v'yom koreinu.*

Now march in the sixth *hakafah*.

Read:

קָדוֹשׁ וְנוֹרָא הוֹשִׁיעָה נָּא, רַחוּם וְחַנּוּן הַצְלִיחָה נָּא, שׁוֹמֵר הַבְּרִית עֲנֵנוּ בְיוֹם קָרְאֵנוּ:

Holy, Awesome One, save us. Compassionate One, cause us to prosper. Perfect in all ways, answer us when we call. *Aneinu v'yom koreinu.*

Read:

תּוֹמֵךְ תְּמִימִים הוֹשִׁיעָה נָּא, תַּקִּיף לָעַד הַצְלִיחָה נָּא, תָּמִים בְּמַעֲשָׂיו עֲנֵנוּ בְיוֹם קָרְאֵנוּ:

Upholder of the innocent, save us. Eternal in power, cause us to prosper. Perfect in Your ways, answer us when we call. *Aneinu v'yom koreinu.*

Now march in the seventh *hakafah*.

Things to remember:

1. Many congregations provide flags to be carried during the *hakafot* processionals on Simchat Torah. You may want to make your own original banner in advance and bring it to services.

2. There are other kinds of processionals besides those during Simchat Torah (and regular Torah readings). At a traditional wedding, for example, the bride circles the groom (three or seven times, depending on the tradition of the community). In Sephardic and Hasidic communities, individuals walk around a coffin seven times prior to the burial. Some people also follow the custom of making a processional around the cemetery when praying for the sick. In addition, Torah scrolls are carried around in a processional circuit during the dedication ceremonies of synagogues and cemeteries.

3. Children often parade with miniature (toy) Torah scrolls.

Key words and phrases:

Aneinu v'yom koreinu עֲנֵנוּ בְיוֹם קָרְאֵנוּ. Answer us when we call.

Hakafah הַקָּפָה (plural, *hakafot* הַקָּפוֹת). Ceremonial processional circuits with Torah scrolls around the synagogue.

Hoshanah הוֹשַׁעְנָה (plural *hoshanot* הוֹשַׁעְנוֹת). Verses asking God to save us.

If you want to know more:

Philip Birnbaum, *A Book of Jewish Concepts* (New York, 1964).

Encyclopaedia Judaica (Jerusalem, 1971), 7:1154.

Ronald H. Isaacs and Kerry M. Olitzky, *Sacred Celebrations: A Jewish Holiday Handbook* (Hoboken, NJ, 1994).

More particulars:

Some people leave the synagogue and do their *hakafot* for Simchat Torah around the outside of the building or parade in the neighborhood.

Instant Information
Who's Who and What's What on a Page of . . . ?
דַּף

The source:

The first five books of the Bible, also known as the Five Books of Moses and as the Pentateuch, are collectively called the *Chumash* and are also often referred to as the Torah; the entire Hebrew Bible is known as the *Tanach.* The Talmud is referred to as the Oral Torah, in contradistinction to the biblical text, which is known as the Written Torah. According to tradition, both Torahs were given by God to Moses on Mount Sinai. Moses immediately wrote down the Written Torah, but it took a long time before the Oral Torah was written down in the form of the two Talmuds, one in Eretz Israel (often referred to as the Palestinian Talmud) and the other in Babylonia (the Babylonian Talmud).

What you need to know:

1. This is what you will find on a page of Torah text in the *Mikra'ot Gedolot,* a classic arrangement of commentaries on the Hebrew Bible.

    a. *Targum.* Aramaic translation of the Torah attributed to Onkelos (2nd cent. C.E.) and therefore referred to as Targum Onkelos. Since all translation is interpretation, this is an important tool for understanding the text. It gives us an idea of how the Hebrew text was understood nearly two thousand years ago and is especially useful in regard to unusual words and ancient customs or practices.
    b. *Rashi's Commentary.* By Rabbi Shlomo Yitzchaki (France, 1040–1105); particularly important because

of Rashi's encyclopedic grasp of the entire Jewish tradition.

c. *Ibn Ezra's Commentary.* By Avraham ben Meir Ibn Ezra (Spain, 1093–1167); stresses grammar and other literary matters.

d. *Supercommentary on Ibn Ezra.* By Rabbi Shlomo Zalman Netter (Austria-Hungary, 19th century): explains difficult points in Ibn Ezra's commentary.

e. *Sforno's Commentary.* By Ovadia Sforno (Italy, 1475–1550); literal explanation of text.

f. *Rashbam's Commentary.* By Shmuel ben Meir (France, 1080–1174), the grandson of Rashi; explicates simple meaning of text.

g. *Masorah.* Notes and rules concerning writing, spacing, paragraphing, and correct vowelization of text (which originally was written without vowels), prepared by Masoretes in Tiberias (6th–10th cent.).

h. *Toldot Aharon.* Cross-references to talmudic passages where biblical text under discussion is cited.

2. This is what you will find on a page of Talmud text:

a. *Mishnah.* Text of Oral Law.

b. *Gemara.* Rabbinic discussions of Mishnah, redacted around 500 C.E.

c. *Rashi.* Commentary on Talmud by Rabbi Shlomo Yitzchaki (France, 1040–1105).

d. *Tosafot.* Collected comments of Rashi's descendants, his disciples and the schools they founded.

e. *Ein Mishpat.* Cross-references to code of Maimonides (*Mishneh Torah*) and other legal collections.

f. *Commentary of Rav Nissim Gaon.* References of quotations encountered in the course of Talmudic study, as well as source and parallels (North Africa, 11th cent.).

g. *Gilyon Hashas.* Textual notes by Rabbi Akiva Eger (Germany, 1761–1837).

h. *Hagahot Ha'bach.* Marginal notes by Rabbi Yoel Sirkes (Poland, 1561–1640).

i. *Mesoret Ha'shas.* Cross-references to other volumes of Talmud.

Things to remember:

1. Traditional writings on the Torah fall into two categories, *midrash halachah* (legal material) and *midrash aggadah* (nonlegal material).

2. The Babylonian Talmud is paginated according to the front (a) and back (b) side of each page; thus, for example, the sequence would be 1a, 1b, 2a, 2b, and so forth.

3. The Mishnah and Gemara together make up the Talmud. The Gemara includes legal discussions as well as historical records, legends, parables, and ethical discussions.

Key words and phrases:

Masorah מְסוֹרָה. Jewish tradition in general; more specifically, rules regarding the traditional text of the Hebrew Bible.

Midrash aggadah מִדְרָשׁ אַגָּדָה. Nonlegal material, as found, for instance, in Midrash Rabbah, Tanhuma, and Pesikta deRab Kahana.

Midrash halachah מִדְרָשׁ הֲלָכָה. Legal material, including Mishnah and Gemara (i.e., the two Talmuds), early (Geonic) responsa, codes (including those by Alfasi, and Rashi as well as the *Mishneh Torah, Tur,* and *Shulchan Aruch*), and later rabbinic responsa.

Mikra'ot Gedolot מִקְרָאוֹת גְדוֹלוֹת. Often called Rabbinic Bible; contains various commentaries.

Mishnah מִשְׁנָה. From the word שָׁנָה meaning "to repeat"; codification of Oral Law prepared by Rabbi Judah Hanasi in 200 C.E., divided into six parts, and subdivided into sixty-three tractates.

Rashbam רַשְׁבַּ"ם. Rabbi Shmuel ben Meir, Rashi's grandson; author of commentary that supplements Rashi's.

Rashi רַשִׁ"י. Rabbi Solomon ben Isaac or Shlomo Yitzchaki, the classic Jewish commentator on both Bible and Talmud.

Supercommentary. Commentary on some other commentary.

If you want to know more:

Joel Lurie Grishaver, *Learning Torah: A Self-Guided Journey Through the Layers of Jewish Learning* (New York, 1990).
A Page from . . . the Torah, Talmud, Midrash, Mishneh Torah, Shulchan Aruch (New York, n.d.).

More particulars:

In the modern sense of the word, one might "study" the Bible by reading its text from beginning to end and thinking about it. In the traditional sense, however, one reads the Torah in uniform increments rather than all at once (the weekly portions read aloud in the synagogue each Sabbath) and gleans an understanding of the text by means of the commentaries found in a source like *Mikra'ot Gedolot*.

Instant Information
Jewish Acronyms
רָאשֵׁי תֵּיבוֹת

The source:

Acronyms are abbreviations derived from the initial letters of combinations of words. They are shortcut for long names and terms. The Jewish cultural universe is replete with acronyms of many kinds. Some, like the word *Tanach,* date back to the talmudic period.

What you need to know:

Rabbinic Acronyms

Besht	Rabbi Israel Baal Shem Tov
HaGra	Rabbi Elijah ben Solomon Zalman (the Vilna Gaon)
Ralbag	Rabbi Levi ben Gerson (Gersonides)
Ramaz	Rabbi Moses Zacuto
Rambam	Rabbi Moses ben Maimon (Maimonides)
Ramban	Rabbi Moses ben Nachman (Nachmanides)
Rashbam	Rabbi Samuel ben Meir
Rashi	Rabbi Solomon bar Isaac
Rif	Rabbi Isaac ben Jacob Alfasi

Religious Organizations

Reform

AAC	American Conference of Cantors
ARZA	Association of Reform Zionists of America
CCAR	Central Conference of American Rabbis
HUC-JIR	Hebrew Union College–Jewish Institute of Religion
NATA	National Association of Temple Administrators

NATE	National Association of Temple Educators
NFTY	North American Federation of Temple Youth
UAHC	Union of American Hebrew Congregations
WRJ	Women of Reform Judaism (formerly, National Federation of Temple Sisterhoods)

Conservative

CA	Cantors' Assembly
EA	Educators' Assembly
JTS	Jewish Theological Seminary of America
RA	Rabbinical Assembly
UJ	University of Judaism
USCJ	United Synagogue of Conservative Judaism (formerly United Synagogue of America)
USY	United Synagogue Youth
UTCJ	Union of Traditional Conservative Judaism

Orthodox

CAA	Cantorial Association of America
RAA	Rabbinical Association of America
RCA	Rabbinical Council of America
UOJCA	Union of Orthodox Jewish Congregations of America (also known as the OU)
UOR	Union of Orthodox Rabbis
YU	Yeshiva University

Reconstructionist

FRSH	Federation of Reconstructionist Synagogues and Havurot
JRF	Jewish Reconstructionist Foundation
RRA	Reconstructionist Rabbinical Association
RRC	Reconstructionist Rabbinical College

Zionist Organizations

ARZA	Association of Reform Zionists of America
AZF	American Zionist Federation
AZYF	American Zionist Youth Foundation
JNF	Jewish National Fund
LZA	Labor Zionist Organization
MERCAZ	Movement to Reaffirm Conservative Zionism
ZOA	Zionist Organization of America

Youth Organizations

BBYO	B'nai B'rith Youth Organization
NCSY	National Council of Synagogue Youth
NFTY	North American Federation of Temple Youth
USY	United Synagogue Youth

Defense Organizations

ADL	Anti-Defamation League of B'nai B'rith
AJC	American Jewish Committee
AJC	American Jewish Congress
JDL	Jewish Defense League

Books

AJYB	*American Jewish Year Book*
EJ	*Encyclopaedia Judaica*
JE	*Jewish Encyclopaedia*
Tanach	The Hebrew Bible, comprising *Torah*, *Nevi'im* (Prophets), and *Ketuvim* (Writings)
UJE	*Universal Jewish Encyclopedia*

Charitable Organizations

AJC	Allied Jewish Charities
CJA	Combined Jewish Appeal
CJF	Council of Jewish Federations
CJP	Council of Jewish Philanthropies
FJC	Federated Jewish Charities

FJP	Federation of Jewish Philanthropies
HIAS	Hebrew Immigrant Aid Society
JFA	Jewish Federated Appeal
UHC	United Hebrew Charities
UJA	United Jewish Appeal

Other Organizations

AAAPME	American Academic Association for Peace in the Middle East
AIPAC	American Israel Public Affairs Committee
AJCW	Association of Jewish Center Workers
AJHS	American Jewish Historical Society
CAJE	Coalition for the Advancement of Jewish Education
GA	General Assembly (annual meeting of Jewish federations)
JDC	Joint Distribution Committee
JESNA	Jewish Education Service of North America
JTA	Jewish Telegraphic Agency
JWV	Jewish War Veterans
NCJW	National Council of Jewish Women
NCSJ	National Conference on Soviet Jewry
NJCRAC	National Jewish Community Relations Advisory Council
SCA	Synagogue Council of America
SSSJ	Student Struggle for Soviet Jewry
WJC	World Jewish Congress
WUJS	World Union of Jewish Students

Key words and phrases:

Rashei tevot רָאשֵׁי תֵּיבוֹת. Abbreviation or acronym.

If you want to know more:

Ronald H. Isaacs, *The Jewish Information Source Book* (Northvale, NJ, 1993).

Richard Siegel and Carl Rheins, eds., *The Jewish Almanac* (New York, 1980).

Instant Information
Jewish Surnames and Their Meanings
שֵׁם הַמִּשְׁפָּחָה

The source:

In ancient and medieval times Jews did not have surnames and were generally known only by their given name and patronymic (father's name), in the form X ben (son of) Y. When Jewish families began adopting surnames in the modern era, they took them from a plethora of sources, including occupations, physical characteristics, nicknames, and geographical locations. Often, surnames were assigned to individuals by government officials.

What you need to know:

The following is a sample of European Jewish surnames and their meanings:

Occupational Names

Abzug: printer
Ackerman: plowman
Alembik: distiller
Antman: handyman
Becker: baker
Berger: shepherd
Bernstein: amber dealer
Braverman: brewer
Bronfman: whiskey dealer
Bulka: baker
Burla: jeweler
Chait: tailor
Chazin: cantor
Citron: lemon seller
Drucker: printer
Einstein: mason

Feder: scribe
Flaxman: flax merchant
Fleischer: butcher
Galinsky: grain merchant
Geiger: violinist
Glass: glass trade
Imber: ginger seller
Kadar: cooper
Klinger: junk dealer
Kolatch: baker
Kushner: furrier
Marmelstein: builder
Messinger: brass dealer
Pechenik: baker
Perlmutter: pearl dealer
Plotkin: fish dealer

Portnoy: tailor
Scharfstein: knife grinder
Schloss: lock maker
Singer: cantor

Tabachnik: snuff maker
Wapner: lime dealer
Weberl: weaver

Physical Characteristics

Album: white
Blau: blonde
Bleich: pale
Dick: stout
Geller: yellow
Gross: large
Jung: young

Klein: small
Kraus: curly
Kurtz: short
Roth: red
Schwartz: black
Stark: strong
Weiss: white

Geographical Names

Altfeld: Poland
Apter: Galicia
Auerbach: Germany
Barr: Ukraine
Bolotin: Poland
Burnstein: Poland
Chomsky: White Russia
Eisenberg: Hungary
Floss: Bavaria
Fuld: Germany
Ginsburg: Bavaria
Halperin: Germany

Jastrow: Prussia
Kissinger: Germany
Kutner: Poland
Lapin: Poland
Lubin: Poland
Mintz: Germany
Pilch: Poland
Sturm: Poland
Teplitz: Czechoslovakia
Warburg: Germany
Yampol: Russia

Names Derived from Religious Status

Kohen	*Levi*
Cohen	Levi
Kogan	Levy
Cogan	Levin
Cohn	Levine
Kahn	Levinsky
Kaplan	Levitt
Katz	Levinthal

If you want to know more:

Heinrich and Eva Guggenheimer, *Jewish Family Names and Their Origins: An Etymological Dictionary* (Hoboken, NJ, 1992).

Benzion C. Kaganoff, *A Dictionary of Jewish Names and Their History* (New York, 1977).

The source:

Rabbi Solomon Yitzchaki (1040–1105), known by the acronym Rashi, was medieval Jewry's foremost commentator on the Bible and Talmud. When the first Hebrew Bibles were printed in the sixteenth century, his commentary was included, but in a distinctive typeface that set it off from the biblical text on the same page. Because of its association with Rashi, the new typeface soon came to be known as "Rashi script." Almost all of the commentaries on the Talmud and Bible are still printed in Rashi script. In fact, the ability to read Rashi script is an essential skill for studying this literature.

What you need to know:

Here is the Hebrew alphabet in Rashi script.

א ב ג ד ה ו ז ח ט י כ ל מ נ ס ע פ צ ק ר ש ת

Key words and phrases:

K'tav Rashi כְּתָב רַשִׁי. Rashi script.

Things to remember:

1. There are other commentaries besides those attributed to Rashi that are written in Rashi script.

2. Rashi's commentary is important because it is encyclopedic in nature (and pre-CD ROM).

If you want to know more:

Encyclopaedia Judaica (London, 1973), 13:1558–65.

Instant Information
Who's Who in the Bible
תַּנַ"ךְ

What you need to know:

The following is an alphabetical list of important personalities in the Torah, the Five Books of Moses:

Aaron: Elder brother of Moses.
Abel: Second son of Adam and Eve.
Abraham: First patriarch and founder of Hebrew nation.
Adam and Eve: First man and woman in the Bible.
Balaam: Heathen prophet whose intended curse of the Israelites turned into a blessing.
Balak: King of Moab.
Benjamin: Youngest son of Jacob.
Cain: Eldest son of Adam and Eve.
Caleb: Leader of tribe of Judah.
Dan: Fifth son of Jacob.
Dinah: Daughter of Jacob and Leah.
Enoch: Eldest son of Cain.
Ephraim: Youngest son of Joseph.
Esau: Son of Isaac and elder twin brother of Jacob.
Gad: Seventh son of Jacob.
Gershon: Eldest of Levi's three sons.
Hagar: Mother of Ishmael and Egyptian handmaid of Sarah.
Ham: Son of Noah.
Haran: Brother of Abraham.
Heth: Son of Canaan.
Isaac: Second of the three patriarchs.
Ishmael: Eldest son of Abraham.
Israel: New name given to Jacob.
Issachar: Fifth son of Jacob and Leah.
Jacob: Third of the patriarchs.
Japheth: Son of Noah.
Jethro: Midianite priest and father of Zipporah.

Joseph: Son of Jacob and Rachel.

Judah: Fourth son of Jacob's first wife, Leah.

Keturah: Abraham's second wife.

Korah: Levite related to Moses who rebelled against Moses and Aaron.

Laban: Brother of Rebeccah.

Lamech: Father of Noah.

Leah: Daughter of Laban and wife of Jacob.

Levi: Third son of Jacob and Leah.

Lot: Son of Abraham's brother Haran.

Manasseh: First son of Joseph and Asenath.

Melchizedek: King of Salem.

Methusaleh: Son of Enoch and oldest person recorded in the Bible.

Miriam: Elder sister of Moses.

Moses: Prophet and founder of Jewish people.

Nahshon: Chief of tribe of Judah.

Naphtali: Sixth son of Jacob.

Noah: Hero of the flood narratives.

Onan: Son of Judah.

Pharaoh: Permanent title of king of Egypt in ancient times.

Phineas. Priest and grandson of Aaron.

Potiphar: Chief of Pharaoh's bodyguard.

Puah: One of midwives who disobeyed Pharaoh's orders to kill the Hebrew male children at birth.

Rachel: Second wife of Jacob.

Rebeccah: Wife of Isaac and mother of Jacob and Esau.

Reuben: Eldest son of Jacob and Leah.

Sarah: Wife of Abraham and mother of Isaac.

Shem: Son of Noah.

Simeon: Second son of Jacob.

Tamar: Wife of Er.

Terah: Father of Abraham.

Zebulun: Sixth son of Jacob and Leah.

Zelophehad: Israelite of the tribe of Manasseh whose five daughters claimed the right, until then reserved to sons, to inherit their father's land.

Zipporah: Wife of Moses.

Judges

The period of the judges, or civic leaders of the community, began with the death of Joshua and ended during the lifetime of the prophet Samuel. This is a list of the judges, as they appear in the **Bible**:

Othniel	Jephthah
Ehud	Ibzan
Shamgar	Elon
Barak	Abdon
Gideon	Samson
Abimelech	Eli, the priest
Tola	Samuel the prophet
Jair	

Kings of Israel

After the period of judges, Israel was ruled by kings. Their names are listed below.

United Kingdom	*Kingdom of Judah*	*Kingdom of Israel*
Saul	Rehoboam	Jeroboam I
David	Abijah	Nadab
Solomon	Asa	Baasha
Judah	Jehoshaphat	Elah
	Jehoram	Zimri
	Ahaziah	Omri
	Athaliah	Ahab
	Jehoash	Ahaziah
	Amaziah	Jehoram
	Uzziah	Jehu
	Jotham	Jehoahaz
	Ahaz	Jehoash
	Hezekiah	Jeroboam II
	Manasseh	Zechariah
	Amon	Shallum
	Josiah	Menahem
	Jehoahaz	Pekahiah
	Jehoiakim	Pekah
	Jehoiachin	Hoshea
	Zedekiah	Joash

Prophets

Prophets acted as spokespersons for God. They often arose at times of political or social crisis. Here is a list of the forty- eight persons granted the gift of prophecy in the period after the conquest of Canaan. Those whose prophetic utterances were set down in writing and included in the Bible are indicated by an asterisk.

Joshua

Phinehas

Elkanah

David

Samuel

Asir

Elkanah, son of Korah

Abiasaph

Gad

Nathan

Asaph

Heman

Ethan

Jeduthun

Ahijah

Shemaiah

Iddo

Azariah

Hanani

Jehu

Micaiah

Eleazar

Elijah

Elisha

Jonah*

Obadiah*

Zechariah

Amoz

Oded

Hosea*

Amos*

Isaiah*

Micah*

Joel*

Nahum*

Habakkuk*

Zephaniah*

Jeremiah*

Uriah

Ezekiel*

Baruch

Seraiah

Daniel

Mordecai

Haggai*

Zechariah*

Malachi*

The seven female prophets were:

Sarah

Miriam

Deborah

Hannah

Abigail

Huldah

Esther

If you want to know more:

Joan Comay, *Who's Who in the Old Testament* (Nashville, 1971).

Kerry M. Olitzky and Ronald H. Isaacs, *A Glossary of Jewish Life* (Northvale, NJ, 1992).

P. Wollman Tsamir, *Graphic History of the Jewish Heritage* (New York, 1963).

More particulars:

In the preceding lists, we have used the conventional English spellings of the names from the Bible. They may differ somewhat from the spellings you will find elsewhere, especially when transliterated directly from the Hebrew.

Instant Information
The 613 Commandments
תַּרְיַ"ג מִצְוֹת

The source:

The total number of biblical commandments (both precepts and prohibitions) is given in rabbinic tradition as 613. Rabbi Simlai, one of the talmudic sages, stated: "613 commandments were revealed to Moses at Sinai, 365 prohibitions equal in number to the solar days, and 248 mandates corresponding to the number of limbs of the human body" (Babylonian Talmud, Makkot 23b).

What you need to know:

The following is a summary of the 613 commandments as prepared by Moses Maimonides in his *Book of Commandments.* His version is accepted by the majority of teachers and scholars.

Positive Commandments

The Jew is required to (1) believe that God exists and (2) acknowledge God's unity; to (3) love, (4) fear, and (5) serve God. The Jew is also instructed to (6) cleave to God (by associating with and imitating the wise) and to (7) swear only by God's name. One must (8) imitate God and (9) sanctify God's name.

The Jew must (10) recite the *Shema* each morning and evening and (11) study the Torah and teach it to others. The Jew must bind *tefillin* on (12) head and (13) arm. The Jew must make (14) *tzitzit* for the garments and (15) fix a *mezuzah* on the door. The people are to be (16) assembled every seventh year to hear the Torah read, and (17) the king must write a special copy of the Torah for himself. (18) Every Jew is to have a Torah scroll. One must (19) praise God after eating.

The Jews are to (20) build a Temple and (21) respect it. It must be (22) guarded at all times, and (23) the Levites are to perform their special duties in it. Before entering the Temple or participating in its service, the priests (24) must wash their hands and feet; they must also (25) light the candelabrum daily. The priests are required to (26) bless Israel and (27) set the shewbread and frankincense before the Ark. Twice daily they must (28) burn the incense on the golden altar. (29) Fire shall be kept burning on the altar continually, and the ashes must be (30) removed daily. Ritually unclean persons must be (31) kept out of the Temple. Israel (32) is to honor its priests, who must be (33) dressed in special priestly raiment. The priests are to (34) carry the Ark on their shoulders, and (35) the holy anointing oil must be prepared according to its special formula. (36) The priestly families are to officiate in rotation. In honor of certain dead close relative the priests must (37) make themselves ritually unclean. The high priest may marry (38) only a virgin.

The (39) *tamid* sacrifice must be offered twice daily, and the (40) high priest must also offer a meal-offering twice daily. An additional sacrifice (*musaf*) must be offered (41) every Sabbath, (42) on the first of every month, and (43) on each of the seven days of Passover. On the second day of Passover (44) a meal offering of the first barley must also be brought. On Shavuot a (45) *musaf* must be offered and (46) two loaves of bread as a wave-offering. The additional sacrifice must also be made on (47) Rosh Hashanah and (48) on the Day of Atonement when the (49) *Avodah* must also be performed. On every day of the festival of (50) Sukkot a *musaf* must be brought, as well as on the (51) eighth day thereof.

Every male [and female] Jew is to make (52) pilgrimage to the Temple three times a year and (53) appear there during the three pilgrim festivals. One must (54) rejoice on the festivals.

On the fourteenth of Nisan one must (55) slaughter the paschal lamb, and one must (56) eat of its roasted flesh on the night of the fifteenth. Those who were ritually impure in Nisan are to slaughter the paschal lamb on the (57) fourteenth of Iyar and eat it with (58) *matzah* and bitter herbs. Trumpets should be (59) sounded when the festive sacrifices are brought and also in times of tribulation.

Cattle to be sacrificed must be (60) at least eight days old and (61) without blemish. All offerings must be (62) salted. It is a *mitzvah* to perform the ritual of (63) the burnt-offering, (64) the sin-offering, (65) the guilt-offering, (66) the peace-offering, and (67) the meal-offering.

Should the Sanhedrin err in a decision, its members (68) must bring a sin-offering, which offering must also be brought (69) by a person who has unwittingly transgressed a *karet* prohibition [i.e., an act which incurs *karet* if done deliberately]. When in doubt as to whether one has transgressed such a prohibition, a (70) "suspensive" guilt-offering must be brought.

For (71) stealing or swearing falsely and for other sins of a like nature, a guilt-offering must be brought. In special circumstances the sin-offering (72) can be according to one's means.

One must (73) confess one's sins before God and repent for them.

A (74) man or (75) woman who has a seminal issue must bring sacrifice; a woman must also bring a sacrifice (76) after childbirth.

A leper must (77) bring a sacrifice after he [or she] has been cleansed.

One must (78) tithe one's cattle. The (79) firstborn of clean [i.e., permitted] cattle are holy and must be sacrificed. Firstborn sons must be (80) redeemed. The firstling of the ass must be (81) redeemed; if not (82) its neck has to be broken.

Animals set aside as offerings (83) must be brought to Jerusalem without delay and (84) may be sacrificed only in the Temple. Offerings from outside the land of Israel (85) may also be brought to the Temple.

Sanctified animals (86) which have become blemished must be redeemed. A beast exchanged for an offering (87) is also holy.

The priests must eat (88) the remainder of the meal-offering and (89) the flesh of sin- and guilt-offerings; but consecrated flesh which has become (90) ritually unclean or (91) which was not eaten within its appointed time must be burned.

A Nazirite must (92) let his hair grow during the period of his separation. When that period is over he must (93) shave his head and bring his sacrifice.

A person must (94) honor his vows and oaths which a judge can (95) annul only in accordance with the law.

Anyone who touches (96) a carcass or (97) one of the eight species of reptiles becomes ritually unclean; food becomes unclean by (98) coming into contact with a ritually unclean object. Menstruous women (99) and those lying-in after childbirth (100) are ritually impure. A leper (101), a leprous garment (102), and a leprous house (103) are all ritually unclean. A man having a (104) running issue is unclean, as is (105) semen. A woman suffering from (106) a running issue is also impure. A human corpse (107) is ritually unclean. The purification water (*mei niddah*) purifies (108) the unclean, but makes the clean ritually impure. It is a *mitzvah* to become ritually clean (109) by ritual immersion. To become cleansed of leprosy one (110) one must follow the specified procedure and also (111) shave off all of one's hair. Until cleansed the leper (112) must be bareheaded with clothing in disarray so as to be easily distinguishable.

The ashes of (113) the red heifer are to be used in the process of ritual purification.

If a person (114) undertakes to give his [or her] own value to the Temple, he [or she] must do so. Should a person declare an unclean beast (115), a house (116), or a field (117) as a donation to the Temple, he must give their value in money as fixed by the priest. If one unwittingly derives benefit from Temple property (118), full restitution plus a fifth must be made.

The fruit of (119) the fourth year's growth of trees is holy and may be eaten only in Jerusalem. When you reap your fields you must leave the corners (120), the gleanings (121), the forgotten sheaves (122), the misformed bunches of grapes (123), and the gleanings of the grapes (124) for the poor.

The first fruits must be (125) separated and brought to the Temple, and you must also (126) separate the great heave-offering (*terumah*) and give it to the priests. You must give (127) one tithe of your produce to the Levites and separate (128) a second tithe which is to be eaten only in Jerusalem. The Levites (129) must give a tenth of their tithe to the priests.

In the third and sixth years of the seven-year cycle you must (130) separate a tithe for the poor instead of a second tithe. A declaration (131) must be recited when separating the various tithes and (132) when bringing the first fruits to the Temple. The first portion of the (133) dough must be given to the priest.

In the seventh year (*shemittah*) everything that grows is (134) ownerless and available to all; the fields (135) must lie fallow and you may not till the ground. You must (136) sanctify the Jubilee [fiftieth] year, and on the Day of Atonement in that year (137) you must sound the *shofar* and set all Hebrew slaves free. In the Jubilee year all land is to be (138) returned to its ancestral owners; and generally, in a walled city (139) the seller has the right to buy back a house within a year of the sale.

Starting from entry into the land of Israel, the years of the Jubilee must be (140) counted and announced yearly and septennially.

In the seventh year (141) all debts are annulled, but (142) one may exact a debt owed by a foreigner.

When you slaughter an animal you must (143) give the priest his share just as you must also give him (144) the first of the fleece. When a person makes a *cherem* [special vow], you must (145) distinguish between what belongs to the Temple [i.e., when God's name is mentioned in the vow] and between what goes to the priests. To be fit for consumption, beast and fowl must be (146) slaughtered according to the law, and if they are not of a domesticated species (147) their blood must be covered with earth after the slaughtering.

Set the parent bird (148) free when taking the nest. Examine beast (149), fowl (150), locusts (151), and fish (152) to determine whether they are permitted for consumption.

The Sanhedrin is to (153) sanctify the first day of every month and reckon the years and the seasons.

You must (154) rest on the Sabbath day and (155) declare it holy at its onset and termination. On the fourteenth of Nisan (156) remove all leaven from your ownership, and on the night of the fifteenth (157) relate the story of the Exodus from Egypt; on that night (158) you must also eat *matzah*. On the (159) first and (160) seventh days of Passover you must rest. Starting from the first day of the first sheaf [the sixteenth of Nisan] you shall (161) count forty-nine days. You must rest on (162) Shavuot and on (163) Rosh Hashanah; on the Day of Atonement you must (164) fast and (165) rest. You must also rest on (166) the first and

(167) the eighth day of Sukkot, during which festival you shall (168) dwell in booths and (169) take the four species. On Rosh Hashanah (170) you are to hear the sound of the *shofar*.

Every male is to (171) give half a shekel to the Temple annually. You must (172) obey a prophet and (173) appoint a king. You must also (174) obey the Sanhedrin; in the case of a division, (175) yield to the majority. Judges and officials shall be (176) appointed in every town and they shall judge the people (177) impartially.

Whoever is aware of evidence (178) must come to court to testify. Witnesses shall be (179) examined thoroughly and, if found to be false, (180) shall have done to them what they intended to do to the accused.

When a person is found murdered and the murderer is unknown, the ritual of (181) decapitating the heifer must be performed.

Six cities of refuge are to be (182) established. The Levites, who have no ancestral share in the land, shall (183) be given cities to live in.

You must (184) build a fence around your roof and remove potential hazards from your home.

Idolatry and its appurtenances (185) must be destroyed, and a city which has become perverted must be (186) treated according to the law. You are instructed to (187) destroy the seven Canaanite nations, and (188) blot out the memory of Amalek, and (189) to remember what they did to Israel.

The regulations for wars other than those commanded in the Torah (190) are to be observed, and a priest must be (191) appointed for special duties in times of war. The military camp must be (192) kept in a sanitary condition. To this end, every soldier must be (193) equipped with the necessary implements.

Stolen property must be (194) restored to its owner. Give (195) charity to the poor. When a Hebrew slave goes free the owner must (196) give him gifts. Lend to (197) the poor without interest; to the foreigner you may (198) lend at interest. Restore (199) a pledge to its owner if he needs it. Pay the worker his wages (200) on time; (201) permit him to eat of the produce with which he is working. You must (202) help unload an animal when necessary, and also (203) help load human or beast [of burden]. Lost property (204) must be restored to its owner. You are required (205) to reprove the sinner, but you must (206) love your neighbor as yourself. You are instructed (207) to love the proselyte. Your weights and measures (208) must be accurate.

Respect the (209) wise; (210) honor and (211) revere your parents. You must (212) perpetuate the human species by marrying (213) according to the law. A bridegroom is to (214) rejoice with his bride for one year. Male children must (215) be circumcised. Should a man die childless, his brother must either (216) marry his widow or (217) release her (*chalitzah*). He who violates a virgin must (218) marry her and may never divorce her. If a man unjustly accuses his wife of premarital promiscuity (219), he shall be flogged, and may never divorce her. The seducer (220) must be punished according to the law. The female captive must be (221) treated in accordance with her special regulations. Divorce can be executed (222) only by means of a written document (*get*). A woman suspected of adultery (223) has to submit to the required test.

When required by the law, (224) you must administer the punishment of flogging and you must (225) exile the unwitting homicide. Capital punishment shall be by (226) the sword, (227) strangulation, (228) fire, or (229) stoning, as specified. In some cases the body of the executed (230) shall be hanged, but it (231) must be brought to burial the same day.

Hebrew slaves (232) must be treated according to the special laws for them. The master is to (233) marry his Hebrew maidservant or (234) redeem her. The alien slave (235) must be treated according to the regulations applying to him.

The applicable law must be administered in the case of injury caused by (236) a person, (237) an animal, or (238) a pit. Thieves (239) must be punished. You must render judgment in cases of (240) trespass by cattle, (241) arson, (242) embezzlement by an unpaid guardian, and in claims against (243) a paid guardian, a hirer, or (244) a borrower. Judgment must also be rendered in disputes arising out of (245) sales, (246) inheritance, and (247) other matters generally. You are required to (248) rescue the persecuted even if it means killing the oppressor.

Prohibitions

It is (1) forbidden to believe in the existence of any but the One God.

You may not make images (2) for yourself or (3) for others to worship or for (4) any other purpose.

You must not worship anything but God either in (5) the manner prescribed for Divine worship or (6) in its own manner of worship.

Do not (7) sacrifice children to Molech.

You may not (8) practice necromancy or (9) resort to familiar spirits; neither should you take idolatry or its mythology (10) seriously.

It is forbidden to construct a (11) pillar or (12) dais even for the worship of God or to (13) plant trees in the Temple.

You may not (14) swear by idols or instigate an idolater to do so, nor may you encourage or persuade any (15) non-Jew or (16) Jew to worship idols.

You must not (17) listen to or love anyone who disseminates idolatry, nor (18) should you withhold yourself from hating him [or her]. Do not (19) pity such a person. If somebody tries to convert you to idolatry (20), do not defend that person or (21) conceal the fact.

It is forbidden to (22) derive any benefit from the ornaments of idols. You may not (23) rebuild what has been destroyed as a punishment for idolatry, nor may you (24) gain any benefit from its wealth. Do not (25) use anything connected with idols or idolatry.

It is forbidden (26) to prophesy in the name of idols or to prophesy (27) falsely in the name of God. Do not (28) listen to the one who prophesies for idols, and do not (29) fear the false prophet or hinder his execution.

You must not (30) imitate the ways of idolaters or practice their customs; (31) divination, (32) soothsaying, (33) enchanting, (34) sorcery, (35) charming, (36) consulting ghosts or (37) familiar spirits, and (38) necromancy are forbidden. Women must not (39) wear male clothing nor men [clothing] (40) of women. Do not (41) tattoo yourself in the manner of the idolaters.

You may not wear (42) garments made of both wool and linen, nor may you shave [with a razor] the sides of (43) your head or (44) your beard. Do not (45) lacerate yourself over your dead.

It is forbidden to return to Egypt to (46) dwell there permanently or to (47) indulge in impure thoughts or sights. You may not (48) make a pact with the seven Canaanite nations or (49) save the life of any member of them. Do not (50) show mercy to idolaters, (51) permit them to dwell in the land of Israel, or (52) intermarry with them. A Jewish woman may not (53) marry an Ammonite or Moabite even if he converts to Judaism, and is to refuse [for reasons of genealogy alone] (54) a descendant of Esau or (55) an Egyptian who is a proselyte. It is prohibited to make (56) peace with the Ammonite or Moabite nation.

The (57) destruction of fruit trees even in times of war is forbidden, as is wanton waste at any time. Do not (58) fear the enemy and do not (59) forget the evil done by Amalek.

You must not (60) blaspheme the Holy Name, (61) break an oath made by it, (62) take it in vain, or (63) profane it. Do not (64) test Adonai, [who is] God.

You may not (65) erase God's name from the holy texts or destroy institutions devoted to Divine worship. Do not (66) allow the body of one hanged to remain so overnight.

Be not (67) lax in guarding the Temple.

The high priest must not enter the Temple (68) indiscriminately; a priest with a physical blemish may not (69) enter there at all or (70) serve in the sanctuary, and even if the blemish is of a temporary nature, he may not (71) participate in the service there until it has passed.

The Levites and the priests must not (72) interchange in their functions. Intoxicated persons may not (73) enter the sanctuary or teach the Torah. It is forbidden for (74) non-priests, (75) unclean priests, or (76) priests who have performed the necessary ablution but are still within the time limit of their uncleanness to serve in the Temple. No unclean person may enter (77) the Temple or (78) the Temple Mount.

The altar must not be made of (79) hewn stones, nor may the ascent to it be by (80) steps. The fire on it may not be (81) extinguished, nor may any other but the specified incense be (82) burned on the golden altar. You may not (83) manufacture oil with the same ingredients and in the same proportions as the anointing oil, which itself (84) may not be misused. Neither may you (85) compound incense with the same ingredients and in the same proportions as that burned on the altar. You must not (86) remove the staves from the Ark, (87) remove the breastplate from the ephod, or (88) make any incision in the upper garment of the high priest.

It is forbidden to (89) offer sacrifices or (90) slaughter consecrated animals outside the Temple. You may not (91) sanctify, (92) slaughter, (93) sprinkle the blood of, or (94) burn the inner parts of a blemished animal even if the blemish is (95) of a temporary nature and even if it is (96) offered by Gentiles. It is forbidden to (97) inflict a blemish on an animal consecrated for sacrifice.

Leaven or honey may not (98) be offered on the altar, neither may (99) anything unsalted. An animal received as the hire of a harlot or as the price of a dog (100) may not be offered.

Do not (101) kill an animal and its young on the same day.

It is forbidden to use (102) olive oil or (103) frankincense in the sin-offering or (104), (105) in the jealousy-offering (*sotah*). You may not (106) substitute sacrifices even (107) from one category to the other. You may not (108) redeem the firstborn of permitted animals. It is forbidden to (109) sell the tithe of the herd or (110) sell or (111) redeem a field consecrated by the *cherem* vow. When you slaughter a bird for a sin-offering you may not (112) split its head.

It is forbidden to (113) work with or (114) shear a consecrated animal. You must not slaughter the paschal lamb (115) while there is still leaven about; nor may you leave overnight (116) those parts that are to be offered up or (117) to be eaten.

You may not leave any part of the festive offering (118) until the third day or any part of (119) the second paschal lamb or (120) the thanksgiving-offering until the morning.

It is forbidden to break a bone of (121) the first or (122) second paschal lamb or (123) to carry their flesh out of the house where it is being eaten. You must not (124) allow the remains of the meal-offering to become leaven. It is also forbidden to eat the paschal lamb (125) raw or sodden or to allow (126) an alien resident, (127) an uncircumcised person, or an (128) apostate to eat of it.

A ritually unclean person (129) must not eat of holy

things, nor may (130) holy things which have become unclean be eaten. Sacrificial meat (131) which is left after the time-limit or (132) which was slaughtered with wrong intentions must not be eaten. The heave-offering must not be eaten by (133) a non-priest, (134) a priest's sojourner or hired worker, (135) an uncircumcised person, or (136) an unclean priest. The daughter of a priest who is married to a non-priest may not (137) eat of holy things.

The meal-offering of the priest (138) must not be eaten, neither may (139) the flesh of the sin-offerings sacrificed within the sanctuary or (140) consecrated animals which have become blemished. You may not eat the second tithe of (141) corn, (142) wine, or (143) oil or (144) unblemished firstlings outside Jerusalem. The priests may not eat the (145) sin-offerings or the trespass-offerings outside the Temple courts or (146) the flesh of the burnt-offering at all. The lighter sacrifices (147) may not be eaten before the blood has been sprinkled. A non-priest may not (148) eat of the holiest sacrifices, and a priest (149) may not eat the first fruits outside the Temple courts.

One may not eat (150) the second tithe while in a state of impurity or (151) in mourning; its redemption money (152) may not be used for anything other than food and drink.

You must not (153) eat untithed produce or (154) change the order of separating the various tithes.

Do not (155) delay payment of offerings—either freewill or obligatory—and do not (156) come to the Temple on the pilgrim festivals without an offering.

Do not (157) break your word.

A priest may not marry (158) a harlot, (159) a woman who has been profaned from the priesthood, or (160) a divorcee; the high priests must not (161) marry a widow or (162) take one as a concubine. Priests may not enter the sanctuary with (163) overgrown hair of the head or (164) with torn clothing; they must not (165) leave the courtyard during the Temple service. An ordinary priest may not render himself (166) ritually impure except for those relatives specified, and the high priest must not become impure (167) for anyone in (168) any way.

The tribe of Levi shall have no part in (169) the division of the land of Israel or (170) in the spoils of war.

It is forbidden (171) to make oneself bald as a sign of

mourning for one's dead.

A Jew may not eat (172) unclean cattle, (173) unclean fish, (174) unclean fowl, (175) creeping things that fly, (176) creatures that creep on the ground, (177) reptiles, (178) worms found in fruit or produce, or (179) any detestable creature.

An animal that dies naturally (180) is forbidden for consumption, as is (181) a torn or mauled animal. One must not eat (182) any limb taken from a living animal. Also prohibited is (183) the sinew of the thigh (*gid ha'nasheh*), as is (184) blood and (185) certain types of fat (*chelev*). It is forbidden (186) to cook meat together with milk or (187) to eat of such a mixture. It is also forbidden to eat (188) of an ox condemned to stoning (even should it have been properly slaughtered).

One may not eat (189) bread made of new corn or the new corn itself, either (190) roasted or (191) green, before the *omer* offering has been brought on the sixteenth of Nisan. You may not eat (192) *orlah* or (193) the growth of mixed planting in the vineyard. Any use of (194) wine libations to idols is prohibited, as is (195) gluttony and drunkenness. One may not eat anything on (196) the Day of Atonement. During Passover it is forbidden to eat (197) leaven (*chametz*) or (198) anything containing a mixture of such. This is also forbidden (199) after the middle of the fourteenth of Nisan [the day before Passover]. During Passover no leaven may be (200) seen or (201) found in your possession.

A Nazirite may not drink (202) wine or any beverage made from grapes; he may not eat (203) grapes, (204) dried grapes, (205) grape seeds, or (206) grape peel. He may not render himself (207) ritually impure for his dead, nor may he (208) enter a tent in which there is a corpse. He must not (209) shave his hair.

It is forbidden (210) to reap the whole of a field without leaving the corners for the poor; it is also forbidden to (211) gather up the ears of corn that fall during reaping or to harvest (212) the misformed clusters of grapes, or (213) the grapes that fall or to (214) return to take a forgotten sheaf.

You must not (215) sow different species of seed together or (216) corn in a vineyard; it is also forbidden to (217) crossbreed different species of animals or (218) work with two different species yoked together.

You must not (219) muzzle an animal working in a field to prevent it from eating.

It is forbidden to (220) till the earth, (221) to prune trees, (222) to reap [in the usual manner] produce or (223) fruit which has grown without cultivation in the seventh year (*shemittah*). One may also not (224) till the earth or prune trees in the Jubilee year, when it is also forbidden to harvest [in the usual manner] (225) produce or (226) fruit that has grown without cultivation.

One may not (227) sell one's landed inheritance in the land of Israel permanently or (228) change the lands of the Levites or (229) leave the Levites without support.

It is forbidden to (230) demand repayment of a loan after the seventh year; you may not, however, (231) refuse to lend to the poor because that year is approaching. Do not (232) deny charity to the poor or (233) send a Hebrew slave away empty-handed when he finishes his period of service. Do not (234) dun your debtor when you know that he [or she] cannot pay. It is forbidden to (235) lend to or (236) borrow from another Jew at interest or (237) to participate in an agreement involving interest either as a guarantor, witness, or writer of the contract.

Do not (238) delay in the payment of wages.

You may not (239) take a pledge from a debtor by violence, (240) keep a poor person's pledge when he [or she] needs it, (241) take any pledge from a widow or (242) from any debtor if he [or she] earns a living from it.

Kidnapping (243) a Jew is forbidden.

Do not (244) steal or (245) rob by violence. Do not (246) remove a land marker or (247) defraud.

It is forbidden (248) to deny receipt of a loan or a deposit or (249) to swear falsely regarding another person's property.

You must not (250) deceive anyone in business. You may not (251) mislead a person even (252) verbally or (253) do him [or her] injury in trade.

You may not (254) return or (255) otherwise take advantage of a slave who has fled to the land of Israel from his master, even if his master is a Jew.

Do not (256) afflict the widow or the orphan. You may not (257) misuse or (258) sell a Hebrew slave; do not (259) treat him cruelly or (260) allow a heathen to mistreat him. You must not (261) sell your Hebrew maidservant or, if you marry her, (262) withhold food, clothing, and conjugal rights from her. You must not (263) sell a female captive or (264) treat her as a slave.

Do not covet (265) another person's possessions even if you are willing to pay for them. Even (266) the desire alone is forbidden.

A worker must not (267) cut down standing corn during his [or her] work or (268) take more fruit than he [or she] can eat.

One must not (269) turn away from a lost article which is to be returned to its owner, nor may you (270) refuse to help a person on an animal which is collapsing under its burden.

It is forbidden to (271) defraud with weights and measures or even (272) to possess inaccurate weights.

A judge must not (273) perpetrate injustice, (274) accept bribes, or be (275) partial or (276) afraid. He [or she] may (277) not favor the poor or (278) discriminate against the wicked; he [or she] should not (279) pity the condemned or (280) pervert the judgment of strangers or orphans.

It is forbidden to (281) hear one litigant without the other being present. A capital case cannot be decided by (282) a majority of one.

A judge must not (283) accept a colleague's opinion unless he [or she] is convinced of its correctness; it is forbidden to (284) appoint as a judge someone who is ignorant of the law.

Do not (285) give false testimony or accept (286) testimony from a wicked person or from (287) relatives of a person involved in the case. It is forbidden to pronounce judgment (288) on the basis of the testimony of one witness.

Do not (289) murder.

You must not convict on (290) circumstantial evidence alone.

A witness (291) must not sit as a judge in capital cases. You must not (292) execute anyone without due proper trial and conviction.

Do not (293) pity or spare the pursuer.

Punishment is not to be inflicted for (294) an act committed under duress.

Do not accept ransom (295) for a murderer or (296) a manslayer.

Do not (297) hesitate to save another person from danger, and do not (298) leave a stumbling block in the way or (299) mislead another person by giving wrong advice.

It is forbidden (300) to administer more than the assigned number of lashes to the guilty.

Do not (301) tell tales or (302) bear hatred in your heart. It is forbidden to (303) shame a Jew, (304) to bear a grudge, or (305) to take revenge.

Do not (306) take the mother when you take the young birds.

It is forbidden to (307) shave a leprous scale or (308) remove other signs of that affliction. It is forbidden (309) to cultivate a valley in which a slain body was found and in which subsequently the ritual of breaking the heifer's neck (*egla arufah*) was performed.

Do not (310) suffer a witch to live.

Do not (311) force a bridegroom to perform military service during the first year of his marriage. It is forbidden to (312) rebel against the transmitters of the tradition or to (313) add or (314) detract from the precepts of the Torah.

Do not curse (315) a judge, (316) a ruler, or (317) any Jew. Do not (318) curse or (319) strike a parent.

It is forbidden to (320) work on the Sabbath or (321) to walk farther than the permitted limits (*eruv*). You may not (322) inflict punishment on the Sabbath.

It is forbidden to work on (323) the first or (324) the seventh day of Passover, on (325) Shavuot, on (326) Rosh Hashanah, on the (327) first and (328) eighth (*Shemini Atzeret*) days of Sukkot, and (329) on the Day of Atonement.

It is forbidden to enter into an incestuous relationship with one's (330) mother, (331) stepmother, (332) sister, (333) half-sister, (334) son's daughter, (335) daughter's daughter, (336) daughter, (337) any woman and her daughter, (338) any woman and her son's daughter, (339) any woman and her daughter's daughter, (340) father's sister, (341) mother's sister, (342) paternal uncle's wife, (343) daughter-in-law, (344) brother's wife, or (345) wife's sister.

It is also forbidden to (346) have sexual relations with a menstruous woman.

Do not (347) commit adultery.

It is forbidden for (348) a man or (349) a woman to have sexual intercourse with an animal.

Homosexuality (350) is forbidden, particularly with (351) one's father or (352) uncle.

It is forbidden to have (353) intimate physical contact (even without actual intercourse) with any of the women with whom intercourse is forbidden.

A *mamzer* (illegitimate child) may not marry (354) a Jewish woman.

Prostitution (355) is forbidden.

A divorcee may not be (356) remarried to her first husband if, in the meanwhile, she had married another.

A childless widow may not (357) marry anyone other than her late husband's brother.

A man may not (358) divorce a wife whom he married after having raped her or (359) after having slandered her.

A eunuch may not (360) marry a Jewish woman.

Castration (361) is forbidden.

You may not (362) elect as king anyone who is not of the seed of Israel.

The king may not accumulate an excessive number of (363) horses, (364) wives, or (365) wealth.

Things to remember:

1. There are 248 positive instructions (in other words, things that we are supposed to do) and 365 negative instructions (or things we are prohibited from doing).

2. According to traditional Jewish law, women were exempt from performing any *mitzvah* that had to be done at a specific time (with exceptions, including the lighting of Sabbath candles).

3. The first attempt at classifying all of the commandments was made in the *Halachot Gedolot* by Rabbi Simeon Kahira (8th cent. C.E.). His example was followed by many others, including Rabbi Saadia Gaon and Maimonides.

4. In Jewish law, boys at thirteen and girls at twelve become subject to the performance of the commandments.

5. There is a tradition that 611 of the 613 commandments were given through Moses (and the other two, the first and second of the Ten Commandments, directly by God

at Mount Sinai). The basis for this tradition is the fact that the numerical value of the word *torah* (תּוֹרָה) is 611. For further discussion of this method of interpretation, see the discussion of gematria on p. 32.

Biblical Sources:

Textual Sources for Positive Commandments

1. Exodus 20:2   2. Deuteronomy 6:4   3. Deuteronomy 6:13   4. Deuteronomy 6:13   5. Exodus 23:25; Deuteronomy 11:13; (Deuteronomy 6:13 and 13:5)   6. Deuteronomy 10:20 7. Deuteronomy 19:20   8. Deuteronomy 28:9   9. Leviticus 22:32 10. Deuteronomy 6:7   11. Deuteronomy 6:7   12. Deuteronomy 6:8 13. Deuteronomy 6:8   14. Numbers 15:38   15. Deuteronomy 6:9 16. Deuteronomy 31:12   17. Deuteronomy 17:18   18. Deuteronomy 31:19   19. Deuteronomy 8:10   20. Exodus 25:8   21. Leviticus 19:30   22. Numbers 18:4   23. Numbers 18:23   24. Exodus 30:19 25. Exodus 27:21   26. Numbers 6:23   27. Exodus 25:30   28. Exodus 30:7   29. Leviticus 6:6   30. Leviticus 6:3   31. Numbers 5:4 32. Leviticus 21:8   33. Exodus 28:2   34. Numbers 7:9   35. Exodus 30:31   36. Deuteronomy 18:6-8   37. Leviticus 21:2-3   38. Leviticus 21:13   39. Numbers 28:3   40. Leviticus 6:13   41. Numbers 28:9   42. Numbers 28:11   43. Leviticus 23:26   44. Leviticus 23:10   45. Numbers 28:26-27   46. Leviticus 23:17   47. Numbers 29:1-2   48. Numbers 28:26-27   49. Leviticus 16   50. Numbers 29:13   51. Numbers 29:36   52. Exodus 23:14   53. Exodus 34:23; Deuteronomy 16:16   54. Deuteronomy 16:14   55. Exodus 12:6 56. Exodus 12:8   57. Numbers 9:11   58. Numbers 9:11; Exodus 12:8 59. Numbers 10:10; 10:9   60. Leviticus 22:27   61. Leviticus 22:21 62. Leviticus 2:13   63. Leviticus 1:2   64. Leviticus 6:18   65. Leviticus 7:1   66. Leviticus 3:1   67. Leviticus 2:1; 6:7   68. Leviticus 4:13   69. Leviticus 4:27   70. Leviticus 5:17-18   71. Leviticus 5:15, 21-25; 19:20-21   72. Leviticus 5:1-11   73. Numbers 5:6-7 74. Leviticus 15:13-15   75. Leviticus 15:28-29   76. Leviticus 12:6 77. Leviticus 14:10   78. Leviticus 27:32   79. Exodus 13:2   80. Exodus 22:28; Numbers 18:15   81. Exodus 34:20   82. Exodus 13:13 83. Deuteronomy 12:5   84. Deuteronomy 12:14   85. Deuteronomy 12:26   86. Deuteronomy 12:15   87. Leviticus 27:33   88. Leviticus 8:9   89. Exodus 29:33   90. Leviticus 7:19   91. Leviticus 7:17 92. Numbers 6:5   93. Numbers 6:18   94. Deuteronomy 23:24 95. Numbers 30:3   96. Leviticus 11:8, 24   97. Leviticus 11:29-31   98. Leviticus 11:34   99. Leviticus 15:19   100. Leviticus 12:2 101. Leviticus 13:3   102. Leviticus 13:51   103. Leviticus 14:44 104. Leviticus 15:2   105. Leviticus 15:16   106. Leviticus 15:19 107. Numbers 19:14   108. Numbers 19:13, 21   109. Leviticus 15:16 110. Leviticus 14:2   111. Leviticus 14:9   112. Leviticus 13:45 113. Numbers 19:2-9   114. Leviticus 27:2-8   115. Leviticus 27:11-12

116. Leviticus 27:14   117. Leviticus 27:16, 22-23   118. Leviticus 5:16   119. Leviticus 19:24   120. Leviticus 19:9   121. Leviticus 19:9   122. Deuteronomy 24:19   123. Leviticus 19:10   124. Leviticus 19:10   125. Exodus 23:19   126. Deuteronomy 18:4   127. Leviticus 27:30; Numbers 18:24   128. Deuteronomy 14:22   129. Numbers 18:26   130. Deuteronomy 14:28   131. Deuteronomy 26:13   132. Deuteronomy 26:5   133. Numbers 15:20   134. Exodus 23:11   135. Exodus 34:21   136. Leviticus 25:10   137. Leviticus 25:9   138. Leviticus 25:24   139. Leviticus 25:29-30   140. Leviticus 25:8   141. Deuteronomy 15:3   142. Deuteronomy 15:3   143. Deuteronomy 18:3   144. Deuteronomy 18:4   145. Leviticus 27:21, 28   146. Deuteronomy 12:21   147. Leviticus 17:13   148. Deuteronomy 22:7   149. Leviticus 11:2   150. Deuteronomy 14:11   151. Leviticus 11:21   152. Leviticus 11:9   153. Exodus 12:2; Deuteronomy 16:1   154. Exodus 23:12   155. Exodus 20:8   156. Exodus 12:15   157. Exodus 13:8   158. Exodus 12:8   159. Exodus 12:16   160. Exodus 12:16   161. Leviticus 23:35   162. Leviticus 23   163. Leviticus 23:24   164. Leviticus 16:29   165. Leviticus 16:29,31   166. Leviticus 23:35   167. Leviticus 23:42   168. Leviticus 23:42   169. Leviticus 23:40   170. Numbers 29:1   171. Exodus 30:12-13   172. Deuteronomy 18:15   173. Deuteronomy 17:15   174. Deuteronomy 17:11   175. Exodus 23:2   176. Deuteronomy 16:18   177. Leviticus 19:15   178. Leviticus 5:1   179. Deuteronomy 13:15   180. Deuteronomy 19:19   181. Deuteronomy 21:4   182. Deuteronomy 19:3   183. Numbers 35:2   184. Deuteronomy 22:8   185. Deuteronomy 12:2; 7:5   186. Deuteronomy 13:17   187. Deuteronomy 20:17   188. Deuteronomy 25:19   189. Deuteronomy 25:17   190. Deuteronomy 20:11-12   191. Deuteronomy 20:2   192. Deuteronomy 23:14-15   193. Deuteronomy 23:14   194. Leviticus 5:23   195. Deuteronomy 15:8; Leviticus 25:35-36   196. Deuteronomy 15:14   197. Exodus 22:24   198. Deuteronomy 23:21   199. Deuteronomy 24:13; Exodus 22:25   200. Deuteronomy 24:15   201. Deuteronomy 23:25-26   202. Exodus 23:5   203. Deuteronomy 22:4   204. Deuteronomy 22:1; Exodus 23:4   205. Leviticus 19:17   206. Leviticus 19:18   207. Deuteronomy 10:19   208. Leviticus 19:36   209. Leviticus 19:32   210. Exodus 20:12   211. Leviticus 19:3   212. Genesis 1:28   213. Deuteronomy 24:1   214. Deuteronomy 24:5   215. Genesis 17:10; Leviticus 12:3   216. Deuteronomy 25:5   217. Deuteronomy 25:9   218. Deuteronomy 22:29   219. Deuteronomy 22:18-19   220. Exodus 22:15-23   221. Deuteronomy 21:11   222. Deuteronomy 24:1   223. Numbers 5:15-27   224. Deuteronomy 25:2   225. Numbers 35:25   226. Exodus 21:20   227. Exodus 21:16   228. Leviticus 20:14   229. Deuteronomy 22:24   230. Deuteronomy 21:22   231. Deuteronomy 21:23   232. Exodus 21:2   233. Exodus 21:8   234. Exodus 21:8   235. Leviticus 25:46   236. Exodus 21:18   237. Exodus 21:28   238. Exodus 21:33–34   239. Exodus 21:37,

22:3   240. Exodus 22:4   241. Exodus 22:5   242. Exodus 22:6-8   243. Exodus 22:9-12   244. Exodus 22:13   245. Leviticus 25:14   246. Exodus 22:8   247. Deuteronomy 25:12   248. Numbers 27:8

Textual Sources for Prohibitions

1. Exodus 20:3   2. Exodus 20:4   3. Leviticus 19:4   4. Exodus 20:20   5. Exodus 20:5   6. Exodus 20:5   7. Leviticus 18:21   8. Leviticus 19:31   9. Leviticus 19:31   10. Leviticus 19:4   11. Deuteronomy 16:21   12. Leviticus 20:1   13. Deuteronomy 16:21   14. Exodus 23:13   15. Exodus 23:13   16. Deuteronomy 13:12   17. Deuteronomy 13:9   18. Deuteronomy 13:9   19. Deuteronomy 13:9   20. Deuteronomy 13:9   21. Deuteronomy 13:9   22. Deuteronomy 7:25   23. Deuteronomy 13:17   24. Deuteronomy 13:18   25. Deuteronomy 7:26   26. Deuteronomy 18:20   27. Deuteronomy 18:20   28. Deuteronomy 13:3–4   29. Deuteronomy 18:22   30. Leviticus 20:23   31. Leviticus 19:26; Deuteronomy 18:10   32. Deuteronomy 18:10   33. Deuteronomy 18:10-26   34. Deuteronomy 18:10-11   35. Deuteronomy 18:10-11   36. Deuteronomy 18:10-11   37. Deuteronomy 18:10-11   38. Deuteronomy 18:10-11   39. Deuteronomy 22:5   40. Deuteronomy 22:5   41. Leviticus 19:28   42. Deuteronomy 22:11   43. Leviticus 19:27   44. Leviticus 19:27   45. Deuteronomy 16:1; 14:1; Leviticus 19:28   46. Deuteronomy 17:16   47. Numbers 15:39   48. Exodus 23:32; Deuteronomy 7:2   49. Deuteronomy 20:16   50. Deuteronomy 7:2   51. Exodus 23:33   52. Deuteronomy 7:3   53. Deuteronomy 23:4   54. Deuteronomy 23:8   55. Deuteronomy 23:8   56. Deuteronomy 23:7   57. Deuteronomy 20:19   58. Deuteronomy 7:21   59. Deuteronomy 25:19   60. Leviticus 24:16; Exodus 22:27   61. Leviticus 19:12   62. Exodus 20:7   63. Leviticus 22:32   64. Deuteronomy 6:16   65. Deuteronomy 12:4   66. Deuteronomy 21:23   67. Numbers 18:5   68. Leviticus 16:2   69. Leviticus 21:23   70. Leviticus 21:17   71. Leviticus 21:18   72. Numbers 18:3   73. Leviticus 10:9-11   74. Numbers 18:4   75. Leviticus 22:2   76. Leviticus 21:6   77. Numbers 5:3   78. Deuteronomy 23:11   79. Exodus 20:25   80. Exodus 20:26   81. Leviticus 6:6   82. Exodus 30:9   83. Exodus 30:32   84. Exodus 30:32   85. Exodus 30:37   86. Exodus 25:15   87. Exodus 28:28   88. Exodus 28:32   89. Deuteronomy 12:13   90. Leviticus 17:3-4   91. Leviticus 22:20   92. Leviticus 22:22   93. Leviticus 22:24   94. Leviticus 22:22   95. Deuteronomy 17:1   96. Leviticus 22:25   97. Leviticus 22:21   98. Leviticus 2:11   99. Leviticus 2:13   100. Deuteronomy 23:19   101. Leviticus 22:28   102. Leviticus 5:11   103. Leviticus 5:11   104. Numbers 5:15   105. Numbers 5:15   106. Leviticus 27:10   107. Leviticus 27:26   108. Numbers 18:17   109. Leviticus 27:33   110. Leviticus 27:28   111. Leviticus 27:28   112. Leviticus 5:8   113. Deuteronomy 15:19   114. Deuteronomy 15:19   115. Exodus 34:25   116. Exodus 23:10   117. Exodus 12:10

118. Deuteronomy 16:4   119. Numbers 9:13   120. Leviticus 22:30   121. Exodus 12:46   122. Numbers 9:12   123. Exodus 12:46   124. Leviticus 6:10   125. Exodus 12:9   126. Exodus 12:45 127. Exodus 12:48   128. Exodus 12:43   129. Leviticus 12.4 130. Leviticus 7:19   131. Leviticus 19:6-8   132. Leviticus 7:18 133. Leviticus 22:10   134. Leviticus 22:10   135. Leviticus 22:10 136. Leviticus 22:4   137. Leviticus 22:12   138. Leviticus 6:16 139. Leviticus 6:23   140. Deuteronomy 14:3   141. Deuteronomy 12:17   142. Deuteronomy 12:17   143. Deuteronomy 12:17   144. Deuteronomy 12:17   145. Deuteronomy 12:17   146. Deuteronomy 12:17   147. Deuteronomy 12:17 148. Deuteronomy 12:17   149. Exodus 29:33   150. Deuteronomy 26:14   151. Deuteronomy 26:14   152. Deuteronomy 26:14 153. Leviticus 22:15   154. Exodus 22:28   155. Deuteronomy 23:22 156. Exodus 23:15   157. Numbers 30:3   158. Leviticus 21:7 159. Leviticus 21:7   160. Leviticus 21:7   161. Leviticus 21:14 162. Leviticus 21:15   163. Leviticus 10:6   164. Leviticus 10:6 165. Leviticus 10:7   166. Leviticus 21:1   167. Leviticus 21:11 168. Leviticus 21:11   169. Deuteronomy 18:1   170. Deuteronomy 18:1   171. Deuteronomy 14:1   172. Deuteronomy 14:7 173. Leviticus 11:11   174. Leviticus 11:13   175. Deuteronomy 14:19   176. Leviticus 11:41   177. Leviticus 11:44   178. Leviticus 11:42   179. Leviticus 11:43   180. Deuteronomy 14:21 181. Exodus 22:30   182. Deuteronomy 12:23   183. Genesis 32:33 184. Leviticus 7:26   185. Leviticus 7:23   186. Exodus 23:19 187. Exodus 34:26   188. Exodus 21:28   189. Leviticus 23:14 190. Leviticus 23:14   191. Leviticus 23:14   192. Leviticus 19:23 193. Deuteronomy 22:9   194. Deuteronomy 32:38   195. Leviticus 19:26; Deuteronomy 21:20   196. Leviticus 23: 29   197. Exodus 13:3   198. Exodus 13:20   199. Deuteronomy 16:3   200. Exodus 13:7   201. Exodus 12:19   202. Numbers 6:3   203. Numbers 6:3   204. Numbers 6:3   205. Numbers 6:4   206. Numbers 6:4   207. Numbers 6:7   208. Leviticus 21:11   209. Numbers 6:5   210. Leviticus 23:22   211. Leviticus 19:9   212. Leviticus 19:10   213. Leviticus 19:10   214. Deuteronomy 24:19 215. Leviticus 19:19   216. Deuteronomy 22:9   217. Leviticus 19:19 218. Deuteronomy 22:10   219. Deuteronomy 25:4   220. Leviticus 25:4   221. Leviticus 25:4   222. Leviticus 25:5   223. Leviticus 25:5 224. Leviticus 25:11   225. Leviticus 25:11   226. Leviticus 25:11 227. Leviticus 25:23   228. Leviticus 25:33   229. Deuteronomy 12:19   230. Deuteronomy 15:2   231. Deuteronomy 15:9 232. Deuteronomy 15:7   233. Deuteronomy 15:13   234. Exodus 22:24   235. Leviticus 25:37   236. Deuteronomy 23:20 237. Exodus 22:24   238. Leviticus 19:13   239. Deuteronomy 24:10   240. Deuteronomy 24:12   241. Deuteronomy 24:17 242. Deuteronomy 24:10   243. Exodus 20:13   244. Leviticus 19:11 245. Leviticus 19:13   246. Deuteronomy 19:14   247. Leviticus 19:13   248. Leviticus 19:11   249. Leviticus 19:11   250. Leviticus

25:14   251. Leviticus 25:17   252. Exodus 22:20   253. Exodus 22:20   254. Deuteronomy 23:16   255. Deuteronomy 23:17 256. Exodus 22:21   257. Leviticus 25:39   258. Leviticus 25:42 259. Leviticus 25:43   260. Leviticus 25:53   261. Exodus 21:8   262. Exodus 21:10   263. Deuteronomy 21:14 264. Deuteronomy 21:14   265. Exodus 20:17   266. Deuteronomy 5:18   267. Deuteronomy 23:26   268. Deuteronomy 23:25 269. Deuteronomy 22:   270. Exodus 23:5   271. Leviticus 19:35 272. Deuteronomy 25:13   273. Leviticus 19:15   274. Exodus 23:8 275. Leviticus 19:15   276. Deuteronomy 1:17   277. Leviticus 19:15: Exodus 23:3   278. Exodus 23:6   279. Deuteronomy 19:13 280. Deuteronomy 24:17   281. Exodus 23:1   282. Exodus 23:2 283. Exodus 23:2   284. Deuteronomy 1:17   285. Exodus 20:16 286. Exodus 23:1   287. Deuteronomy 24:16   288. Deuteronomy 19:15   289. Exodus 20:13   290. Exodus 23:7   291. Numbers 35:30   292. Numbers 35:12   293. Deuteronomy 25:12 294. Deuteronomy 22:26   295. Numbers 35:31   296. Numbers 35:32   297. Leviticus 19:16   298. Deuteronomy 22:8   299. Leviticus 19:14   300. Deuteronomy 25:2-3   301. Leviticus 19:16 302. Leviticus 19:17   303. Leviticus 19:17   304. Leviticus 19:18 305. Leviticus 19:18   306. Deuteronomy 22:6   307. Leviticus 13:33   308. Deuteronomy 24:8   309. Deuteronomy 21:4   310. Exodus 22:17   311. Deuteronomy 24:5   312. Deuteronomy 17:11 313. Deuteronomy 13:1   314. Deuteronomy 13:1   315. Exodus 22:27   316. Exodus 22:27   317. Leviticus 19:14   318. Exodus 21:17   319. Exodus 21:15   320. Exodus 20:10   321. Exodus 16:29   322. Exodus 35:3   323. Exodus 12:16   324. Exodus 12:16 325. Leviticus 23:21   326. Leviticus 23:25   327. Leviticus 23:35 328. Leviticus 23:36   329. Leviticus 23:28   330. Leviticus 18:7 331. Leviticus 18:8   332. Leviticus 18:9   333. Leviticus 18:11 334. Leviticus 18:10   335. Leviticus 18:10   336. Leviticus 18: 10 337. Leviticus 18:17   338. Leviticus 18:17   339. Leviticus 18:17 340. Leviticus 18:12   341. Leviticus 18:13   342. Leviticus 18:14 343. Leviticus 18:15   344. Leviticus 18:16   345. Leviticus 18:18 346. Leviticus 18:19   347. Leviticus 18:20   348. Leviticus 18:23 349. Leviticus 18:23   350. Leviticus 18:22   351. Leviticus 18:7 352. Leviticus 18:14   353. Leviticus 18:6   354. Deuteronomy 23:3 355. Deuteronomy 23:18   356. Deuteronomy 24:4   357. Deuteronomy 25:5   358. Deuteronomy 22:29   359. Deuteronomy 22:19 360. Deuteronomy 23:2   361. Leviticus 22:24   362. Deuteronomy 17:15   363. Deuteronomy 17:16   364. Deuteronomy 17:17 365. Deuteronomy 17:17

Key words and phrases:

Mitzvah מִצְוָה. (plural, *mitzvot* מִצְווֹת). Commandment (or instruction).

Mitzvat aseh מִצְוַת עֲשֵׂה. Positive commandment.

Mitzvat lo ta'aseh מִצְוַת לֹא תַעֲשֶׂה. Negative commandment.

Taryag mitzvot תַּרְיַ"ג מִצְוֹת. The 613 commandments; the word *taryag* is a mnemonic for remembering the number.

If you want to know more:

Gersion Appel, *A Philosophy of Mizvot* (Hoboken, NJ, 1975).

Philip Birnbaum, *A Book of Jewish Concepts* (New York, 1964).

Abraham Chill, *The Mitzvot* (New York, 1974).

Encyclopaedia Judaica (Jerusalem, 1975), 5:760 ff.

Aaron HaLevi, *The Book of Mitzvah Education*, 5 vols. (Jerusalem, 1978).

Ron Isaacs *The Book of Commandments: A Source Book* (Northvale, NJ, forthcoming).

Instant Information
Magazines, Newspapers and Journals

What you need to know:

Many of these periodicals are sponsored by religious or ideologically-based organizations. Thus, some of them express viewpoints different from those expressed by others on the same list. Taken together, however, these journals, magazines, and newspapers present a cross-section of the attitudes and opinions of Jews around the world. Thus, they are important for the modern Jew who wishes to function in the contemporary Jewish world.

Periodicals

AJS Review

Academic journal for members of the Association of Jewish Studies.

Brandeis University
Waltham, MA 02254

American Jewish Archives

Academic journal published by the institution of the same name, primarily devoted to the preservation and study of the American Jewish experience.

American Jewish Archives
3101 Clifton Avenue
Cincinnati, OH 45220

American Jewish History

Academic journal primarily devoted to the study of the American Jewish experience and sponsored by the American Jewish Historical Society.

American Jewish Historical Society
2 Thornton Road
Waltham, MA 02154

Biblical Archaeology Review

Independent and sometimes controversial magazine aimed at both general readers and those well-versed in archaeology.

Biblical Archaeology Society
4710 41st Street NW
Washington, DC 20016

CCAR Journal

Professional journal of the Central Conference of American Rabbis, the international organization of Reform rabbis.

Central Conference of American Rabbis
192 Lexington Avenue
New York, NY 10016

Commentary

Generally representing a politically conservative point of view; sponsored by the American Jewish Committee.

American Jewish Committee
165 East 65th Street
New York, NY 10022

Congress Monthly

Sponsored by the American Jewish Congress, historically a liberal organization.

American Jewish Congress
15 East 84th Street
New York, NY 10028

Conservative Judaism

Professional journal of Rabbinical Assembly of America, the international organization of Conservative rabbis.

Rabbinical Assembly of America
3080 Broadway
New York, NY 10027

Cross-Currents

Interfaith publication sponsored by Association for Religion and Intellectual Life.

Association for Religion and Intellectual Life
College of New Rochelle
New Rochelle, NY 10805

Dimensions

Holocaust education publication of Anti-Defamation League of B'nai B'rith and its Braun Center for Holocaust Studies.

Anti-Defamation League
823 United Nations Plaza
New York, NY 10017

European Judaism

Published in association with Leo Baeck College, the liberal rabbinical training institution in London, and the Michael Goulston Education Foundation.

The Manor House
80 East End Road
London N32SY
United Kingdom

Hadassah

House organ of the women's Zionist organization, includes excellent articles on education and parenting.

Hadassah
50 West 58th Street
New York, NY 10019

Humanistic Judaism

House organ of Society for Humanistic Judaism.

Society for Humanistic Judaism
28611 West Twelve Mile Road
Farmington Hills, MI 48334

Jerusalem Report

Leading popular Jewish periodical today, covering Israel and the Middle East.

Jerusalem Report
1212 Avenue of the Americas
New York, NY 10036
or 22 Rehov Yosef Rivlin
Jerusalem 91017 Israel

National Jewish Monthly

Sponsored by B'nai B'rith International; easy-to-read magazine with information about popular Jewish culture.

B'nai B'rith International
1640 Rhode Island Avenue
Washington, DC 20036

Jewish Quarterly

Arts and literature journal.

Jewish Quarterly
P.O. Box 1148
London NW5 ZAZ
United Kingdom

Jewish Spectator

Excellent thinker's magazine with a long track record, founded by Trude Weiss-Rosmarin.

American Friends of the Center
for Jewish Living and Values
4391 Park Milana
Calabasas, CA 91302

Journal of Psychology and Judaism

Independent journal edited by a rabbi, with an excellent annual issue on aging.

Human Sciences Press
233 Spring Street
New York, NY 10013

Judaism

Sponsored by American Jewish Congress and representing a wide perspective of opinions.

American Jewish Congress
15 East 84th Street
New York, NY 10028

Lilith

Leading Jewish feminist magazine.

Lilith
250 West 57th Street
New York, NY 10107

Midstream

General journal on Zionism.

Theodor Herzl Foundation
110 East 57th Street
New York, NY 10022

Moment

Independent magazine, founded by Leonard Fein, features popular articles about contemporary Jewish culture.

Jewish Educational Ventures
4710 41st Street NW
Washington, DC 20016

Near-East Report

Weekly report out of Washington on American Middle Eastern policy.

Near East Research
440 First Street NW, Suite 607
Washington, DC 20001

Reconstructionist

House organ of Reconstructionist movement, published by its rabbinical college.

Reconstructionist Rabbinical College
Church Road and Greenwood Avenue
Wyncote, PA 19095

Reform Judaism

House organ of Union of American Hebrew Congregations, national organization of Reform synagogues.

Union of American Hebrew Congregations
838 Fifth Avenue
New York, NY 10021

Sh'ma: A Journal of Jewish Responsibility

Started by philosopher/theologian Eugene B. Borowitz, now published by CLAL (Center for Jewish Learning and Leadership).

CLAL
99 Park Avenue South, Suite 300
New York, NY

Tikkun

Relatively young publication, edited by Michael Lerner, representing a liberal political perspective.

Tikkun
P.O. Box 1758 Cathedral Station
New York, NY 10025

Torah Umada'a Journal

Orthodox journal about Jewish law, sponsored by the rabbinical seminary at Yeshiva University.

Rabbi Isaac Elchanan Theological Seminary
500 West 185th Street
New York, NY 10033

Tradition

Orthodox journal of thought sponsored by the Rabbinical Council of America, a centrist Orthodox rabbinical organization.

Rabbinical Council of America
275 Seventh Avenue
New York, NY 10011

United Synagogue Review

House organ of United Synagogue for Conservative Judaism, the national organization of Conservative synagogues.

United Synagogue for Conservative Judaism
155 Fifth Avenue
New York, NY 10010

Newspapers

Forward

The newspaper that Americanized your grandparents and great-grandparents, while teaching them English at the same time. In its current form, it is geared to young intellectuals.

44 East 33rd Street
New York, NY 10016

Jerusalem Post

The only English-language daily in Israel, also available in a weekend overseas edition, this newspaper has become very right wing since it changed ownership several years ago.

6 Oholiav Street
Jerusalem 91000
211 East 43rd Street, Suite 601
New York, NY 10017

(Philadelphia) Jewish Exponent

Excellent community newspaper.

226 South 16th Street
Philadelphia, PA 19102

(National) Jewish Post and Opinion

National newspaper with regional editions, of limited journalistic quality.

611 North Park Avenue
Indianapolis, IN 46204

(Baltimore) Jewish Times

Excellent local newspaper.

2104 North Charles Street
Baltimore, MD 21218

(New York) Jewish Week

Keeps you informed about the largest Jewish community in North America.

3 East 40th Street
New York, NY 10016

If you want to know more:

The Jewish Telegraphic Agency (JTA) keeps you informed about things taking place in the Jewish world. While many local Jewish papers carry material from JTA, you can subscribe directly.

Jewish Telegraphic Agency
165 West 46th Street, Room 511
New York, NY 10036

Instant Information
Videos and Video Distributors

What you need to know:

There are literally hundreds of videos of Jewish interest available at your local video store; there are also distributors which specialize in Jewish content and interest. We are including some of these distributors below. Try your local Bureau of Jewish Education or local Jewish book store, especially if you live in a large metropolitan area. But don't forget, everyone has a telephone!

If you want to know more:

1. For fun, why not try studying the Bible by watching a good video? Here are some titles to look for:

> *Queen Esther,* starring Victoria Principal
> *Samson and Delilah,* starring Joan Collins
> *Samson and Delilah* with Victor Mature and Hedy Lamar
> *Solomon and Sheba* with Yul Brynner
> *David and Bathsheba* with Gregory Peck
> *King David,* starring Richard Gere
> *The Ten Commandments,* directed by Cecil B. De Mille

2. You'll also want to look for classics like *Cast a Giant Shadow,* starring Kirk Douglas; *Exodus,* starring Paul Newman; and *Marjorie Morningstar,* with Natalie Wood and Gene Kelly.

3. Hanna Barbera has a modest series of children's Bible cartoons, called *The Greatest Adventure,* available through:
UAHC Television and Film Institute
838 Fifth Avenue
New York, NY 10021
or
Hanna-Barbera
3900 Cahuenga Boulevard
Hollywood, CA 90068

357

Rabbit Ears Productions (of Rowayton, CT) also has an excellent Bible story series (called *The Greatest Stories Ever Told*), read by actors and actresses, like *Noah and the Ark* read by Kelly McGillis.

4. Don't forget the Israeli *Sesame Street* program, which has been adapted for American distribution under the *Shalom Sesame* label. Two volumes (on holidays and places of interest in Israel) are available.

5. Companies well known for their ability to put award-winning children's books on films have many tapes of Jewish interest, like Barbara Cohen's *Molly's Pilgrim* and Isaac Bashevis Singer's *Zlateh the Goat*. Many are available from:
Weston Woods
Weston, CT 06883

6. Here are some films that made it to the big screen and are now available in video. When you are looking for a film for a Saturday night at home, why not rent one of the following:

> *Au Revoir les Enfants*
> *The Boat Is Full*
> *The Boys from Brazil*
> *The Chosen*
> *Crossing Delancey*
> *The Delta Force*
> *Hanna's War*
> *Hester Street*
> *Judgment at Nuremberg*
> *Music Box*
> *Oh God (I and II)*
> *Raid on Entebbe*

7. Here are some children's films to look for that may have been broadcast over your local PBS or Disney station:

> *An American Tale*
> *The Animated Haggadah*
> *Lights*

8. These were made for TV:

> *Holocaust*

The House on Garibaldi Street
The Impossible Spy
Operation Thunderbolt

10. There are some which only made it to the arts cinemas, like *Wedding in Galilee*.

More particulars:

For more specific information, contact:

Columbia House Video Library
(including *Masters of the Bible* series)
1-800-638-2922

Ergo Media
668 Front Street
P.O. Box 2037
Teaneck, NJ 07666

Jewish Educational Video
713 Crown Street
Brooklyn, NY 10010

Jewish Video Library
300 Raritan Avenue
Highland Park, NJ 08904

National Center for Jewish Film
Lown Building 102
Brandeis University
Waltham, MA 02254

Sisu Home Entertainment
475 Fifth Avenue, 23rd Floor
New York, NY 10017

Instant Information
The Electronic Arts

What you need to know:

Please note: Much of this material is for the serious student and often quite expensive. Some of the material requires Hebrew language skills. [The material in this chapter was prepared with the assistance of Professor Marc Bregman, Hebrew Union College–Jewish Institute of Religion, Jerusalem.]

CD-ROM and Hard Disk

CD-ROM Judaic Classics Library, *Babylonian Talmud,* Soncino Edition (Hebrew and English)
for MAC or PC with windows, Davka Corporation

Midrash Rabbah, Soncino Edition (Hebrew and English) on CD-ROM, Davka Corporation

ServiceMaker—program for creating liturgies designed and distributed by Joel M. Hoffman (joel@wam.umd.edu)

Talmud Text Data Bank (Hebrew)
Index of references dealing with talmudic literature
Line Collation Software,
Saul Lieberman Institute of Talmudic Research, Jewish Theological Seminary of America

Bar-Ilan University Responsa Project (Hebrew)
Includes Bible, Commentaries, Talmuds, Midrash, Poskim, and Responsa
distributed in the United States by Torah Educational Software

If you want to know more:

Internet

Libraries (on-line catalogs and data bases):

Harvard University
telnet hollis.harvard.educ or telnet 128.103.60.31

University of California
telnet melvyl.ucop.edc or telnet 192.35.222.222

ALEPH (Israel University Libraries)
telnet aleph.huji.ac.il or telnet 128.139.4.15
telnet ram2.huji.ac.il or telnet 128.139.4.3
Data bases:
RAMBI (Index to Articles in Jewish Studies) [LB/JNL.RBI]
IHP (Index to Hebrew Periodicals) [LB/IHP]—includes all Israeli newspapers

Uncover (article access and delivery by fax)/fee for service
E-mail: database@carl.org, tel. 303/758-3030

Jewish Networks

SHAMASH: Jewish Networking Project
(gopher israel.nysernet.org)

Jerusalem One: Global Jewish Networking
(gopher jerusalem1.datasrv.co.il)

Discussion Groups, Forums, Lists

Clari.News.Jews: ClariNet wire service articles about Jewish matters/ fee for service
    (info@clarinet.com)
Ioudaios: Judaism in the Greco-Roman world
    (ioudaios-l@lehigh.edu)
Israeline: Israel press clippings via the Israeli Consulate
  in New York
    (nycon@israel-info.gov.il)
Israel-Mideast: information and editorials from the Israeli press via Foreign Ministry
    (analysis%israel-infor.gov.il@vm.tau.ac.il)
Jewish-psy: Judaism and mental health
    (Jewish-psy@jerusalem1.datasrv.co.il)
PJAL: Discussion forum for progressive Jews
    (pjal@israel.nysernet.ORG)
PJML: Discussion forum for progressive Jews
    (pjml@israel.nyscrnet.ORG)
Postmodern Jewish Philosophy Network
    (Journal: pmassa@drew.edu; Discussion group:
  poch@drew.edu)

Sh'ma Online: sponsored by *Sh'ma* Magazine
     (shma@shamash.nysernet.org; contact Derek Fields
   derek@bellcore.com)
UAHCampus: List for people concerned about Reform
   Judaism on the college campus
     (uahcampus@israel.nysernet.ORG)

More particulars:

Davka
7074 N Western Avenue
Chicago, IL 60645

The Educational Software Company (TES)
c/o Jerusalem Sales Co.
4 College Road
Monsey, NY 10452

Kabbalah Software
8 Price Drive, Dept. CJ
Edison, NJ 08817

Lev Software
P.O. Box 17832
Plantation, FL 33318

Saul Lieberman Institute of Talmudic Research
Jewish Theological Seminary of America
3080 Broadway
New York, NY 10027

Torah Educational Software.
1-800-925-6853

Extra Holiday How-To
Making (International) *Charoset*
חֲרוֹסֶת

The source:

Charoset is a paste made of fruit, spices, wine, cinnamon, and nuts which forms part of the *seder* rite on the evening of Passover. It is symbolic of the mortar that the Jews made when they were slaves in Egypt. Some say that the name *charoset* is derived from the Hebrew word *cheres*, meaning "clay," because the food mixture resembles the color of clay. In Exodus 12:8 the Israelites are instructed to eat bitter herbs (*maror*). The rabbis suggested that we dip the *maror* in the *charoset* to temper the bitterness of the bitter herbs.

What you need to know:

1. Ingredients with which to make *charoset* vary from community to community. In most Western Jewish communities, *charoset* is made using apples, chopped walnuts, cinnamon, and red wine.

2. In many Sephardic communities, *charoset* is made using the biblical fruits of the Land of Israel: grapes, wheat (matzah meal), figs, olives, pomegranates, and dates.

3. Jews from North Africa often use pine nuts and hard-boiled eggs when making their *charoset,* flavoring it with piquant and pungent spices, such as ginger.

4. Jews from Yemen add other seasonings, such as chili pepper, when they make their *charoset.*

5. Israeli Jews often turn *charoset* into an actual dessert by adding bananas, dates, candied fruit peel, orange juice, and sugar.

Things to remember:

1. Be creative. Start with the basics and add the flavor of your community to the *charoset*. Make the new recipe your family's new tradition.

Key words and phrases:

Charoset. חֲרוֹסֶת Mixture eaten at Passover *seder* to symbolize mortar used to build the pyramids.

Maror. מָרוֹר Bitter herbs dipped into *charoset* over which the blessing on the herbs is said.

If you want to know more:

Philip Goodman, *The Passover Anthology* (Philadelphia, 1962).

Ronald H. Isaacs and Kerry M. Olitzky, *The Discovery Haggadah* (Hoboken, NJ, 1993).

More particulars:

Here are some international *charoset* recipes:

American *Charoset*
1 pound peeled, cored, finely chopped apples
1 cup chopped walnuts
1–2 teaspoons cinnamon (or to taste)
Sweet red wine
Add wine until mixture forms a paste, or to taste.

European *Charoset*
1 pound apples, cored and grated
1/2 cup chopped almonds or walnuts
2 tablespoons honey
1 teaspoon ground cinnamon
1/4 cup sweet red wine

Yemenite *Charoset*
15 pitted dates, chopped
15 dried figs, chopped
2 tablespoons sesame seeds (optional)
1 teaspoon ground ginger
dash of coriander
red wine to taste
1 small chili pepper or pinch of cayenne pepper (optional)

Turkish *Charoset*

1/2 cup finely chopped pitted dates
1/2 cup finely chopped figs
1/2 cup finely chopped dried apricots
1/2 cup finely chopped walnuts or almonds
1 apple, peeled, cored, and grated

Moroccan *Charoset*

1 cup chopped dates
1 cup chopped walnuts
sweet red wine to taste

Greek *Charoset*

1/2 cup black currants, finely chopped
1/2 cup raisins, finely chopped
1/2 cup almonds or pine nuts, finely chopped
1/2 cup dates, finely chopped
2 tablespoons honey (optional)
sweet red wine to taste

Extra Holiday How-To
Baking *Hamantaschen*
הָמָן־טַאשֶׁן

The source:

The commandments in the Scroll of Esther to observe Purim as a day of feasting and gladness (Esther 9:22) gave rise to the creation of many delicacies for this festival. The traditions of having a Purim *seudah* (meal) and *mishlo'ach manot* (sending gifts of food) resulted in the introduction of many new Purim delicacies. One of the most popular is *hamantaschen,* baked dough filled with poppy seeds. Because of the association of this pastry with Purim, its original name, *mohntaschen,* from the German *mohn* (poppy seed) and *taschen* (pockets), was revised to *hamantaschen,* recalling Haman, the enemy of the Jews in the Persian empire.

What you need to know:

1. Some people have suggested that the three-cornered shape of the *hamantaschen* is meant to recall the distinctive hat worn by Haman as prime minister of Persia.

2. In recent years, many new kinds of *hamantaschen* fillings have been introduced. These include prunes, cherries, and even cream cheese and chocolate chips (our favorite)!

3. There are many different recipes for baking *hamantaschen.* Here is one of our favorites:

1 pound vegetable shortening
5 cups flour
1 teaspoon salt
1 cup pineapple juice
1/2 cup sugar
Mix and refrigerate roll of sugared flour. Cut and fill. Bake at 400 degrees for 20–25 minutes.

Cream Cheese Filling
3/4 cup brown sugar

3 ounces cream cheese
1/2 teaspoon salt (may be omitted)
1 teaspoon vanilla
1/2 cup nuts, chocolate chips (our favorite), coconut, or peanut brittle.
Best if chilled. Mix all ingredients. Fill dough and bake.

Things to remember:

1. It is a good idea to give yourself plenty of time when preparing the *hamantaschen* for your food baskets as well as your Purim meal.

2. Be as creative as possible, and try to create your own original *hamantaschen* recipe.

3. Another favorite traditional Purim dish is *kreplach*, triangular pieces of dough filled with chopped meat. Purim shares the eating of *kreplach* with the evening of the Day of Atonement; meat is often viewed as a symbol of God's stern judgment.

4. In some places it is also customary to eat *nahit*, cooked chickpeas. This vegetarian dish recalls Esther's diet while she lived in the court of Ahasuerus. According to tradition, she ate vegetables in order not to violate the Jewish dietary laws.

Key words and phrases:

Hamantaschen. הָמָן־טַאשֶׁן/הָמָנטַאשֶׁן Triangular Purim pastries.

Mishlo'ach manot. מִשְׁלֹחַ מָנוֹת Sending of gifts, often food baskets, to one's friends and the needy.

Oznai Haman. אָזְנֵי הָמָן Literally, "Haman's ears." Hebrew name for *hamantaschen.*

Purim seudah. סְעוּדַת פּוּרִים Purim feast, characterized by frivolity and merrymaking.

If you want to know more:

Philip Goodman, *The Purim Anthology* (Philadelphia, 1973).

Ronald H. Isaacs and Kerry M. Olitzky, *Sacred Celebrations: A Jewish Holiday Handbook* (Hoboken, NJ, 1994).

Extra Holiday How-To
Making *Etrog* Jam
רִבָּה שֶׁל אֶתְרוֹג

The source:

"On the first day, you shall take the fruit of the hadar tree, branches of the palm tree, boughs of leafy trees, and willows of the brook" (Leviticus 23:40).

What you need to know:

The *etrog* is one of the four species that are part of the ritual for Sukkot. At the end of the holiday it can be used to make jam.

Ingredients
1 *etrog*
2 lemons
1 cup preserving sugar

1. Slice the fruit into thin cross-sections. Remove the pits and white membranes as far as possible.

2. Place the fruit into a bowl of tepid water for three days. Change the water daily. (This removes some of the bitterness.) On the third day, taste the water. If it is not acidic, the fruit is ready.

3. Dry the fruit with a paper towel. (Water will retard the set of the jam.)

4. Add enough water to the sugar to cover. Then cook it over a low heat. Be careful not to burn the sugar (or yourself). Add the softened lemon slices and several teaspoons of water. When the sugar is syrupy, add the *etrog*. Continue cooking until the *etrog* gets glossy.

5. Test the jam for a set with a sugar thermometer (about 220°F. or 104°C.). As an alternative, take a few small plates; put them in the freezer for a few minutes with a spoonful of jam on each plate. (Remember to take the

368

jam off the stove while you are testing.) If the jam puckers and has formed a thin skin when you push it with a spoon, then it is ready. If not, cook it for a few more minutes.

6. Let the jam cool. Then place it in a jar. It should keep for up to two years.

Things to remember:

1. Try to use an *etrog* that is just underripe.

2. Use preserving sugar, not brown or white sugar.

Key words and phrases:

Etrog. אֶתְרוֹג Citron.
Pitam. פִּטָם Stemlike protrusion on the bottom of the *etrog*.

If you want to know more:

Ronald H. Isaacs and Kerry M. Olitzky, *Sacred Celebrations* (Hoboken, NJ, 1994).

Extra Holiday How-To
Sending *Mishlo'ach Manot*
מִשְׁלֹחַ מָנוֹת

The source:

"On those days, the Jews rested from their enemies, the month was turned from sorrow to gladness, from mourning to joy. Thus, they should make them days of feasting and exhilaration, sending portions to one another and gifts to the poor" (Esther 9:22).

What you need to know:

1. Send money to the poor, and food, pastries, and something to drink to friends, as an expression of joy over Esther's victory and the survival of the Jewish people.

2. There is no need to be fancy or expensive. Send raisins, fruits, and nuts. You may also want to include something about celebrating Purim for your friends. You can include a *gragger* (noisemaker).

3. It's nice to deliver the goodies yourself or leave them on neighbors' doorsteps so that they can find them when they return home.

Things to remember:

1. Send two food items for *mishlo'ach manot* to at least one person and give *tzedakah* to the poor (*matanot la'evyonim*). Try to give your *tzedakah* on Purim itself. If this is not possible, do so later. Make it a family *mitzvah*. Decide where you want the money to go and then deliver it yourself. With all the homeless and hungry on the streets of our cities, it shouldn't be too difficult to deliver the *tzedakah* directly to people in need.

2. Make sure to include pastries relevant to the festival of Purim, like *hamantaschen*.

Key words and phrases:

Matanot la'evyonim. מַתָּנוֹת לָאֶבְיוֹנִים Gifts to the poor, mandated as part of the observance of Purim.

Mishlo'ach manot. מִשְׁלֹחַ מָנוֹת The sending of portions, often referred to as *shalach manos* by Ashkenazim and Yiddish speakers.

If you want to know more:

Ronald Isaacs and Kerry Olitzky, *Sacred Celebrations: A Jewish Holiday Handbook* (Hoboken, NJ, 1994).

More particulars:

Some congregations use *mishloach manot* baskets as fund-raisers for sisterhood, brotherhood (men's club), or youth groups.

Extra Holiday How-To
Making Cheese Blintzes
בְּלִינְצִים

The source:

Two sources have been suggested as the primary explanation for eating dairy products on Shavuot: (1) "Your lips, O my bride, drop honey; honey and milk are under your tongue" (Song of Songs 4:11). This is an allusion to the sweetness of Torah. Thus, children traditionally begin learning on Shavuot with honey dripped on the pages of text. (2) "Bring to Adonai's house the choicest first fruits. You shall not seethe a kid in its mother's milk" (Exodus 23:19). The juxtaposition of these texts suggests a relationship between Shavuot and dairy.

What you need to know:

Cheese blintzes are a traditional Shavuot food. Here is how to make them:

Batter
3 eggs (or egg substitutes for the cholesterol conscious)
2 tablespoons oil, plus additional oil for frying (not for the fat-free dieter)
1-1/4 cups milk (you can use skim)
1-1/2 tablespoons sugar
dash of salt
1. In a large bowl, mix together eggs, oil, and milk.
2. Stir in the flour, sugar, and salt.
3. In a 7-inch frying pan, heat a very small amount of oil.
4. Pour in just enough batter to cover the bottom of the pan lightly.
5. Fry for 1 minute, until the bottom of the blintze shell is light brown.
6. Remove the blintze from the pan and place it on a paper towel to drain.
7. Repeat frying process until all of the batter is used. This recipe makes about 12 blintzes.

Filling

1 pound dry cottage cheese
1/4 cup sour cream
1 egg white, beaten
dash of cinnamon
1/2 teaspoon vanilla flavoring

1. In a large bowl, mix filling ingredients together.
2. Place a tablespoon of filling in the center of each blintze (on the brown side, since the other side will become brown when the blintzes are baked.
3. Wrap the blintze around the filling like a jelly roll, then fold sides in so that the filling can't fall out.
4. Bake on a greased cookie sheet in a preheated oven at 350° F. for 30 minutes.
5. Serve hot with sour cream and jam or let cool, freeze, then reheat and serve at a later time.

Things to remember:

1. Another explanation for the association of cheese blintzes with Shavuot relates to the fact that it was on Shavuot that the Torah was given to Israel. Normally so auspicious an event would have been celebrated with a meat meal, but on the first Shavuot this was not possible, because the Israelites had not previously known the dietary laws and therefore had no supply of kosher meat readily available. Thus they had to make do with dairy.

2. Other traditional Shavuot foods include kreplach, because the three sides of this triangular-shaped food symbolize the triad of Torah-God-Israel. Cheesecake is also a popular item on this occasion. Many people also use dairy foods for their first meal after the Yom Kippur fast.

If you want to know more:

Hanna Goodman, *Jewish Cooking from Around the World* (Philadelphia, 1969).

More particulars:

Some suggest that two cheese blintzes represent the two tablets of the Ten Commandments. Two *challot* are used during Shavuot for the same reason.

Extra Holiday How-To
Making a Tu Bishevat *Seder*
סֵדֶר לְט״וּ בִּשְׁבָט

The source:

Sixteenth-century Kabbalists gathered on the eve of Tu Bishevat for singing, dancing, and the tasting of fruits and wines.

What you need to know:

1. To prepare for the Tu Bishevat *seder,* you will need the following:

> a. Red and white wine or grape juice, enough to serve each person four cups.
>
> b. *Seder* fruit plates. You will need three platters of fruits.
>
> Choose at least five with an inedible shell: tangerine, kiwi, walnut, pomegranate, pistachio, grapefruit, coconut, almond, orange.
>
> Choose at least five fruits with an inedible seed: peach, avocado, olive, apricot, plum, date, cherry, mango.
>
> Choose at least five fruits which are completely edible: grape, fig, apple, raisin, cranberry, pear, carob.
>
> These fruits should be cut into pieces in advance of the *seder.*

2. Serve four cups of wine during the Tu Bishevat *seder.* For the first cup, use entirely white wine or juice, which symbolizes the winter. The second cup is a mixture of white wine and a bit of red wine, symbolic of the thawing earth. The third cup has red wine with a bit of white wine, reflecting the flowers blooming in the summer. The fourth and last cup uses all red wine, suggesting the beginning of autumn.

3. Recite the blessing before drinking each cup:

בָּרוּךְ אַתָּה יהוה אֱלֹהֵינוּ מֶלֶךְ הָעוֹלָם, בּוֹרֵא פְּרִי הַגֶּפֶן:

Baruch atah Adonai elohaynu melech ha'olam borei p'ri ha'gafen.

Praised are You, Adonai our God, Sovereign of the Universe, who creates the fruit of the vine.

Now all drink the wine.

4. After each cup of wine, recite the blessing, then taste the fruit.

בָּרוּךְ אַתָּה יהוה אֱלֹהֵינוּ מֶלֶךְ הָעוֹלָם, בּוֹרֵא פְּרִי הָעֵץ:

Baruch atah Adonai elohaynu melech ha'olam borei p'ri ha'etz.

Praised are You, Adonai our God, Sovereign of the Universe, who creates the fruit of trees.

Now share the fruit.

5. Sometime during the *seder* you may want to invite someone to ask Four Questions about the *seder*. All of these questions should focus on the theme of trees and fruit, growth and ecology. For example, someone might ask: On all of the other days of the year we rarely mention the importance of trees and fruit. Why on this day do we think of fruit and trees?

6. Each participant needs a Tu Bishevat Haggadah. There are a variety of different *seder* booklets designed for Tu Bishevat that will assist you in conducting your own *seder*. Feel free to make your own.

Things to remember:

1. There is a tradition which suggests that trees are judged by God on Tu Bishevat just as all people are judged on Rosh Hashanah. That is why Tu Bishevat is also called the New Year for Trees.

2. In Israel, Tu Bishevat is an official holiday, involving elaborate parades, songs, and general merriment.

3. The organization that works to reforest Israel is the Jewish National Fund (JNF).

4. In addition to having a Tu Bishevat *seder,* you may want to consider an activity such as maple sugar sapping. (Check with your community park service to see whether this is permitted.)

5. There is a custom of giving multiples of 91 cents to various charities on Tu Bishevat. In gematria, 91 is the numerical equivalent for the Hebrew word for "tree" (*ilan*).

Key words and phrases:

Keren Kayemet L'Yisrael. קֶרֶן קַיֶּמֶת לְיִשְׂרָאֵל Hebrew name of the Jewish National Fund.

Rosh Hashanah La'ilanot. רֹאשׁ הַשָּׁנָה לָאִילָנוֹת New Year for Trees; another name for Tu Bishevat.

If you want to know more:

Harlene Winnick Appelman et al., *A Seder for Tu Bishevat* (Baltimore, 1984).

Adam Fisher, *Seder Tu Bishevat: The Festival of Trees* (New York, 1989).

Voice of the Trees. This is the newspaper of Shomrei Adamah, a Jewish organization devoted to ecology and the environment. Write them at Church Road and Greenwood Avenue, Wyncote, PA 19095, for information.

More particulars:

Here are several Tu Bishevat table songs to sing at your Tu Bishevat *seder.*

1. *Hashkediya porachat*
V'shemesh paz zorachat
Tziporim merosh kol gag
M'vasrot et bo hechag
Tu Bishevat higiyah Chag ha'ilanot (2)

The almond tree is growing
A golden sun is glowing
Birds sing out in joyous glee
From every roof and every tree.
Tu Bishevat is here
The Jewish Arbor Day
Hail the trees' New Year
Happy holiday.

2. *Tzaddik katamar yifrach yifrach*
K'erez ba'levanon yisgeh
Shetulim bevayt Hashem.

Righteous people will grow mightly like the palm and
flourish like the cedars of Lebanon.

3. *Atzuy zaytim omdim la la la . . .*

The olive trees are standing.

4. *Eytz chayyim hee la'machazikim bah ve'tomcheha
me'ushar*
Deracheha darchay no'am ve'chol netivoteha shalom.
*Hasheevaynu Adonai eylecha ve'nashuvah chadesh ya-
maynu ke'kedem.*

It is a tree of life to those who hold fast to it, and
those who uphold it are happy. Its ways are ways of
pleasantness and all its paths turn to peace. Return
us to You, O God, and we shall return. Renew our
days as of old.

5. *Eytz chayyim hee la'machazikim bah ve'tomcheha
me'ushar. Deracheha darchay no'am ve'chol netivoteha
shalom.*

It is a tree of life to those who hold fast to it, and
those who uphold it are happy. Its ways are ways of
pleasantness and all its paths turn to peace. Shalom

Extra Holiday How-to
Dipping Apples in Honey (and Not Getting Stuck)
תַּפּוּחִים

The source:

On Rosh Hashanah, people customarily eat apples dipped in honey. This custom symbolically expresses the hope that there will be many sweet times in the coming year. We will all learn ways of being sweeter in everything we say and do (*Turei Zahav,* chap. 583).

What you need to know:

1. It is customary to eat apples and honey on the eve of Rosh Hashanah before the festive meal.

2. Take apples, cut them into pieces, and give a piece to each member of the family. Dip the apples into the honey, then say the following blessings before eating the apples and honey.

יְהִי רָצוֹן מִלְּפָנֶיךָ יְיָ אֱלֹהֵינוּ וֵאלֹהֵי אֲבוֹתֵינוּ שֶׁתְּחַדֵּשׁ עָלֵינוּ שָׁנָה טוֹבָה וּמְתוּקָה.

Yehi ratzon milfanecha Adonai elohaynu vaylohay avotenu she-te-cha-desh alaynu shanah tova u'metukah.

May it be Your will, Adonai our God, that You renew for us a good and sweet year.

בָּרוּךְ אַתָּה יהוה אֱלֹהֵינוּ מֶלֶךְ הָעוֹלָם, בּוֹרֵא פְּרִי הָעֵץ:

Baruch atah Adonai elohaynu melech ha'olam boray p'ri ha'etz.

Praised are You, Adonai, our God, Sovereign of the Universe, who creates the fruit of the tree.

Things to remember:

1. Many families go apple picking before the festival of Rosh Hashanah. Some wait for the week of Sukkot. It is a nice idea to pick extra apples and give them to a local food bank.

2. There are many biblical references to honey, one of the sweetest products of nature. The Land of Israel is called the land of milk and honey in the Bible (Exodus 3:8). Bees are still abundant even in the remote parts of Israel's desert, where they deposit their honey in the crevices of rocks or in hollow trees. Honey was not to be used in sacrifices (Leviticus 2:11), but the first fruits of honey, as of other kinds of produce, were to be presented to God, for the use by God's priests. Here are some of the other biblical references to honey:

> a. "On that day I lifted My hand to them, to bring them out of Egypt into a land flowing with milk and honey" (Ezekiel 20:6).
> b. "And the House of Israel called its name manna, and it was like coriander seed, white. Its taste was like wafers made with honey" (Exodus 16:31).
> c. "Then Jonathan said, 'How my eyes are brightened, because I have tasted a little of this honey'" (I Samuel 14:29).
> d. "More to be desired are the ordinances of God than much fine gold, sweeter also than honey and the honeycomb" (Psalm 19:10).
> e. "My child, eat honey, for it is good, and the honeycomb is sweet to your taste" (Proverbs 24:13).

Key words and phrases:

D'vash. דְּבַשׁ Honey.
Shanah tovah. שָׁנָה טוֹבָה Happy New Year.

If you want to know more:

Philip Goodman, *The Rosh Hashanah Anthology* (Philadelphia, 1973).
Arthur I. Waskow, *Seasons of Our Joy* (New York, 1982).

Life-Cycle Checklists

BRIT MILAH AND NAMING PLANS (including *Simchat Bat*)

This list will help you to keep track of the organization for your *Brit Milah* and naming plans.

___Date and time of birth _____

___Date and time of *Brit Milah* _____

___Date and time of naming ceremony _____

___Name of *mohel/mohelet* or Jewish physician _____

___Officiating clergy _____

___Hebrew/Jewish name for our child _____

___We have notified all of our guests.

___We have selected for our twinning ceremony.

___The *kvater* is _____

___The *kvaterin* is _____

___The *sandek* is _____

___We have arranged for a *shalom zachor/nekevah* which will take place at _____.

___We have arranged for the *seudat mitzvah*.

___Our participants at the *seudat mitzvah* will be _____to lead *Hamotzi* over the bread and _____to lead the *Birkat Hamazon* (grace after the meal).

PIDYON HABEN/HABAT

This list will help you to keep track of your plans for organizing a *Pidyon Haben/Habat*.

___Date and time of *Pidyon Haben/Habat* _____

___Name of officiating clergy _____

___Name of *kohen* _____

___We have contacted all of our guests.

___We have obtained five silver shekels (silver dollars).

___We have arranged for the *seudat mitzvah*.

___*Kiddush* (blessing over the wine) will be recited by ___

___*Hamotzi* (blessings over the bread) will be said by ____

___*Birkat Hamazon* (grace after the meal) will be led by _

BAR/BAT MITZVAH

This list will help you to keep track of the organization for your Bar/Bat Mitzvah.

___Hebrew/English date of Bar/Bat Mitzvah _____

___Names(s) of Torah portion and Haftarah _____

___I have sent out invitations
___Name of person with whom twinning will take place _
___Name of florist _____
___Name of photographer _____
___Name of caterer _____
___We have selected our participants in the service and reminded those that will chant blessings to review them. They are:
Ark Openers and Closers
(English Names) _____
(Hebrew Names) _____
Aliyot:
___ 1. English and Hebrew name: _____
___ 2. English and Hebrew name: _____
___ 3. English and Hebrew name: _____
___ 4. English and Hebrew name: _____
___ 5. English and Hebrew name: _____
___ 6. English and Hebrew name: _____
___ 7. English and Hebrew name: _____
___ 8. (*Maftir*) Bar/Bat Mitzvah: English and Hebrew name: _____
___*Hagbahah* (lift Torah): English and Hebrew name: ___
___*Gelilah* (dress Torah): English and Hebrew name: ___
Other parts in service: Name _____ Part _____
___Name of *Kiddush* chanter _____
___Name of person leading *Hamotzi* _____
___Name of person leading *Birkat Hamazon* (grace after the meal) _____
___List of new *mitzvot* that Bar/Bat Mitzvah will consider doing the first year:
1. _____
2. _____
3. _____
4. _____
5. _____
___*Tzedakah* organizations for contributions: _____
_____

A JEWISH WEDDING
This list will help you to keep track of your wedding plans:
___Wedding date _____
___Officiants _____

___Place of wedding _____
___Place of reception _____
___Our meeting with the rabbi/cantor will take place on
___We have selected our wedding ring(s).
___We have ordered our wedding invitations.
___We have selected our *chuppah*.
___We have selected our *ketubah*.
___Our two witnesses will be _____
___Our attendants will be: Best man_____
       Maid/Matron of honor _____
___Our other attendants in our wedding procession are:
___We have chosen these musical selections: _____
_____
___We have taken our blood tests and applied for the civil license.
___We have arranged for an *aufruf.*
___We have arranged for an organization that will use food left over from the reception _____.
___In honor of our wedding, we will contribute *tzedakah* to these organizations:

_____

CLERGY CARD FOR FUNERAL
___English/Hebrew name of deceased _____
___English/Hebrew date of death _____
___Officiating clergyperson _____
___Name and location of cemetery _____
___Location of plot in cemetery _____
___Names of pallbearers

_____
_____
_____
_____
_____
_____

___Contact person for the cemetery _____
___Funeral Home _____
___Contact person at the funeral home _____
___Contact person for the Chevra Kaddisha _____

SHABBAT *ALIYOT*

PARASHAT _____ DATE _____

ALIYOT—ENGLISH / HEBREW /
FATHER (H) / MOTHER (H)

KOHEN I: _____ _____
_____ _____

LEVI II: _____ _____
_____ _____

III: _____ _____
_____ _____

IV: _____ _____
_____ _____

V: _____ _____
_____ _____

VI: _____ _____
_____ _____

VII: _____ _____
_____ _____

MAFTIR: _____ _____
_____ _____

LIFT: _____ _____
_____ _____

TIE: _____ _____
_____ _____

ARK OPENING BEFORE BARCHU
1. _____
2. _____

CURTAIN OPENING BEGINNING OF TORAH SER-
VICE
1. _____
2. _____

TAKE TORAH FROM ARK
1. _____
2. _____

CURTAIN OPENING END OF TORAH SERVICE
1. _____
2. _____

REPLACE TORAH IN ARK
1. _____

2. _____

CLOSE ARK AFTER MOURNER'S KADDISH

1. _____
2. _____

B'NAI MITZVAH NAME _____

NOTES: _____
_____
_____

The Third "How to" Handbook for Jewish Living

Interpret Dreams

The source:

Babylonian Talmud, *Berakhot* 56b–57b.

What you need to know:

1. Almost all people dream. Dreams are a necessary outlet for the mind.

2. Professional dream interpreters were prominent in ancient Mesopotamia and Egypt, and manuals since that time have revealed hundreds of dream interpretations.

3. Dream interpretation has been a major component of psychoanalysis since that discipline was born. Freud and his disciples spent a great deal of time applying their knowledge to the field of dream study.

4. While many believe that the importance of dreams was neglected until the advent of psychology, Jewish sources spoke of the meaning of dreams centuries ago. The Torah itself, in the stories of Joseph and Pharaoh, emphasizes that dreams are a matter to be dealt with seriously.

5. The Bible often views dreams as signs or omens. The book of Daniel is filled with them. Daniel gains his reputation as an interpreter of dreams for Nebuchadnezzar, the king of Babylon (Daniel 2). He interprets a second dream for the king (Daniel 3:31–5:30) and then wrestles with the meaning of his own dream (Daniel 7). Many Talmudic sages discussed dreams and taught specific doctrines about them. A variety of symbols that may present themselves in dreams are also discussed in rabbinic literature. Here are some basic teachings (taken from the Babylonian Talmud, *Berakhot* 56b–57b):

    i. If you see a reed in a dream, you may hope for wisdom.

    ii. If you dream of an ox that eats flesh, you will become rich.

iii. If you dream of riding on an ox, you will rise to greatness.

iv. If you see a donkey in a dream, you may hope for salvation.

v. If you see white grapes in a dream, that is a good sign.

vi. If you see an elephant in a dream, a miracle will occur.

vii. If you see wheat in a dream, you will see peace.

viii. If you see myrtle in your dream, you will have good luck with your property.

ix. If you see a goose in a dream, then you may hope for wisdom.

x. If you dream that you are entering a large town, your desire will be fulfilled.

xi. If you dream that you are sitting in a small boat, you will acquire a good name.

xii. If you dream that you go up on a roof, you will attain a high position.

Things to remember

"Neither a good dream nor a bad dream is wholly fulfilled" (Babylonian Talmud, *Berakhot* 55a).

Key words and phrases:

Chalom: Dream

If you want to know more:

Solomon ben Almoli, *Dream Interpretations from Classical Jewish Sources*. Translated and annotated by Yaakov Elman. Hoboken, NJ: KTAV Publishing House, 1996.

Ronald Isaacs, *Divination, Magic and Healing: The Book of Jewish Folklore*. Northvale, NJ: Jason Aronson, 1998.

Ameliorate a Bad Dream

The source:

Babylonian Talmud, *Ta'anit* 12b; *Berakhot* 55b.

What you need to know:

1. Many famous Talmudic teachers frequently discussed dreams and developed their own interpretations of them, as well as ways to deal with them.

2. Some of these teachers believed that a person's dreams were a direct result of his or her thoughts from the day that immediately preceded it.

3. Fasting became customary in rabbinic times when a person had a bad dream. (In Hebrew, this fast was called a *ta'anit chalom*.)

4. Giving *tzedakah* may also help, say the Sages.

5. The rabbinic sages suggested some verses to be recited upon awakening from a bad dream. For instance, when Samuel the sage had a bad dream, he used to say: "The dreams speak falsely" (Zechariah 10:2). They also instituted a special prayer that was supposed to nullify a dream. This was called *hatavat chalom*. In some synagogues, the nullification prayer is said by congregants as they are being blessed by the descendants of the priests (in *Birkat HaKohanim* during the *Amidah*). This time was chosen in the liturgy because this portion of prayer is a time of general good will. This is the nullification prayer text:

If one has seen a dream and does not remember what one saw, let that person stand before the priests at the time when they spread out their hands and say as follows: "Sovereign of the Universe, I am Yours and my dreams are Yours. I have dreamt a dream and I do not know what it is. Whether I have dreamt about myself or my companions have dreamt about me, or I have dreamt about others, if they are good dreams, confirm them and reinforce them like the dreams of Joseph. If they require a remedy, heal them, as the waters of Marah were healed by Moses, our teacher, and as Miriam was healed of her leprosy, and Hezekiah of his sickness, and the waters of Jericho by Elisha. As you did turn the curse of the wicked Bilaam into a blessing, so turn all my dreams into something good for me."

One should conclude one's nullification prayer at the same time as the priests conclude their benediction, so that surrounding worshipers may answer "Amen" (may it be so). If one is unable to conclude the prayer at the same time as the priests, then, according to the Talmud, one should conclude by saying: "You who are majestic on high, who abides in might, You who are peace and Your name is peace, may it be Your will to bestow peace upon us" (Babylonian Talmud, *Berakhot* 55b)

5. The Talmud also prescribes a procedure for turning an evil dream into a good one. This procedure takes its lead from the number three. Three verses are recited, three instances of the dream are good, and so on. This procedure is suggested in the Talmud as follows:

Rabbi Huna ben Ammi said in the name of Rabbi Pedat, who heard it from Rabbi Yochanan: If a person has a dream which makes one sad, one should go and have it interpreted in the presence of three. Has not Rabbi Chisda said: A dream which is not interpreted is like a letter which is not read and therefore can do no harm? Say, rather, then, one should have a good construction given to it in the presence of three. Let one bring three and say to them: I have seen a good dream. And they will say to that one: Good it is and good may it be. May the All-Merciful turn it to good. Seven times may it be decreed from heaven that it should be good and may it be good. They should say three verses with the word *hafakh* (turn) and three with the word *padach* (redeem) and three with the word *shalom* (peace):

These three verses with the word "turn":

1. "You did **turn** for me my mourning into dancing. You did loosen my sackcloth and gird me with gladness" (Psalm 30:12).

2. "Then shall the virgin rejoice in the dance, and the young men and the old together. For I will **turn** mourn-

390

ing into joy and will comfort them and make them re-joice from their sorrow" (Jeremiah 31:13).

3. "Nevertheless, Adonai your God would not hearken unto Bilaam, but the Lord your God **turned** the curse into a blessing for you" (Deuteronomy 23:6).

These three verses with the word "redeem":

1. "God has **redeemed** my soul in peace, so that none can come near to me" (Psalm 55:19).

2. "And the **redeemed** of Adonai shall return and come with singing to Zion, and sorrow and sighing shall flee away" (Isaiah 35:10).

3. "The people said to Saul: Shall Jonathan die, who has wrought this great salvation in Israel? . . . So the people **redeemed** Jonathan that he died not" (I Samuel 14:45).

These three verses with the word "peace":

1. "'**Peace**, peace to the one who is far and to the one who is near,' says God, who creates the fruits of the lips; and I will heal that person" (Isaiah 57:19).

2. "Then the spirit clothed Amasai, who was chief of the captains: Yours are we, David, and on your side, you, son of Yishai: **Peace**, peace be unto you and peace be your helpers, for your God helps you" (I Chronicles, 12:19).

3. "Thus you shall say: All hail, and **peace** be both to you and peace be to your house, and peace be to all that you have" (I Samuel 25:6).

Things to remember:

The Talmudic sages were known to provide a variety of instructions concerning what to do after dreaming a particular kind of dream. The Talmud also presents a long list of symbols that might be found in a dream and the things that these symbols represent. Most of these are found in the Babylonian Talmud, *Berakhot* 56b–57b. For further details, see the section entitled "Interpreting Dreams" in this "How to" handbook.

Key words and phrases:

Chalom: Dream
Hatavat Chalom: Prayer for nullifying a dream
Ta'anit Chalom: Dream fast

If you want to know more:

Solomon ben Almoli, *Dream Interpretations from Classical Jew-*
    ·ish Sources. Translated and annotated by Yaakov El-
    man. Hoboken, NJ: KTAV Publishing Co., 1996.
Shmuel Boteach, *Dreams*. Brooklyn: B.P., 1991.

Add Meaning to the Bar/Bat Mitzvah Party

The source:

There is no classic source for this "How to".

What you need to know:

1. The festive meal that follows the ceremony of bar or bat mitzvah is an opportunity for family and friends to celebrate the joy (*simcha*) of the occasion. The meal after the religious ceremony is called a *seudat mitzvah* (religious meal). It may take some effort to create a context in which the party takes on an aura of sanctity.

2. Since many families have already developed ways that invest the party with added sanctity, here are some simple ideas that work:

   i. Instead of using flowers as centerpieces, use Jewish books as your table decorations. Then donate the books to your local synagogue library or community center.

   ii. With each place card, include information about MAZON: A Jewish Response to Hunger. Encourage your guests to contribute to it.

   iii. In advance, arrange to give leftover food to a local food bank.

   iv. Instead of giving souvenir party favors to the guests, plant trees in Israel in their honor and give out the tree certificates as mementoes.

   v. Ask guests to bring canned food, clothing, or toys to the party for distribution to the needy.

   vi. Give a percentage of the total cost of your Bar/Bat Mitzvah celebration to a hunger relief organization.

   vii. Be sure to begin your meal with the *hamotzi*, the blessing over the bread.

   viii. Be sure to conclude your meal with the *birkat hamazon*, the blessing after the meal. The text for both *hamotzi* and *birkat hamazon* can be printed

in booklets with explanations and guidelines so that people can continue to adopt the practices as part of their home routine.

ix. Instead of a D.J. or band, consider Israeli dancing and Jewish music to help further invest the party with deeper Jewish feeling. As an alternative, use these when the band or D.J. takes a break.

Things to remember:

In 1595 in Cracow, Poland, the rabbinic authorities levied a communal tax on bar mitzvah feasts so as to keep them within the bounds of good taste. Judaism has always urged people to use moderation in their celebrations to ensure that the spiritual significance of the event is not lost.

Key words and phrases:

Birkat Hamazon: Blessing after the meal
Hamotzi: Blessing over the bread
Seudat Mitzvah: Religious meal

If you want to know more:

Ronald H. Isaacs, *Reaching for Sinai: A Practical Handbook for Bar/Bat Mitzvah and Family*. Hoboken, NJ: KTAV Publishing House, Inc., 1999.
Jeffrey K. Salkin, *Putting God on the Guest List*. Woodstock, VT: Jewish Lights Publishing, 1992.

Prepare a Meaningful Passover Family *Seder*

The source:

Mishnah, *Pesachim* 10.

What you need to know:

1. It is a tradition on the first two nights of Passover to have a family gathering and recite the narrative of Passover using the *Haggadah*. This gathering is known as the Passover *seder*. As a result, more Jews celebrate the Passover *seder* in one form or another than any other holiday observance, including Hanukkah.

2. Make the *seder* interactive. Even if the gathering is all adult, use props, games, and engaging questions. Keep the *seder* lively.

3. Here are some suggestions to help lift up the *seder*.

   i. **Karpas**: Although it is early evening, go outside. Find a new spring blossom and recite the special blessing when you see a blossom or flower for the first time: "Praised are You, Adonai, Sovereign of the universe, who has not left the world lacking in anything and has created in it good trees to give pleasure to people." While this blessing can be recited at various times of the year (during the spring or late winter), it is only recited once a year according to tradition.

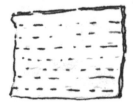

   ii. **Yachatz**: Place the afikoman in a bag and throw it over your shoulder. Have participants rise and follow the leader as he or she carries the afikoman around the *seder* table in a reenactment of the Exodus.

   iii. **Ma Nishtana**: Ask additional contemporary questions during the Ma Nishtana part of the *seder*. For example, "Why must the proliferation of nuclear weapons continue?" or "Why is there homelessness when our society is so wealthy?"

iv. **Maggid**: An interesting custom is to have the leader or one of the participants leave the room and return with a napkin containing the afikoman slung over one's shoulder. Everyone at the table then asks: "Who are you?" The answer from the person acting out the Exodus: "A Jew." The dialogue continues: "Where do you come from?" "From Egypt." "What did you do there?" "I was a slave." How many years did it take for you to come here?" "Forty years." Let the dialogue continue.

v. **Ten Plagues**: Ask the participants to list ten contemporary plagues which "plague" us today. In addition, prepare simulations for each of the ten plagues in advance. For example: for blood, use magic trick blood that changes water to blood; for frogs, use rubber frogs; for lice, use plastic bugs. You get the idea. As the plagues are read, have *seder* participants open the bags and show the "plague."

vi. **Afikoman**: Play the Afikoman game. Participants sing a Passover song while the "searcher" looks for the afikoman. As the searcher gets closer to the afikoman, those at the Seder table sing the song more loudly. As the searcher moves further away from the afikoman, the participants sing more softly.

vii. **Elijah the Prophet**: Have a participant leave in advance and re-enter, dressed as Elijah. Then give participants a chance to ask Elijah questions about himself, his life and the purpose of his visit.

viii. **Sing Chad Gadya:** Take each character in the story in Chad Gadya and as you sing the song and the character or object is about to be sung, create a sound for the character. For example, when the cat is mentioned, someone says "meow." When the dog is mentioned someone says "bow wow." It may sound childish, but take it from us, it is a lot of fun with families and friends.

Things to remember:

The *Haggadah* is not just a book of stories from the distant past. It is a living record of Jewish history which we add to each year as we participate in the *seder*. Thus, we are reminded during the *seder* that we must feel as if we were in Egypt ourselves and were personally freed. Invite participants to talk about what it was like when they were slaves in Egypt. Have them also share one of the first things that they would have done once they were liberated.

Key words and phrases:

Haggadah: Book read at the *seder* that contains the narrative of the Israelite journey from slavery into freedom
Seder: Passover meal

If you want to know more:

Philip Goodman, *The Passover Anthology*. Philadelphia: Jewish Publication Society, 1961.

Ronald Isaacs, *Every Person's Guide to Passover*. Northvale, NJ: Jason Aronson, 1999.

Ben Kamin, *Think Passover*. New York: Dutton, 1997.

Joy Leavitt and Michael Strassfeld, *A Night of Questions*. Philadelphia: Reconstructionist Press, 2000.

Rachel Musleah, *Why on This Night: A Passover Haggadah for Family Celebration*. New York: Aladdin Paperbacks/Simon & Schuster, 2000.

Kerry M. Olitzky and Ronald H. Isaacs, *The Discovery Haggadah*. Hoboken, NJ: KTAV Publishing, 1992.

Shoshana Silberman, *In Every Generation: A Family Haggadah*. Rockville, MD: Kar-Ben Copies, 1987.

A Survivor's Haggadah. Philadelphia: Jewish Publication Society, 2000.

Noam Zion and David Dishon, *A Different Night*. Jerusalem: Shalom Hartman Institute, 1997.

Celebrate Lag B'Omer

The source:

Leviticus 23:15–16: "You shall count from the day after [the first day of] Passover, when an *omer* of grain is brought as an offering, seven complete weeks".

What you need to know:

1. Lag B'Omer, literally the "33rd day of the Omer" occurs on the 18th day of Iyar. It serves as a break in the semi-mourning *sefirah* days between Passover and Shavuot.

2. Many synagogues hold picnics and outings on Lag B'Omer, with food, music, dance, sporting events (often in the form of a competitive Maccabiah), and other festivities. Some synagogues hold bonfires and cookouts on Lag B'Omer, which often include Israeli singing and dancing. If your synagogue does not have a Lag B'Omer program, be the first to start one.

3. Use the occasion to go on a family outing or picnic.

4. Get together with several families and make a campfire which includes good eating and singing.

5. Each night, before the counting of the omer (which begins on the second evening of Passover), take a nonperishable grain product and place it in a box. On Lag B'Omer, take all of the grain products to a local food pantry as your way of helping the hungry.

More particulars

Lag B'Omer is not a major holiday. It is not mentioned in the Bible and there are no specific prayers associated with it. However, there are several historical events that have been associated with the holiday. In Roman times, according to tradition, a great plague which ravaged the students of Rabbi Akiva came to an end on the 18th of Iyar, which is Lag B'Omer. Another tradition concerns Rabbi Shimon bar Yochai, a disciple of Rabbi Akiva, who was sentenced to death by the Romans for his participation in a revolt against them. He hid in a cave and did not come out until Lag B'Omer, when he learned that the enemy had been defeated. Because of the connection to Rabbi Akiva and his students, Lag B'Omer is also known as the Scholar's Festival, and Jewish children throughout the world hold special celebrations to mark the occasion.

Key words and phrases:

Lag: Hebrew letters (*lamed-gimel*) with the alpha-numeric value of 33

Omer: Measure of barley brought to the Temple on the second day of Passover. From that day we count every day until Shavuot to show the connection between the two holidays.

If you want to know more:

Ronald H. Isaacs and Kerry M. Olitzky, *Sacred Celebrations: A Jewish Holiday Handbook*. Hoboken, NJ: KTAV Publishing, 1994.

Kerry M. Olitzky and Rachel Smookler, *Anticipating Revelation: Counting Our Way Through the Desert: An Omer Calendar of the Spirit*. New York: Synagogue 2000, 1998.

Improve your *Derekh Eretz*

The source:

Various sections of *Shabbat, Pesachim, Baba Kamma,* and *Derekh Eretz Zuta* in the Babylonian Talmud; as well as the entire book of Proverbs and the mishnah of *Pirke Avot.*

What you need to know:

1. *Derekh Eretz* is a term referring to good behavior, courtesy, politeness, etiquette.

2. The rabbis were intent on setting rules of behavior to establish a good name for oneself and promote the welfare of society.

3. The Talmudic tractate called *Derekh Eretz Zuta* is a collection of ethical teachings containing rules of conduct. It urges gentleness, patience, respect for age, readiness to forgive. Many of its teachings are directed to scholars.

4. Following are ten guidelines for improving your *derekh eretz* as culled from various rabbinic sources:

    1. **Address people by their names**: "A person spoken to must first be addressed by one's name, just as God first called to Moses and then spoke to him." (Babylonian Talmud, *Yoma* 4b)
    2. **Do not suddenly enter a neighbor's home, but wait until someone opens the door:** "The answer 'yes' to a knock on the door does not mean enter but wait." (Babylonian Talmud, *Baba Kamma* 33a)
    3. **Be careful with your words:** "Rabbi Joshua ben Levi said: Never use an indecent expression, even if you have to use more words to complete the sentence." (Babylonian Talmud, *Pesachim* 3a)
    4. **Be humble**: "God is a friend of the person who is humble." (Zohar ii, 233b)
    5. **Be compassionate:** "The person who has compassion for other people will receive compassion from Heaven." (Babylonian Talmud, *Shabbat* 151b)
    6. **After offending, be sure to reconcile:** "Whoever

offends one's fellow human being, even if only with words, should endeavor to reconcile with that person." (Babylonian Talmud, *Yoma* 87a)

7. **When criticizing, do so in a *menschlikhkeit* way:** "A person who rebukes another should administer the rebuke privately, speak to the offender gently and tenderly, and point out that he is speaking only for the wrongdoer's own good. (Maimonides, *Mishneh Torah,* Laws Concerning Moral Dispositions and Ethical Conduct 6:7.)

8. **Don't meddle:** "Do not inject yourself into someone else's quarrel. It's none of your business!" (*Sefer Chasidim,* paragraph 73)

9. **Be a happy person:** "A happy heart is good medicine." (Proverbs 17:22)

10. **Be generous:** "One who says: what is mine is yours, and what is yours is yours, is saintly. (*Pirke Avot* 4:12)

11. **Overlook an insult:** A person should overlook an insult and not glorify himself by his fellow person's humiliation. (*Derekh Eretz Zuta* 6:4)

Things to remember:

Pirke Avot 5:19 sums up the ideal character in this way:

Whoever has these three attributes is of the disciples of our ancestor Abraham: a good eye, a humble mind, and a lowly spirit.

Key words and phrases:

Derekh Eretz: Proper behavior

If you want to know more:

Ronald H. Isaacs *The Jewish Book of Etiquette*. Northvale, NJ: Jason Aronson, 1998.

S. Wagschal, *Guide to Derech Eretz.* New York: Feldheim Publishers, 1993.

Kerry M. Olitzky and Rachel T. Sabath, *Striving Toward Virtue: A Contemporary Guide for Jewish Ethical Behavior.* Hoboken: NJ: KTAV Publishing, 1996.

Annul a Vow

The source:

Kitzur Shulchan Arukh, chapter 67 (section on vows and oaths).

Things to remember:

1. Judaism is a religion of values and concepts which is deeply invested in words. The power of words, when spoken in the form of a promise, is likened to a belief in God, in whose name that vow is made.

2. Jewish law requires that one must keep a commitment, for commitments are tied to one's belief in God and in God's presence in the world and in the lives of people.

3. Rabbinic advice generally states that one should avoid making vows.

4. When wanting to annul a vow one should consult one's local rabbi. According to the *Code of Jewish Law,* vows made to consecrate certain objects to God must be fulfilled. ("I will pay my vows to God" Psalm 116:18).

5. Following is a formula for annulling a vow, which is customarily done on the morning before Rosh Hashanah in the presence of three, who constitute an improvised court:

   I request annulment for the vows that I have made, whether they were matters relating to money, or to the body, or whether they were matters related to the soul.

   The three members of the "court" repeat three times: May everything be permitted you, may everything be forgiven you, may everything be allowed you.

   The petitioner concludes: Behold, I make formal declaration before you and I cancel from this time onward all vows and oaths. Regarding all of them, I regret them from this time and forever.

Things to remember:

1. The popular Hebrew expression *blee neder* (without vow), accompanying any statement concerning some future action contemplated by the speaker, is in keeping with the idea that we are expected to carry out everything we say, unless we specify that it is not a solemn promise but a mere thought expressed in words.

2. Before you think otherwise, please note that the annulment of vows does not pertain to vows that were made to other people, especially those involving financial obligations.

More particulars

The best-known statement about promises and vows occurs on the eve of Yom Kippur, the Day of Atonement, at the Kol Nidre Service. This declaration specifies that all the promises that one has made to God that have gone unfulfilled are null and void.

Key words and phrases:

Blee Neder: Without vow
Hatarat nedarim: The annulment of vows
Neder: Vow

If you want to know more:

Solomon Ganzfried, *Code of Jewish Law* (Abridged). New York: Hebrew Publishing Company, 1961.

Choose a Synagogue

The source:

"Let them make Me a sanctuary, so I may dwell among them" (Exodus 25:8).

What you need to know:

1. The Israelites built a tabernacle to God in the wilderness in Bible times. There they offered sacrifices to God.

2. It is likely that the synagogue originated after the destruction of the First Temple when those exiled to Babylonia would gather together for mutual strength and consolation. After the destruction of the Second Temple, the synagogue became the only method of worship.

3. Your local synagogue can be a most powerful ally in realizing the Jewish aspirations you have for yourself and your children.

4. Some synagogues, by virtue of the caliber of their rabbinic and lay leadership, set religious, moral, and ethical expectations for a congregation. Families should seek out a congregation that will help them maintain religious standards with which they are comfortable and grow spiritually.

3. When seeking out a synagogue, call the local Jewish Federation to get the names of ones in your area. You will want to begin by finding out whether there is a local synagogue that matches the branch of Judaism with which you feel most comfortable (e.g., Orthodox, Conservative, Reform, Reconstructionist).

4. Begin by making an appointment with the rabbi to determine the mission statement of the synagogue, the rabbi's philosophy, educational goals of the religious school, and so forth.

5. Meet with the synagogue's educational director to discuss the school's curriculum, its teaching staff, and teaching mission.

6. Ask to see copies of the Adult Education brochure and a brochure that details and describes all of the offerings and organizations within the synagogue (e.g., Sisterhood, Men's Club, Couples Club, and Youth groups).

7. Speak to families that are already members to determine their evaluation of the synagogue and its professional staff.

8. Try to attend a worship service and several programs to get a sense of the culture of the synagogue and its members.

Things to remember:

1. If you are newly married, many synagogues will offer you a free year's membership.

2. Synagogues will be prepared to make a special arrangement if you feel that paying full dues is an undue financial hardship. Also, they often have a special rate for families whose head of household is under 30 years of age.

3. No human institution has a longer continuous history than the synagogue, and none has done more for the uplifting of the human race.

Key words and phrases:

Bet Knesset: Synagogue
Shule: Yiddish for "synagogue"

If you want to know more:

Hayim Halevy Donin, *To Pray as a Jew*. New York: Basic Books, 1980.

Do *Ushpizin* for Sukkot

The source:

Zohar 5:103b.

What you need to know:

1. According to the tradition of kabbalah, these seven mystical guests visit the sukkah during the days of the festival of Sukkot: Abraham, Isaac, Jacob, Moses, Aaron, Joseph and David

2. Recently, some people have advocated inviting the matriarchs and other important women of the Bible and in Jewish life to also be *ushpizin* guests in the sukkah. The most popular list includes: Sarah, Rebecca, Rachel, Leah, Miriam, Abigail and Esther.

3. Invite the spiritual guest of each day before the meal, using this text as invitation: "Enter, exalted guests. Be seated, guests of faithfulness. Be seated in the shade of the Holy Blessed One. Worthy is our portion, worthy is the portion of Israel, as it is written: 'For God's portion is God's people, Jacob the lot of God's heritage.' For the sake of the unification of the Holy Blessed One and God's Presence, to unify the Name *Yud-Hei* with *Vav-Hei* in perfect unity through God who is hidden and inscrutable. May the pleasantness of my God be upon us. May God establish our handiwork for us."

4. Sephardic Jews set aside an ornate chair for the honored guest and recite: "This is the chair of the *ushpizin*."

5. Rabbi Zalman Schachter-Shalomi suggests that one treat each *ushpizin* as a real presence in the sukkah. Set aside a chair for him or her. Try to see the world through the eyes of an Abraham or Rachel. What idols would Abraham smash today? If you are with your family or some other group, ask each person to have a conversation with the *ushpizin*.

Things to remember:

1. Decorate the sukkah with a wall plaque which bears an inscription of the seven guests.

2. Some families have the custom of making up a list of their contemporary heroes, and each night having a different family member invite a new imaginary guest into the sukkah. This activity can be enhanced by having a family member "role play" a contemporary guest. Family members are asked to guess the identity of the contemporary guest.

More particulars

There is an interesting connection between the *ushpizin* and Sukkot. All of the *ushpizin* were wanderers or exiles. Abraham left his father's house to go to Israel. All three patriarchs wandered in the land of Canaan, dealing with the rulers from a position of disadvantage. Jacob fled to Laban. Joseph was exiled from his family. Moses fled Egypt for Midian. Together with Aaron, Moses led the people for forty years as they wandered in the desert. David fled from Saul. The theme of wandering and homelessness symbolized by the temporariness of the sukkah is reflected in the lives of the *ushpizin*.

Key words and phrases:

Ushpizin: Guests

If you want to know more:

Ronald Isaacs and Kerry M. Olitzky, *Sacred Celebrations: A Jewish Holiday Handbook*. Hoboken: NJ: KTAV Publishing, 1994.

Spiritualize Your Morning Waking Moments

The source

Code of Jewish Law (Abridged) Chapter 1: Rules of Conduct upon Arising in the Morning.

What you need to know:

1. According to Jewish tradition, an individual is encouraged to direct one's mind to God and to be aware of God's presence, as soon as he or she awakens in the morning.

2. The first traditional practice upon awakening is the recitation of the prayer for thankfulness to God, named by its opening words, *Modeh Ani* (I thank You). The text of this prayer can be found at the beginning of most prayer books. It is a response to the statement from the previous evening before sleep. At that time one gives one's soul into God's hands for safekeeping. At that time one says: "Into Your hand I commit my spirit." In the morning one expresses gratitude at receiving it back:

מוֹדֶה* אֲנִי לְפָנֶיךָ, מֶלֶךְ חַי וְקַיָּם, שֶׁהֶחֱזַרְתָּ בִּי נִשְׁמָתִי בְּחֶמְלָה רַבָּה אֱמוּנָתֶךָ.

*females say: מוֹדָה

Modeh ani lefanekha melekh chai v'kayam she-he-che-zarta bee nishmatee be'chemlah; rabbah emunatekha.

I am grateful to You, living and enduring Sovereign, for restoring my soul to me in compassion. You are faithful beyond measure.

3. The second practice required by traditional Jewish law is the ritual of washing of the hands. Jewish mystics explains this practice: When we sleep, the holy soul departs, and an unclean spirit rests in our body. When we awaken, this unclean spirit departs from

the entire body except the fingers, from which it does not pass until water is poured on them with this blessing:

בָּרוּךְ אַתָּה יְיָ אֱלֹהֵינוּ מֶלֶךְ הָעוֹלָם אֲשֶׁר קִדְּשָׁנוּ בְּמִצְוֹתָיו, וְצִוָּנוּ עַל נְטִילַת יָדָיִם:

Barukh ata Adonai Eloheinu melekh ha'olam asher kidshanu be'mitzvotav v'tzivanu al nitalat yadayim.

Praised are You, Adonai our God, Sovereign of the Universe, who adds holiness to our life and who has given us the *mitzvah* of washing our hands.

4. After handwashing it is a good idea to direct your mind to God and God's service through meditation, and to remind yourself of reverence for God. An excellent *kavanna* (sacred mantra) for this purpose is also found in the early pages of most prayer books:

אֱלֹהַי! נְשָׁמָה שֶׁנָּתַתָּ בִּי טְהוֹרָה הִיא.

Elohai neshama sh'nata bee tehorah hee
God, the soul that you have given me is pure.

Key words and phrases:

Modeh Ani: Thank you
Netilat yadayim: Washing the hands

If you want to know more:

Yitzhak Buxbaum, *Jewish Spiritual Practices*. Northvale, NJ: Jason Aronson, 1990.
Solomon Ganzfried, *Code of Jewish Law* (Abridged). New York: Hebrew Publishing Company, 1961.

Kasher a Home

The source:

1. "You shall not cook a kid in its mother's milk." (Exodus 23:19)

2. "You shall set apart the ritually clean beast from the unclean." (Leviticus 20:25)

3. "You must not eat flesh torn by beasts." (Exodus 22:30)

4. "You shall not eat anything that died a natural death." (Deuteronomy 14:21)

What you need to know:

1. *Kashrut* is about holiness and spiritual direction. It is not about health and hygiene (although both may be a benefit of keeping kosher).

2. The laws of *kashrut* regulate eating. Jews are not permitted to eat whatever they may want. Even permitted foods must be prepared in a special way. For instance, the only animals designated by the Torah as kosher are those that have cloven hooves and that chew their cud (i.e., process their food through regurgitation). But even these animals must be slaughtered by a *shochet* (ritual slaughterer).

3. Among fish, only those with fins and scales are designated kosher.

4. Jewish law forbids consuming an animal's blood. It was not enough that the animal must be killed in the most humane way, but even the symbol of life, the blood, must be removed.

5. In three separate places in the Torah, the Torah legislates that one shall not seethe a kid in its mother's milk. The rabbis deduced from this that not only is it forbidden to cook meat and milk products together but also to eat them or derive any benefit from them. The rabbis also forbade the eating of meat and milk together at the same meal even if they were not cooked together. Be-

410

cause of this law, kosher homes have two sets of dishes and cutlery, one for meat and the other for dairy.

6. Foods such as fish, fruits, and vegetables, which are neither milk nor meat, are called *pareve* and may be eaten with either milk or meat meals.

7. It is important to remember that within the Jewish community one finds many variations in the way Jews observe the dietary laws. Different authorities prescribe a variety of interpretations.

8. Following are some guidelines for making a home kosher:

   i. The basic requirements for having a kosher kitchen are twofold: there should be nothing nonkosher in it, and it should provide for separation of meat and dairy foods and utensils. Today kosher symbols abound on food products, certifying them as kosher.

   ii. There are two basic methods of *kashering* utensils. Most cooking utensils can be made kosher by immersion in boiling water. This includes metal pots, most pans including nonstick pans, flatware, plastic with high heat tolerance and many other kinds of kitchenware. The procedure is as follows:

      a. Thoroughly scour the article to be made kosher.
      b. Set the article aside and do not use it for 24 hours.
      c. Completely immerse the article in a pot of boiling water.
      d. If the pot is too large to fit into another pot, the pot to be kashered is filled to the brim with water, and that water is brought to a boil. While the water is still boiling, a hot stone or piece of metal is dropped into the pot in order that the water remain at its peak heat and also that it boil over the side of the pot.
      e. Rinse the articles immediately under cold water.
      f. The pot in which the articles were *kashered* is then itself *kashered*.

411

iii. Any utensil which comes in direct contact with fire, such as a barbecue spit or grill, a broiling pan, or rack, is *kashered* by open flame. The procedure is as follows:

    a. Thoroughly scour the article.

    b. Set the article aside and do not use it for 24 hours.

    c. Put the article under or over an open flame and thoroughly heat it until the metal glows red hot or is so hot that a piece of paper is singed when it is touched to the metal.

iv. Among Conservative Jews, glassware, when washed, is considered as new. However, there is a more elaborate process for *kashering* glassware among Orthodox Jews.

v. A sink is *kashered* like a large pot, by scouring, filling with boiling water, and dropping a hot stone or hot piece of metal into it.

vi. To *kasher* a dishwasher, scour the interior. The dishwasher should then not be used for 24 hours and then it should be run through a complete wash cycle without soap.

vii. To *kasher* a refrigerator/freezer, remove the shelves and bins in order to facilitate cleaning. Then carefully wash the shelves, bins and walls.

viii. Countertops and tables made of formica should be thoroughly scoured. Those made of wood are scraped with a steel brush, and the surface is then left bare for 24 hours. After that the surface is completely splashed with boiling water, poured directly from the pot in which the water was boiled.

ix. To kasher a microwave oven, clean it thoroughly, and place a cup of water inside. The microwave should then be turned on until the water boils out. (But be careful not to let the microwave run too long; you will burn *it* out.)

Key words and phrases:

Fleishig (Yiddish): A product deriving from meat

Kosher: Fit and proper to eat

Kashering: The process of making utensils kosher for use
Kashrut: The system of the Jewish dietary laws
Milchig: A dairy-based food
Pareve: Something neutral, neither meat nor dairy (all eggs, fish, fruits, vegetables and grains are *pareve*)

If you want to know more:

Samuel H. Dresner and Seymour Siegel, *The Jewish Dietary Laws*. New York: Rabbinical Assembly, 1982.

James M. Lebeau, *The Jewish Dietary Laws: Sanctify Life*. New York: United Synagogue Department of Youth Activities, 1983.

Behave in a Synagogue

The source:

Code of Jewish Law (abridged), The Sanctity of Synagogue and the House of Study, Vol. 1, Ch. 13.

What you need to know:

1. Each synagogue has its own *minhag hamakom* (community custom) with regard to behavior and dress, particularly for worship services. Some are Friday night casual and Saturday morning formal—with no special expectations for weekday and Sunday morning *minyanim* (usually dependent on what else is going on or where the worshiper is going following the service). And while certain holidays may be formal (such as Sukkot, Pesach and Shavuot), others may be more casual (such as Hanukkah and Purim). Therefore, it is important to check with the specific synagogue prior to services.

2. There are specific times during which synagogues close the entry doors to the sanctuary, indicating that it is probably an inappropriate time to enter. These usually include the rabbi's sermon (simply a matter of respect) and while the congregation is standing (for example, for the reader's repetition of the *Amidah*).

3. While it may be impolite to speak while others are praying throughout the service (or even when the rabbi is talking), and therefore it is discouraged, there are times in the service when we are actually prohibited by Jewish law from talking. The primary time when we are prohibited from speaking is during the reading of the Torah since, traditionally, we are simulating revelation and listening for God's voice speaking to us (which is rather difficult to do when people are talking). This is the general rule: don't talk while others are praying.

4. Don't wait for "stage directions" from the rabbi. Stand or sit when appropriate. Many prayer books help you

with this if you are unfamiliar with the service. However, the Reform and Conservative movements may differ somewhat as to standing/sitting during certain parts of the service and even congregations within the same movement differ on other parts. If you are unfamiliar with the custom of the congregation, take your cue from someone sitting nearby.

5. In Orthodox, Conservative, and many Reform and Reconstructionist congregations, certain activities are prohibited on Shabbat and holidays, such as using telephones (including cellular telephones) or any other electronic devices, smoking (some synagogues are smoke-free all the time as a health precaution), and the use of cameras. Since it is traditionally forbidden to drive on the Sabbath and holidays, many Orthodox congregations actually secure their parking lots with a chain or gate.

Things to remember:

1. Men can't go wrong dressed in suits. And women can't go wrong in dresses. It is always better to be more formally dressed, rather than more casually dressed. Women should keep their shoulders covered. No sleeveless tops, plunging necklines, or short skirts. Modesty is the goal.

2. Men should keep their head covered. Bring a *kipah* with you (if you do not wear one regularly). While it is customary for women in some synagogues to cover their heads, others only do so if they are married. Even in synagogues where only married women cover their heads, single women may be required to cover their heads when they ascend the *bimah* for an *aliyah* to the Torah. Of course, generally, this is only relevant in an egalitarian congregation.

3. On mornings men should bring a *tallit* with them. However, most synagogues that require men to wear *tallitot* usually have an ample supply available. Yet, when there are many guests (such as during a *bar/bat mitzvah*), this supply dwindles rather rapidly. It is the custom in some congregations for only married men to wear *tallitot*.

415

However, this presupposes that those unmarried men are each wearing a *tallit katan* under their garments.

4. On mornings during which *tefillin* is worn, men (and women who do so) should bring their *tefillin* with them. Few congregations have an adequate supply for those who do not bring them. And if you need help with putting on *tefillin*, don't be afraid to ask.

Key words and phrases:

Minhag hamakom: prevailing custom of the community or of the synagogue
Tzniut: modesty
Zenut: promiscuous sexual behavior, exploiting the body (the opposite of *tzniut*)

If you want to know more:

Kerry M. Olitzky and Rachel T. Sabath, *Striving Toward Virtue: A Contemporary Guide for Jewish Ethical Behavior*. Hoboken, NJ: KTAV Publishing House, 1996. (See "Exploiting the Body/Protecting the Spirit, pp. 60–67).

More particulars:

Some congregations are used to people coming and going throughout the service. It is ok, goes the logic, to be fashionably late. Others put it rather sharply, "The Reform movement has no *musaf* and the Conservative movement has no *shacharit*." Be on time. Stay for the entire service.

Count a Minyan

The source:

Numbers 14:27, the story of the ten spies; alternatively, Genesis 18:32, where Abraham argues with God on behalf of the possibility of finding ten righteous men in Sodom.

What you need to know:

1. A *minyan* (ten men in Orthodox Judaism or ten men and/or women in other movements) is the minimum number of persons that constitute a religious community; a prayer quorum.

2. A person may hallow God's name by moral acts in private, God's name cannot be hallowed in public prayer unless it is in the presence of a congregation of ten adult "witnesses."

Things to remember:

1. A *minyan* is required for the repetition of the *amidah* with the *kedusha*; reading the Torah and haftarah; reciting the priestly benediction; and the *kaddish*. Most also require a *minyan* for the call to prayer, the invitation of *barekhu*.

2. A *minyan* is required for a mourner to be able to say *kaddish* and thereby be comforted by this "community."

3. A *minyan* is required for the recital of the seven wedding blessings.

4. The Reform movement historically rejected the requirement of *minyan*, although many Reform rabbis have reinstated it.

5. Some Conservative congregations do not count women to make up the requirement of ten adults, but the Reform and Reconstructionist movements do so.

Key words and phrases:

Minyan: literally means number; refers to the smallest unit of a community

If you want to know more:

Simon Glustrom, *Language of Judaism*. Northvale, NJ: Jason Aronson, 1988.

More particulars:

1. Children are not counted as part of the *minyan*, but a ten-year-old child or older may count as the tenth in the presence of nine adults.

2. A long-standing custom is not to count Jews in order to determine whether a *minyan* is present. Counting in the Bible was often connected to census-taking for wars of aggression. Thus, counting is considered an act that is alien to Judaism. In order to determine if the proper number of people are present for a *minyan*, several ten-word liturgical passages are recommended. For example, "*Hoshiyah et amekha u'varekh et nachalatekha ooreym v'naseym ad olam*." Alternatively, some people add the word "not" (or *nisht* in Yiddish) before each number.

Devise a Mitzvah Performance Plan

The source:

Six hundred and thirteen commandments were commanded to Moses (Babylonian Talmud, *Makkot* 23b).

What you need to know:

1. Set a goal for yourself that you think is feasible. A new mitzvah a day, a week, a month. Work it into your daily routine. Find a place where it is comfortable for you. After it is part of you (and only you know it when you miss it and you *really* miss it), then go on to the next one on your list.

2. While it is easier for members of a family to support one another in the acquisition of *mitzvot*, this is not always possible. So if you can't get family members to join you, then at least ask for their support and understanding.

3. It usually helps to focus on an area or two of *mitzvot*. For example, begin by working on Shabbat *mitzvot* or the *mitzvot* regarding *kashrut* and eating. Then you can easily make the connection from one behavior to another. Sometimes, there are clusters of *mitzvot* that are difficult to separate one from another.

4. Don't focus on what you have ahead of you to do. Instead, concentrate on the progress you have made and luxuriate in each *mitzvah* as it takes you closer in your relationship to God.

5. Make a chart and keep a journal. The goal is not quantity. It is the soulful depth of the experience.

Things to remember:

1. Some people may try to tell you that it is all or nothing. Don't believe them. We grow in *mitzvot* just as we grow in other aspects of our lives. Our relationship with the tradition is dynamic—as it should be.

419

2. There are several different listings of the 613 commandments.

3. Many of the commandments are restricted to the land of Israel, and the sacrificial system. Therefore, we are unable to fulfill many of them.

4. Often, we learn Jewish behaviors by observing, then emulating (really mimicking) others. Make sure that the person you are following has it right. It is best to develop a relationship with a teacher (like your rabbi) and follow his or her guidance and advice. And don't be afraid to ask questions or ask for assistance.

Key words and phrases:

M'tzaveh: *the* commander, that is, God

Mitzvah: commandment, sacred obligation, a Divine instruction; not to be confused with *mitzveh* (as influenced by the Yiddish) a good deed

Taryag hamitzvot: an abbreviation/acronym for 613 commandments based on the Hebrew alpha-numeric for the number 613

If you want to know more:

Aaron HaLevi, *The Book of Mitzvah Education*, 5 vols. Jerusalem: 1978.

Ronald Isaacs, *The Book of Commandments*. Northvale, NJ: Jason Aronson, 1992.

More particulars:

Most *mitzvot* begin with a blessing. The traditional form of blessing is "*Barukh ata Adonai Elohenu Melekh Ha-olam . . .*" then it continues either with a reference first to *mitzvot* (*asher kidshanu b'mitzvotav v'tzivanu*—who has made us holy with *mitzvot*) or directly to the theme or behavior. This is what Jewish tradition considers the best way to access God's address, so to speak. It is the traditional vehicle for establishing a line of communication, a dialogue with the Divine. Most behaviors are preceded by a blessing. Some, like the ritual washing of hands before eating bread, are done before saying the blessing. Others seem to be delayed, such as the blessing over wine during *Havdalah*, but what is really taking place is the reciting of a series of blessings before drinking the wine.

Do Jewish Meditation

The source:

God can be found wherever God is sought.

What you need to know:

1. Rabbi Zalman Schacter-Shalomi suggests that having a visual image of *kavannah* is important as you try to align your will with the will of God. Thus, close your eyes and visualize God's will flowing through your body, becoming united with your soul and all aspects of your body, flowing through your veins and arteries, filling your limbs, organs, senses, brain, and nerves.

Some people use the following (from a midrash) as a visualization before meditating:

> In the name of Adonai, the God of Israel,
> At my right is Michael (love),
> at my left is Gabriel (strength),
> ahead of me is Oriel (light of the mind),
> behind me is Raphael (healing).
> Above me—and all around me—is the *Shekhinah* of God.

2. Start out slowly. Perhaps begin with ten minutes the first day. You can start by meditating without a text. Just meditate on God. For help, think about a text that describes something about God, such as "How great are Your works, God" (*Mah rabu maasekha Yah!*). Or choose a text that you are familiar with that brings spiritual pleasure to you. Then repeat it over and over, softly aloud at first, and then just in your head, until the words are indistinguishable one from the other.

2. You may want to meditate only a couple times a week until it has become part of your daily routine and don't rush ahead to find another phrase on which to meditate. The phrase only gets you started until you can transcend it fully. One can meditate for an entire life on just one meditation.

Things to remember:

1. Meditation takes time over time. So plan on spending at least a half hour a day meditating.

2. Meditation is about the direction and intention, the *kavannah*, of your activity. In this case, it is to direct yourself toward God.

3. You can use meditation as part of your prayer and ritual life, as well. Spend a few minutes meditating after you have said a blessing over bread before you eat it, for example. Or use the time to put on *tallit* and *tefillin* in the morning to meditate before reciting the morning service.

Key words and phrases:

Kavannah: a mantra, comprised of a small unit of sacred text

If you want to know more:

Nan Fink Gefen, *Discovering Jewish Meditation: A Beginner's Guide to an Ancient Spiritual Practice*. Woodstock, VT: Jewish Lights Publishing, 1999.
Aryeh Kaplan, *Jewish Meditation: A Practical Guide*. New York: Schocken Books, 1995.

More particulars:

Before you go to sleep each night, follow the practice of Levi Yitzchak of Berditchev and take a *cheshbon hanefesh*, an accounting of the soul. Recall the name of anyone who may have wronged you during the day and as you recall his or her name, forgive that person and pray for his or her welfare. Then affirm the Oneness of God, your longing to be united with the Divine and then say the *Shema*. Finally, review all of your actions during the day. Start by taking only a few minutes to do this and increasing the amount of time devoted to this activity over time. Select one or two actions in which you believe that you acted wrongly and humbly ask God to help you remove this kind of action from your daily life.

Make a *Havdalah* Kit

The source:

If the Sabbath is to be remembered, then its departure must be noted.

What you need to know:

1. At approximately 42 minutes after sunset on Saturday evening (which is 25 hours after candle lighting on Friday evening), *havdalah* is made at the conclusion of *maariv*. Some wait 72 minutes. For many Jews, particularly among the Orthodox, 60 minutes after sunset is the norm or after three stars can be seen in the sky.

2. All you need is a candle made of up at least two separate wicks, preferably more; a full cup of wine (or grape juice); and a small container (referred to as a spice box) for spices (like cloves or cinnamon) or flowers. Put this together in a container or sack and pack it to take with you whenever you will be out-of-town for Shabbat. You can purchase small "single-size" bottles of grape juice for just such a purpose. (It also makes a nice "care package" for kids away at camp or college.)

Things to remember:

1. *Havdalah* is a ceremony that marks the transition between special time (like Shabbat and the holidays) and regular time (like ordinary days of the week). *Havdalah* prayers are also included during the *maariv* service itself, during the *Amidah*.

2. The order of *havdalah* is simple: introductory paragraph; wine (blessing but no drinking yet); spices (blessing then sniff); fire (blessing then we extend our hands toward the flame in order to see its reflection in our fingernails); then the final *havdalah* blessing (we drink the wine and then extinguish the flame in it). [If you use brandy—which is a wine—instead of regular wine, it will usually go aflame when the candle is set to it. If you are careful, this adds a lovely ending to the ritual.]

Key words and phrases:

Besamim: spices
Havdalah: a distinction or something that has been made
  separate
Ner havdalah: a *havdalah* candle, usually twisted to emphasize the mingling of the sacredness of Shabbat with the
  routine of the everyday
Shavuah tov: a good week; greetings extended to one another at the conclusion of *havdalah*

If you want to know more:

Ronald H. Isaacs, *Shabbat Delight: A Celebration in Stories,
  Games, and Songs*. Hoboken, NJ and New York: KTAV
  Publishing and the American Jewish Committee,
  1987.
Kerry Olitzky and Ronald Isaacs, *The "How to" Handbook for
  Jewish Living*, Vol. 1. Hoboken, NJ: KTAV Publishing,
  1993.

More particulars:

1. When a holiday falls on weekday, there are certain
   changes to be made in the *havdalah* ritual. The introductory verses, candle and spices are omitted. At the
   conclusion of Yom Kippur, when it does not coincide
   with Shabbat, the introductory verses and the spices
   are omitted. However, the blessing over the flame is
   recited from a candle that has been lit with a fire that
   had been burning throughout Yom Kippur. According to traditional Jewish law, if one is not available,
   then the blessing over the flame is omitted.

2. *Havdalah* is said standing or sitting, depending on the
   custom of the community. Most people stand for it. If
   havdalah is made in the synagogue, in some communities the first paragraph is omitted.

3. Since you cease from creation during Shabbat, lighting
   the candle as the first act following Shabbat indicates
   that you have re-entered the creative mode. According
   to a midrash, fire was created on the first Saturday
   night (see Babylonian Talmud, *Pesachim* 54a).

4. We use spices (a symbol of the spiritual pleasures of Shabbat) to enliven our senses once the extra soul that we gain during Shabbat is gone and to raise our spirits following the departure of the Sabbath queen.

5. Most people sing a *shavuah tov* song at the end of the ceremony, following the singing of *Eliahu Hanavi*.

Move Toward Greater Shabbat Observance

The source:

"Remember the Sabbath day and keep it holy" (Exodus 20:8).

What you need to know:

1. Assess your current pattern of observance (or non-observance) of Shabbat. What do you do on Friday night, Saturday morning and afternoon? Then choose what will be easiest to change. Leave the hard things for last. For example, it will probably be easiest to transform Friday night dinner into a family Shabbat dinner if you already get together as a family for that dinner. Take it slowly. One thing at a time. Make a list of what changes you plan on doing and how quickly you think you can integrate them into your life. Some things will take longer than others. Begin simply by moving your Friday night dinner from the kitchen into the dining room. Put a table cloth on the table. Set it with flowers. Start the meal with blessings (wine or grape juice; *challah*). Bless your children and speak words of praise to a spouse. Review the week with those assembled at the table, but stay away from discussing challenges at work that require resolution. And avoid any discussions about money and finance. And don't forget to intersperse the courses with song—much better than intermezzo sorbet! At the end of the meal, express your gratitude to God for the food on the table and the friends and family with whom you are sharing it. When you are ready, use *birkat hamazon* at the end of the meal. Start with the short version, then add elements in the weeks following.

2. Next, focus on your preparation for Shabbat. When do you begin? How do you plan ahead? Then, determine a routine for Friday afternoon. Leave work early. Be conscious of doing errands on time, such as picking

427

up last-minute things that you will need. Take a shower. Change your clothes. Dress in things that you don't wear from day to day.

3. For some people, it is easier to start Friday evenings by going to the synagogue. For others, it makes more sense to *daven* at home rather than rush to a late-night service.

4. Turn off the telephone—or let the answering machine pick it up. People will soon realize that Shabbat is not the time to call you. And you don't want to be bothered by solicitations in any case. And leave the TV and radio off, as well. Let the natural sounds entertain you one day a week. And stay out of the shopping malls and away from the movie theaters. Instead use this time of leisure to read or study.

5. Begin your Saturday at the synagogue. Go early and stay for the entire service. Luxuriate in the fact that you don't have to rush off to go anywhere. Come home for a leisurely meal. Invite your friends to join you. (Shabbat is always nicer when you share it with others.) After this lunch has become part of the routine (even the menu does not vary much in our home), then you may want to introduce some more traditional elements into it, such as table blessings and songs. (Don't forget *kiddush* wine and *challah* for this meal too.)

6. Next comes the best part of Shabbat: a nap, something that we anticipate with as much enthusiasm and longing as we do the more potentially ethereal aspects of Shabbat such as prayer and study. One would think that you can easily add this into your Shabbat schedule, but it is not so easy. Shabbat naps are only possible when demands are not being made on the rest of your time.

7. Following your nap, it should be time for *mincha*. Just as this service is the most challenging in our daily routine (even if it is the simplest and least complicated) since we are in the midst of other things and have to break away from them in order to *daven mincha,* it is hard to return to the synagogue in the afternoon. That is why some synagogues schedule *mincha*

either after the *kiddush* following morning services (within the parameters set forward by Jewish law) or just before *maariv* and *havdalah* in the evening. Usually, some study separates the two services, regardless of whether it is held early or late in the afternoon. However, some communities use the reading of the Torah on Saturday afternoon for study. Late afternoon/early evening is a particularly nice time in the summer to study, since sunset is much later than it is the rest of the year. And the third *shabbat meal* (called *seudah shlishit* in Hebrew or *shalosh seudos* in Yiddish) which is usually lighter fare is eaten between *mincha* and *maariv*.

For some, it is easier to get into the routine of Shabbat *mincha* by *davening* at home. For others, it is easier to establish the routine by joining with the community at prayer.

8. At the end of Shabbat, gather together and bid it farewell. This is accomplished ritually in *havdalah*. While the ceremony is rather brief, and people are often in a hurry to go out on Saturday night, feel free to add other elements into the ritual. For example, share with one another your plans for the week ahead, the challenges you face, or what you would like to accomplish.

9. This is the time of Shabbat that is often most difficult. That is why *havdalah* is bittersweet. We want to re-enter secular time, but we hesitate to leave holy time behind. What is even more difficult for those of us who live in mixed communities is the fact that during the summer when Shabbat ends around 9 p.m., our friends may not be willing to wait for us to go out. That's why it is important to try to develop relationships with those who are on the path to their own renewal of Jewish observance, rather than compromising your own Shabbat observance to meet the social needs of your friends. Once you change this rhythm and you let Shabbat become embedded in your soul, none of this will seem strange to you. What may seem strange instead is going to the movies on a late Friday afternoon, early evening in the summer since Shabbat begins—as it ends—very late.

Things to remember:

1. Shabbat is not a burden. Its goal is the exact opposite: to ease the burdens of daily living by making them unimportant one day a week. It is an opportunity to bring joy and tranquility into your life by collapsing ancient time (of Paradise) with future (messianic) time and thereby making time as we know it irrelevant.

2. People observe Shabbat in various ways regardless of the particular community in which they live. Once you have determined the community of religious observance in which you feel most comfortable, use the observance patterns of others to guide you, but do not use what they do as a measuring stick for what you have chosen for your own life, and the life of your family.

3. You will not be able to recreate the pattern of observance of your parents or grandparents—if they had one. Instead, you must create your own, one that feels comfortable for you and helps to create Jewish memories for your children, as it affirms your own. Be creative. Be open.

Key words and phrases:

Birkat hamazon: grace after meals
Challah: special bread, twisted like the braids of the hair of the mystical Sabbath bride
Daven: pray
Havdalah: ritual that marks the separation between Shabbat and the rest of the week
Kiddush: prayer of sanctification said over wine
Maariv: evening service
Mincha: afternoon service

If you want to know more:

Ronald H.Isaacs, *Shabbat Delight: A Celebration in Stories, Games, and Songs*. Hoboken, NJ and New York: KTAV Publishing and the American Jewish Committee, 1987
Kerry M. Olitzky and Ronald H. Isaacs, *Sacred Celebrations: A Jewish Holiday Handbook*. Hoboken, NJ: KTAV Publishing Co., 1994.

More particulars:

1. Because of the impact of Jewish law on our routine as we usher in Shabbat and bid it farewell (through *havdalah*), Shabbat is actually 25 hours long. It begins approximately 18 minutes before sunset on Friday and concludes when there are three stars evident in the sky on Saturday evening (or 42 minutes after sunset). Shabbat does not begin or end when you are ready.

2. "More than Israel has kept the Sabbath, has the Sabbath kept Israel." (Ahad Ha-am)

Observe *Yom Hashoah*

The source:

A resolution of the Knesset, Israel's national legislature, on April 12, 1951 designated the 27th of Nisan as "Holocaust and Ghetto Uprising Day, a day of perpetual remembrance for the House of Israel."

What you need to know:

1. Yom Hashoah marks the anniversary of the Holocaust. While there are those who believe that its observance should be part of Tisha B'av, most members of the Jewish community have fixed it on their calendars.

2. Yom Hashoah has become more of a public community observance than a personal observance. However, of late, introduced by the Federation of Men's Clubs of the Conservative movement (United Synagogue of Conservative Judaism), many people light yellow candles that function in much the same way as *yahrzeit* candles (that burn for 24 hours). Some people light six candles (white or yellow) in order to acknowledge the six million of our people who perished.

3. Since this is a day like no other, find some time for yourself to reflect on the tragedy of the Holocaust. Take a few moments to think about those in your family who perished. Study in their memory. Give *tzedakah* in their memory. Teach in their memory.

Things to remember:

1. In the synagogue, the observance of Yom Hashoah is usually held in combination with the evening service. Candles are lit and special prayers such as *El Maleh Rachamim* and *kaddish* are added. Holocaust poems and literature are often read and public testimony by survivors is usually offered. Songs of the partisans may be sung (often in Yiddish, the Jewish folk language that was nearly destroyed in the Holocaust along with the people who spoke it). And the *ani ma'amin* prayer

is generally sung in a dirge-like melody that was sung by the victims of the Holocaust often as they were marched to their deaths.

Key words and phrases:

Shoah: holocaust, literally "conflagration by fire"
Yahrzeit: anniversary of one's death

If you want to know more:

Kerry M. Olitzky and Ronald H. Isaacs, *Sacred Celebrations: A Jewish Holiday Handbook*. Hoboken, NJ: KTAV Publishing Co., 1994.

More particulars:

1. Yom Hashoah is observed a week before Yom Haatzmaut, in order to emphasize the fact that the Jewish people emerged from the ashes of the Holocaust in order to build the modern state of Israel.

2. Outside Israel, in the early years of the observance, it was customary to memorialize the Holocaust on April 19, the day on which the Warsaw Ghetto uprising began.

3. The tenth of Tevet was designated by the Israeli Chief Rabbinate as the day of *yahrzeit* for *kaddish* to be said by relatives of those who had lost family in the Holocaust and who did not know the exact day they perished.

Personalize a Bar/Bat Mitzvah

The source:

At 13, one is ready for the *mitzvot* (Pirke Avot 5:23).

What you need to know:

1. Bar/Bat Mitzvah is not something that is bestowed on you or something that you do. It is a state of being that is determined by your age. Once boys become 13 or girls become 12 (though most non-Orthodox congregations no longer make a distinction of age between boys and girls), according to their birthdays as reckoned by the Hebrew calendar, you gain certain privileges in the community. With these privileges, you also incur certain responsibilities. This time of transition from childhood—where these privileges and obligations had no impact on you—and adulthood is marked by the most salient of these privileges, that is, the right to be called to the Torah for an *aliyah*.

2. As you think about personalizing your bar/bat mitzvah, make sure that it enhances the ceremony and celebration (and thereby becomes *hiddur mitzvah*) and neither eclipses it or replaces it in importance. That is why it is important that the process of personalization emerge out of Jewish tradition. For example, since the *haftarah* reading is supposed to be educational (unlike the Torah reading which is primarily intended to simulate the experience at Sinai) and highlight the theme of the Torah reading, you may want to narrate the *haftarah* reading for those in the congregation. Place it in context. Help people to understand what is being read and why it is being read and how it really relates to the Torah reading. As another option, particularly for those unfamiliar with the service, you may want to provide a guide and commentary to the service. These can be distributed with the prayer books as people enter the synagogue. Similarly, you may want to distribute something ahead of time that helps visitors to understand what is so important about the ceremony they will be attending. This is more than rules and regulations for guests to the syn-

agogue. This is about what the ceremony means to you and your family and how you prepared for it.

3. There are many things that are now common in many synagogues that may need rethinking if you want to personalize the ceremony and make it more meaningful to you. What will you do with the flowers that are placed on the *bimah*—if they are there at all? If there is a reception or *kiddush*, will people be invited to donate to *tzedakah* the equivalent of what they might have spent had they paid for the meal? Or alternatively, will the leftover food be given (within the bounds of local health department standards) to a local "feed the hungry" program? Perhaps you may want to consider identifying a charitable cause that you can champion (or already have) so that people can provide funds in your honor to the organization. Make sure that you include information on the organization either in the invitation or on the day itself.

Things to remember:

1. Each community has its parameters with regard to bar/bat mitzvah, as well as worship in general. Make sure that you review with your rabbi what options are available to you. Plan well in advance since some of these things may have to be reviewed by the congregation's ritual committee. The bar/bat mitzvah is placed in the context of regular community worship. The challenge, therefore, is to personalize the bar/bat mitzvah in such a way that it does not compromise the experience of worship for the community.

2. Review what responsibilities and obligations, rights and privileges accrue to the bar/bat mitzvah in your community. After you decide how to personally respond to these, you will then be able to develop a more complete plan for personalizing the bar/bat mitzvah.

Key words and phrases:

Aliyah: Torah honor, may also refer to immigrating to Israel
Bar: son, from the Aramaic
Bat: daughter
Bimah: raised platform at the front of the synagogue

Hiddur mitzvah: beautifying the mitzvah
Mitzvah: commandment, sacred obligation

If you want to know more:

Ronald Isaacs, *Reaching for Sinai: A Practical Handbook for Bar/Bat Mitzvah and Family*. Hoboken, NJ: KTAV Publishing, 1989.

Jeffrey Salkin, *For Kids—Putting God on the Guest List: How to Claim the Spiritual Meaning of Your Bar or Bat Mitzvah*. Woodstock, VT: Jewish Lights Publishing, 1999.

———, *Putting God on the Guest List: How to Reclaim the Spiritual Meaning of Your Child's Bar or Bat Mitzvah*. Woodstock, VT: Jewish Lights Publishing, 1992.

Plan a Spiritual Trip to Israel

The source:

God said to Abram, "Raise your eyes and look out from where you are, to the north and south, to the east and west, for I give you all the land that you see, to you and your ancestors forever" (Gen. 13: 14–15).

What you need to know:

1. Use a layered approach to your trip, what Rabbi Larry Hoffman labels as "anticipate, approach, acknowledge, and afterthought."

   A. Anticipate: once you have determined where you want to go, spend some time thinking about the place. Read a little about it in history, but don't get bogged down. Just get a feel for the place and what happened there.

   B. Approach: since you are coming as a pilgrim to the site, prepare yourself accordingly, maybe a poem, a prayer. Think about the way you should dress, as well.

   C. Acknowledge: Once you have arrived, take note of the place. Don't rush for photo opportunities. Simply drink in the environment. Say a blessing. Study a bit of Torah or repeat something that you have learned and share it with others. This is about spiritual feelings, not facts and figures.

   D. Afterthought: How do you keep the experience alive? Some people like to write things down in a journal. This is not "what I did on my summer vacation." Instead, write down what you felt, the smells, the sounds and the sights. Bits of conversation that you might have heard, even something simple like children playing outside and the sound of their laughter and the sweetness of their innocent voices.

Things to remember:

1. Plan well in advance but be flexible enough so that you are open to spontaneous experiences while you are in Israel. Start your trip even before you leave. Ask your rabbi for an *aliyah* to the Torah prior to making your trip (and remember to *bentsch gomel* when you return safely, please God). Then make sure that you say *tefillat haderekh* once you get situated on the airplane. Add your own prayers to those that have been stipulated by our tradition. You are going home as a pilgrim to the land, not a tourist.

2. Bring a *siddur* and *tanakh* with you with which you are familiar and comfortable. Bring a map of Israel that is easy to read and highlights the places that you want to visit.

3. Be realistic about what you will be able to accomplish in the number of days that you plan on being in Israel and the often competing demands of those with whom you are traveling.

4. Use your trip to Israel as a way of trying out things like daily prayer and daily study that you will want to incorporate into your routine when you return home. Start slowly, perhaps with a daily psalm or one of the fixed prayer services and work your way toward a more extensive routine. Choose those experiences that speak directly to you out of the experience of our tradition. For example, beginning your first day in Israel by saying the daily blessings brings that memory with their recitation each time you say them.

5. Much of the trip will be about how you visit, rather than where you visit. Even breathing the crisp morning air in Jerusalem while walking through its streets can be a spiritual experience. It certainly is for us!

6. Don't try to read too much about the sites you will be visiting. Try to read one thing about each place that you want to remember. Then carry that with you as a kind of sacred mantra, a *kavannah*, for that particular place.

Key words and phrases:

Bentsch gomel: blessing after having survived a traumatic event, such as travel

Eretz Yisrael: the land of Israel

Tefillat haderekh: traveler's prayer

If you want to know more:

Lawrence A. Hoffman, *Israel, A Spiritual Travel Guide: A Companion for the Modern Jewish Pilgrim*. Woodstock, VT: Jewish Lights Publishing, 1998.

Pray with *Kavannah*

The source:

Babylonian Talmud, *Berakhot* 13a.

What you need to know:

1. Schedule for yourself enough time to pray. If you are more focused on the time you have to conclude your prayer, then it will be difficult for you to find the *kavannah* with which to pray.

2. Find a comfortable place for prayer, one that is pleasant but whose aesthetic will not be distracting. Try to avoid influencing the senses, particularly with any background noises, except perhaps those of nature.

3. Be conscious of the way you are dressed for prayer. Your mode of dress helps you with the way you feel about prayer and approach it.

4. Take it slowly. The goal of prayer is not how much you can say and how fast you can say it. (Avoid what we like to call "mumble-*davening*.") This is particularly true with the preliminary material in a formal service such as *pesuke d'zimra*. These "verses of song," as they are called, are supposed to be just that. So choose a verse in a psalm that speaks to you and repeat it over and over again until you are able to transcend the words themselves. Let them imprint themselves on your soul so that you can carry their lingering memory throughout the day. Let them be the prism through which you experience the world around you. Sing the verse aloud if you know a particular melody for it. Don't feel obligated to rush through the entire psalm, nor each and every one of them in the prayer book. The goal of prayer is to create a pathway through which your prayers can reach God and open up the dialogue with the Divine.

5. Don't be afraid to use your body in prayer. When we are lucky, community prayer breaks into dance (such as on Erev Shabbat). But *shukeling* (swaying) also reflects the rhythm of Jewish prayer. People *shukel* dur-

ing prayer in much the same way as they tap their feet to music. It is the way we keep in tune with the prayers. It also serves to disorient ourselves from regular space and enter into the space of prayer. Try it. Don't be too self-critical and certainly don't be critical of others who do. And please don't assign certain prayer movements to specific groups of Jews. All of Jewish tradition, custom, and ritual is ours to embrace.

Things to remember:

1. *Kavannah* is more about the attitude with which we pray, rather than the words of prayer themselves. Some people even think that the words are irrelevant, as long as the heart and soul are directed to Heaven.

2. Don't confuse being an expert in liturgy with being able to pray with *kavannah*. Sometimes, a lot of knowledge gets in the way when we confuse prayer with liturgy. And sometimes we get in our own way when we worry about how much we do not know, or how inadequate is our Hebrew. You can also pray in English (but don't deceive yourself into believing that translating makes the praying any easier or that responsive readings are prayers).

3. Leave your critical self at the door. Prayer is a meta-rational experience.

4. Leave your burdens of the day at the door, as well. Try to shake off any residual memory of yesterday's challenges and try not to enter into today's challenges either. If you have had any recent arguments with those you love, try to bring them to closure before you pray. Sometimes a simple "I'm sorry" is all that it takes.

Key words and phrases:

Kavannah: the sacred intention with which one prays; the technical term for spontaneous prayer (in distinction to the *keva* of fixed prayer); a mantra of sorts made up of words or texts, primarily of sacred origin
Keva: fixed prayer, the daily routine of prayer
Pesuke d'zimra: verses of song, from the morning service

If you want to know more:

Yitzchak Buxbaum, *Real Davening*. Flushing, NY: Jewish Spiritual Booklet Series, 1996.

Lawrence A. Hoffman, *The Art of Public Prayer*. Woodstock, VT: Jewish Lights Sky Paths Publishing, 1999.

_____, *My People's Prayer Book* series. Woodstock, VT: Jewish Lights Publishing, 1997ff.

Ellen Singer, ed., *Paradigm Shift: The Jewish Renewal Teachings of Reb Zalman Schachter-Shalomi*. Northvale, NJ: Jason Aronson, 1993. (See section on *Davvenology*.)

More particulars:

Some people find that using sign language during prayer helps them to find the right posture for their prayers. Find someone in your community that can help you sign those prayers that you find are pivotal to your experience of worship.

Start a Study *Chavurah*

The source:

"Get a study buddy" (*Pirke Avot* 1:6).

"The study of Torah is equal to them all (that is, *mitzvot* that have no specific measure), because it leads to them all" (Mishnah *Peah* 1:1, also included in the *siddur*).

What you need to know:

1. To begin, a good-sized group should be about 12 people. This allows for some flexibility should people not be able to attend each session.

2. While no one should be in charge, it is sometimes helpful for an individual to chair each meeting. We recommend a rotating chairperson. This person would be responsible for planning and guiding the study session in any given week. But the responsibility of leading the group remains in the hands of the entire group. Since this is a peer group, it is important that each person take an equal role in it.

3. Choose a subject that you think will be of interest to people. You may want to begin with the weekly Torah or Haftarah reading or you may want to choose a classic of sacred literature such as *Pirke Avot* since it is easily accessible. As an alternative, books like *Sefer Hakhinukh* (lit. Book of Education, a book of mitzvah education) or *Mesillat Yesharim* (a classic work on ethical piety) are excellent choices for groups and are available in English translation. You may also want to consult Michael Katz and Gershon Schwartz, *Swimming in the Sea of Talmud* (Philadelphia: Jewish Publication Society, 1997).

4. Invite two friends to participate. And ask them to invite two of their friends and so on until you have a group of 12 people.

5. At the outset, don't be too democratic. As the founder of the group, you can make certain logistical decisions

until the group takes shape. Be sensitive to the needs of others, but choose the venue, the time for the first meeting, etc.

6. Be clear about the expectations from the beginning. If this is to be a group that only studies when it meets, then be sure that everyone knows that. However, if members of the group want a more extensive study experience and are willing to study independently at times when the group is not meeting, then that has to be made clear to potential group members, as well.

7. Start each session with the blessing for the study of Torah as a way of reminding the participants of the sacred nature of Jewish study. *Barukh ata Adonai Elohenu Melekh Ha-olam asher kidshanu bemitzvotav vitzivanu la'asok bidivrei Torah.* "Praised are You, Adonai our God, Sovereign of the Universe who makes us holy with *mitzvot* and instructs us to busy ourselves with the words (and works) of Torah."

Things to remember:

1. In a study group, everyone is equal even if some of its members have certain Hebrew or text skills or background that are superior to others.

2. The group should meet on a regular basis so that it is something that its members can fit into their regular routine and they come to expect it.

3. It is good to build into your study *chavurah* a Jewish calendar rhythm so that its nuances can be included in your study.

4. A study group can begin with two people committed to study.

5. Depending on when you meet, include the routine of *tefillah* in your meetings.

6. Try to make a schedule of your subject matter, but let the learning lead you. Some people prefer to use the weekly Torah portion as a guide. Others choose to start at Genesis and then just keep going.

7. Take note of all practical considerations:

a. Where should the meeting take place?
b. Will the meeting schedule accommodate all who are invited to participate?
c. Is there room for more people to join as the group evolves?
d. Does everyone have transportation?

Key words and phrases:

Chavurah: fellowship (surrogate extended family)
Chevruta: study partner; study buddy
Talmud torah: classical Jewish study

If you want to know more:

Sharon Strassfeld and Michael Strassfeld, *The Third Jewish Catalogue*. Philadelphia: Jewish Publication Society of America, 1980.

Talk to Your Kids About God

The source:

"I am Adonai Your God who brought you out of the land of Egypt, out of the house of bondage. You shall worship only Me" (Exodus 20:1–2).

What you need to know:

1. Make sure that you have provided an open environment in which your children feel comfortable in talking to you about God (or anything else, for that matter).

2. Since most people think that Godtalk is closely related to patterns of religious observance, it is important for your children to realize that their relationship to God is not limited to the confines of their religious school classroom or the synagogue (that you may have chosen not to attend very frequently).

3. Children take their cues from what they hear and what they observe more than what we tell them.

4. While no one is certain about their relationship to God, it will be important for you to reflect on your own feelings before talking with your children. You may want to begin by talking with your spouse or an intimate friend. (Sometimes it is helpful for older children to speak to younger children.)

5. Begin these conversations while they are young. Let them evolve from their experiences with God and the world rather than a decision that you may have made that it is time to talk about God. Also, this allows God to be discussed in the context of an experience with the Divine rather than limited to merely an intellectual discussion. You may want to read books together that provide a viewpoint on God for your child to understand in order to foster such a conversation.

6. Help them to understand something that many of our rabbis and cantors don't fully understand: that heartfelt prayer should be the foundation for worship. However, prayer should not be limited to the words in

the prayer book. It should be an expression of our hearts and souls.

7. Finally, our understanding of God grows as we grow, as we experience attributes of the Divine in our own lives. It is a dynamic understanding and a dynamic relationship.

Things to remember:

1. Be honest. Share your struggles and your doubts as your children are ready to understand them. Admit to inconsistencies, as well. And invite them to join you on a journey of exploration.

2. Remember that most children cannot think abstractly. That is why the narrative material in the Torah speaks so vividly to them in concrete terms. Don't dismiss these stories as primitive myths.

3. Because of the covenant between God and the Jewish people (and therefore with each of us), we are never alone. Our obligation is to live a life reflective of that covenant.

4. Don't try to tell your children everything at once.

5. Even if your posture is rational with little room for the metarational, don't rob your children of the mystery that a relationship with God can offer.

6. Don't confuse your experience with God with the ways in which your children might experience God.

Key words and phrases:

Adonai: the conventional euphemism used for the unspeakable name (the tetragrammaton) of the personal God of Israel

Elohim: the way the Torah generally speaks of God in abstract terms.

If you want to know more:

Ronald Isaacs, *Close Encounters: Jewish Views About God.* Northvale, NJ: Jason Aronson, 1996.

Harold Kushner, *When Children Ask About God*. New York: Schocken Books, 1971.

David Wolpe, *Teaching Your Children About God*. New York: HarperTrade, 1994.

More particulars:

In an essay entitled, "Talking to Kids About God," Rabbi Daniel Syme offers these guidelines for parents:

1. Do not offer the biblical notion of God—or any one concept—as "the" Jewish God idea.

2. When you speak to your children about God, state your personal beliefs, but clearly indicate that they are *your* beliefs.

3. Use appropriate language when discussing God with children of younger ages.

4. When your child volunteers a personal notion as to the nature of God, try to tie that affirmation to a great Jewish thinker.

5. Never be embarrassed to respond, "I don't know" to a child's question about God.

6. Do not hesitate to consult with your rabbi, Jewish educator, or others to deal with difficult questions.

7. Encourage your children to share their thoughts about God and instances when they feel they have experienced God in their lives.

8. Listen better.

9. Emphasize to your children that our personal ideas of God grow as we grow, both in depth and in complexity.

10. Help your child see ritual, prayer, and holiday observances as ways in which the Jewish people express their attachment to God.

11. Do not be reluctant to share stories of times in your life when you experienced or felt close to God.

Use the Book of Psalms

The source:

Jewish custom.

What you need to know:

1. Keep a book of psalms handy. Some people keep a copy in their briefcases or purses, as well as on the table next to their bed. In this way, they can access the psalms easily, review them when they awaken in the morning (in order to help start the day) and reflect on them at night (to help them reflect on the day that just passed).

2. Read each psalm that you have chosen slowly. Focus on one verse or even one word.

Things to remember:

1. People read psalms at various times in their lives. Such reading helps people focus and offers direction, particularly in time of need. The reading of psalms can raise the spirit when it is low or offer direction and insight when one feels lost or misguided. The reading of psalms takes place when a body is being watched over following death. A traditional groom recites psalms while his bride makes the circuit around him. Psalms are said for people to bring them healing. And they have found their way in whole or in part throughout Jewish liturgy.

2. The service called *kabbalat Shabbat*, which grew out of the mystical tradition in Judaism, includes a series of psalms. One is supposed to reflect on the past week, one day at a time, as each psalm is read.

Key words and phrases:

Kabbalat Shabbat: service for welcoming Shabbat that precedes the Shabbat evening service
Tehillim: psalms

If you want to know more:

Yitzchak Buxbaum, *Jewish Spiritual Practices*. Northvale, NJ: Jason Aronson, 1994.

Simkha Y. Weintraub, ed. *Healing of Soul, Healing of Body: Spiritual Leaders Unfold the Strength and Solace in Psalms*. Woodstock, VT: Jewish Lights Publishing, 1994.

More particulars:

1. Rabbi Nachman of Bratslav designated these psalms as psalms for healing for what he called a *tikkun klali*, a complete remedy: 16, 32, 41, 42, 59, 77, 90, 105, 137, 150.

2. The twenty-third psalm is well-known for its ability to provide comfort. Therefore, it is associated with mourning.

3. Just as there are many translations of the Bible, there are many translations of the various books in the Bible, including the book of Psalms. Since all translation is interpretation, you may find that one translation of a particular psalm speaks to you differently than does another translation.

4. Many psalms speak to people in different ways. After you become more familiar with individual psalms, you may find that you resonate with each one differently depending on the context in which you are reciting a particular one. Start with these (feel free to copy this list and place it inside your own book of Psalms)[1]

   a. When studying Torah: 1, 19, 119
   b. In the synagogue: 5,26, 27, 63, 65, 73, 84, 96, 122, 135
   c. In nature: 19, 104, 148
   d. Desire to repent: 40, 51, 90
   e. After committing sin: 25, 32, 51, 130
   f. Sad, depressed: 30, 42, 43
   g. Cannot sleep: 4

[1] Adapted from Yitzchak Buxbaum, *Jewish Spiritual Practices*. Northvale, NJ: Jason Aronson, 1994, p. 366.

h. Lonely: 25
i. Disruptive changes in your life; personal tragedy: 46, 57
j. Frustration at the evil of people: 36, 52, 53, 58
k. Anxiety from those who seek to do you harm: 3, 5, 6, 7, 9, 17, 22, 25, 31, 35, 38, 43, 54, 55, 56, 57, 59, 71, 140, 142
l. Anxious concern about livelihood: 23, 62, 68
m. Suffering, afflicted: 38, 102
n. Want to pray, say psalms, speak to God: 51
o. Need to increase your trust in God: 22, 23, 56, 62, 84, 123, 125, 128, 131, 146
p. Single, hoping to find soulmate: 68
q. Feeling uplifted: 8, 19, 24, 47, 48
r. Need God's help, protection: 70, 91, 121, 130
s. Confused by success of wicked, envious of rich: 1, 37, 49, 73
t. Beset by the challenges of old age: 71
u. Perplexed by injustice and God's distance: 10
v. Doubts about faith: 1, 2, 19, 37
w. Feeling confused about your faith: 25, 143
x. Israel, Jews, Judaism pressed, abused, threatened: 53, 74, 83, 124
y. Betrayed, hurt by others, particularly someone close to you: 35, 41, 55
z. Feel abandoned: 27, 88, 142
aa. Feeling of thankfulness to God: 9, 18, 65, 66, 116
bb. Grateful to God for success, prosperity: 65, 144, 147
cc. Feel threatened, anxious or afraid: 4, 22, 23, 56
dd. Slandered, abused verbally, victim of wrongdoing: 39, 64, 120
ee. Great troubles and distress: 6, 31, 34, 55, 69, 77 86, 88, 107, 121, 138, 142
ff. Feel humiliated by people: 22

Choose a Religious School

The source:

"You shall teach them diligently to your children" (Deuteronomy 6:7).

What you need to know:

1. There are several important questions that concerned parents ought to be thinking about when choosing a school for their child:

   a. When should we begin our child's Jewish education?
   b. What is the right kind of school for our child?
   c. How do we decide among schools of different sponsorships—private, communal, denominational, congregational?
   d. What if there is only one school available in our community? Do we still have options?

2. It is important to enroll early, as early as preschool and primary programs. Before enrolling in such programs, consider the goals of the school and whether they coincide with your own. Don't be persuaded by the reputation of the school in the community. Check it out yourself. And trust your "gut."

3. Although no single factor can account for the effectiveness or so-called ".quality" of any school, here are some guidelines you may wish to look for when choosing a Jewish school.

Characteristics of Effective Schools

What Parents should look for when choosing a religious school

Well-defined philosophy and mission
>   Ask to see a copy of school's goals and mission statement.

A system of evaluation to frequently monitor student progress
>   Look for ways in which school determines whether

students are learning what school is teaching (achievement tests, report cards, etc.).

Sequential curriculum that matches philosophy
Does school have written curriculum that lists teachers' goals and student objectives for each grade?

School climate and plant
Tour the school and see if you can be given a chance to see school in action.
Is the school environment conducive for learning?

Strong educational director
Meet and get to know school principal.

Experienced teaching staff
Ask for information about teachers.
What are their backgrounds, teaching styles, etc?

Strong community support
Is there adequate financial support and advocacy for school in the community?

Things to remember:

1. Your ability to analyze a school assumes that there are options in the community. This is not always the case. Always keep in mind that the school should not represent the only option for Jewish education. It is just one of them. Jewish home experiences, camping experiences, and community and youth programs all contribute to one's Jewish education. One has to provide support for the other.

2. If you have a Jewish day school in your community, you will certainly want to learn more about it as a possibility for your children. Since there is a high correlation between the number of hours of Jewish education a child receives and the development of one's Jewish identity, the day school is more likely to provide a student with better resources for living a Jewish life. Day school education also means additional financial obligation. Most day schools also expect more parental involvement than do most congregational schools, especially in the area of fundraising and policy making.

More particulars:

1. Learning-disabled children are entitled to a Jewish education. Be an advocate in your community. Make sure that all children receive a Jewish education, according to their need and ability. *P'tach*, which stands for "**P**arents for **T**orah for **A**ll **C**hildren" is a national organization devoted to making sure that learning-disabled kids get a Jewish education. *P'tach* headquarters are located at 1363 49th Street, Brooklyn, NY 11219. There are branches all around North America, as well as in Israel.

2. Be aware of any challenges that your children face concerning their Jewish education. The earlier, the better.

Key words and phrases:

Bet Sefer: School
Bet Sefer Yomi: Day school

If you want to know more:

Hayim Halevy Donin, *To Raise a Jewish Child: A Guide for Parents*. New York: Basic Books, 1977.

Teach Civil Responsibility

The source:

"Do not separate yourself from the community" (*Pirke Avot* 2:5).

What you need to know:

1. Jewish teachers have always stressed responsible citizenship in the community in which one resides. The prophet Jeremiah (29:7) taught: "Seek the peace of the city where I have caused you to be carried away, and pray to God for it."

2. Since values and attitudes related to any ideology are initially formed in the home, show your own children that Jewish people care not only about the Jewish community but the community at large.

3. There are many windows of opportunity that Judaism provides for transmitting notions of civic responsibility. For example, the *mitzvah* of *tzedakah* (righteous giving) reminds us of our responsibility of reaching out to the needy. Use the *pushke* (charity box) each week and let all family members share in placing coins into it before Shabbat, the traditional time to do so. If there are marches for the hungry, food collections sponsored by local synagogues or your local Jewish Federation, or clothes drives for the needy, donate to them as a family. When children see parents reach into their pockets, they are immediately impressed with the value of giving to others.

4. As your children grow older you will want to encourage them to show that your family cares not only about Jewish concerns but concerns of the general community at large. Encourage your children to read and discuss both the daily newspaper and your local Jewish Federation's publication. At election time, have a family discussion related to the various candidates, and talk about which ones would be the best leaders based on their values of goodness and justice. Have your kids write letters to their leaders when they feel that a

particular wrong needs to be corrected. By reaching out as a family to all of those who are less fortunate than we, we can express the Jewish value of community—that all members are ultimately responsible for one another.

Key words and phrases:

Achrayoot ezrachee: Civic responsibility
Tzedakah: Righteous giving.

If you want to know more:

Kathy Green and Sharon Strassfeld, *The Jewish Family Book*. New York: Bantam Books, 1981.

Explain Death to Children

The source:

There is no classic source for this "How to."

What you need to know:

1. Children growing up today are more aware of death than most adults realize. They are confronted with it in TV, word and song, in the natural world of plants and animals, and among their friends and family.

2. Children may not understand what they see when they are ignored during the grieving process. Too often we heighten the child's feeling of isolation when we pretend that the loved one is still living.

3. A child's ability to understand the meaning of death and loss is dependent on his or her cognitive development and life experiences.

4. A child of two years of age can sense loss and suffer the feelings that go with that loss, but is not likely to comprehend death in an intellectual sense. Parents of children this age can respond to a child's feelings, but explanations are not likely to be of substantial value.

5. Children aged three or four tend to think of death as a temporary condition and view it as separation.

6. Children between ages five and nine are much better able to understand the meaning of physical death. At this age, they may begin to worry about the time when those close to them will no longer "exist."

7. By the time children are aged nine or ten, they begin to formulate more realistic conceptions of death based on biological observances and their wider experience of the world. They begin to understand that death is the final end of bodily life.

8. There is no one proper way to tell a child about death. Although what is said is significant, how it is said is also very important. Consider carefully the tone of your

457

voice and the context in which the information is being shared.

9. Don't overwhelm children with too much detail. Remember to keep in mind the child's level of comprehension.

10. Avoid theological abstractions and detailed explanations, so that death will not be linked to sin or divine punishment.

11. Avoid myths and fairy tales that will later have to be rejected (e.g., Grandpa went away on a long trip; God took Daddy because your father was so good that God wanted him; Grandma has just gone to sleep).

12. Allow children time to express themselves and ask questions. Also allow them to talk about their fears and anxieties.

13. It is useful to explain in advance to children who will be attending the funeral what the chapel might look like, where the casket will be placed, where the family will be sitting, what the rabbi might say. Make sure that a member of the family or a close relative or friend sits with the children.

Things to remember

Speak from the heart and from your own belief. Be direct and truthful, always guided by the age of the child. Answer the questions asked, as they are asked. Be supportive and understanding. And don't be afraid to say, "I just don't know. Perhaps we can find out together."

If you want to know more:

Earl Grollman, ed., *Explaining Death to Children*. Boston: Beacon Press, 1969.

_____, *Talking About Death*: *A Dialogue Between Parent and Child*. Boston: Beacon Press, 1990.

Honor the Memory of the Deceased

The source:

Code of Jewish Law, Orach Chayim 568:8; Yoreh Deah 402:12.

What you need to know:

1. While there are certain activities that are required by Jewish law for those in mourning that honor the memory of the deceased (such as *shiva*, *sheloshim*, twelve months, *yahrzeit*, *yizkor*), there are many opportunities to honor the memory of the deceased beyond these specific obligations.

2. According to traditional law, there are certain family members obligated to say *kaddish* in memory of the deceased. However, others may assume this obligation, particularly when there are none who are alive to say *kaddish* or who are unable to do so for other reasons. Jewish law requires a *minyan* to be present when *kaddish* is said. If a *minyan* is not present, mourners are urged to study in memory of the deceased. Thus, study becomes a model for honoring the memory of the one who has died.

3. Similarly, when one teaches something that he or she has learned from another, that person is obligated to recall the teacher's name publicly as if he or she were in the room. This is particularly important when something was learned from someone who is no longer living. In addition, when Torah is taught, it can be taught to honor the memory of another.

4. The giving of *tzedakah* which is customarily tied to the daily routine of fixed prayer (three times daily) is also a means through which one can honor the memory of the deceased. Among people of means, this is extended on a larger scale in the form of programs and projects and even buildings.

5. Acts of *gemilut chasadim* also honor the memory of the deceased, particularly when the work that they started is carried on.

Things to remember:

When a person is recalled in conversation by name, Jewish etiquette suggests adding the words, "may s/he rest in peace"or "of blessed memory." Another customary phrase to honor the deceased is "may his or her memory be a blessing."

Key words and phrases:

Alav hashalom: may peace be unto him
Aleha hashalom: may peace be unto her
Gemilut chasadim: loving acts of kindness
Sheloshim: first 30 days of mournng
Shiva: first seven days of mourning
Twelve months: also referred to as *yud-bet chodesh* (a way of saying "twelve months" in Hebrew), marks the first twelve months of mourning (sometimes observed as eleven months in some communities with regard to the recitation of *kaddish*)
Tzedakah: charitable giving
Yahrzeit: (called *anos*, among Sephardic Jews), anniversary of a death, marked by saying *kaddish* by mourners
Yizkor: memorial service, part of the holiday liturgy
Zikhrona livrakha: may her memory be a blessing
Zikhrono livrakha: may his memory be a blessing

If you want to know more:

Kerry M. Olitzky, *Grief in Our Seasons*. Woodstock, VT: Jewish Lights Publishing, 1998.
Ron Wolfson, *"A Time to Mourn, a Time to Comfort."* New York: Federation of Jewish Men's Clubs, 1993.

More particulars:

There are others ways to remember our loved ones. Consider making *tzedakah* contributions in their memory to scholarship and lecture funds that will perpetuate their name, particularly to a cause or organization in which they were active or interested.

Do an Unveiling

The source:

"Jacob set up a pillar on Rachel's grave" (Genesis 35:20).

What you need to know:

1. Gather at the graveside of the deceased.

2. Read a few psalms that offer comfort such as Psalms 23 and 121.

3. Offer a few words in memory of the deceased, something that you want him/her to be remembered for.

4. Remove the cloth covering the gravestone.

5. Read the inscription on the stone.

6. Chant *El Malei Rachamim*.

7. Recite mourner's *kaddish,* if a minyan is present. (Reform Judaism historically does not require the presence of a *minyan*. However, a growing number of Reform rabbis require it nonetheless.)

8. Encourage each person present to place a small stone on the grave marker. (Laying stones on monuments is a sign that someone has visited the cemetery and is thus an acknowledgment that the deceased is still loved and remembered.)

Things to remember:

1. There is no specific time to erect a grave marker. It has become customary to do so at the conclusion of the first year of mourning, but it can take place anytime after thirty days. Unveilings may take place whenever grave visitations in general are permissible.

2. The custom of the unveiling is a Western custom that has evolved over time. Since the tombstone is covered with a cloth by many non-Orthodox families in North America—when it is installed—it is taken off by the family during the service. This ritual has come to be called an unveiling.

3. This is not to be another funeral. It is appropriate for immediate family and close friends to be invited, however. Although a rabbi frequently officiates, it is a brief, uncomplicated ceremony that can easily be led by a member of the family.

Key words and phrases:

Bet chayim: lit., house of life; cemetery
Chevrah kaddisha: burial society
Matzevah: headstone or grave marker
Sheloshim: period marking the first 30 days of mourning, following and including *shiva*
Shiva: the first seven days of mourning
Yahrzeit: anniversary of a person's death (called *anos* among Sephardim), based on the Hebrew date

If you want to know more:

Ronald H. Isaacs and Kerry M. Olitzky, *A Jewish Mourner's Handbook*. Hoboken, NJ: KTAV Publishing House, 1991.

More particulars:

1. There are a variety of markings that people use on headstones. It is common among Ashkenazim, to write the Hebrew letters *peh-nun*, the initials for *poh nach* or "here rests." Sephardim often use the Hebrew letters *mem-kuf*, the initials for *matzevet kevurah* or "monument of the grave of." Underneath the inscription on the headstone, one often finds the Hebrew letters *tav-nun-tzadee-bet-heh* for *tehi nishmato/nishmatah tzerurah bitzeror ha-chayyim* or "May his/her soul be bound up in the bond of eternal life."

2. A descendant of the Levites may have a ewer carved over the inscription since Levites washed the priests' hands in the ancient Temple prior to the recitation of the priestly blessing. This is still done is some synagogues prior to the offering of the priestly blessing by descendants of the priests. This is called *duchanen*.

3. The stone of a descendant of the priests (*kohanim*) is often marked by the carving of hands raised in the priestly blessing.

Do a *Taharah*

The source:

"As one came so shall one go" (Ecclesiastes 5:5); *Kitzur Shulchan Arukh*, chapter 197.

What you need to know:

1. Before the deceased is placed into his/her coffin, the custom is to wash the body in a ritual known as a *taharah* (ritual purification). Those who perform this ritual are generally members of the Holy Burial Society, known as the *Chevra Kaddisha* or *Chevra Kavod Hamet*. Some congregations have made this function part of their Caring Committee (or other committee that looks out for the welfare of the congregation and its members).

2. This is a general outline of the procedure for doing *taharah*. (Note: the precise procedure may vary from one *Chevra Kaddisha* or community to another.)
   i. The purification rite of the *taharah* generally takes place in a specially designated room in a mortuary.
   ii. Before the *taharah* begins, if you are participating in the *taharah*, wash your hands three times using a utensil.
   iii. The body lies facing up during the entire *taharah* procedure.
   iv. Using a large container, wash the body in lukewarm water in the following order: head, neck, right side of body, left side of body. Raise the deceased and wash the back in a similar manner beginning with the right side and then the left.
   v. Clean the nails of the hands and feet thoroughly.
   vi. It is also customary among some communities to comb the hair of the deceased.
   vii. Wash your hands again and wash the body again with 24 quarts of water poured over the head, so that the water flows down over the entire body.
   viii. Move the deceased and place him or her on a dry sheet and wipe him or her dry.

ix. According to some communities, mix the white of a raw egg with a little wine or vinegar and then wash the head with the mixture.

x. Now dress the body with *tachrichim* (white linen shrouds), consisting of several garments. Place the *mitznefet* (head dress) on the head and draw it down to cover the head and neck. Extend the *michnasayim* (trousers) from the belly to the ankles and tie them by making three forms that are shaped to resemble the Hebrew letter *shin*, a symbol of *Shaddai* (Almighty God). Around the ankles, tie each foot with a band, but do not form any knots. The *ketonet* (chemise) has an opening at the top to be slipped over the head and sleeves for the arms. At the neck, knot the bands with bows to resemble the Hebrew letter *shin*. The *kittel* (upper garment) has sleeves for the arms; draw it over the body. Wind the *avnet* (belt) around the body three times over the *kittel*, Make sure that both ends are knotted over the belly with three bows in the shape of the Hebrew letter *shin*.

xi. Choose the *tallit* (prayer shawl) that the deceased wore while praying when he was alive. Place the body in the coffin and wrap the *tallit* around the body. Tear one of the *tzitzit* (fringes) from the *tallit*. Then wrap the *sovev* (linen) sheet around the head.

xii. Place broken pieces of earthenware and a handful of earth from Israel (put into a linen bag) into the casket before it is closed.

xiii. Ask forgiveness of the deceased and then close the casket.

Things to remember:

1. If the deceased died instantaneously through violence or accidents, and his/her body and garments were completely spattered with blood, no washing or *taharah* is performed. The body is placed in the casket without the clothes being removed, and a sheet is wrapped over the clothes.

2. The custom of dressing in plain linen shrouds was to

prohibit a family from showing off its wealth by dressing the deccased in fancy clothing.

Key words and phrases:

Chevra Kaddisha/Chevra Kavod Hamet: Holy Burial Society
Tachrichim: Burial shrouds
Taharah: Ritual purification
Met: Deceased

If you want to know more:

Maurice Lamm, *The Jewish Way in Death and Mourning*. New York: Jonathan David, 1969.

Instant Information
Seven Laws of Noah

The source:

Babylonian Talmud, *Sanhedrin* 56a.

What you need to know:

1. While non-Jews are obviously not required to keep the *mitzvot*, Jewish tradition holds that non-Jews are bound by seven laws. These laws (which are called the Noahide Laws) are presumed to date from the time of Noah who is considered to be a righteous gentile. There are six negative laws and one positive one:

    a. Not to deny God (for example, idolatry)
    b. Not to blaspheme God
    c. Not to murder
    d. Not to engage in incest, adultery, bestiality, or homosexuality.
    e. Not to steal
    f. Not to eat a limb torn from a living animal
    g. To set up courts to ensure obedience to the other six laws.

2. Judaism regards any non-Jew who keeps these laws as a righteous person who is guaranteed a place in the world-to-come.

3. The medieval philosopher/theologian Moses Maimonides believed that a non-Jew was regarded as righteous only if the non-Jewish person observed the laws, because Maimonides believed that God commanded them, as well.

Things to remember:

1. The seven Noahide laws constitute the standard by which Jews assess the morality of a non-Jewish society.

2. The Noahide laws represent a theory of universal religion, emphasizing good actions rather than right be-

lief, ethical living rather than creedal statements. They require only loyalty to a basic code of ethical conduct, and rest upon the recognition of a divine Creator.

More particulars:

Traditional Judaism rejects homosexuality. In recent years, this posture has come under attack by various Jewish movements and organizations. In 1972, the Reform movement (through its lay organization, the Union of American Hebrew Congregations) accepted a gay synagogue into its membership. Both Hebrew Union College–Jewish Institute of Religion, the rabbinical seminary of the Reform movement, and the Reconstructionist Rabbinical College have accepted gay members to study for the rabbinate. As a result, its rabbinical organizations have embraced these rabbis as members. The Conservative movement (through its United Synagogue of Conservative Judaism, the Jewish Theological Seminary of America, and the University of Judaism) is continuing to explore the issues of homosexuality.

Key words and phrases:

B'nai Noach: All the descendants of Noah who survived the flood along with his closet kin

If you want to know more:

Encyclopaedia Judaica. Jerusalem: Keter Publishing Co., 1975, 2:1189 ff.

Aaron Lichtenstein, *The Seven Laws of Noah.* New York and Brooklyn: Rabbi Jacob Joseph School Press and Z. Berman Books, 1981.

Psalm 31: Woman of Valor

The source:

Proverbs 31:10–31.

What you need to know:

1. It is traditional for a husband to read this section of Proverbs in honor of his spouse. This selection from Proverbs has become known as the "woman of valor" because of its descriptive opening phrase. It is read on Friday evening at the Sabbath dinner table before *kiddush* is recited. The passage describes the ideal wife.

2. Since the text is available in any volume of Hebrew Scriptures, here is an alternative translation by Rabbi Susan Grossman:

   A good wife, who can find her?
   She is worth far more than rubies.
   she brings good and not harm
   all the days of her life.
   She girds herself with strength
   and find her trades profitable.

   Wise counsel is on her tongue
   and her home never suffers for warmth.
   She stretches her hands to the poor,
   reaches her arms to the needy.
   All her friends praise her.
   Her family blesses her.
   She is known at the gates
   as she sits with the elders.
   Dignity, honor are her garb.
   She smiles at the future.

3. Some spouses choose to read a selection to honor their husbands. This translation takes the same text from Proverbs and modifies it for use by a woman for her husband. It is also by Rabbi Susan Grossman:

A good man, who can find him?
He is worth far more than rubies.
All who trust in him
never lack for gain.
He shares the household duties
and sets a goodly example.
He seeks a satisfying job
and braces his arms for work.
He opens his mouth with wisdom.
He speaks with love and kindness.
His justice brings him praises.
He raises the poor, lowers the haughty.

Sometimes, their children are invited to add:

These two indeed do worthily
True leaders in Zion.
Give them their due credit.
Let their works praise them at the gates.

Things to remember

While it is traditional for a husband to read the text from Proverbs in honor of his wife, and the wife responds in many household in a like-mannered fashion, and children are blessed by their parents, there is no traditional provision for children to say anything in honor of their parents. Thus, children may want to write something and read it aloud at the Sabbath dinner table.

Key words and phrases

Eishet Chayil: Woman of valor

If you want to know more:

Ronald Isaacs, *Every Person's Guide to Shabbat*. Northvale, NJ: Jason Aronson, 1998.

Instant Information
Shalom Aleikhem

Source:

Rabbi Yossi, son of Rabbi Judah said: "Two ministering angels accompany an individual on the eve of the Sabbath from the synagogue to home. One is a good angel and one is an evil one. And when the individual arrives home and finds the lamp burning, the table set, and the couch covered with a spread, the good angel exclaims, 'May it be even thus on another Sabbath too,' and the evil angel unwillingly responds 'Amen'. But if not [if the house is not prepared for Shabbat], the evil angel exclaims, 'May it be even thus on another Sabbath too,' and the good angel unwillingly responds 'Amen'."

Based on the Babylonian Talmud, *Shabbat* 119b.

What you need to know:

1. *Shalom Aleikhem* is a traditional hymn chanted on Friday nights, upon returning home from the Sabbath eve services. However, some synagogues sing it at the beginning of late Friday evening services (particularly in the Reform movement). Others sing it after services, before *kiddush*, in the synagogue, when late services are held.

2. This song of peace was said to be introduced by the kabbalists four centuries ago. It invites Sabbath angels to accompany the individual at the onset of Shabbat and stay with that person throughout Shabbat and then depart in peace at its conclusion.

שָׁלוֹם עֲלֵיכֶם מַלְאֲכֵי הַשָּׁרֵת מַלְאֲכֵי עֶלְיוֹן,
מִמֶּלֶךְ מַלְכֵי הַמְּלָכִים הַקָּדוֹשׁ בָּרוּךְ הוּא.

Shalom aleikhem malakhei ha-sharet malakhei elyon
Mi-melekh malkhei ha-mlakhim ha-kadosh barukh hu.

Peace be unto you, ministering angels, angels of the
   most High,
The Ruler of Rulers, the Holy Blessed One.

בּוֹאֲכֶם לְשָׁלוֹם מַלְאֲכֵי הַשָּׁלוֹם מַלְאֲכֵי עֶלְיוֹן,
מִמֶּלֶךְ מַלְכֵי הַמְּלָכִים הַקָּדוֹשׁ בָּרוּךְ הוּא.

Bo'akhem le-shalom malakhei ha-shalom malakhei elyon,
Mi-melekh malkhei ha-mlakhim ha-kadosh barukh hu.

Enter in peace, angels of peace, angels of the most
   High,
The Ruler of Rulers, the Holy Blessed One.

בָּרְכוּנִי לְשָׁלוֹם מַלְאֲכֵי הַשָּׁלוֹם מַלְאֲכֵי עֶלְיוֹן,
מִמֶּלֶךְ מַלְכֵי הַמְּלָכִים הַקָּדוֹשׁ בָּרוּךְ הוּא.

Barkhuni le-shalom malakhei ha-shalom malakhei elyon,
Mi-melekh malkhei ha-mlakhim ha-kadosh barukh hu.

Bless me with peace, angels of peace, angels of the
   most High.
The Ruler of Rulers, the Holy Blessed One.

צֵאתְכֶם לְשָׁלוֹם מַלְאֲכֵי הַשָּׁלוֹם מַלְאֲכֵי עֶלְיוֹן,
מִמֶּלֶךְ מַלְכֵי הַמְּלָכִים הַקָּדוֹשׁ בָּרוּךְ הוּא.

Tzetkhem le-shalom malakhei ha-shalom malakhei elyon,
Mi-melekh malkhei ha-mlakhim ha-kadosh barukh hu.

Depart in peace, angels of peace, angels of the most
   High,
The Ruler of Rulers, the Holy Blessed One.

Things to remember:

In many communities and in many families, individuals
either hold hands or embrace one another's shoulders
while singing *Shalom Aleikhem* and swaying back and forth.
This adds to the special time of the Sabbath.

Key words and phrases:

Malakhei Ha-sharet: Ministering angels
Shalom Aleikhem: Welcome

If you want to know more:

Encyclopaedia Judaica. Jerusalem: Keter Publishing House, 1975, 14:1286.

Instant Information
Jewish Ethical Advice

The source:

Various biblical and rabbinic sources, including Leviticus 19:18, Micah 6:8, Jeremiah 9:22–23, Psalm 15:1–5, Isaiah 33:15–16, Babylonian Talmud, *Makkot* 23b–24a, *Shabbat* 31a; Mishneh Peah 1:1.

What you need to know:

1. Ethics is part of the essence of Judaism. While the Reform movement describes Judaism as ethical monotheism, traditional Judaism argues that one of God's first concerns is with a person's decency. According to the Talmud, "In the hour when a person is brought before the heavenly court for judgment, one will be asked: 'Did you conduct your business affairs honestly? Did you set aside regular time for study? Did you try to have children? Did you look forward to the world's redemption?'"

2. Judaism teaches that it is through Torah study that a person learns to be a moral and ethical person. In addition, Jews have the obligation to perfect the world.

3. Here are some guiding principles culled from the Bible:

    i. God has told you what is good, and what is required of you:
       Do justly. love goodness and walk humbly with your God. (Micah 6:8)
    ii. Thus said God: Let not the wise person glory in one's wisdom, nor the strong one glory in one's strength. Let not the rich person glory in one's riches. Only in this should one glory: In one's earnest devotion to Me. For I God act with kindness, justice and equity in the world, and in these do I delight. (Jeremiah 9:22–23)
    iii. Love your neighbor as yourself. (Leviticus 19:18)

iv. God, who may sojourn in Your tent, and who may dwell in Your holy mountain? One who lives without blame, does right, and in one's heart acknowledges the truth. One whose tongue is not given to evil, who has never done harm to one's fellow human being or borne reproach for one's acts toward one's neighbor. For whom a contemptible person is abhorrent, but who honors those who fear God, who stands by one's oath even to one's own harm, who has never lent money at interest or accepted a bribe against the innocent. (Psalm 15:1–5)

v. One [is ethical] who walks in righteousness, speaks uprightly, spurns profit from fraudulent dealings, who waves away a bribe instead of taking it, who closes one's ears and does not listen to malicious words, who shuts one's eyes against looking at evil. (Isaiah 33:15–16)

4. Here are some guiding principles culled from rabbinic literature:

i. When Habakkuk came, he summed up the 613 commandments in one principle, for he said, "The righteous shall live according to his faith [2:4]." (Babylonian Talmud, *Makkot* 23b–24a)

ii. The world endures because of three things: Torah study, worship of God and deeds of kindness. (*Pirke Avot* 1:2)

iii. What is hateful to you, do not do to your neighbor. (Babylonian Talmud, *Shabbat* 31a)

Things to remember

According to the medieval philosopher/theologian Moses Maimonides, the purpose of the laws of the Torah is to bring mercy, lovingkindness and peace into the world. (*Mishneh Torah,* Laws of Shabbat, 2:3)

Key words and phrases:

Tikkun Olam: Perfection of the world
Ve'ahavta le'ray'ekha kamokha: Love your neighbor as yourself

If you want to know more:

Ronald Isaacs, *Derech Eretz: The Path to an Ethical Life*. New
   York: United Synagogue of Conservative Judaism,
   Department of Youth Activities, 1998.

Instant Information
Redeeming Captives

The source:

Babylonian Talmud, *Horayot* 13a; *Bava Batra* 8a–8b.

What you need to know:

1. It is a *mitzvah* to redeem captives and ransom Jews who are being held hostage. It is one of only a few commandments that deal with matters of life and death.

2. When several people are held hostage, Jewish law requires that women are to be ransomed first, because it is assumed that they will suffer greater abuse in captivity.

3. According to the rabbis, if a man and his father and his teacher are incarcerated, and the man only has enough money to redeem one person, then he (i.e., the man) takes precedence over his teacher in procuring ransom, while his teacher takes precedence over his father. He must procure the ransom of his teacher before that of his father. But his mother takes precedence over them all. A scholar takes precedence over a king, for if a scholar dies there is none to replace him, while all are eligible for kingship. (Babylonian Talmud, *Horayot* 13a)

4. Captives were not to be ransomed for more than their value, as a precaution for the general good. (Babylonian Talmud, *Gittin* 4:6)

5. According to Maimonides, there is no greater *mitzvah* than redemption of captives, for the problems of the captive include the problems of the hungry, the naked and those in mortal danger.

6. In recent years oppressed Jews of the Soviet Union, Ethiopia and Syria required the attention of the Jewish community. Thankfully many of them have

been successfully redeemed. But there is still more work to do, for even after they have been redeemed, they have to be absorbed into the community.

Things to remember:

1. In the 17th century, the Jewish community of Venice organized its own society for the redemption of captives (*chevrat pidyon shevuyim*) for the liberation of Jews incarcerated by pirates. Many other communities, from their example, appointed communal wardens to collect funds for the purpose of ransoming captives.

Key words and phrases:

Pidyon Shevuyim: Redeeming of captives

If you want to know more:

Barbara Fortgang Summers. *Community and Responsibility in Jewish Tradition*. New York: United Synagogue of America, Department of Youth Activities, 1978.

The Biblical Precepts Relevant to the Founding of the United States

Source:

Various Bible passages, including: Leviticus 25:10; Deuteronomy 16:20; Micah 6:8; Amos 5:26; Malachi 2:10; Psalm 133:1; and Proverbs 14:34.

What you need to know:

Many American founding documents are clearly related to biblical precepts. Following is a listing of some of the more famous ones, along with their biblical counterparts.

1. "We hold these truths to be self-evident, that all men are created equal, that they are endowed by their Creator with certain inalienable rights, that among these are life, liberty and the pursuit of happiness" (Declaration of Independence).

   "Have we not all one Parent? Has not one God created us? Why should we be faithless to each other, profaning the covenant of our ancestors" (Malachi 2:10).

2. "We, the people of the United States, in order to form a more perfect union, establish justice, insure domestic tranquility, provide for the common defense, promote the general welfare, and secure the blessings of liberty to ourselves and our posterity, do ordain and establish a Constitution for the United States of America" (United States Constitution).

   "Justice, justice, shall you pursue, that you may thrive in the land which the Lord your God gives you" (Deuteronomy 16:20).

3. "Congress shall make no law respecting an establishment of religion, or prohibiting the free exercise thereof; or abridging the freedom of speech, or of the press; or of the right of the people to assemble, and to

petition the government for a redress of grievances" (The Bill of Rights).

"Proclaim liberty throughout the land, for all of its inhabitants" (Leviticus 25:10).

4. "Of all the dispositions and habits which lead to political prosperity, religion and morality are indispensable supports. Where is the security for property, for reputation, for life, if the sense of religious obligation desert the oaths which are the instruments of investigation in courts of justice? And let us with caution indulge the supposition that morality can be maintained without religion" (George Washington, Farewell Address).

"It has been told to you what is good, and what God requires of you: to act justly, to love mercy and to walk humbly with your God" (Micah 6:8).

5. "For happily the government of the United States which gives to bigotry no sanction, to persecution no assistance, requires only that they who live under its protection should demean themselves as good citizens in giving it on all occasions their effectual support" (George Washington, Letter to Newport Synagogue).

"Righteousness raises a nation to honor, but sin is disgraceful for any people" (Proverbs 14:34).

6. "We here highly resolve that these dead shall not have died in vain, that this nation, under God, shall have a new birth of freedom, and that government of the people, by the people, and for the people, shall not perish from the earth" (Abraham Lincoln, Gettysburg Address).

"How good and how pleasant it is when brothers [and sisters] live together in unity" (Psalm 133:1).

7. "With malice toward none, with charity for all, with firmness in the right as God gives us to see the right, let us strive to finish the work we are in . . . to do all which may achieve and cherish a just and lasting peace among ourselves, and with all nations" (Abraham Lincoln, Second Inaugural Address).

"Let justice roll on like a mighty river, righteousness like a never-ending stream" (Amos 5:26).

Things to remember:

There are many Bible phrases that continue to be used in everyday speech. Here are some examples:

1. "I have escaped with the **skin of my teeth**" (Job 19:20)

2. "**Am I my brother's keeper?**" (Genesis 4:9)

3. "Those who **spare the rod spoil the child**" (Proverbs 13:24)

4. "A person has no better thing under the sun, than to **eat, drink, and be merry**" (Ecclesiastes 8:15)

5. "I am **holier than thou**" (Isaiah 65:5)

6. "**Man does not live by bread alone**" (Deuteronomy 8:3)

7. "**Pride goes before a fall**" (Proverbs 16:18)

8. "**There is nothing new under** the sun" (Ecclesiastes 1:9)

Key words and phrases:

Tzedek, tzedek teerdof: Justice, justice you shall pursue

If you want to know more:

Ronald H. Isaacs. *The Jewish Bible Almanac*. Northvale, NJ: Jason Aronson, 1981.

Instant Information
Who's Who in Bible Commentators

Source:

Most of the classical commentators can be found in what is called *The Rabbis' Bible*: *Mikraot Gedolot*. Others are found in various sacred texts.

What you need to know:

Over the centuries numerous people have added their personal commentary to the Bible. Following is a partial listing of some of these commentators.

Ancient

Mekhilta: Oldest rabbinic commentary on Exodus (3rd century C.E.)

Midrash: Ancient sermonic explanations of the Torah and the Five Scrolls (1st through 10th century C.E.)

Philo Judaeus: Renowned Jewish philosopher in Alexandria, author of symbolic (allegorical) commentaries on the Five Books of Moses (2 B.C.E.–40 C.E.)

Septuagint: Greek translation of the Bible made by the Jews in Egypt (3rd century B.C.E.)

Sifra: Oldest rabbinic commentary on Leviticus

Sifre: Oldest rabbinic commentary on Numbers and Deuteronomy (4th century C.E.)

Medieval

Abraham ibn Ezra: Spanish biblical commentator (1092–1167)

Chizkuni: French commentator (13th century)

David Kimchi: French-Spanish biblical scholar (1160–1235)

Moses ben Nachman: Called the Ramban, a leading Spanish commentator (1194–1270)

Don Isaac Abarbanel: Spanish Bible commentator (1437–1509)

Joseph Bechor Shor: French commentator (12th century)

Obadiah Sforno. Italian commentator (1475–1550)

Rashi: Considered one of the greatest of all Bible commentators, this French Bible scholar was known for his literal interpretation of the Bible (1040–1105)

Modern

Israel Abrahams. Anglo-Jewish commentator (1858–1925)

David Altshul. Wrote popular commentaries on prophetic books (17th century)

Umberto Cassuto. Italian-Jewish commentator (1883–1951)

Samson Raphael Hirsch. German commentator (1808–1888)

Marcus Jastrow. American Bible scholar (1829–1903)

S. D. Luzzatto. Italian Hebraist and commentator (1800–1865)

Nehama Leibowitz. A Bible professor and commentator at the Hebrew University of Judaism

Malbim: Russian commentator (1809–1879)

Leopold Zunz: Edited and translated the Bible that is most used among German-speaking Jews (1794–1886)

Things to remember:

Various commentators were known to specialize in a particular style of explanation. The early rabbis compared the Torah to a beautiful garden whose fruits might be extracted by using four different methods signified by the Hebrew letters for the word for "orchard" or "paradise" *PaRDeS*:

P=Peshat: Commentator is interested in the literal interpretation of the Bible text (i.e., what the Bible meant to say at the time in which the passage was written). The commentator Rashi was master of the *Peshat* methodology.

R=Remez: The allegorical interpretation of the Bible, used by Philo, which hinted at information.

D=Derash: The sermonic, interpretative style, leading to the path of ethical and aggadic (stories, fables, legends) commentary.

S=Sod: The secretive and mystical interpretation of the Bible text, often used by students of the Kabbalah.

Key words and phrases:

Parshanut: Field of literature made up of commentaries and commentators.

If you want to know more:

Encyclopaedia Judaica. Jerusalem: Keter Publishing Co., 1975, 4:890–892.

Joseph Hertz, ed., *The Pentateuch and Haftorahs*. London: Soncino Press, 1987.

Instant Information
Rabbinic Remedies for Illness

The source:

Various Talmudic sources, including these tractates of the Babylonian Talmud: *Pesachim* and *Horayot*, *Gittin* and *Shabbat*.

What you need to know:

Much of ancient medicine consisted of a combination of science, superstition and folklore. As we explore "alternative" or "complementary" forms of medicine in the postmodern world, the challenge remains as to how to determine one from the other! Supernatural agencies were often considered as causes of illness and disease, and remedies often included incantations accompanied by other rites and rituals. Following are several rabbinic passages which reflect the many recipes that belong to the category of folk medicine.

1. **Remedy for an intermittent fever:** Rabbi Huna said: As a remedy for a fever, one should procure seven prickles from seven date palms, seven chips from seven beams, seven pegs from seven bridges, seven handfuls of ash from seven ovens, seven pinches of earth from seven graves, seven bits of pitch from seven ships, seven seeds of cumin, and seven hairs from the beard of an old dog, and tie them inside the collar of his shirt with a band of twined strands of wool. (Babylonia Talmud, *Shabbat* 67a)

2. **Remedy for depression:** If a person is seized by depression, eat red meat broiled over coals and drink diluted wine. (Babylonian Talmud, *Gittin* 67b)

3. **Remedy for a migraine headache**: For a migraine, one should take a woodcock and cut its throat with a white silver coin over the side of the head where the pain is concentrated, taking care that the blood does not blind the eyes. Then hang the bird on the doorpost, so that

the person can rub against it when coming in and when exiting. (Babylonia Talmud, *Gittin* 69a)

4. **Remedy for cataracts:** Take a seven-hued scorpion, dry it out in the shade, and mix two parts of ground kohl to one part of ground scorpion. Then, with a paintbrush, apply three drops to each eye—no more, lest the eye burst. (Babylonian Talmud, *Gittin* 69a)

5. **Remedy to stop a nosebleed**: Call a priest whose name is Levi and write "Levi" backward, or else call any other man and write backward, "I am Papa Shila bar Sumki," or else write "the taste of the bucket in water of blemish." (Babylonian Talmud, *Gittin* 69a)

6. **Remedy for a toothache:** For a toothache, Rabbah bar R. Chuna said: Take a whole head of garlic, grind it with oil and salt and apply it on his thumbnail to the side where the tooth aches. Put a rim of dough around it, thus taking care that it does not touch the flesh, as it may cause leprosy. (Babylonian Talmud, *Gittin* 69a)

7. **Remedy for heartburn:** Take black cumin regularly. (Babylonian Talmud, *Berakhot* 40a)

8. **Remedy for bad breath:** After every food eat salt, and after every beverage drink water and you will come to no harm. (Babylonian Talmud, *Berakhot* 40a)

Things to remember:

Because of the importance of medicine and the treatment of the body, the Babylonian Talmud (*Sanhedrin* 17b) enumerates ten things that must be in a city where a scholar lives. Among these requirements are a physician and a surgeon.

Key words and phrases:

Rofeh: doctor

If you want to know more:

Ronald H. Isaacs, *Judaism, Medicine and Healing*. Northvale, NJ: Jason Aronson, 1998.

Instant Information
Prophets of the Bible

The source:

Rashi's commentary on the Talmud lists the prophets (Babylonian Talmud, *Megillah* 14), as do the collections of *Halakhot Gedolot* and *Seder Olam*. Some of the information in this section can be culled directly from a reading of the Bible itself.

What you need to know:

1. The Hebrew word for "prophet," *navi*, signifies a spokesperson, one who speaks for God to human beings.

2. Foreseeing the outcome of national crises and evil practices, the prophets fearlessly criticized the morals of their own day while teaching a nobler way of living.

3. The message of the prophets was usually one of warning and exhortation, including a prediction of coming events in the near or distant future.

4. While we may not normally have called some of the following individuals prophets, according to the medieval commentator Rashi, these are the forty-eight male prophets and seven female prophets:

Male Prophets

1. **Abraham**: (18th century B.C.E.) The son of Terach and a descendant of Eber, Abraham was the father of the Israelite nation and the first to preach monotheism to the world.

2. **Aaron**: (13th century B.C.E.) Brother of Moses, served as intermediary between Moses and Pharaoh because of his eloquence.

3. **Ahijah the Shilonite**: (10th century B.C.E.) Active toward the end of Solomon's reign, speaking in God's

name, he prophesied the division of the kingdom "because they have forsaken Me and they have not walked in My ways, to do that which is right in my eyes, and to keep My statutes and My ordinances, as did David" (I Kings 11:33).

4. **Amos**: (8th century B.C.E.) Native of Tekoa, this minor prophet prophesied in the days of Uzziah, Jeroboam II, Jotham, Ahaz, and Hezekiah. He was the first prophet whose utterances have been transmitted to us in a separate book.

5. **Amoz**: (8th century B.C.E.) According to the sages, he was the brother of King Amaziah. He opposed the importing of troops from the Northern Kingdom to aid Judah (II Chronicles 25:15–16).

6. **Azariah, son of Oded**: (8th century B.C.E.) During the reign of Asa, King of Judah, Azariah prophesied: "God is with you, while you are with God. Be strong, and let not your hands be slack, for your work shall be rewarded" (II Chronicles 15:1–2, 7). Asa eventually removed the detestable idols from the land of Judah and Benjamin.

7. **Baruch, son of Neriah**: (6th century B.C.E.) Scribe and student of Jeremiah, Baruch "wrote from the mouth of Jeremiah all the words of God, which God has spoken to him, upon a roll of a book" (Jeremiah 36:4).

8. **Chaggai:** (10th century B.C.E.) This post-exilic prophet, whose book is the tenth of the minor prophets, called for rebuilding of the Temple.

9. **Chanani the Seer**: (5th century B.C.E.) He rebuked Asa, king of Judah, for relying on the king of Aram when in danger, and not upon God (II Chronicles 16).

10. **David**: (10th century B.C.E.) The rabbinic sages observed that David, too, was a prophet, because the Bible says, "to whom David and Samuel the seer did ordain in their office" (I Chronicles 9:22).

11. **Eli the Priest:** (11th century B.C.E.) He was the predecessor of Samuel, the last of the judges, and was the last High Priest in the Tabernacle of Shiloh.

Eli was revered by all, and his blessing was prized as one that came from the lips of the holy man of God (I Samuel 1:17).

12. **Eliezer, son of Dodavahu**: (9th century B.C.E.) A Judean prophet, Eliezer told Jehoshaphat, "Because you have joined yourself with Ahaziah, God has made a breach in your works." Jehoshaphat, refusing to heed the prophet's words, made an agreement with the king of Israel to have ships built in Ezion-geber. However, before the vessels were able to sail for Tarshish, their destination, they were destroyed (II Chronicles 20:35–37)

13. **Elijah**: (9th century B.C.E.) Native of Gilead, he prophesied and brought miracles in the kingdom of Ephraim during the reigns of Ahab and his son Ahaziah. He waged an endless struggle against Jezebel and the Baal cult which she had brought to Israel from her birthplace (I Kings 19:1–21). Because of his ascent to heaven while still alive, Jewish tradition holds that he will announce the arrival of the Messiah.

14. **Elisha:** (9th century B.C.E.) Son of Shaphat, he was the disciple and successor of Elijah. He had an extraordinary career, performing even more miracles than did Elijah. For instance, he purified the fountain in Jericho (II Kings 2:19–22) and miraculously increased a widow's supply of oil (II Kings 4:1–7).

15. **Elkanah:** (11th century B.C.E.) Son of Jeroham, a family of the tribe of Levi (I Chronicles 6:19–24). According to rabbinic tradition (Babylonian Talmud *Megillah* 14), he was one of the major prophets, unparalleled in his generation.

16. **Ezekiel**: (6th century B.C.E.) Third of the three major prophets, he witnessed the destruction of Jerusalem and Judea and went into exile to Babylonia. Chapter 37 of his book describes his famous vision of the valley of dry bones that are resurrected, symbolizing the rebirth of Israel.

17. **Gad the Seer**: (10th century B.C.E.) The Bible refers to Gad as both prophet and seer (I Chronicles 29:29).

He helped David to organize the Levitical singers in the Temple (I Chronicles 23:27).

18. **Habakkuk**: (7th century B.C.E.) His book is the eighth of the minor prophets. It is an outcry against the victory of the Chaldeans and the rule of iniquity in the world.

19. **Hosea**: (8th century B.C.E.) He was the first man whose own failed marriage symbolized Israel's relationship with God. His book is considered to be one of the minor prophetic books.

20. **Iddo the Seer**: (10th century B.C.E.) According to the sages, Iddo preached during the reign of Jeroboam, son of Nebat. It was he who came from Judah to Bethel and prophesied the destruction of the altar that Jeroboam had built there and had sacrificed upon.

21. **Isaac**: (17th century B.C.E.) Only son of Abraham by his wife Sarah, Isaac was the second of the patriarchs.

22. **Isaiah**: (8th century B.C.E.) He prophesied from the year of Uzziah's death until the beginning of Manasseh's reign. He is considered one of the three major classical prophets.

23. **Jacob**: (16th century B.C.E.) Son of Isaac, Jacob was the third of the patriarchs and father of the twelve tribes of Israel.

24. **Jehu son of Chanani**: (9th century B.C.E.) Prophesying during the reign of Asa, he declared that Baasa, ruler of the Northern Kingdom, would suffer Jeroboam's fate. Jehu also wrote the chronicles of Jehoshaphat (II Chronicles 20:34).

25. **Jeremiah:** (7th century B.C.E.) This major prophet with his own book belonged to a priestly family in Anatot near Jerusalem. His prophecies foretold the doom of his people as punishment for their sins.

26. **Joel**: (5th century B.C.E.) Second in the order of the twelve minor prophets, Joel called the people of Judea to repent because the Day of Judgment was at hand.

27. **Jonah, son of Amittai**: (8th century B.C.E.) According to the book that bears his name, Jonah was sent to

Nineveh to make the people repent of their evil doing. He fled the country, only to be swallowed by a large fish. In the end he was forced to come to Nineveh, and there successfully encouraged its inhabitants to repent.

28. **Joshua**: (13th century B.C.E.) Son of Nun, Joshua belonged to the tribe of Ephraim. He led the Israelites in battle in the desert against Amalek whom he defeated in Rephidim. (Exodus 17:8) He succeeded Moses and conquered the seven nations of Canaan.

29. **Machseiah**: (7th century B.C.E.) He was the father of Neriah and grandfather of Baruch, the scribe of Jeremiah (Jeremiah 32:12).

30. **Malachi**: (5th century B.C.E.) Last of the biblical prophets, he protests against transgressions in matters of sacrifices and tithes and complains of mixed and broken marriages.

31. **Micah**: (12th century B.C.E.) This minor prophet spoke out against the social evils of his time, maintaining that they would bring about the nation's downfall.

32. **Micaiah, son of Imlah**: (9th century B.C.E.) In the days of Ahab, Micaiah was the only true prophet among some 400 court prophets who told the king whatever he wanted to hear (I Kings 22:8). According to the Bible, he beheld God and the heavenly angels: "I saw God sitting on the throne, and all the heavenly host standing by God on the right hand and on the left" (I Kings 22:19).

33. **Mordecai**: (5th century B.C.E.) A descendant of Kish, he lived in Shushan and reared Esther, his cousin. With her help, he was able to thwart the evil Haman's schemes and bring retribution upon the enemies of Israel.

34. **Moses:** (13th century B.C.E.) Considered the greatest of the prophets. Of him the Bible says: "There has not arisen a prophet since in Israel like Moses, whom God knew face to face" (Deuteronomy 34:10). Moses had a strong influence on all the prophets who followed him. The Jewish people received the Torah through Moses at Sinai.

35. **Nahum**: (7th century B.C.E.) He lived during the reign of Manasseh and foretold the fall of Nineveh.

36. **Nathan the Prophet:** (10th century B.C.E.) Nathan was a prophet in the generation that followed Samuel. He admonished David fearlessly for the latter's misconduct with Bathsheba (II Samuel 12:13 ff.).

37. **Neriah**: (7th century B.C.E.) He was the father of Baruh and one of the eight prophets descended from Rahab, a woman of Jericho (Jeremiah 36:4).

38. **Obadiah**: (5th century B.C.E.) He was the fourth of the so-called minor prophets. In his one-chapter book, he predicts the destruction of Edom and condemns the Edomites for having refused to assist Jerusalem in the days of calamity.

39. **Oded**: (10th century B.C.E.) Oded prophesied in Samaria during the reign of Ahaz, king of Judah, and Pekah, son of Remaliah, king of Israel.

40. **Pinchas:** (11th century B.C.E.) Grandson of Aaron, in reward for his zealous action against Zimri, he and his descendants were promised the priesthood (Numbers 25).

41. **Samuel**: (11th century B.C.E.) Son of Elkanah and the last judge of Israel. As an adult he attained fame as a prophet throughout the land.

42. **Seraiah, son of Neriah**: (6th century B.C.E.) According to the sages, he prophesied during the second year of Darius' reign. He appears in the fifty-first chapter of the Book of Jeremiah.

43. **Shemaiah**: (10th century B.C.E.) A Judean, Shemaiah prophesied during the reign of Rehoboam when the latter mustered his army in hopes of regaining his sovereignty over the Northern Kingdom.

44. **Solomon**: (10th century B.C.E.) The rabbinic sages included King Solomon among the prophets because of his dream at Gibeon. God appeared to him there and said, "Ask what I shall give you." Solomon requested "an understanding heart" to judge the people (I Kings 3:5, 9).

45. **Uriah, son of Shemaiah**: (6th century B.C.E.) Native of Kiriath-jearim, Uriah prophesied during the reign of Jehoiakim. He foretold the destruction of the city and the country in much the same way as did Jeremiah.

46. **Yechaziel the Levite**: (10th century B.C.E.) In II Chronicles 20:14, we learn that "the spirit of God came upon Yechaziel." He encouraged Jehoshaphat prior to the battle against Ammon, Moab and Seir.

47. **Zechariah:** (6th century B.C.E.) This minor prophet's prophecies are concerned with contemporary events and foretell the ingathering of the exiles and the expansion of Jerusalem.

48. **Zephaniah:** (7th century B.C.E.) The prophecies of this minor prophet were mostly eschatological. Described in his book is the Day of the Lord, when God will punish all the wicked and God will be universally acknowledged.

Female Prophets

1. **Abigail**: (10th century B.C.E.) The Bible records that Abigail prophesied to David: "God will certainly make my lord a sure house" (I Samuel 25:28–31).

2. **Channah**: (11th century B.C.E.) She was the mother of the prophet Samuel.

3. **Chuldah:** (7th century B.C.E.) The wife of Shallu, she lived near the courts of learning in Jerusalem during the reign of Josiah (II. Kings 22:14). The sages (Babylonian Talmud, *Megillah* 14b) declared that Chuldah was one of the three prophets of that generation; the other two were Zephaniah and Jeremiah.

4. **Deborah**: (12th century B.C.E.) The Bible refers to Deborah as "a prophet, the wife of Lapidot." She fought a famous battle against Sisera and successfully defeated his army (Judges 4).

5. **Esther**: (5th century B.C.E.) The rabbis regarded Esther as a prophet because the Bible says of her: "Esther put on her royal apparel" (Esther 5:1) This

was interpreted to mean that she was clothed with the divine spirit, as it is similarly written: "The spirit clothed Amasai" (I Chronicles 12:19; cf. Babylonian Talmud, *Megillah* 4b).

6. **Miriam**: (13th century B.C.E.) The Bible explicitly refers to Miriam as a prophet: "And Miriam the prophet took the timbrel" (Exodus 15:20). She was the sister of Moses, considered the greatest prophet to have ever lived.

7. **Sarah**: (18th century B.C.E.) Sarah, the wife of Abraham, bore Isaac. Today she is considered one of the four Jewish matriarchs.

Things to remember:

1. The literary prophets were so called because their words were written down in books that were named for them.

2. Many of the prophets preached the importance of being ethical and moral.

3. The fundamental experience of the prophet is a fellowship with God.

Key words and phrases:

Navi: prophet

If you want to know more:

Ronald Isaacs, *Messengers of God: A Jewish Prophets Who's Who*. Northvale, NJ: Jason Aronson, 1998.

Names of God

The source:

A cross-section of some of the names of God, culled from the Bible, the prayer book, and various rabbinic sources.

What you need to know:

1. Jewish tradition says that the name of God, which consists of the four Hebrew letters *yod*, *heh*, *vav*, *heh*, was revealed to Moses at the burning bush. Its exact pronunciation was passed on to his brother Aaron and kept a secret among the priests.

2. The only time when the High Priest actually pronounced the name of God was on Yom Kippur (Day of Atonement), during the confession of sins.

3. When people were not in the ancient sanctuary, the euphemism *Adonai* was used as the name for God.

4. In conversation, the term *HaShem* ("The Name") is often used to protect God's name from possible blasphemy and improper use, particularly among traditional Jews.

God in the Bible

1. *El*: The oldest Semitic term for God, it is a descriptive name, often used in combination with other names for God. For example, *El Olam* (Eternal God) or *El Shaddai* (Almighty God).

2. *Elohim*: Appears in the opening verse of the Torah: "In the beginning, God (Elohim) created the heaven and the earth" (Genesis 1:1).

3. *YHVH* (alternatively *YHWH*): An ancient biblical name for God, possibly pronounced Yahweh. The consensus of scholarly opinion is that *YHVH* is derived from a form of the verb "to be."

4. *El Shaddai*: Divine Name frequently found in the Bible and often translated "Almighty."

5. *Adonai*: Derived from the Hebrew *Adon* (Lord).

6. *Yah*: A short form of the Divine Name (*Yh*), Yah may represent the original form from which YHVH was expanded. Yah also appears in biblical names such as Elijah (*Eliyahu* in Hebrew).

7. *Adonai Tzeva'ot*: "Lord of Hosts (i.e., God's angels) is the traditional translation of this Divine Name. Some say that it means "One who brings the angelic hosts into being."

8. *Kadosh*: The Holy One.

9. *Tzur*: The Rock.

10. *Ehyeh asher Ehyeh*: "I am that I am" (Exodus 3:14).

Rabbinic Names for God

1. *HaKadosh Barukh Hu*: The Holy Blessed One.

2. *Ribbono shel Olam*: Sovereign of the Universe.

3. *Hamakom*: The Place or the Omnipresent One.

4. *Avinu Shebashamayim*: Our Father in Heaven.

5. *Ein Sof*: Kabbalistic name, meaning "Without End."

6. *Shalom*: Peace.

7. *Temira detemirin*: Kabbalistic name, meaning "Hidden of Hiddens."

God's Names in the Prayerbook

1. *Elohay Avraham*: God of Abraham.

2. *Elohay Yitzchak*: God of Isaac.

3. *Elohay Ya'akov*: God of Jacob.

4. *Shomer Yisrael*: Guardian of Israel.

5. *Melekh Malkhai hamelakhim*: Sovereign of Sovereigns.

6. *Adon Olam*: Eternal God.

7. *Harofe*: The Healer.

8. *Tzur Yisrael*: Rock of Israel.

Things to remember:

1. The various names of God reflect descriptions of different aspects of God as our ancestors experienced the Divine.

2. The rabbis prescribed injunctions regarding the writing of God's name. For example, if the name of God is written, it cannot be erased. It can be discarded only through ritual burial, just like sacred texts.

Key words and phrases:

Chillul HaShem: Profaning of God's Name
Kiddush Hashem: Sanctification of God's Name

If you want to know more:

Steven Brown, *Higher and Higher: Making Jewish Prayer Part of Us*. New York: United Synagogue of America, Department of Youth Activities, 1985.
Ronald Isaacs, *Close Encounters: Jewish Views About God*. Northvale, NJ: Jason Aronson, 1996.

Instant Information
Jewish Numerology

The source:

The Bible and various rabbinic sources.

What you need to know:

1. The Jewish Bible is full of numbers. Some were to be taken literally, while others are symbols or metaphors.

2. With the advent of *gematria* (i.e., rabbinic numerology), rabbis began to use *gematria* to explain various Jewish texts.

3. A cross-section of interesting numbers from Jewish life:

   a. **Longest verse in the Bible**: Appears in the Book of Esther (8:9) which has 43 words in Hebrew.
   b. **Rabbinic teacher mentioned the most times**: Rabbi Yehuda bar Ilai is mentioned 607 times in the Mishnah.
   c. **The human life cycle**: This passage from *Pirke Avot* presents the ages of readiness for responsibilities in life.

   The age of 5 for the study of Bible.
   The age of 10 for the study of Mishnah.
   The age of 13 for being responsible for the commandments.
   The age of 15 for the study of Talmud.
   The age of 18 for marriage.
   The age of 20 for earning a living.
   The age of 30 for power.
   The age of 40 for understanding.
   The age of 50 for giving advice.
   The age of 60 for old age.
   The age of 70 for gray hairs.
   The age of 80 for special strength.
   The age of 90 for bowed back.

The age of 100—it is as if one had died and passed away.

d. **The number 7 as a rabbinic remedy for fever**: To cure a fever, take 7 prickles from 7 palm trees, 7 chips from 7 beams, 7 nails from 7 bridges, 7 ashes from 7 ovens, 7 scoops of earth from 7 door sockets, 7 pieces of pitch from 7 ships, 7 handfuls of cumin, and 7 hairs from the beard of an old dog, and tie them to the neck hole of the shirt with a twisted cord. (Babylonian Talmud, *Shevuot* 15b)

e. **The number 12 in Jewish life:** Following are the appearances of the number 12 in Jewish life:

12 tribes of Israel (Reuben, Simeon, Levi, Judah, Issachar, Zebulun, Joseph, Benjamin, Dan, Naphtali, Gad, and Asher)

12 stones in the breastplate of the High Priest

12 minor prophets: Hosea, Joel, Amos, Obadiah, Jonah, Micah, Nachum, Habakkuk, Zephaniah, Haggai, Zechariah, and Malachi

12 months in the year

12 constellations

Jewish girl is obligated to fulfill *mitzvot* at age 12

12 loaves of shewbread used in the tabernacle

12 portions in the Book of Genesis

At age 12 King Solomon became king.

f. **Bible Statistics:** The Bible has more than 773,000 words and 3.5 million letters. There are 39 books in the Jewish Bible, 929 chapters, and 23,214 verses.

g. **Number 70 in the writings of the Rabbis**:

   i. Gog and Magog have the numerical value of 70, namely the 70 nations.

  ii. The Torah was transmitted to the 70 elders. *(Midrash Yelamdeinu)*

 iii. There are 70 facets to the Torah. (*Zohar Bereshit* 36)

  iv. Seventy facets to the Torah were translated into 70 languages in order to make it more understandable to the 70 nations. (Babylonian Talmud, *Sotah* 32a)

v. On the Festival of Sukkot, 70 sacrifices were offered for the sake of the 70 nations of the world who have 70 representatives among the heavenly angels. *(Midrash Alpha Beita)*

If you want to know more:

Ronald Isaacs, *The Jewish Book of Numbers*. Northvale, NJ: Jason Aronson, 1996.

The source:

Various rabbinic sources, including the Talmud and other kabbalistic sources.

What you need to know:

1. Over time each community has developed its own particular folk customs and practices that are associated with it. Within the world of folklore one will usually find a variety of superstitions.

2. A superstition is generally defined as any custom or act that is based on an irrational fear rather than on tradition, belief, reason, or knowledge.

3. Many Jewish superstitions evolved with the goal of safeguarding a person from danger and evil.

4. A cross-section of Judaism's superstitions, many of which continue to play an important role in the life of a contemporary Jew:

   i. **Superstition related to circumcision:** Place red ribbons and garlic on a baby's crib to ward off evil spirits. Also, keep candy under the bed to draw attention of evil spirits away from baby.

   ii. **Superstition related to naming a child:** Some Jews have the custom of refusing to marry a person who has the same name as their mother or father. This custom arose from fear that the Angel of Death might confuse two persons with the same name, leading to the premature death of one or the other.

   iii. **Superstition and the wedding:** Brides often carried a lighted torch or candle as a way of warding off evil spirits. Also, the custom of the fast of a bride and groom on the day of their wedding is intended to fool the evil spirits into thinking that it is a day of mourning rather than one of ultimate joy.

iv. **Superstition and death**: Watching and caring for a deceased person (before burial) while reading various psalms was considered a strong antidote to evil spirits.

v. **Superstition and saliva:** Expectorating and using one's saliva was an ancient way of repelling evil spirits. Today, saying the phrase "pooh pooh pooh" after witnessing or acknowledging something wonderful or beautiful such as a newborn baby is considered an antidote to evil.

vi. **Superstition and books**: Closing books that are left open is a superstitious practice that likely relates to the ancient belief that an open book can be more easily inhabited by an evil spirit who can work to distort its meaning.

vii. **Superstition and the evil eye:** Put a piece of matzah into the pocket of a particularly handsome child to protect him or her against the evil eye. Qualify any praise that you give a beautiful object or person with the phrase *kein hore* (Yiddish for "no evil") or *kein ayen hore* (Yiddish for "no evil eye"), often shortened to *kaynahora*.

viii. **Superstition and counting people**: Never count people using one, two, three, etc., because numbering people creates a special susceptibility to the evil eye. If you need to count people, count "not one," "not two," and so on.

Key words and phrases:

Ayin Hara: Evil eye

If you want to know more:

Brenda Z. Rosenbaum and Stuart Copans, *How to Avoid the Evil Eye*. New York: St Martin's Press, 1985.

Joshua Trachtenberg, *Jewish Magic and Superstition: A Study in Folk Religion*. New York: Behrman House, 1939.

Instant Information
Notable Quotations from the Bible

The source:

The Jewish Bible, especially the Book of Proverbs.

What you need to know:

1. The Bible is filled with pithy sayings and proverbs, many of which have entered into contemporary conversation.

2. The fifteenth book of the Bible, called Proverbs, contains a plethora of sayings concerning industry, sobriety, honesty, caution and learning.

3. A cross-section of proverbs and notable sayings from various Bible sources:

   a. The fear of God is the beginning of knowledge. (Proverbs 1:7)
   b. The one who spares the rod spoils the child. (Proverbs 13:24)
   c. Go to the ant, you sluggard, consider her ways and be wise. (Proverbs 6:6)
   d. Hate stirs up strife, but love covers all transgressions. (Proverbs 10:2)
   e. A word fitly spoken is like apples of gold in settings of silver. (Proverbs 25:1)
   f. Am I my brother's keeper? (Genesis 4:9)
   g. Cast your bread upon the waters, for after many days you will find it. (Ecclesiastes 11:1)
   h. An eye for an eye, a tooth for a tooth. (Exodus 21:24)
   i. Not by might, nor by power, but by My spirit, says the Lord of Hosts. (Zechariah 4:6)
   j. The Lord is my shepherd and I shall not want. (Psalm 23:1)

If you want to know more:

A. Colin Day, *Roget's Thesaurus of the Bible*. San Francisco: Harper Collins, 1992.

Instant Information
Best Times to Get Married

The source:

Various rabbinic and talmudic sources.

What you need to know:

1. Weddings among traditional Jews are not performed:

   on Sabbaths and festivals; during the intermediate days of Passover and Sukkot;

   during periods of national mourning, such as the days of *sefirah* (counting the omer) between Passover and Shavuot and what are called the "three weeks" between the seventeenth of Tammuz and the Ninth of Av.

2. One should consult his or her own rabbi concerning days when weddings may take place, since there are also times when it is considered inconvenient for the community or inappropriate even if there is no Jewish law preventing it.

3. Certain days are considered lucky for wedding ceremonies. They include:

   a. Tuesdays, because in describing the third day of creation (i.e., Tuesday), the Bible twice uses the expression "God saw that this was good" (Genesis 1:10, 12).
   b. Wednesdays for virgins, and Thursday for widows
   c. Israel Independence Day, Lag B'Omer and Tu B'Av (the 15th day of Av)
   d. During the month of Elul, before the High Holidays. Elul is considered a month for love because the word Elul is an acronym formed from the Hebrew words in the Song of Songs, *Ani Le-dodi, Ve-dodi Li*, "I am my beloved's and my beloved is mine."

Key words and phrases:

Ani Le-dodi: I am my beloved's and my beloved is mine.

If you want to know more:

Maurice Lamm, *The Jewish Way in Love and Marriage*. San
    Francisco: Harper and Row, 1980.

Instant Information
The Confessional

The source:

"When a person is sick and near death, that person is required to make confession" (Babylonian Talmud, *Shabbat* 32a).

What you need to know:

1. Observant Jews make confession on their deathbed, in keeping with the talmudic instruction that one who is near death is asked to do so.

2. While there are a variety of texts that may be used for the confessional, here is one that is commonly used:

    My God and God of my ancestors, accept my prayer. Do not turn away. Forgive me for all the times I may have disappointed You. I am aware of the wrongs I have committed.

    May my pain and suffering serve as atonement. Forgive my shortcomings, for against You I have sinned.

    May it be Your will, Adonai my God and God of my ancestors, that I live now with a clear conscience and in accordance with Your will. Send a *refuah sheleimah*, a complete healing, to me and to all who suffer.

    My life and death are in Your hands, Adonai my God. May it be Your will to heal me.

    Guardian of the bereaved, protect my beloved family; our souls are bound together. In Your hands lies my spirit.

    Hear O Israel: Adonai is our God, Adonai is One.

    Adonai is God. Adonai is God.[1]

---

[1]Excerpted from the *Rabbis Manual*. New York: Rabbinical Assembly, 1998.

More Particulars

Since the only way to complete full *teshuva*, according to many authorities, is through one's death, even criminals are urged to confess within a short distance of the scene of their execution. If they have nothing to confess, they are instructed to say: "Let my death be an atonement for all of my transgressions" (Babylonian Talmud, *Sanhedrin* 6:2).

Key words and phrases:

Vidui: Confession

If you want to know more:

Simon Glustrom, *The Language of Judaism*. Northvale, NJ: Jason Aronson, 1966.

Instant Information
Sing *Hava Nagilah*

The source:

Lyrics composed by Cantor Moshe Nathanson (cantor of the Society for the Advancement of Judaism). Based on the verse from the Book of Psalms (118:24): "*Zeh hayom asah Adonai nagilah v'nismecha bo.* This is the day that God has made, let us be happy and rejoice on it."

What you need to know:

1. *Hava Nagilah* is probably the world's most famous Hebrew song of joy.

2. The melody for *Hava Nagilah* was composed by A. Z. Idelsohn, famous Jewish musicologist, who is often considered the founder of modern Jewish musicology

3. The text for *Hava Nagilah*, often accompanied by a dance (the *hora* circle dance):

הָבָה נָגִילָה

וְנִשְׂמְחָה

הָבָה נְרַנְּנָה

וְנִשְׂמְחָה

עוּרוּ עוּרוּ אַחִים

עוּרוּ אַחִים בְּלֵב שָׂמֵחַ

Hava Nagilah (3)
V'nismecha
Hava n'ranana (3)
V'nismecha
Uru uru achim
Uru achim b'lev sameach

Come, let us be joyful
And let our happiness overflow.
Come, let us rejoice

And let our happiness overflow.
Rise, rise, O brethren,
Rise, O brethren.

Things to remember:

The melody for *Hava Nagilah* was adapted from a hasidic tune. Few songfests, Jewish weddings, bar or bat mitzvah celebrations are considered complete without the singing of *Hava Nagilah*.

Key words and phrases:

Hava Nagilah: Come, let us be joyful

If you want to know more:

Sheldon Feinberg, *Hava Nagila: The World's Most Famous Song of Joy*. New York: Shapolsky Publishers, 1988.

Instant Information
Who's Who in Rabbinic Commentators

The source:

Various editions of the Talmud contain commentaries on the Talmud. Some include biographical information of sorts. Easier access for this information is provided in: Moses Mielziner, *Introduction to the Talmud*. New York: Bloch Publishing, 1925.

What you need to know:

1. A knowledge of the dates of the rabbinic commentators (known as Tannaim—the early teachers—and the Amoraim—the later teachers) and the chronological order of the generations in which they lived can be of help in understanding different aspects of Talmudic discussion.

2. Amoraim is the title given to Jewish scholars in Palestine and Babylonia in the 3rd through the 6th centuries C.E. The Amoraim continued the work of the Tannaim, teachers living during the first two centuries C.E. in Palestine.

3. The chronology of rabbinic scholars can help to demonstrate the evolution of opinions among the rabbis, as well as how they conflict and contrast with one another.

4. Many sages had identical names. Thus, it is often difficult to determine whether a statement should be ascribed to the first, second, or even third scholar bearing that name.

5. Following is a summary of the important rabbinic scholars during both the Tannaitic and Amoraic periods:

Tannaitic Period

Date	Tannaim	Historical Events in Israel
3rd cent. B.C.E.	Shimon HaTzaddik	Conquest of Israel by Alexander the Great
	Antigonos of Sokho	
2nd cent. B.C.E.	Yose ben Yoezer Yose ben Yochanan Nitai HaArbeli	Maccabees
1st cent. B.C.E.	Yehudah ben Tabbi Alexander Yannai Shimon ben Shetach Shemayah, Avtalyon	
30 B.C.E.– 20 B.C.E.	Hillel, Shammai	Herodian period
20 C.E.–40 C.E.	Gamliel HaZaken	Herodian period
40 C.E.–80 C.E.	Shimon ben Gamliel I Yochanan ben Zakkai	Second Temple destroyed
80 C.E.–110 C.E.	Gamliel II of Yavneh Eliezer ben Hyrcanus	
110 C.E.–135 C.E.	Akiva	Bar Kokhba revolt
135 C.E.–170 C.E.	Shimon ben Gamliel II Shimon bar Yochai	
170 C.E.–200 C.E.	Yehudah HaNasi	Final redaction of Mishnah

Amoraic Period

Dates	Israel	Babylonia	World Events
200 C.E.–220 C.E.	Oshaya Rabbah Bar Kappara Hiyya		
220 C.E.–250 C.E.	Hanina ben Hama	Rav, Shmuel	Sassanid kingdom
250 C.E.–290 C.E.	Yochanan ben Nappacha Resh Lakish	Huna Yehudah	
290 C.E.–320 C.E.	Ammi, Assi, Zera	Rabbah, Yosef	Sassanid kingdom
320 C.E.–350 C.E.	Hillel II, Yonah, Yose	Abaye, Rava,	Christianity
350 C.E.–375 C.E.	Mana II Tanchuma bar Abba Mar ben Rav Ashi	Ashi, Ravina I	Jerusalem Talmud
460 C.E.–500 C.E.	Rabbah Tosafa'ah Ravina II		Final redaction of Babylonian Talmud

Key words and phrases:

Amora (plural, *Amoraim*: Title given to Jewish scholars in Palestine and Babylonia in the 3rd–6th centuries.

Tanna (plural, *Tannaim*): Teacher mentioned in Mishnah (first two centuries C.E.)

If you want to know more:

Jacob Neusner, *Invitation to Talmud*. New York: Harper and Row, 1973.

Instant Information
Sephardic Customs

The source:

The best source for this information is through the observance and participation in Sephardic communities. However, it should be noted that customs differ depending on country of origin, community of origin, and individual synagogues.

What you need to know:

1. The Jewish community is primarily divided into Ashkenazic and Sephardic Jews, although these distinctions have less and less significance. Most Jews whose families come from Europe are regarded as Ashkenazim, and those whose families come from either Spain or the Arab world are called Sephardim.

2. Today, Sephardic Jews constitute a vital force in world Jewry and a majority in Israeli Jewry.

3. There are numerous differences in the religious and cultural practices of Ashkenazic and Sephardic Jews. What follows is a list of some of the better-known differences:

Custom	Sephardim	Ashkenazim
Hebrew Pronunciation	Pronounce ת as "t" and ָ as "ah"	Pronounce ת as "s" and ָ as "aw"
Naming	Name children after living relatives	Name after relatives who have died
Torah	Torah kept in hard wooden case and is read standing upright	Torah kept in soft fabric cover and read lying flat on table
Ark	Ark is kept open with Torah scrolls exposed	Ark is covered with a *parochet* (curtain)
Tefillin	Wrapped clockwise	Wrapped counter-clockwise

Language	Ladino	Yiddish
Nusach (chanting of liturgy)	Use distinct nusach derived from Spanish and Near Eastern cultures	Use distinct nusach derived from European cultures
Bar Mitzvah	Celebrate Yom Tefillin First time a boy puts on tefillin For two years prior to a Bar Mitzvah	Observed by boys and girls
Wedding	Bride and groom stand together wrapped in single tallit	Bride and groom stand separately
Shiva	*Keriah* (rending of garments) is done upon return from cemetery Mourners sit on floors or pillows At end of *shiva* a special meal and study session, called a *mishmara* is held	*Keriah* is done at funeral parlor Mourners sit on low stools No special meal served at shiva's end
Foods	Favor spicy Near Eastern delicacies	Favor well-cooked meals and rich cakes
Name for Torah receptacle	Heichal	Aron HaKodesh
Name for yearly anniversary remembrance of loved one	Anos	Yahrzeit

Things to remember:

It is estimated that worldwide, some 80 percent of all Jews are *Ashkenazim,* and only 20 percent *Sephardim.* In the United States, *Ashkenazim* outnumber *Sephardim* by an even greater percentage. In Israel, more than half of the Jewish population is Sephardic.

More Particulars

Who's Who Among Sephardic Jewry
Many notable figures in history boasted Sephardic heritage. Here is a brief listing:

Solomon ibn Gabirol: Poet of the Golden Age of Spain, his works served as models for later poets and also have become part of the High Holy Day liturgy.

Yehoram Gaon: One of Israel's leading entertainers has made his mark as a singer and movie star both in Israel and in the United States.

Judah HaLevi: As a poet/philosopher, he became an inspiration to all the Jews of Spain. His best-known works are *Ode to Zion* and *The Kuzari*.

Joseph Karo: The author of the *Shulchan Arukh*, considered Judaism's most authoritative law code.

Moshe Katzav: The first Sephardic president of the State of Israel.

David Levy: Was the first serious contender of Sephardic descent for the Israeli Prime Minister's position. He narrowly lost out to Yitzchak Shamir in the wake of Prime Minister Begin's resignation.

Moses Maimonides: Also known as Rabbi Moshe ben Maimon (the Rambam), he was born in Cordova in 1135. His great works include *Guide for the Perplexed* and the *Mishneh Torah*.

Joseph Nasi: He spent much time traveling with his aunt Gracia Mendes before rising to power in his own right as an advisor to the Turkish sultan. He used his influence to help his people, including the resettlement of Jewish refugees in Palestine.

Hasdai ibn Shaprut: Living in 10th century Spain, this court physician rose to high government office and used his position to influence policy for the good of the people.

Naomi Shemer: Israel's foremost contemporary songwriter, she is the child of an Ashkenazi/Sephardi marriage. Her most well-known song is probably *Yerushalayim Shel Zahav* (Jerusalem of Gold), released just after the Six-Day War in 1967.

Key words and phrases

Ladino: Spanish-Jewish folk language

If you want to know more:

Robert Sugar, *Our Story: The Jews of Sepharad*. New York: Coalition for the Advancement of Jewish Education, 1991.

Joseph Teleushkin, *Jewish Literacy*. New York: William Morrow, 1991.

Instant Information
Twenty-Year Calendar of Jewish Holidays

The source:

The Jewish calendar, established by Hillel II in 350 C.E.

What you need to know:

1. While many people think that the Jewish calendar is a lunar calendar, it is really a soli-lunar calendar. This means that it is a lunar calendar that is adjusted by the seasons (which are governed by the sun). This approach prevents holidays from occurring in different seasons each year—as they do in the calendar of Islam. As a result, the Jewish calendar has 354 days, while the secular (solar) calendar has 365 days. Thus, Jewish holidays fall on different days of the secular calendar each year. That's where we get the expression "The holidays are late—or early—this year."

2. Jews in Israel observe one-day festivals, as the Torah prescribes, and continue to do so to this day (except for Rosh Hashanah). The Orthodox and Conservative movements insist that Jews in the Diaspora observe two days of all the holy days. Reform Judaism generally consider such double celebrations unnecessary. However, some congregations have chosen to observe a second day of holidays in order to celebrate at the same time as does the rest of the Jewish world and to increase the opportunities for celebration and observance.

3. Jewish holidays begin in the evening with sunset. This is based on the biblical verse in the story of creation which states that "there was evening and then there was morning."

4. Twenty-Year Calendar of Jewish Holidays:

(dates are listed for the first day of multiple-day holidays only)

2001/5762

Rosh Hashanah	Sept. 18
Yom Kippur	Sept. 27
Sukkot	Oct. 2
Hanukkah	Dec. 10

2002

Purim	Feb. 26
Passover	March 28
Shavuot	May 17

2002/5763

Rosh Hashanah	Sept. 7
Yom Kippur	Sept. 16
Sukkot	Sept. 21
Hanukkah	Nov. 30

2003

Purim	March 18
Passover	April 17
Shavuot	June 6

2003/5764

Rosh Hashanah	Sept. 27
Yom Kippur	Oct. 6
Sukkot	Oct. 11
Hanukkah	Dec. 20

2004

Purim	March 7
Passover	April 6
Shavuot	May 26

2004/5765

Rosh Hashanah	Sept. 16
Yom Kippur	Sept. 25
Sukkot	Sept. 30
Hanukkah	Dec. 8

2005

Purim	March 25
Passover	April 24
Shavuot	June 13

2005/5766

Rosh Hashanah	Oct. 4
Yom Kippur	Oct. 13
Sukkot	Oct. 18
Hanukkah	Dec. 26

2006

Purim	March 14
Passover	April 13
Shavuot	June 2

2006/5767

Rosh Hashanah	Sept. 23
Yom Kippur	Oct. 2
Sukkot	Oct. 7
Hanukkah	Dec. 16

2007

Purim	March 4
Passover	April 3
Shavuot	May 23

2007/5768

Rosh Hashanah	Sept. 13
Yom Kippur	Sept. 22
Sukkot	Sept. 27
Hanukkah	Dec. 5

2008

Purim	March 21
Passover	April 20
Shavuot	June 9

2008/5769

Rosh Hashanah	Sept. 30
Yom Kippur	Oct. 9
Sukkot	Oct. 14
Hanukkah	Dec. 22

2009

Purim	March 10
Passover	April 9
Shavuot	May 21

2010/5770

Rosh Hashanah	Sept. 19
Yom Kippur	Sept. 28
Sukkot	Oct. 3
Hanukkah	Dec. 12

2010

Purim	Feb. 28
Passover	March 30
Shavuot	May 19

2010/5771

Rosh Hashanah	Sept. 9
Yom Kippur	Sept. 18
Sukkot	Sept. 23
Hanukkah	Dec. 2

2011

Purim	March 20
Passover	April 19
Shavuot	June 8

2011/5772

Rosh Hashanah	Sept 29
Yom Kippur	Oct 8
Sukkot	Oct. 13
Hanukkah	Dec. 21

2012

Purim	March 8
Passover	April 7
Shavuot	May 27

2012/5773

Rosh Hashanah	Sept. 17
Yom Kippur	Sept. 26
Sukkot	Oct. 1
Hanukkah	Dec. 9

2013

Purim	Feb. 14
Passover	March 26
Shavuot	May 15

2013/5774

Rosh Hashanah	Sept. 5
Yom Kippur	Sept. 14
Sukkot	Sept. 19
Hanukkah	Dec. 28

2014

Purim	March 16
Passover	April 15
Shavuot	June 4

2014/5775

Rosh Hashanah	Sept. 25
Yom Kippur	Oct. 4
Sukkot	Oct. 9
Hanukkah	Dec. 17

2015

Purim	March 5
Passover	April 4
Shavuot	May 24

2015/5776

Rosh Hashanah	Sept. 14
Yom Kippur	Sept 23
Sukkot	Sept. 28
Hanukkah	Dec. 7

2016

Purim	March 24
Passover	April 23
Shavuot	June 12

2016/5777

Rosh Hashanah	Oct. 3
Yom Kippur	Oct. 12
Sukkot	Oct. 17
Hanukkah	Dec. 25

2017

Purim	March 12
Passover	April 11
Shavuot	May 31

2017/5778

Rosh Hashanah	Sept. 21
Yom Kippur	Sept. 30
Sukkot	Oct. 5
Hanukkah	Dec. 13

2018

Purim	March 1
Passover	March 31
Shavuot	May 20

2018/5779

Rosh Hashanah	Sept. 10
Yom Kippur	Sept. 19
Sukkot	Sept. 24
Hanukkah	Dec. 3

2019

Purim	March 21
Passover	April 20
Shavuot	June 9

2019/5780

Rosh Hashanah	Sept. 30
Yom Kippur	Oct. 9
Sukkot	Oct. 14
Hanukkah	Dec. 23

2020

Purim	March 10
Passover	April 19
Shavuot	May 29

2020/5781

Rosh Hashanah	Sept. 19
Yom Kippur	Sept. 28
Sukkot	Oct. 3
Hanukkah	Dec. 11

Key words and phrases:

Luach: Calendar

If you want to know more:

Kerry M. Olitzky and Ronald H. Isaacs, *Rediscovering Judaism: Bar and Bat Mitzvah for Adults*. Hoboken, NJ: KTAV Publishing House, Inc., 1997.

More particulars:

If an American Jew travels to Israel, he or she must follow the diaspora observance pattern (regarding one- or two-day holidays) unless he or she is going to be there for all three pilgrimage festivals. However, since it is permissible "to extend holiness," Israeli Jews who are going to be outside Israel may extend their observance of the holidays. Nevertheless, most authorities suggest that Israelis who will be abroad on the second day of holidays should put on *tefillin* at home and not at the synagogue.

Instant Information
Sabbath Table Songs

The source:

"When Jewish people eat and drink, they begin with words of Torah and hymns of praise" (Babylonian Talmud, *Megillah* 12b).

What you need to know

1. *Zemirot* (table songs) sung during Sabbath meals provide us with the atmosphere to promote Sabbath joy. They add light and joy to the soul. Since Sabbath table songs are unique, they help to create Jewish memories for our children and ourselves. Composed at an early date, these songs became particularly popular during the 16th century through the influence of the mystics.

2. The tunes of the *zemirot*, reflecting the experiences of Jewish people throughout history, are mostly adapted local folk tunes that eventually became characteristically Jewish.

3. Some popular *zemirot* for you to sing at your Sabbath dinner table:

מְנוּחָה וְשִׂמְחָה אוֹר לַיְּהוּדִים,

יוֹם שַׁבָּתוֹן יוֹם מַחֲמַדִּים,

שׁוֹמְרָיו וְזוֹכְרָיו הֵמָּה מְעִידִים,

כִּי לְשִׁשָּׁה כֹּל בְּרוּאִים וְעוֹמְדִים.

שְׁמֵי שָׁמַיִם אֶרֶץ וְיַמִּים,

כָּל צְבָא מָרוֹם גְּבוֹהִים וְרָמִים,

תַּנִּין וְאָדָם וְחַיַּת רְאֵמִים,

כִּי בְּיָהּ יְיָ צוּר עוֹלָמִים.

1. ***Menukha V'simcha***
Menukha v'simcha
Or la-y'udim

521

Yom Shabbaton yom machmadim
Shomrav v'zochrave heima m'idim
Ki l'shisha b'rurim v'omdim.
Sh'mei shamayim eretz v'yamim
Kol tz'va marom g'vohim v'ramim
Tanim v'adam v'chayat r'eimim
Ki b'yah Adonai tzur olamim.

To rest and rejoice is a Jewish right,
This Sabbath day of sheer delight
Those who keep it say this Friday night
In six days God made the mighty world
The highest heavens, earth and sea,
The angels above, in majesty,
Monsters and humans and beasts running free,
The strengths of the world, Almighty is God.

צוּר מִשֶּׁלּוֹ

צוּר מִשֶּׁלּוֹ אָכַלְנוּ, בָּרְכוּ אֱמוּנַי
שָׂבַעְנוּ וְהוֹתַרְנוּ כִּדְבַר יְיָ.
הַזָּן אֶת עוֹלָמוֹ, רוֹעֵנוּ אָבִינוּ, אָכַלְנוּ
אֶת לַחְמוֹ, וְיֵינוֹ שָׁתִינוּ, עַל כֵּן נוֹדֶה
לִשְׁמוֹ, וּנְהַלְלוֹ בְּפִינוּ, אָמַרְנוּ וְעָנִינוּ,
אֵין קָדוֹשׁ כַּיְיָ.

2. *Tzur Mishelo*
Tzur mishelo achalnu
Bar'khu emunai
Savanu v'hotarnu kidvar Adonai
Hazan et olamo, ro-einu avinu
Akhalnu et lachmo v'yeinu shatinu,
Al ken nodeh lishmo un-hal'lo b'finu
Amarnu v'aninu ein kadosh kadonai.

We've eaten God's food; let's adore and bless God in
   one accord
We've had enough and more, by the word of God.
God keeps the world well fed, this Shepherd Parent of
   mine
We ate God's tasty bread and drank God's goodly wine
Let's thank God, feeling glad, and praise God as
   we dine,
Singing as we recline: None is holy like God.

522

דרור יקרא

דְּרוֹר יִקְרָא לְבֵן עִם בַּת. וְיִנְצָרְכֶם
כְּמוֹ בָבַת. נְעִים שִׁמְכֶם וְלֹא
יֵשָׁבַת. שְׁבוּ וְנוּחוּ בְּיוֹם שַׁבָּת.
דְּרוֹשׁ נָוִי וְאוּלָמִי. וְאוֹת יֶשַׁע עֲשֵׂה
עִמִּי. נְטַע שׂוֹרֵק בְּתוֹךְ כַּרְמִי. שְׁעֵה
שַׁוְעַת בְּנֵי עַמִּי.

3. Dror Yikra

D'ror yikra, l'vein ul-vat
V'yin tzorkhem k'mo vavat,
N'im shimkhem v'lo yushbat,
Sh'vu v'nu'chu b'yom Shabbat.
D'rosh navi v'ulami
V'ot yesha asei imi,
N'ta soreik b'tokh karmi
Sh'ei shav'at b'nei ami.

God invites God's children to partake of Shabbat
To rest from labor, anxiety, and strife.
Shabbat renews the heart, inspires wisdom,
And restores dignity of life.
God will proclaim freedom for all the children
And will keep you as the apple of God's eye
Pleasant is your name and will not be destroyed
Repose and rest on the Sabbath day.

מפי אל

מִפִּי אֵל מִפִּי אֵל יְבֹרַךְ יִשְׂרָאֵל
אֵין אַדִּיר כַּיְיָ, אֵין בָּרוּךְ כְּבֶן עַמְרָם,
אֵין גְּדוֹלָה כַּתּוֹרָה, אֵין דּוֹרְשֶׁיהָ
כְּיִשְׂרָאֵל.

4. Mipi Eil

Mipi Eil mipi Eil
Y'vorakh yisrael.
Ein adir kadonai
Ein barukh k'ven amram
Ein g'dolah katorah
Ein dorsheha k'yisrael.

There is no other as powerful as God,
None as blessed as Moses, the son of Amram.
There is no other as great as the Torah
And who profess, as Israel.
God will bless Israel.

לֹא יִשָׂא גוֹי

לֹא יִשָׂא גוֹי אֶל גוֹי חֶרֶב
וְלֹא יִלְמְדוּ עוֹד מִלְחָמָה.
לֹא יִשָׂא גוֹי אֶל גוֹי חֶרֶב
וְלֹא יִלְמְדוּ עוֹד מִלְחָמָה.

5. *Lo Yisa Goy*
Lo yisa goy el goy cherev
Lo yilmedu od milchama
Lo yisa goy el goy cherev
Lo yilmedu od milchama

Nation shall not lift up sword against nation
Neither shall we learn war anymore.

Key words and phrases:

Zemer (plural, *Zemirot*): Sabbath and Festival hymns

If you want to know more

Ronald Isaacs, *Every Person's Guide to Shabbat*. Northvale, NJ: Jason Aronson, 1998.

_____, *Shabbat Delight: A Celebration in Stories, Games and Songs*. Hoboken, NJ and New York: KTAV and the American Jewish Committee, 1987.

Instant Information
Healing Prayers

The source:

"O God, heal her now" (Numbers 12:13).

What you need to know:

1. The obligation to heal in Jewish tradition dates back to biblical times, when prayers were used in time of illness. Abraham prayed for the recovery of Avimelech (Gen. 20:17) and God healed him. Moses prayed for the recovery of his sister Miriam with the words "O God, heal her now." (Numbers 12:13) and she recovered from (what most commentators say was) leprosy. This short, simple prayer became the model for all prayers.

2. Years ago, the 18th-century Hasidic master Rabbi Nachman of Bratslav identified ten specific psalms that have inherent power to bring a true and complete healing of both body and spirit. He designated the ten psalms (numbers 16, 32, 41, 42, 59, 77, 90, 105, 137, 150) as a *Tikkun Haklali*—the Complete Remedy. (See Healing Psalms section in Instant Information for the complete texts of these psalms.)

3. Since the *mi sheberakh* requires a *minyan*, it is generally said while the congregation is engaged in the Torah service, following an *aliyah*.

4. Some congregations offer *mi sheberakh* prayers individually. Others offer them on behalf of all those who are ill.

4. The prayer takes its name from the first two words— *mi sheberakh*, "the One who blessed," namely God. While most people use this name to refer to the prayer for healing, there are a variety of *mi sheberakh* prayers. What they share in common is a request of God to bless a specific person or persons. Besides healing, they ask God to reward various individuals including those who have come up for the Torah

reading, those who make donations to the synagogue and other worthy causes, bar and bat mitzvah celebrants, wedding celebrants, and those who have been circumcised and/or named.

5. There are many prayers found in the *siddur*, the Bible, and in contemporary writings that include healing prayers and texts. Some common examples:

    i. Praised are You, Sovereign our God, Ruler of the Universe, who with wisdom fashioned the human body, creating openings, arteries, glands and organs, marvelous in structure, intricate in design. Should but one of them, by being blocked, fail to function, it would be impossible to exist. Praised are You, God, Healer of all flesh, who sustains our bodies in wondrous ways. (From the liturgy, *Asher Yatzar*)

    ii. Our Parent, Our Sovereign, send complete healing to those who are ill. (From the liturgy, *Avinu Malkenu*)

    iii. May God who blessed our ancestors Abraham, Isaac and Jacob, Sarah, Rebecca, Rachel and Leah, bless and heal _____. May the Holy One in kindness strengthen him (her) and heal him (her) speedily, body and soul, together with all others who are ill.

    iv. O God, I turn to You in prayer,
You who bind up wounds and heal the sick.
I put my trust in You.
Knowing that I am in Your hands, O God,
I have faith that You will not forsake me.
Give me courage now and in the days ahead,
Grant wisdom and skill to my physician.
Make all those who are assisting me
Instruments of Your healing power.
Give me strength for this day
And grant me hope for tomorrow.
Hear my prayer, be with me and protect me.
Restore me to health, O God
So that I may serve You. (Prayer before an operation)

    vi. Hear my voice O God, when I call,
Be gracious to me and answer me. (Psalm 27:7)

vii. Heal me, O God, and I shall be healed.
Saved me and I shall be saved;
For You are my praise. (Jeremiah 17:14)

Things to remember:

1. The *mi sheberakh* should be said in the context of a community. Thus, a *minyan* is required.

2. The person for whom the *mi sheberakh* is said is mentioned as the son or daughter of his or her mother (rather than father as is the case in most other traditional Jewish contexts).

Key words and phrases:

Mi sheberakh: (May) The One who blesses . . .
Refuah shleima: complete healing (used as an expression from one person to another, often when speaking of a third person)

If you want to know more:

David L. Freeman and Judith Z. Abrams, eds., *Illness and Healing in the Jewish Tradition: Writings from the Bible to Today*. Philadelphia: Jewish Publication Society of America, 1999.

Ronald Isaacs, *A Gabbai's How To Manual*. Hoboken, NJ: KTAV Publishing, 1996.

_____, *Judaism, Medicine and Healing*. Northvale, NJ: Jason Aronson, 1998.

Kerry M. Olitzky, *Jewish Paths to Healing and Wholeness*. Woodstock, VT: Jewish Lights Publishing, 2000.

Simkha Y. Weintraub, ed., *Healing of Soul, Healing of Body*. Woodstock, VT: Jewish Lights Publishing, 1994.

Instant Information
Basic Jewish Library

The source:

"Study is the most basic *mitzvah* of them all" (Babylonian Talmud, *Shabbat* 127a).

What you need to know:

1. Mohammed is credited with naming the Jews "the People of the Book." From the days of Ezra, the Torah and the books added to it were so intimately a part of the Jewish people that they could not easily conceive of another way of life. Not even the king was exempt from reading and studying the Torah.

2. The life and destiny of the Jewish people was formed not only by the Bible but also by the many volumes that were inspired by the Bible, including both classic and contemporary texts.

3. Following are some suggestions for your home library and your reading table:

Basic Reference

Kerry M. Olitzky and Ronald Isaacs, *A Glossary of Jewish Life*. Northvale, NJ: Jason Aronson, 1992.

Life Cycle

Ronald Isaacs, *Rites of Passage: A Guide to the Jewish Life Cycle*. Hoboken, NJ: KTAV, 1992. (Conservative)

Isaac Klein, *A Guide to Jewish Religious Practice*. New York and Jerusalem: Jewish Theological Seminary of America, 1979, 1992. (Conservative)

Simeon J. Maslin, ed., *Gates of Mitzvah: A Guide to the Jewish Life Cycle*. New York: Central Conference of American Rabbis, 1979. (Reform)

Philosophy/Theology

Eugene B. Borowitz, *Choices in Modern Jewish Thought: A Partisan Guide*. New York: Behrman House, 1983.

Elliot Dorff, *Knowing God*. Northvalc, NJ: Jason Aronson, 1992.

Neil Gillman, *Sacred Fragments: Recovering Theology for the Modern Jew*. Philadelphia: Jewish Publication Society, 1990.

Ronald Isaacs, *Every Person's Guide to Jewish Philosophy and Philosophers*. Northvale, NJ: Jason Aronson, 1999.

Harold Kushner, *When Bad Things Happen to Good People*. New York: Schocken, 1981.

_____, *When Children Ask About God*. New York: Schocken, 1976.

Daniel Syme, *Finding God*. New York: Union of American Hebrew Congregations, 1986.

Bibles with Commentary

Bernard Bamberger, William W. Hallo, and W. Gunther Plaut, eds., *The Torah: A Modern Commentary*. New York: Union of American Hebrew Congregations, 1981. (Reform)

Joseph H. Hertz, *Pentateuch and Haftorahs*. New York: Soncino Press, 1988. (Traditional)

The J.P.S. Commentary. 5 volumes. Philadelphia: Jewish Publication Society, 1996.

Prayer Books

Jules Harlow, ed., *Siddur Sim Shalom*. New York: Rabbinical Assembly and United Synagogue of America, 1985. (Conservative)

Joseph H. Hertz, ed., *Authorized Daily Prayer Book*. New York: Bloch, 1961. (Traditional)

Chaim Stern, ed., *Gates of Prayer*. New York: Central Conference of American Rabbis, 1972. (Reform)

David Teutsch, ed., *Kol Haneshama*. Wyncote, PA.: Reconstructionist Press, 1994. (Reconstructionist)

Text Study

Barry Holtz., ed., *Back to the Sources: Reading the Classic Jewish Text*. New York: Summit Books, 1984.

Michael Katz and Gershon Schwartz, *Swimming in the Sea of Talmud*. Philadelphia: Jewish Publication Society, 1997.

Leonard Kravitz and Kerry M. Olitzky, *Pirke Avot: A Modern Commentary on Jewish Ethics*. New York: UAHC Press, 1993.

_____, *Shemonah Perakim: A Treatise on the Soul*. New York: UAHC Press, 1999.

Holiday and Festival Observances

Penina V. Adelman, *Rituals for Jewish Women Around the Year*. New York: Biblio Press, 1986.

Nahum N. Glatzer, ed., *The Passover Haggadah*. New York: Schocken, 1981.

Philip Goodman, ed., *The Passover, Purim, Rosh Hashanah, Shavuot, Sukkot and Simchat Torah* and *Yom Kippur Anthologies*. 6 volumes. Philadelphia: Jewish Publication Society, 1970–1973.

Kerry M. Olitzky, *Eight Nights, Eight Lights: Family Values for Hanukkah*. Los Angeles: Alef Design Group, 1994.

_____ and Ronald Isaacs, *Sacred Celebrations*. Hoboken, NJ: KTAV, 1994.

Ron Wolfson, *The Art of Jewish Living: Hanukkah*. New York: Federation of Jewish Men's Clubs, 1990.

_____, *The Art of Jewish Living: Passover*. New York and Los Angeles: Federation of Jewish Men's Clubs and University of Judaism, 1988.

_____, *The Art of Jewish Living: The Shabbat Seder*. New York and Los Angeles: Federation of Jewish Men's Clubs and University of Judaism, 1985.

General History

Abba Eban, *Heritage: Civilization and the Jews*. New York: Summit Books, 1984.

Steven Bayme, *Understanding Jewish History: Texts and Commentaries*. Hoboken, NJ: KTAV, 1997.

Paul Johnson, *A History of the Jews*. New York: Harper and Row, 1987.

Abram Leon Sachar, *A History of the Jews*. New York: Knopf, 1967.

Israel

Abraham Joshua Heschel, *Israel: An Echo of Eternity*. New York: Farrar, Straus and Giroux, 1969.

Howard Morley Sachar, *A History of Israel: From the Rise of Zionism to Our Time*. New York, Knopf, 1976.

Sol Scharfstein, *Understanding Israel*. Hoboken, NJ: KTAV, 1994.

The American Jewish Experience

Nathan Glazer, *American Judaism*. 2nd edition. Chicago: University of Chicago Press, 1972.

Jacob Rader Marcus, *United States Jewry, 1776–1985*. Detroit: Wayne State University Press, 1989.

Key words and phrases:

Am hasefer: People of the book

Instant Information
Avoiding *Lashon Hara*

The source:

You shall not go about spreading slander among your people. (Leviticus 19:16)

What you need to know:

1. Words can be powerful objects. When used properly, they can soothe and comfort. However, when they are used improperly, they can hurt, injure and curse. The power of words was described this way in the book of Proverbs: "Death and life are in the power of the tongue." (18:21)

2. Words are used so frivolously at times that we do not often stop to think about them and the way in which they ought to be used. Taking them for granted, we often value their power less than we should.

3. The specific vice of slander is condemned in all Jewish writings. The term slander (*lashon hara*) has been defined as the utterance or dissemination of false statements or reports concerning a person, or malicious representation of that person's actions, in order to defame or injure. According to the Talmud, it is a hideous crime which can easily destroy a person's life and reputation.

4. A cross-section of practical advice culled from a variety of Jewish sources to help prevent you from engaging in *lashon hara*:

   i. **Don't speak too much**: "A person should try to discipline himself not to speak too much so that he should not come to the point of uttering *lashon hara* or indecent words and should not become a chronic complainer. Instead, he should stress silence." (*Menorat HaMaor*)

   ii. **Keep a civil tongue**: "A person should always try to keep a civil tongue in his head, whether engaged in Torah study or discussing worldly affairs." (*Menorat HaMaor*)

iii. **Study Torah**: "If your tongue turns to uttering slander, go and study the words of Torah." (Midrash on Psalms)

iv. **Put your hands in your ears**: "If you hear something unseemly, you should put your hands in your ears." (Babylonian Talmud, *Ketubot* 5a-b)

Key words and phrases:

Lashon hara: Slander

If you want to know more:

Ronald Isaacs, *The Jewish Book of Etiquette*. Northvale, NJ: Jason Aronson, 1998.

Zelig Pliskin, *A Practical Guide to the Laws of Loshon Hara Based on Chofetz Chayim*. Jerusalem: NP, 1975.

Yehudah HeChasid, *The Book of the Pious*. Northvale, NJ: Jason Aronson, 1997.

Instant Information
Basic Terms in Kabbalah

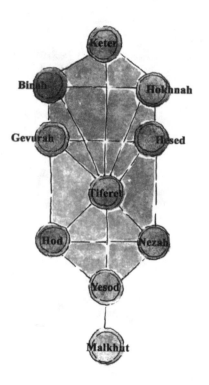

The source:

Kabbalah is the term generally used to describe the esoteric teachings of Judaism and Jewish mysticism. It literally means the "received tradition."

What you need to know:

Adam kadmon: primordial man, the first human spiritual prototype

Bittul hayesh: annihilation of individuality, through direct communion with God

Devekut: spiritual communion with God, where the ego is nearly annihilated

Ein Sof: the Infinite, a name for God

Hitbodedut: solitude, being alone with God

Histavvut: equanimity, the indifference of the soul to praise or blame

Kavannah: meditative verses, or the attitude or intent with which one does something

Kelippot (*kelippah*, sing.): husks or shells of evil that were embedded in the earth following creation

Nitzotzot: sparks of holiness that need to be released from the earth

Orot: lights of holiness

Sefirot (*sefirah*, sing.): mystical emanations of God, an idea influenced by I Chronicles 29:11

> *Keter* (*elyon*): (supreme) crown
> *Chokhmah*: wisdom
> *Da'at*: knowledge
> *Binah*: intelligence
> *Gedulah* (or *chesed*): greatness (or love)
> *Gevurah* (or *din*): power (or judgment)
> *Tiferet* (or *rachamim*): beauty (or compassion)
> *Netzah*: lasting endurance
> *Hod*: majesty

> *tzadik* or (*yesod olam*): righteous one or foundation of
> the world
>
> *malkhut* (or *atarah*): sovereignty (or diadem)

Shekhinah: God's indwelling presence, and feminine
attributes

shemittot (*shemittah*, sing.): cosmic cycles

shevirat kelim: breaking of the vessels at creation

sitra achra: the other side, the domain of dark emanations
and demonic powers

tikkun: repair of the world (and of the self)

tzimtzum: contraction of God for the purpose of creation
of the world

Things to remember:

While kabbalah is one of many terms referring to mysticism (from the 14th century on), the Talmud speaks of
sitrei Torah and *razei Torah* (both, secrets of the Torah). Parts
of this secret tradition are called *ma'aseh bereishit* (literally,
the work of creation) and *ma'aseh merkabah* (work of the
chariot).

Key words and phrases:

Anshei emunah: men of belief

Ba'alei hasod: masters of mystery, a mystical group during
the period following the close of the Talmud

Ba'alei hayediah: masters of knowledge

Chokhmah: wisdom, part of the inner truth

Chokhmah penimit: inner wisdom, from the period of the
Provencal and Spanish kabbalists

Chokhmat ha-emet: the science of truth

Chokhmat hatzeruf: meditations on letter combinations

Chokhmei halev: the wise-hearted, following Exodus 28:3

Derekh ha-emet: the way of truth

Emet: truth, the inner truth

Emunah: faith, part of the inner truth

Hayodim: those who know

Maskilim: the enlightened ones, a reference to Daniel
12:10, not be confused with those of the later
Enlightenment period

Yordei merkabah: those who descend to the chariot, the name of a mystical group

If you want to know more:

David S. Ariel, *The Mystic Quest: An Introduction to Jewish Mysticism*. Northvale, NJ: Jason Aronson, 1988.
David A. Cooper, *God Is a Verb*. New York: Riverhead Books, 1997.

More particulars:

The Zohar (ca. 1280) is the core book in Jewish mysticism and is a commentary or midrash on the Torah. However, there are other mystical volumes, such as *Sefer Yetzirah* (ca. 1130).

Instant Information
Books of the Talmud

The source:

Babylonian Talmud.

What you need to know:

There are six orders or sections of the Babylonian Talmud. These are divided into sections called tractates, sometimes referred to as books. Next to the Hebrew name is the subject matter (in parentheses). An asterisk means that this tractate appears in the Talmud of Eretz Yisrael (the land of Israel), inaccurately called by most people the Jerusalem Talmud, as well. However, the material may not be the same.

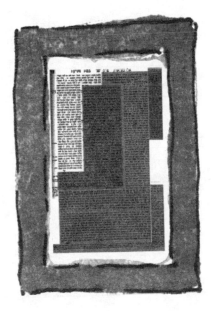

Seder Zeraim
Berakhot (blessings)*
Peah (gleanings of the field)*
Demai (doubtfully tithed produce)*
Kilayim (diverse kinds)*
Shevi'it (Sabbatical year)*
Terumot (heave offering)*
Ma'aserot (tithes)*
Ma'aser Sheni (second tithe)*
Challah (dough offering)*
Orlah (the fruit of young trees)*
Bikkurim (first fruits)*

Seder Moed
Shabbat (Sabbath)*
Eruvim (Sabbath limits)*
Pesachim (Passover)*
Shekalim (shekel dues)*
Yoma (Day of Atonement)*
Sukkah (Feast of Tabernacles)*
Beitzah (festival laws)*
Rosh Hashanah (various new years)*
Ta'anit (fast days)*
Megillah (Purim)*

Moed Katan (intermediate days of festivals)*
Chagigah (festival offering)*

Seder Nashim
Yevamot (levirate marriage)*
Ketubot (marriage contracts)*
Nedarim (vows)*
Nazir (the Nazirite)*
Sotah (one suspected of adultery)*
Gittin (divorce)*
Kiddushin (marriage)*

Seder Nezikin
Bava Kamma (torts)*
Bava Metziah (civil law)*
Bava Batra (property law)*
Sanhedrin (judges and courts)*
Makkot (flagellation)*
Shevuot (oaths)*
Eduyyot (traditional testimonies)
Avodah Zarah (idolatry)*
Avot (ethical maxims)
Horayot (erroneous rulings of the court)*

Seder Kodashim
Zevachim (animal offerings)
Menachot (meal offerings)
Chullin (animals slaughtered for food)
Bekhorot (firstlings)
Arakin (vows of valuation)
Temurah (substituted offering)
Keritot (extirpation)
Me'ilah (sacrileges)
Tamid (the daily sacrifice)
Middot (measurements of the Temple)
Kinnim (the bird offering)

Seder Tohorot
Kelim (uncleanness of articles)
Oholot (uncleanness through overshadowing)
Negaim (leprosy)
Parah (the red heifer)
Tohorot (ritual cleanness)
Mikvaot (ritual ablution)
Niddah (the menstruant)*

Makhshirin (liquid that predisposes food to become
ritually unclean)
Zavim (fluxes)
Tevul Yom (ritual uncleanness between immersion
and sunset)
Yadayim (ritual uncleanness of the hands)
Uktzin ("stalks"; part of plant that is susceptible to
uncleanness)

Things to remember:

1. Pages of the Talmud are numbered on both sides of
   the page: A, then B.

2. Because the cover is counted as a page, each book
   starts on page two.

Key words and phrases:

Talmud means "study" or "learning." It refers to a specific collection of oral law (either the Babylonian or Eretz
Yisrael/Jerusalem Talmud)—the body of teaching that
comprises the commentary and discussions of the rabbis
on the mishnah compiled by Rabbi Judah Hanasi. It can
also refer to the whole body of one's learning (in much the
same way that the word Torah is used). It can also be used
as part of a technical phrase regarding a teaching that
emerges from a Biblical text (as in *talmud lomar*).
Alternatively, the Talmud is called *shas*, an acronym for
shisah sidrei (the six orders of the mishnah) or *gemara* (the
specific Aramaic commentary/discussion on the mishnah).

If you want to know more:

Michael Katz and Gershon Schwartz, *Swimming in the Sea of
Talmud: Lessons for Everyday Living*. Philadelphia: Jewish
Publication Society of America, 1997.

We have included Biblical sources for each of the following
selected tractates for which its Torah source is readily
ascertained. Not all tractates are listed below.

Seder Zeraim
Peah (see Lev. 19:9–10)
Kitayim (see Deut. 22:9–11)

Shevi'it (see Exod. 23:10–11)
Terumot (see Lev. 22:10–14)
Ma'aserot (see Num. 18:21)
Ma'aser Sheni (see Deut. 14:22ff.)
Challah (see Num. 15:17–21)
Orlah (see Lev. 19:23–25)
Bikkurim (see Lev. 26:1–11)

Seder Moed
Shekalim (see Exod. 30:11–16)
Chagigah (see Deut. 16:16–17)

Seder Nashim
Yevamot (see Deut. 25:5–10)
Nedarim (see Num. 30)
Nazir (see Num. 6)
Sotah (see Num. 5:11ff.)

Seder Nezikin
Makkot (see Deut. 25:2)
Horayot (see Lev. 4:22ff.)

Seder Kodashim
Bekhorot (see Deut. 15:19ff.)
Arakin (see Lev. 27:1–8)
Terumah (see Lev. 27:10)
Keritot (see Lev. 18:29)
Me'ilah (see Lev. 5:15–16)
Tamid (see Num. 28:3–4)
Kinnim (see Lev. 5:7ff.)

Seder Tohorot
Oholot (see Num. 19:14–15)
Negaim (see Lev. 13, 14)
Parah (see Num. 19)
Makhshirin (see Lev. 11:37–38)
Zavim (see Lev. 15)
Tevul Yom (see Lev. 22:6–7)

Instant Information
Fifteen Morning Blessings

The source:

Babylonian Talmud, *Berakhot* 60b

What you need to know:

This series of 15 blessings emerges from the Talmud, where the rabbis teach that we should praise God as we experience each activity in a new day. For example, one thanks God for giving us the crucial ability to make various distinctions in life, such as the difference between night and day, when we rub our eyes and see things for the first time in the morning. Some of these activities are obvious from the text of the blessing. Others are not so obvious. Among them are: sitting up and stretching (who has made me to be free); getting out of bed (gives strength to the weary); stands on the floor (established firm ground amidst the waters); putting on shoes, which demonstrates our ability to make our way in the world (provides for all my needs); setting on toward one's destination (makes firm each person's steps); fastening one's clothing (girds Israel with strength); putting on a hat, which reminds us that God is above us (crowns Israel with splendor); feeling the passing of nighttime exhaustion (gives strength to the weary and removes sleep from the eyelids).

Blessings of the Morning

בִּרְכוֹת הַשַּׁחַר

בָּרוּךְ אַתָּה יְיָ אֱלֹהֵינוּ מֶלֶךְ הָעוֹלָם, אֲשֶׁר נָתַן לַשֶּׂכְוִי בִינָה לְהַבְחִין בֵּין יוֹם וּבֵין לָיְלָה.

Barukh ata Adonai Elohenu melekh ha-olam asher natan la-sekhvi vina le-havchin bein yom u'vein laila.

Praised are You, Adonai our God, Sovereign of the Universe, who has given me the ability to distinguish between day and night.

541

בָּרוּךְ אַתָּה יְיָ אֱלֹהֵינוּ מֶלֶךְ הָעוֹלָם, שֶׁעָשַׂנִי בְּצַלְמוֹ.

Barukh ata Adonai Elohenu melekh ha-olam she'asani betzalmo.

Praised are You, Adonai our God, Sovereign of the Universe, who has made me in the Divine image (alt: who has not made me a woman; who has made me according to Divine will).

בָּרוּךְ אַתָּה יְיָ אֱלֹהֵינוּ מֶלֶךְ הָעוֹלָם, שֶׁעָשַׂנִי יִשְׂרָאֵל.

Barukh atah Adonai Elohenu melekh ha-olam she'asani yisrael.

Praised are You, Adonai our God, Sovereign of the Universe, who has led me to my Jewish heritage (alt: who has not made me a Gentile).

בָּרוּךְ אַתָּה יְיָ אֱלֹהֵינוּ מֶלֶךְ הָעוֹלָם, שֶׁעָשַׂנִי בֶּן (בַּת־) חוֹרִין.

Barukh atah Adonai Elohenu melekh ha-olam she'asani ben (bat) chorin.

Praised are You, Adonai our God, Sovereign of the Universe, who has made me free (alt: who has not made me a slave).

בָּרוּךְ אַתָּה יְיָ אֱלֹהֵינוּ מֶלֶךְ הָעוֹלָם, פּוֹקֵחַ עִוְרִים.

Barukh atah Adonai Elohenu melekh ha-olam poke'ach ivrim.

Praised are You, Adonai our God, Sovereign of the Universe, who opens the eyes of those who would not see.

בָּרוּךְ אַתָּה יְיָ אֱלֹהֵינוּ מֶלֶךְ הָעוֹלָם, מַלְבִּישׁ עֲרֻמִּים.

Barukh atah Adonai Elohenu melekh ha-olam malbish arumim.

Praised are You, Adonai our God, Sovereign of the Universe, who clothes the naked.

בָּרוּךְ אַתָּה יְיָ אֱלֹהֵינוּ מֶלֶךְ הָעוֹלָם, מַתִּיר אֲסוּרִים.

Barukh atah Adonai Elohenu melekh ha-olam matir asurim.

Praised are You, Adonai our God, Sovereign of the Universe, who brings freedom to the captive.

בָּרוּךְ אַתָּה יְיָ אֱלֹהֵינוּ מֶלֶךְ הָעוֹלָם, זוֹקֵף כְּפוּפִים.

Barukh atah Adonai Elohenu melekh ha-olam zokef kefufim.

Praised are You, Adonai our God, Sovereign of the Universe, who girds us with courage (alt: who straightens the bent).

בָּרוּךְ אַתָּה יְיָ אֱלֹהֵינוּ מֶלֶךְ הָעוֹלָם, רוֹקַע הָאָרֶץ עַל הַמָּיִם.

Barukh atah Adonai Elohenu melekh ha-olam roka ha'aretz al ha-mayim.

Praised are You, Adonai our God, Sovereign of the Universe, who establishes firm ground amidst the waters.

בָּרוּךְ אַתָּה יְיָ אֱלֹהֵינוּ מֶלֶךְ הָעוֹלָם, שֶׁעָשָׂה לִי כָּל צָרְכִּי.

Barukh atah Adonai Elohenu melekh ha-olam she'asah lee kol tzorkee.

Praised are You, Adonai our God, Sovereign of the Universe, who provides for all my needs.

בָּרוּךְ אַתָּה יְיָ אֱלֹהֵינוּ מֶלֶךְ הָעוֹלָם הַמֵּכִין מִצְעֲדֵי גָבֶר.

Barukh atah Adonai Elohenu melekh ha-olam ha-maykhin mitz'adei gaver.

Praised are You, Adonai our God, Sovereign of the Universe, who makes firm each person's steps.

בָּרוּךְ אַתָּה יְיָ אֱלֹהֵינוּ מֶלֶךְ הָעוֹלָם, אוֹזֵר יִשְׂרָאֵל בִּגְבוּרָה.

Barukh atah Adonai Elohenu melekh ha-olam ozer yisrael bigevurah.

Praised are You, Adonai our God, Sovereign of the Universe, who girds Israel with strength.

543

בָּרוּךְ אַתָּה יְיָ אֱלֹהֵינוּ מֶלֶךְ הָעוֹלָם, עוֹטֵר יִשְׂרָאֵל
בְּתִפְאָרָה.

Barukh atah Adonai Elohenu melekh ha-olam oter yisrael be-tifarah.

Praised are You, Adonai our God, Sovereign of the Universe, who crowns Israel with splendor.

בָּרוּךְ אַתָּה יְיָ אֱלֹהֵינוּ מֶלֶךְ הָעוֹלָם, הַנּוֹתֵן לַיָּעֵף כֹּחַ.

Barukh atah Adonai Elohenu melekh ha-olam ha-noten la-aiyef koach.

Praised are You, Adonai our God, Sovereign of the Universe, who gives strength to the weary.

בָּרוּךְ אַתָּה יְיָ אֱלֹהֵינוּ מֶלֶךְ הָעוֹלָם, הַמַּעֲבִיר שֵׁנָה מֵעֵינַי
וּתְנוּמָה מֵעַפְעַפָּי.

Barukh atah Adonai Elohenu melekh ha-olam ha'ma'avir sheina may'aynai ut'numah may'afapai.

Praised are You, Adonai our God, Sovereign of the Universe, who removes sleep from my eyes and slumber from my eyelids.

Some *siddurim* attach this additional paragraph to the last blessing:

Yehi ratzon

Yehi ratzon milfanekha Adonai elohenu vaylohay avotaynu she'-targeelaynu betoratekha ve-dabkeinu bemitzvotekha ve'al te'veeyanu lo leeday chet velo leeday aveirah ve'avon velo lee-day neesayon velo leeday veezayon ve'al tashlet banu yetzer ha'ra ve-harcheekaynu may'adam rah u'maychaver rah ve-dabkeinu beyetzer ha-tov uv-ma'asim tovim vechof et yeet-zraynu le-heeshtabed lakh u'tneinu hayom u'vechol yom le-chen ul'chesed ul'rachamim be'aynekha uv'aynay khol ro'aynu ve-teegmelaynu chasadim tovim. Barukh atah Adonai gomel chasadim tovim le'amo yisrael.

May it be your will, Adonai our God, and God of our ancestors, that you accustom us to study the Torah and attach us to your *mitzvot*. Do not bring us into the power of error nor into the orbit of transgression and sin, nor into the influence of challenge, nor be drawn into scorn. Do not let the inclination to do evil dominate us. Distance us from an evil person and an evil companion. Attach us to the inclination to do good and to do good deeds. Compel our inclination to do evil to be subservient to you. Grant us today and every day grace, kindness, and mercy in Your eyes and in the eyes of all who see us, and bestow beneficent kindness upon us. Praised are You, Adonai our God, who bestows kindness on the people Israel.

Things to remember:

1. These blessings should be said while standing.

2. These blessings are said before the morning service and should be recited prior to breakfast.

Key words and phrases:

Barukh ata Adonai Elohenu Melekh ha-Olam is the formula used to initiate a formal blessing. Some prayer books have translated this as "Praised be the Source of Life" in order to avoid any gender reference.

If you want to know more:

Joel Lurie Grishaver, *And You Shall Be a Blessing: An Unfolding of the Six Words That Begin Every Berakhah.* Northvale, NJ: Jason Aronson, Inc., 1994.

Reuven Hammer, *Entering Jewish Prayer: A Guide to Personal Devotion and the Worship Service.* New York: Schocken Books, 1995.

More particulars:

Rabbi Isaac Luria taught that a righteous person should respond to a minimum of 90 blessings each day and recite no less than 100 blessings each day. To assure these 90 Amen responses, some people recite these 15 blessings aloud for one another.

The paragraph attached to the last blessing that begins "May it be Your will" was the personal prayer recited by Rabbi Yehudah Hanasi every day after *shacharit*, according to the Talmud (*Berakhot* 16b). It is a prayer that asks God for divine protection during our everyday dealings with others. One commentator suggests that after its recitation, we should add our personal requests for God's help during the day.

Instant Information
Healing Psalms

The source:

Rabbi Nachman's Psalms of Healing[2] are taken from his *Comprehensive Remedy.*

What you need to know:

Psalm 16
These are among David's golden words:
Watch over me, God,
> for I seek refuge in You.
You said to Adonai:
> "You are my Master,
>> but my good fortune is not Your concern.
"Rather, the holy ones on the earth
>> —You care for them
>> and the great ones who I should emulate.
"When the pain multiplies,
> they know to speedily turn to another,
But I cannot even pour their libations because of guilt,
> I cannot even lift their names to my lips."
Adonai is the Portion, which is mine by right,
> my Cup.
> You nurture my destiny.
Labor pains turn into pleasantness—
> so, too, I must see my inheritance of beauty.
I will bless Adonai who counsels me,
> though at night my conscience afflicts me.
I will keep Adonai continually before me;
> because of God-Who-is-my-Right-Hand,
> I shall not break down.
So my mind is happy,
> my whole being is joyful;
>> even my body rests secure.

[2]Translations adapted from Simkha Y. Weintraub, ed., *Healing of Soul, Healing of Body: Spiritual Leaders Unfold the Strength and Solace in Psalms.* Woodstock, VT: Jewish Lights Publishing, 1994.

For You shall not abandon my soul
>> to the world of the dead,
>>> nor let the one who loves You
>>>> see one's own grave.
Give me directions on life's road.
>> With Your presence,
>>> I am filled with joys,
>>>> with the delights that ever come
>>>>> from Your Strong Arm.

Psalm 32

A Song of David, of instruction:

Happy is one whose sins are forgiven,
>> whose transgressions are wiped away.
Happy is one whose wrongdoing Adonai passes over,
>> whose Spirit is without deceit.
When I kept silent, my bones wore out;
>> I groaned all day in fear.
Day and night Your Hand weighed heavily upon me;
>> My marrow turned dry, parched as by the heat of
>>> summer,
>> *Selah.*
So now, I will acknowledge my transgression,
>> I will no longer obscure wrongdoing;
>>> Even as I began to say, "I admit my sins
>>>> before Adonai,"
>>> You forgave my errors and misdeeds, *Selah.*
Let one devoted to You offer this prayer
>> at those moments when You may be found:
>>> *"When trials and troubles come,*
>>>> *may they not flood in a deluge of destruction!"*
You are my Shelter,
>> You protect me from distress, from enemies,
>>> You surround me with the joy of deliverance,
>>>> *Selah.*
(You have said:)
>> "I will teach you Wisdom,
>> I will illumine the path you must take,
>> My eye will advise you and guide you."
>> Do not be like a horse or a mule who cannot
>>> understand,
>>>> who, with a bit and a bridle,

  must be restrained during grooming,
   so that they do not come too close and
    attack.
Many are the troubles of the wicked,
  but one who trusts in Adonai
   will be enveloped by loving abundance of
    kindness.
Rejoice in Adonai!
  Exult, righteous ones!
   Shout for joy, all who are upright in heart!

Psalm 41

To the Chief Musician: A Song of David

Happy is the one who attends to the needy;
  On an evil day, Adonai will rescue her
Adonai will guard her, Adonai will give her life;
  She will be considered fortunate on this earth,
   not subject to the whims of enemies.
Adonai will nurture her on her sickbed;
  Even when her illness advances, and her rest is
   disturbed,
  You will attend to her and turn things around.
As for me, I said,
  "Adonai, have pity;
  Heal my soul, for I have sinned against You."
My enemies speak evil against me:
  "When will she die and her name be obliterated?"
Even when my enemy comes to visit me,
  her concern is empty and false;
  her heart gathers malicious thoughts,
   which she then goes out and spreads.
Together, they whisper against me, all my enemies,
  they plot evil against me, they explain my suffer-
  ing away.
"All her evil has returned to haunt her through this illness,"
  they say,
  "And now that she has succumbed,
  she will never get up again."
Even my intimate friend,
  whom I trusted, who ate my bread,
  has turned on me, has ambushed me!

But You, Adonai,
     Take pity on me,
     Be gracious to me,
     Lift me up and I shall repay them.
By Your healing, I will know that You accept me,
     that my enemy does not shout triumphantly
          over me.
You will support me because of my integrity,
     You will let me abide in Your presence forever.
Praised is Adonai, God of Israel,
     from eternity to eternity—
     Amen and Amen!

Psalm 42

To the Chief Musician; Instruction to the Sons of Korach

Like a hind crying for springs of water,
     so my soul cries out to You, O God.
My soul thirsts for God,
     for the living *El*/Almighty;
     O, when will I come to appear before God?
My tears have been my food,
     day and night;
     my enemies taunt me all day, asking,
     "Where is your God?"
This I remember, and pour out my soul within me—
     how I used to walk with the crowd,
          moving with them, the festive throng, up to the
House of God,
               with joyous shouts of praise to God
                    a multitude celebrating the festival!
Why so downcast, my soul?
     Why disquieted within me?
          Have hope in God!
               For I will yet praise God
                    for deliverance, for God's presence.
My God, my soul is cast down within me;
     as I remember You in the land of the Jordan River,
          and Mount Hermon's peaks,
               and the smaller mountain of Sinai.
Deep cries out to deep,
     the sounds of the opened sluices of heaven;

all Your breakers and Your billows
have swept over me.
By day, Adonai will command Divine loving abundance
of kindness,
and at night, God's resting place will be with me;
This is my prayer to the Almighty, God of
my life.
I say to the Almighty, my Rock:
"Why have You forgotten me?
"Why must I walk in dark gloom,
oppressed by enemies?"
Crushing my bones
my adversaries revile me,
taunting me all day with,
"Where is your God?"
Why so downcast, my soul?
Why disquieted within me?
Have hope in God!
I will yet praise God,
My ever-present Help,
my God.

Psalm 59

To the Chief Musician, a precious song of David:

"Destroy not!"
Composed when Saul sent messengers to surround
David's house and kill him.
Rescue me from enemies, my God;
from those who rise up against me—strengthen
me!
Rescue me from those who act treacherously;
from bloodthirsty people—save me!
For they lie in ambush for my soul,
brazen ones gather against me;
yet I have not transgressed,
nor sinned against them, Adonai!
With no wrongdoing on my part,
they run and prepare themselves—
Awake, come towards me and see!
You, Adonai, God of Hosts,
God of Israel,
Rise up,

Hold all peoples accountable;
Show no favor to sinful traitors, *Selah*.
They return toward evening, howling
like dogs,
going round about the city;
Mouths barking,
Swords in their lips,
"Who hears it? Who cares?" they say.
But You, Adonai, You laugh at them,
You scorn the evil among the nations.
My strength—
for Your Help I wait,
for God is my Haven.
God, my Faithful One,
You will go before me;
God will let me gaze upon watchful foes.
Do not kill them, lest my people forget;
remove them from prosperity, with Your power,
and bring them down,
Our Shield, my Master.
For the sin of their mouth is the word of their lips,
their very pride will trap them,
because of the curses and lies that they tell.
Consume them in wrath;
Consume them that they exist no more:
and then they will know
That God rules in Jacob
to the ends of the earth, *Selah*.
The wicked may return toward evening,
howling like dogs,
going round about the city;
wandering about, searching for food,
they do not sleep until they are satiated.
But as for me
I will sing of Your strength
I will sing out loud in the morning,
rejoicing in Your loving abundance of
kindness;
For You have been my Stronghold,
a Refuge for me on my day of
trouble.

My Strength—

to You I will sing praises,
    for God is my Tower of Strength,
        God is my loving abundance of
            kindness.

Psalm 77

To the Chief Musician:

On the sufferings of evil decrees; A song of Asaph.
I lift my voice to God and cry out;
    I lift my voice to You
    and You turn Your ears to hear.
On my day of suffering
    I seek out my Master;
    At night, my hand reaches out,
        without ceasing;
            My soul refuses to be comforted.
I remember God—and I moan;
    When I talk,
        my spirit faints, *Selah.*
You gripped the lids of my eyes;
    I throbbed in pain, and could not speak.
I recall former days—
    ancient years, time long past;
    I remember my song, well into the night;
        I delve into my heart,
        My spirit searches and seeks.
    Will my Master cast me off forever?
    Will You not show favor to me once again?
    Has Your loving abundance of kindness disap-
        peared once and for all?
    Has Your word come to an end—
        for all generations?
    Has the Almighty forgotten how to be gracious?
    Has Your anger shut out Your mercy, *Selah*?
I said, "It is to terrify me, to inspire me with fear,
    that the Right Hand of the Most High has shifted."
I remember the deeds of God,
    I remember Your wonders from days long ago.
        I meditate on all Your work, Your actions,
            I speak of Your deeds.
God: Holiness is Your way—
    What power is as great as God?

You are the Almighty who does wonders,
  You have let the nations know of Your strength.
You redeemed Your people with an outstretched arm,
  the children of Jacob and Joseph, *Selah*.
The waters saw you, God,
  the waters saw you and were terrified;
    The depths trembled in turmoil!
The clouds poured out water,
  the skies emitted thunderclaps,
    Your hailstone arrows flew about!
The sound of Your thunder
  whirled like a wheel,
    Bolts of lightning illumined the world,
      the earth trembled and quaked.
Your way was in the sea
  Your path was in the great waters
    Your footsteps were not visible.
You led Your people as a flock,
  by the hand of Moses and Aaron.

Psalm 90

A prayer of Moses, a man of God:

    Adonai, You have been a refuge for us
    in every generation.
Before the mountains were born,
  before You brought forth the earth and the
                inhabited world.
      from world to world—
        You are the Almighty.
You bring people down
  from arrogance to contrition;
    You say,
      "Return to Me, children of Adam
        and Eve!"
For a thousand years are in Your eyes
  like yesterday, which has just passed,
    like a watch in the night.
The stream of human life is like a dream;
  In the morning, it is as grass, sprouting fresh;
  In the morning, it blossoms and flourishes;
    but by evening, it is cut down and shrivels.
So are we consumed by Your anger;

we are terrified by Your rage.
You have placed our sins before You;
>Our hidden misdeeds
>>are exposed by the light of Your counte-
>>nance.
All our days vanish
>in the glare of Your wrath;
>We have used up our years,
>>which pass like a word unspoken.
The days of our years may total seventy;
>if we are exceptionally strong, perhaps eighty;
>>but all their pride and glory is toil and
>>falsehood,
>>>and, severed quickly, we fly away.
Who can know the force of Your fury?
>Your rage is as awful as our fear!
To count every day teach us,
>so we will acquire a heart of wisdom.
Return, Adonai—how long?
>Take pity, have compassion on Your servants.
Satisfy us in the morning
>with Your loving abundance of kindness,
>and we will sing and rejoice all our days!
Give us joy
>that will challenge the days of our affliction,
>>the years we have seen evil.
Let Your work be revealed to Your servants,
>let Your splendor be on their children.
May the pleasantness of my Master, our God, rest upon us,
>and may the work of our hands be established;
>>Establish the work of our hands!

Psalm 105

Give thanks to Adonai, call upon God's name;

>Let all nations know about God's deeds!
Sing to God, compose songs, play instruments for God;
>Tell all about God's wondrous acts!
Take pride in God's Holy reputation;
>The heart of those who seek God rejoices!
Search for Adonai and for God's might,
>Seek God's presence always!
Remember the wonders God has performed,

God's miracles, and the laws from God's mouth.
Seed of Abraham, God's servant,
Children of Jacob, God's chosen:
You are Adonai, our God;
The whole earth is governed by Your laws.
You remembered Your eternal covenant,
the word which You commanded to a thousand
generations.
The covenant which You made with Abraham,
Your oath to Isaac—
You established it as a statute for Jacob,
for Israel—an everlasting covenant.
Saying,
"To you I will give the land of Canaan,
the portion of your inheritance."
When they were only few in number,
and had scarcely dwelled in the land;
when they wandered from nation to nation,
from one kingdom to another people—
You permitted no one to oppress them;
You admonished kings on their behalf:
"Do not touch My anointed ones,
and to My prophets do no harm."
You called a famine in the land,
their staff of life, their bread, You broke off.
Before them, You sent a man—
Joseph, sold as a slave.
They weighed his legs down in fetters,
an iron chain on his soul.
Until Your word came to pass,
the word of Adonai purified him.
The king sent messengers and released him,
the ruler of many peoples set him free.
He appointed him master over his house,
ruler over his possessions,
binding his ministers to his soul,
making his elders wise.
Israel then came down to Egypt
Jacob sojourned in the land of Ham.
God made God's people extremely fruitful,
You made them stronger than their adversaries,
whose hearts You turned to hate Your
people,

to conspire against Your servants.
You sent Moses, Your servant,
        and Aaron, whom You had chosen.
They performed among them
        words of Your signs,
                wonders in the land of Ham.
You sent darkness—and it was dark;
        they did not rebel against Your word.
You turned their waters into blood,
        causing their fish to die.
Their land swarmed with frogs,
        reaching the very chambers of the kings.
You spoke, and wild beasts came,
        lice throughout their borders.
You turned their rains into hail,
        flaming fire in their land.
        The hail struck their vines and fig trees,
                shattered the trees within their borders.
God spoke and locusts came,
        beetles beyond number.
        They ate every herb in their land,
                they devoured the fruit of their soil.
You struck all the firstborn in their land,
        the prime of their strength.
You brought them out, carrying silver and gold,
        and none among Your tribes stumbled.
Egypt rejoiced when they departed,
        for their terror had fallen upon them.
You spread out a cloud as a sheltering cover,
        a fire to illumine the night.
Israel asked and You provided quail,
        You satisfied them with bread from Heaven.
You broke open a rock and waters gushed out,
        rushing through dry places like a river.
For You remembered Your holy word, Your promise
        to Abraham, Your servant.
You brought out Your people with gladness,
        Your chosen ones with joyful singing.
You gave them the lands of nations,
        they inherited that which nations acquire by labor.
So that they might keep Your statutes,
        and treasure Your teachings,
                Halleluyah!

Psalm 137

By the rivers of Babylon,
      there we sat and we wept
            as we remembered Zion.
Upon the willows on its banks
      we hung up our harps.
For there our captors demanded of us
      words of song;
            Our tormentors asked of us (with) joy:
                  "Sing to us from the songs of Zion!"
But how shall we sing the song of Adonai
      on alien soil?
If I ever forget you, Jerusalem,
      may my right hand forget its cunning!
May my tongue cleave to the roof of my mouth,
      if I remember you not;
            if I do not set Jerusalem
                  above my highest joy!
Remind the sons of Edom, Adonai, about the day of
Jerusalem—
      remind those who said,
            "Raze it, raze it to its very foundation!"
Daughter of Babylon,
      it is you who are the annihilated one;
            Happy is the one who will repay you
                  For all that you have done to us!
Happy is the one who will grab your little ones,
      dashing them against the rock!

Psalm 150

Halleluyah. Praise God!
      Praise God in God's Sanctuary;
      Praise God
            in the vast expense of Heaven!
Praise God for mighty deeds;
      Praise God
            according to God's abundant greatness!
Praise God
      with the blowing of the *shofar;*
            Praise God
                  with the lyre and the harp!
Praise God

with drum and dance;
        Praise God
                with instruments and flute!
Praise God
        with resounding cymbals!
                Praise God
                        with clanging cymbals!
Let every breath of life praise God,
        Halleluyah. Praise God!

Things to remember:

Rabbi Nachman of Bratzlav was a Hasidic master who lived from 1772–1810. He identified ten psalms that he believed to contain the power to bring a complete healing to body and spirit. He called these psalms a *tikkun klali*, a complete healing. Nachman was the great-grandson of the Baal Shem Tov, the founder of Hasidism. Although he was joyful, there was a pessimistic streak in him which is epitomized in his often-quoted teaching (frequently put to music), "The world is a narrow bridge. The important thing is not to be afraid." When Rabbi Nachman died, his followers did not select a successor to him.

Key words and phrases:

Tehillim: psalms
Tikkun klali: complete healing or complete remedy

If you want to know more:

Simkha Y. Weintraub, ed., *Healing of Soul, Healing of Body: Spiritual Leaders Unfold the Strength and Solace in Psalms.* Woodstock, VT: Jewish Lights Publishing, 1994.

Index